Higher Education
in Latin America

Higher Education in Latin America

The International Dimension

Editors
Hans de Wit, Isabel Christina Jaramillo,
Jocelyne Gacel-Ávila, and Jane Knight

THE WORLD BANK
Washington, D.C.

ISBN 0-8213-6209-7
ISBN 978-0-8213-6209-9
eISBN 0-8213-6210-0
DOI: 10.1596/978-0-8213-6209-9

Library of Congress Cataloging-in-Publication Data

Higher education in Latin America : the international dimension / edited by Hans de
    Wit . . . [et al.]
        p. cm. – (Directions in development)
    Includes bibliographical references and index.
    ISBN 0-8213-6209-7
    1. Education, Higher–Latin America.   2. Education and globalization—Latin America.
3. International cooperation.   I. Wit, Hans de, 1950- II. World Bank.   III. Directions
in Development (Washington, D.C.)

LA543.H56 2005
378.8—dc22

                                                                                          2005048535

Contents

Tables

Figures

Foreword

When reading about the lives of those who have made a difference to their societies and their communities, I have always been struck by the impact they attribute to having studied outside their own countries. Many of us and our colleagues and family members have had the same experience. There seems to be a "before" and "after," which has been key in shaping our views of the town, the city, the country, the world, and of those who live in them—an experience that not only brings geographical knowledge but, more importantly, enriches one's personal horizon.

International mobility of students has been a driver of cultural exchange, knowledge acquisition, and innovation for centuries. Human ingenuity thrives when minds meet across cultures, and new ideas flourish when young people interact with the most accomplished and experienced scholars and scientists.

The international dimension of higher education responds to the challenges of globalization. The interdependence of today's economies and societies profoundly affects higher education, and higher education in turn shapes globalization—through teaching, research, and other services.

Broadening access to international higher education and research systems for talented Latin American students, irrespective of their background or country of origin, is at the heart of strengthening knowledge and innovation in their countries. An estimated 1.5 million young students worldwide currently study abroad. Roughly half of them come from countries in the Organisation for Economic Co-operation and Development (OECD), and more than 40 percent from East and South Asia. Only a few students from Africa, the Middle East, and Latin America get the opportunity to mix with their peers in other countries.

With this book—published with the OECD in Spanish, French, and English—the World Bank hopes to contribute to advancing the cause of international higher education in Latin America. Throughout Latin America, the World Bank supports targeted investments in science and higher education and efforts to strengthen Latin America's research capacity and the "circulation of brains."

Latin American countries are embracing the agenda of international higher education, and I wish them well in this endeavor.

Pamela Cox
Vice President
Latin America and the Caribbean Region
The World Bank

Preface

In response to globalization, institutions of higher education, national governments, and regional and international organizations are placing greater priority on the international dimension of higher education. Doing so helps the sector respond to some of the challenges that globalization creates.

In Latin America internationalization is becoming recognized as an important phenomenon that is influencing the direction of education and society. Little is known, however, about the development of this process or the trends, issues, and opportunities for internationalization within specific Latin American countries or the region as a whole. This book looks at the "Latin American way" in which the international dimension is evolving, recognizing the cultural, linguistic, political, and economic characteristics of the region, its countries, and its institutions of higher education.

The book compares internationalization issues, trends, and opportunities in higher education in selected Latin American countries at the institutional, national, and regional levels. It addresses the specific elements of the internationalization process, such as mobility, curriculum, linkages, and networks. Rather than investigating these issues in detail, however, it examines them as part of a more comprehensive overview of policies, programs, and activities at all three levels.

The volume examines these elements and the broader process of internationalization in the context of the overall development of higher education. It analyzes the potential contribution of internationalization to institution and nation building, examining such issues as the implications of trade, new forms of delivery, new providers, and the relevance of accreditation and quality assurance for higher education and their international dimensions.

The study is based on studies of seven countries (Argentina, Brazil, Chile, Colombia, Cuba, Mexico, and Peru), which together represent about 90 percent of the region's Spanish- and Portuguese-speaking population. It does not cover the small island countries of the Caribbean, Central America, or the French- and English-speaking countries of the region.

All of the contributors to this volume have worked on international relations issues at public or private institutions of higher education, in two cases at the sector and ministerial level. They bring a diverse academic perspective, coming from a variety of academic fields (education, law, languages, and archaeology). The contributors are actively involved in international officers networks, giving them a broad picture of national developments in their respective countries.

The methodology used for the country studies combines interviews with key decisionmakers at the national and institutional level; analyses of documents, publications, and Web sites; and data collection. The chapters on Colombia and Mexico include analyses of national surveys of international officers at institutions of higher education; the chapters on Argentina and Chile analyze smaller surveys. The paucity of data on internationalization made collecting information a challenge for all of the contributors. For that reason, the emphasis is on the qualitative rather than quantitative analysis of information.

The country studies are based on a common conceptual framework, presented in chapter 1, and each chapter follows a similar format. At the same time, each country has its own characteristics and perspectives and is at a different stage of development in terms of internationalization. Each chapter therefore includes a different emphasis. The chapter on Argentina, for instance, focuses on subregional cooperation within Mercosur and the active participation of national instructions in international and regional networks. In that chapter, as well as in the chapters on Chile, Colombia, and Mexico, there is a strong emphasis on the balanced relation between national policies and programs and internationalization at the institutional level. The chapter on Brazil focuses on the leading role the government plays in the internationalization process and on research cooperation, particularly by public universities. The chapter on Cuba emphasizes the role of national policy and ideology as key drivers for internationalization at both the national and institutional levels. The chapter on Peru analyzes the implications of the fact that international cooperation still consists primarily of development cooperation.

Networking has become a key driver and means for Latin American governments and their universities to stimulate the internationalization process. Networks connect institutions to what is going on regionally and internationally, increase institutions' profile and status, and inform them of opportunities and challenges. Chapter 10 provides an overview and analysis of the key actors and programs in the region.

Chapter 11 summarizes the key findings from the country studies. It examines the key issues at the institutional, national, and regional levels; compares developments in Latin America with developments in other parts of the world; identifies opportunities that internationalization provides for institution and nation building in the region; and shows how internationalization can contribute to higher education.

This publication builds on and contributes to previous studies by the World Bank and the Program on Institutional Management in Higher

Education (IMHE) of the OECD on the international dimension of higher education. IMHE has examined internationalization of higher education at the institutional and system levels in Australia, Canada, Europe, and the United States and in the Asia Pacific countries. With the Academic Cooperation Association and the European Association for International Education, it has developed an instrument with which to evaluate the quality of the international dimension of higher education in institutions.

This publication was coordinated by a project team, whose members also acted as the volume's editors. The team included Hans de Wit, Project Director, Universiteit van Amsterdam; Isabel Cristina Jaramillo, Project Coordinator, Asociación Colombiana de Universidades (ASCUN); Jocelyne Gacel-Ávila, Universidad de Guadalajara, Mexico; and Jane Knight, University of Toronto. The project team hopes that this volume will increase awareness, strengthen knowledge, and enhance opportunities for further internationalization at the regional and international level.

Acknowledgments

This book is the first attempt to analyze the internationalization of higher education both for Latin America and for most of the countries studied. Very little has been written on the topic, and data are scarce. The authors of the country studies and the volume editors collected as much relevant information as they could and based their analysis on that information. The editors see this study not as an end but as the beginning of the analysis of the international dimension of higher education in the region and hope that the references included in this volume will serve as a useful source for further study.

The editors would like to thank the contributors: Jocelyne Gacel-Ávila (Universidad de Guadalajara, Mexico); Jorge Balán (Ford Foundation); José Joaquín Brunner (University Adolfo Ibáñez, Chile); Luis Jaime Castillo Butters (Pontificia Universidad Católica del Perú); Pamela Lastres Dammert (Pontificia Universidad Católica del Perú); Raúl Hernández (Ministerio de Educación Superior/Universidad de Habana, Cuba); Lauritz B. Holm-Nielsen (World Bank); Isabel Cristina Jaramillo (Universidad del Rosario, Colombia); Sonia Pereira Laus (Universidade do Estado de Santa Catarina, Brazil); Marília Morosini (Universidade Luterana do Brasil); Leena Bernuy Quiroga (Pontificia Universidad Católica del Perú); Carlos Alberto Ramirez Sánchez (Universidad de Valparaiso, Chile); Julio César Teichler (Universidad Nacional del Litoral, Argentina); and Kristian Thorn (World Bank).

To ensure that the analysis was as complete as possible, we involved a broader group of experts as peer reviewers. We would like to thank the following reviewers for their invaluable comments: Dr. Mario Albornoz (Director de Redes, Centro de Estudios sobre Ciencia, Desarrollo y Educación Superior, Buenos Aires); Dr. Luis E. Aragón (Coordinador Núcleo de Altos Estudios Amazónicos, Universidade Federal do Pará, Belém, Brazil); Dr. Leonidas Lóz Herrán (Rector de la Corporación Universitaria de Ibagué, Colombia); Dr. Julio Castro Lamas (Director de Posgrado, Ministerio de Educación Superior, Cuba); Lic. Norberto Fernández Lamarra (Director Núcleo Interdisciplinario de Formación y Estudios para el Desarrollo de la Educación, Universidad Nacional de Tres de Febrero, Buenos Aires); Dr. Cristóbal Aljovín de Losada (Director of the Master's Program in History at the Universidad Nacional Mayor de San Marcos in Lima, Peru); Profa. Maria Beatriz Luce (Diretor do Núcleo de Estudos de Política e Gestão dai Educação, Universidade Federal do Rio Grande do

Sul, Porto Alegre, Brazil); Dr. Francisco Marmolejo (Executive Director of the Consortium for North American Education Collaboration, the University of Arizona, Tucson); Dr. Francisco José Piñón (Secretario General de la Organización de Estados Iberoamericanos para la Educación, la Ciencia y la Cultura, Buenos Aires); Prof. Marco Antonio Rodrigues Dias (Special Advisor to the Rector of the United Nations University, Paris); Daniel Samoilovich (Director of the Columbus Program, Paris); Lic. Ernesto F. Villanueva (Presidente de la Comisión Nacional de la Educación y Acreditación Universitaria, Buenos Aires); and Dra. Haydée Azabache Zenaida (Directora del Proyecto Especial de Educación a Distancia, Pontificia Universidad Católica del Perú, Lima).

We would like to thank the World Bank's Higher Education and Science and Technology Program for Latin America and the Caribbean, particularly Lauritz Holm-Nielsen, its leader, who from the beginning inspired and guided this project. Thanks are also due to Jamil Salmi, director of the World Bank's network for education, and to Eduardo Velez Bustillo, manager for education in the World Bank's Latin America and Caribbean Region, for their support. Finally, we would like to thank Kristian Thorn and Jette Samuel Jeppesen at the World Bank for editing the manuscript and the Programme on Institutional Management of Higher Education (IMHE) of the OECD for its support throughout the study. The content of this study is, of course, solely the responsibility of the authors.

Jocelyne Gacel-Ávila,
Isabel Cristina Jaramillo,
Jane Knight, and Hans de Wit
The Project Team

Abbreviations

AECI	Agency for International Cooperation
AGCI	Chilean International Cooperation Agency
ALFA	Latin America Academic Training
AlßAN	High Level Latin-American Scholarship
AMPEI	Mexican Association for International Education
ANUIES	National Association of Universities and Institutions of Higher Education (Mexico)
APCI	Peruvian International Cooperation Agency
ARCAM	Interuniversity Group
ASCUN	Association of Colombian Universities
AUALCPI	Latin America and Caribbean Association of Universities for Integration
AUGM	Montevideo Group University Association
AUIP	Iberoamerican University Association of Graduate Education
CAPES	Coordinating Agency for Graduate Education (Brazil)
CEC	Canadian Education Centre
CEPRES	Regional Planning Councils for Higher Education
CIDA	Canadian International Development Agency
CINDA	Interuniversity Development Center
CLACSO	Latin American Council of Social Sciences
CNPq	Brazilian National Council for Scientific and Technological Development (Brazil)
COLCIENCIAS	Colombian Institute for the Development of Science and Technology
COLFUTURO	Foundation for the Future of Colombia
CONACYT	National Council for Science and Technology (Mexico)
CONAHEC	Consortium for North American Higher Education Collaboration
CONCYTEC	National Council for Science and Technology (Peru)
CONEAU	National Commission for Evaluation and University Accreditation (Argentina)
CONICET	National Council of Scientific and Technological Research (Argentina)
CONICYT	National Commission for Scientific and Technological Research (Chile)

CRISCO	Council of University Presidents for the Integration of the West-Central Sub-Region of South America
CSUCA	Central American Higher University Council
CUIB	Iberoamerican University Council
CYTED	Iberoamerican Program of Science and Technology for Development
DAAD	German Academic Exchange Service
DANIDA	Danish International Development Agency
ESCALA	Common Academic Space Program
EU	European Union
FIMPES	Mexican Federation of Private Institutions of Higher Education
FLACSO	Latin American Faculty of Social Sciences
FO-AR	Argentine Fund for Horizontal Cooperation
FOMEC	Fund for the Enhancement of Educational Quality
FOMES	Fund for the Modernization of Higher Education (Mexico)
FTAA	Free Trade Area of the Americas
GATS	General Agreement on Trade in Services
IAESTE	International Association for the Exchange of Students for Technical Experience
IAU	International Association of Universities
IAUP	International Association of University Presidents
ICETEX	Colombian Institute for Educational Loans and Technical Studies Abroad
LASPAU	Academic and Professional Programs for the Americas
IDB	Inter-American Development Bank
IDRC	International Development Research Centre
IESALC	International Institute for Higher Education in Latin America and the Caribbean
IGLU	Inter-American Organization for Higher Education
IIE	Institute of International Education
IMHE	Program on Institutional Management in Higher Education
INABEC	National Institute of Scholarships and Educational Credit (Peru)
INCO-DEV	Scientific and Technological Cooperation with Developing Countries
IOHE	Inter-American Organization for Higher Education
IOM	International Organization for Migration
ISPJAE	José Antonio Echeverría Advanced Polytechnic Institute
ITESM	Technological Institute of Monterrey (Mexico)

JICA	Japanese International Cooperation Agency
KOICA	Korea International Cooperation Agency
LAMUN	Latin American Macro Universities Network
MBA	Master of Business Administration
Mercocyt	Common Market of Scientific and Technological Knowledge Program
Mercosur	Common Market of the South
MEXA	Mechanism for the Accreditation of University Programs
NAFTA	North American Free Trade Agreement
NGO	nongovernmental organization
NORAD	Norwegian Agency for Development Cooperation
NUFFIC	Netherlands Organizations for International Cooperation in Higher Education
OECD	Organisation for Economic Co-operation and Development
OEI	Iberoamerican Organization for Education, Science and Culture
PAME	Academic Program for Student Mobility
PCI	Inter-University Cooperation Program
PEC-G	Undergraduate Student Program Agreement (Brazil)
PEC-PG	Graduate Student Program Agreement (Brazil)
PIMA	Academic Exchange and Mobility Program
PROMESAN	Program for the Mobility of Students in North America
R&D	research and development
RCI	Colombian Network for the Internationalization of Higher Education
RedCIUN	Network of Heads of International Cooperation of the National Universities (Argentina)
REDUNIV	University Network for Scientific and Technological Information of the Ministry of Education (Cuba)
RIACES	Iberoamerican Network for the Accreditation and Quality of Higher Education
RICYT	Iberoamerican Network of Science and Technology Indicators
RLCU	Iberoamerican Network on University Cooperation
SAREC	Swedish Department for Research Cooperation
SEM	Educational Sector of Mercosur
SIDA	Swedish International Development Agency
SOFES	Society for the Promotion of Higher Education (Mexico)
UDUAL	Latin American Universities Union
UNAM	National Autonomous University of Mexico

UNAMAZ	Association of Universities of the Amazon
UNDP	United Nations Development Programme
UNESCO	United Nations Educational, Scientific and Cultural Organization
UNICEF	United Nations Children's Fund
USAID	United States Agency for International Development
WTO	World Trade Organization

About the Authors

Jorge Balán
Jorge Balán is Senior Program Officer in Education and Scholarship at the Ford Foundation in New York. He served as Executive Director of the National Commission on University Evaluation and Accreditation, Senior Researcher and Director of the Center for the Study of State and Society (CEDES), and Professor of Sociology at the University of Buenos Aires. He holds a bachelor's degree in sociology from the University of Buenos Aires and PhD in sociology from the University of Texas at Austin.

José Joaquín Brunner
José Joaquín Brunner is Professor at the School of Government at the University Adolfo Ibáñez, Chile, and Director of Fundación, Chile's Education Program. A former minister of the Chilean government, he was president of the Higher Council for Education, the National Television Council, and the Commission on Modernization of Chilean Education. He has been a visiting professor at universities in Colombia, Mexico, and Spain and a Pearson Fellow at the International Development Research Centre in Canada. He is a member of the governing board of UNESCO's International Institute for Educational Planning and a recipient of the 2004 International and Comparative Education Society Kneller Award.

Luis Jaime Castillo Butters
Luis Jaime Castillo Butters is Director of International Relations and Cooperation at Pontificia Universidad Católica del Perú and Associate Professor and Chair of the School of Archaeology. His office plays a key role in the internationalization of Peruvian and Latin American universities, through work done for the Latin American Universities Union (UDUAL) and other consortia. He is currently leading the student exchange program for the Interuniversity Development Center (CINDA). Prof. Castillo has published several articles on the role of international student mobility. He holds a BA in archaeology from PUCP and an MA and PhD in anthropology from UCLA.

Pamela Lastres Dammert
Pamela Lastres Dammert is Executive Officer and Professor of Philosophy at Universidad del Pacífico of the AlßAN Scholarship Program in

Peru. She has organized conferences on international education in Peru and abroad and led workshops on the management of international relations in the Peruvian provinces. She holds bachelor's and master's degrees in philosophy from the Pontificia Universidad Católica del Perú.

Jocelyne Gacel-Ávila

Jocelyne Gacel-Ávila is the General Coordinator for Cooperation and Internationalization and a researcher and professor at the University of Guadalajara. She is a member of Mexico's National System of Investigators and a founding member of the Mexican Association for International Education, which she led as president from 1996 to 2000. She is a member of the Advisory Board of the Consortium for North American Higher Education (CONAHEC); the founder and president of the editorial board of the journal *Global Educación*; and the author of *The Internationalization of Higher Education: Paradigm for the Global Citizenship, Internationalization of Higher Education in Latin America and the Caribbean: Reflections and Guidelines*, and *The Internationalization of the Mexican Universities: Political and Institutional Strategies*. She holds a PhD in higher education from the University of Morelos, Mexico.

Lauritz B. Holm-Nielsen

Lauritz B. Holm-Nielsen is the World Bank's Lead Specialist for Higher Education and Science and Technology. While President of the Nordic Academy for Advanced Study in Oslo, he was responsible for integrating higher education, science, and research and development in the Nordic region. He was Rector of the Danish Research Academy, Dean of the Faculty of Sciences of Aarhus University, and Director of the Institute of Biology at Pontificia Universidad Católica del Ecuador. He chaired the Danish Environment Research Program, the Danish National Research Council, the Council for Development Research, and the Board of Trustees of the Institutes for Tropical Agriculture (CIAT) in Cali and Plant Genetic Resources (IPGRI) in Rome. He co-chaired the White Paper on research and development for Denmark in 2001.

Isabel Cristina Jaramillo

Isabel Cristina Jaramillo is Executive Officer at Universidad del Rosario, Bogota; coordinator of COLCIENCIAS' research center on internationalization; and a consultant to the World Bank. She was International Relations Coordinator for the Association of Colombian Universities and leader of the Colombian Network for the Internationalization of Higher Education, an organization that includes most of the international relations offices of higher education institutions in Colombia. She has published several articles on the subject. Her latest book, published in 2003, analyzes the development of the international dimension of higher education in Colombia. She holds an MBA from the Technological Institute of Monterrey in Mexico.

Jane Knight

Jane Knight is an expert on the international dimension of higher education at the institutional, system, national, and international levels. She is the author or editor of many publications on internationalization strategies, quality assurance, management, and mobility, including regional comparative studies of international education for the OECD and World Bank. Dr. Knight is an adjunct professor at the Ontario Institute for Studies in Education at the University of Toronto. She is a member of the editorial board of the *Journal of Studies in International Education* and the *Indian Journal on Higher Education: Policy and Practices*. She holds a PhD in higher education from Michigan State University.

Sonia Pereira Laus

Sonia Pereira Laus is Director of International Cooperation of Santa Catarina State University, Brazil. She was President of the Brazilian International Relations Officers Forum (FAUBAI) from 1996 to 2002 and has been the South Brazil Universities Representative in FAUBAI since 2000. She is involved in the Environment and Development Program (LEAD) of The Rockefeller Foundation. She was a member of the Ibero-American States Organization. In 2002–03 she sat on the selection committee of the Ibero-American Program for Academic Mobility and served as Higher Education Secretary Commission Advisor to the Brazilian Ministry of Education for the creation of a common higher education space by the European Union, Latin America, and Caribbean. She is a member of the selection committee for foreign students applying to the Undergraduate Foreign Students Agreement Program and a member of the International Publishing Commission of the Ibero-American Dialogue Bulletin of the University of Granada (Spain). She is the author of several articles on international academic cooperation published in Brazil, China, Mexico, and Spain. She holds a mater's degree in history from the Federal University of Santa Catarina.

Marilia Costa Morosini

Marilia Costa Morosini is a professor at the Pontificia Universidad Católica de Rio Grande do Sul, a professor emeritus at the Universidad Federal de Rio Grande do Sul (UFRGS), a researcher at the National Council of Scientific and Technological Development, and a visiting scholar at the Tereza Lozano Long Institute of Latin American Studies of the University of Texas, Austin. She holds a PhD in humanities from the UFRGS.

Raúl Hernández Pérez

Raul Hernandez Perez served as Deputy-Director of Teaching Staff, Director of Education, Sub-Director for Scholarships, and Professor of Pedagogy and Law at the Universidad de La Habana. Since 1982 he has headed the Department of Cooperation and Agreements of Cuba's Ministry of Higher Education. He has participated in many national and international activities in higher education, including missions for international cooperation to more than 35 countries. He has received awards in Cuba and abroad, including the Medal for Cuban Education and the Medal for Cooperation of the Minister of Foreign Affairs of France. He holds an MA in pedagogy and law from the Universidad de Habana.

Leena Bernuy Quiroga

Leena Bernuy Quiroga is the Executive Director of Cooperation at the International Relations and Cooperation Office at Pontificia Universidad Católica del Perú (PUCP). A graduate of PUCP, she is a specialist in the planning and management of projects for development cooperation in higher education, science, and culture.

Carlos Ramírez Sánchez

Carlos Ramírez Sánchez is Director of Interinstitutional Relations and International Cooperation of the University of Valparaiso and a professor of history, geography, education, and teaching methodology. He has participated in and directed several ALFA projects and cooperation networks with European universities. He has served as President of the Committee for International Cooperation of the Rectors Council of Chilean Universities, has represented Chilean universities, and spoken on the internationalization of higher education at international meetings in Europe, the United States, and Latin America. He is a member of the Andes Foundation Selection Committee and the Cultural Regional Council of Chile. He holds an MA in education and is pursuing a PhD in economics at the University of Cadiz, Spain.

Julio César Theiler

Julio César Theiler is Secretary of Science at the Universidad Nacional del Litoral, in Santa Fe, Argentina. For eight years, he was Dean of the engineering and hydric sciences faculty. He was President of the Federal Council of Engineering Deans of the Republic of Argentina, a member of the Advisory Committee of the National Commission of Evaluation and University Certification, and Secretary of International Cooperation of the Universidad Nacional del Litoral. He founded the network for international relations for public universities of Argentina, which he currently represents in the Ibero-American Space. He designed and implemented the International Program of Student Mobility of the Universidad Nacional del Litoral and co-designed the exchange program of the Association of Universities of the Montevideo Group.

Kristian Thorn

Kristian Thorn is a political scientist working in the World Bank's Human Development Department and part of the task team on higher education and science and technology operations in Latin America and the Caribbean. He has published on accountability for results, the financing of higher education, and science and technology. Before joining the Bank, Mr. Thorn was head of the section in the Danish Ministry of Finance responsible for public sector modernization, quality assurance, and e-government. He holds a master's degree from the University of Aarhus, Denmark.

Hans de Wit

Hans de Wit is Senior International Advisor at the University of Amsterdam. He is a founding member and past President of the European Association for International Education, a consultant for the Programme on Institutional Management of Higher Education of the OECD, and the editor of the *Journal of Studies in International Education*. He has written several books and articles on the internationalization of higher education and been involved in institutional reviews of internalization policies in different parts of the world. He is the project leader of the World Bank study on the internationalization of higher education, "The Latin American Way." Dr. de Wit holds a master's degree in social sciences and a PhD in humanities from the University of Amsterdam.

1

An Internationalization Model: Responding to New Realities and Challenges

Jane Knight

This chapter focuses on the meaning, rationales, approaches, and strategies for internationalization and identifies core issues. It introduces a generic model of internationalization of higher education, which is used as a framework for analyzing the international dimension of higher education in Latin America and other regions.

The rest of this volume looks at the status, issues, and challenges for internationalization of higher education in selected Latin American countries and the region as a whole. This chapter complements the approach taken in the country analyses by examining internationalization at both the institutional level and the national/sectoral levels. Both levels are important. The national/sectoral level has an important influence on the international dimension of higher education through policy, funding, programs, and regulatory frameworks. But it is usually at the individual institutional level that the real process of internationalization takes place. The analysis of internationalization in this chapter therefore uses a bottom-up (institutional) approach and a top-down (national/sectoral) approach, examining the dynamic relationship between the two levels.

The world of higher education and the world in which higher education plays a significant role are changing, for many reasons. Key drivers include the development of advanced communication and technological services, increased international labor mobility, greater emphasis on the market economy and trade liberalization, the focus on the knowledge society, increased private investment and decreased public support for education, and the growing importance of lifelong learning. The international dimension of higher education is therefore becoming increasingly important and, at the same time, more complex. The analysis of major higher education trends in Latin America, presented in chapter 2, illustrates this complexity. This chapter takes an in-depth and holistic look at the concept of internationalization within this transformative environment.

What Is Internationalization?

Internationalization means different things to different people and is thus used in a variety of ways. While it is encouraging to see the increased use and attention being given to internationalization, there is a great deal of confusion about exactly what it means. For some it means international activities, such as academic mobility for students and teachers; international linkages, partnerships, and projects; and new international academic programs and research initiatives. For others it means the delivery of education to other countries through new types of arrangements, such as branch campuses or franchises, and the use of a variety of face to face and distance techniques. To many it means the inclusion of an international, intercultural, or global dimension in the curriculum and the teaching/learning process. Still others see international development projects and the increasing emphasis on trade in higher education as internationalization. There is frequent confusion and some tension over the fact that the term *internationalization* is used to describe three very different types of cross-border activities: international exchanges and partnerships, cross-border commercial trade ventures, and international development projects. There is also continuing debate and exploration of the relationship between internationalization and globalization. Is internationalization the same as globalization? If not, how is it different and what is the relationship between these two dynamic processes?

Clearly, *internationalization* is interpreted and used in different ways in different countries and by different stakeholders. This reflects the realities of today and presents new challenges in terms of developing a conceptual framework that can provide some clarity on meaning and some principles to guide policy and practice.

In addition to questions about what exactly internationalization means, other very important issues are being raised. What is the purpose of internationalization? What are the expected benefits or outcomes? What values underpin it? Who are the main actors, stakeholders, and beneficiaries? What are the positive consequences, the unintended results, and the negative implications? Is internationalization a passing fad? Is it sustainable? If so, how? How are institutions responding to competing interests within the domain of internationalization? What are the policy and funding implications of increased emphasis on internationalization at both the national and institutional levels? How are governments and non-governmental organizations (NGOs) addressing the issue and moving forward? Is internationalization a response to or an impetus for globalization? Does internationalization play a role in the brain drain, the homogenization/hybridization of culture, and the international mobility of labor? How does the gradual but discernible shift from development aid to commercial trade affect internationalization?

Terminology

A few words about terminology are necessary, as the language of internationalization is changing and differs within and between countries and regions. Although one of the objectives of this chapter is to examine the meaning and definitions of internationalization, it is important to be clear at the outset about how key concepts are interpreted and used in this book.

The terms *postsecondary, tertiary,* and *higher education* are often confused. In this volume, the narrower term *higher education* is used to mean educational institutions, providers, and programs that lead to credit or award at the undergraduate or graduate levels through full-time, part-time, or continuing education. The country reports focus primarily on universities and degree-granting institutions; they do not fully address the nondegree institutions or informal and nonformal continuing education and professional training that are important components of the tertiary and broader postsecondary education sector.

International, transnational, and *global* are used in ways that differentiate among the three terms (Knight 1999b). The term *international* emphasizes the notion of nation and refers to the relationship between nations. *Transnational* is used in the sense of "across nations" and does not specifically address the notion of relationships. *Transnational* is used interchangeably with *cross-border. Global* refers to worldwide in scope and substance and does not highlight the concept of nation. *Globalization* and *internationalization* are viewed as very different, albeit related, processes (as addressed in more detail below).

Higher Education Institutions and Providers

To meet the increase in demand for higher education, new providers, new delivery methods, and new types of programs have been developed. As a result, new types of providers are active in the delivery of higher education programs, both domestically and internationally. These new providers include media companies, such as Pearson (United Kingdom) and Thomson (Canada); multinational companies, such as Apollo (United States), Informatics (Singapore), and Aptech (India); corporate universities, such as those run by Motorola and Toyota; and networks of professional associations and organizations. Generally, these new commercial providers are occupied mainly with teaching and training or providing services; they do not focus on research per se. They can complement, cooperate with, or compete with public and private higher education institutions whose mandate is traditionally the trinity of teaching, research, and service. Because many of the new providers focus on delivering education across borders, they must be included as actors in the internationalization scene. The main focus of this book is traditional public and private higher education institutions; where the new providers are active, they are addressed, however.

Institutional, Sectoral, and National Levels

This book focuses on internationalization at the institutional level and at the national/sectoral level. The institutional level is relatively clear. The national level is more complicated, as it can include different governmental entities or NGOs active in the internationalization of higher education. On the government side, this can include departments of education, foreign affairs, science and technology, culture, employment, immigration, and trade and commerce, all of which have a primary or peripheral interest in the international dimension of higher education. However, in many instances, the internationalization of higher education is on the agenda only of the education-related government departments, agencies, and NGOs. In these cases, the education sector is the key actor. The term *sectoral level* is used to refer to efforts by the national education sector.

International Cooperation: Vertical and Horizontal

Like *internationalization*, the term *international cooperation* is often used as a catch-all phrase. It has very different meanings depending on the country and the actor or stakeholder. In some cases it is used as a generic term to describe the myriad relationships an institution or sector has with partners in other countries. In Latin America the term is also used to refer to international development cooperation. The inclusion of the word *development* implies the existence of funding or support from a bilateral or multilateral body that can be used for a variety of higher education purposes, such as institutional capacity building, human resource development, or academic mobility. It is revealing that the donor countries are more likely to refer to this type of technical assistance relationship as *international development cooperation*, while receiving countries use the term *international cooperation*.

It is important to note the shift from vertical to horizontal cooperation. These terms are used in a variety of ways, but the key elements are the following. Vertical cooperation usually describes donor-recipient relationships in which development is oriented to aid or assistance. Horizontal cooperation reflects more of a mutual benefit and partnership relationship. There is a clear movement in policy and program development toward horizontal, or partnership, cooperation, with or without external funding, often involving a developed and developing country. Yet another interpretation of *horizontal cooperation* is the idea of collaboration among developing countries, often referred to as South-South cooperation. Use of the term horizontal cooperation to describe this kind of relationship becomes murky when the relationships or partnerships among the developing countries (often forged on a regional or subregional basis) are funded by a bilateral or multilateral agency.

The seven country reports use these terms in ways that are consistent with the way each country conceives and approaches the international dimension of higher education. The key common thread is that internationalization is interpreted and used in a broad and inclusive manner and is not limited to one particular set of international activities or programs, such as mobility, development cooperation, research, curriculum development, or trade.

Changes and Challenges

It is impossible to look at new conceptual frameworks for internationalization without considering the realities of the environment in which higher education is operating. There are many changes and new challenges in terms of how the environment is affecting internationalization and how the growing international dimension of higher education is an agent of change itself. Globalization is probably the most pervasive and powerful feature of the changing environment.

Globalization

Globalization is on the minds of policymakers, academics, and practitioners across sectors and disciplines. Education, particularly postsecondary education, as both agent and reactor to globalization, is a critical area of debate and study. Many different views have been expressed about the nature, causes, elements, consequences, and future implications of globalization for education (Scott 2000; Salmi 2001; Marginson 2001; Marquez 2002; Breton and Lambert 2003; Enders and Fulton 2002).

The dynamic relationship between globalization and the internationalization of education is an important area of study that deserves further exploration. Parameters need to be established to frame the discussion. For the purposes of this chapter, *globalization* is defined neutrally and viewed as a key environmental factor that has multiple effects—both positive and negative—on education. The discussion does not center on the globalization of education. Rather, globalization is presented as a phenomenon that affects internationalization.

Substantial efforts have been made during the past decade to maintain the focus on the internationalization of education and to avoid using the term *globalization of education*. These efforts have had mixed results, but some success has been achieved in ensuring that the two terms are not seen to be synonymous and are not used interchangeably.

Globalization is defined as "the flow of technology, economy, knowledge, people, values, ideas . . . across borders. Globalization affects each country in a different way due to a nation's individual history, traditions, culture and priorities"(Knight and de Wit 1997, p. 6). This definition acknowledges that globalization is a multifaceted process that can affect countries in vastly different ways; it does not take a position as to whether this impact is positive or negative. As discussed later, definitions that include rationales or consequences can be very limiting because they cannot be applied across national contexts.

Another key aspect of this definition is that it refers to crossing borders and infers a worldwide scope. This is consistent with the definitions introduced earlier, in which *global* was defined as meaning *worldwide*, and *nation* is not seen as a critical aspect of the term *globalization*.

The concepts of worldwide movement and flow are key to the interpretation of globalization in this chapter. A number of factors are closely related to this flow and seen as integral elements of globalization. These include the knowledge society, information and communication technologies, the market economy, trade liberalization, and changes in governance structures. It can be debated whether these are catalysts for or consequences of globalization; for this discussion they are presented as elements or factors of globalization that have an enormous impact on the education sector.

Table 1.1 describes each of these five elements of globalization and notes some of the key implications for higher education in general and the international dimension in particular. It illustrates some of the major environmental changes shaping the responses and actions of internationalization to globalization. These changes affect all aspects of internationalization, including the curriculum and teaching process, student and academic mobility, the cross-border delivery of education programs, international development projects, the study of foreign languages, commercial trade, and staff development.

Diversification of Funding Sources

Funding and support for higher education represent key changes and challenges for internationalization. Several trends are converging and

Table 1.1 Implications of Globalization for Internationalization of Higher Education

Element of globalization	Impact on higher education	Implications for the international dimension of higher education
Knowledge society Increasing importance attached to the production and use of knowledge as a wealth creator for nations.	Growing emphasis on continuing education, lifelong learning, and continual professional development is creating unmet demand for higher education.	New types of private and public providers (private media companies, networks of public and private institutions, corporate universities, multinational companies) are delivering education and training programs across borders.
	Need to develop new skills and knowledge is resulting in new types of programs and qualifications. Role of universities in research and knowledge production is changing and becoming more commercialized.	Programs are more responsive to market demand. Specialized training programs are being developed for niche markets and professional development purposes and distributed worldwide. Students, academics, education and training programs, research, providers, and projects are increasingly mobile, physically and virtually.
Information and communication technologies New developments in information and communication technologies and systems.	New delivery methods, especially on-line and satellite-based methods, are being used for domestic and cross-border education.	Innovative international delivery methods, such as e-learning, franchises, and satellite campuses, require more attention to accreditation of programs and providers and recognition of qualifications.

(continued)

Table 1.1 *(Continued)*

Element of globalization	*Impact on higher education*	*Implications for the international dimension of higher education*
Market economy Growth in number and influence of market-based economies around the world.	Higher education and training are increasingly commercialized and commodified at the domestic and international levels.	New concerns are arising about the appropriateness of curriculum and teaching materials in different cultures and countries and the potential for homogenization, as well as new opportunities for hybridization.
Trade liberalization New international and regional trade agreements developed to decrease barriers to trade.	The import and export of educational services and products have increased as barriers have been removed.	More emphasis is being placed on commercially oriented export and import of education programs, and less on international development projects.
Governance Creation of new international and regional governance structures and systems.	The role of national-level education actors, both government and non-government, is changing. New regulatory and policy frameworks are being considered at all levels.	New international and regional frameworks are being considered to complement national and regional policies and practices, especially in the areas of quality assurance, accreditation, credit transfer, recognition of qualifications, and mobility of students.

Source: Knight (2004).

have a major impact. The growing demand for higher education is making it difficult for governments to meet demand. At the global level, private investment in education is rising more rapidly than public funding (Levy 2003). This has resulted in several important trends, including the diversification, privatization, and commercialization of higher education and its funding sources.

It is more and more common and necessary for institutions, both public and private, to search for alternative sources of income. These sources include funding from social foundations and the private corporate sector, income from the commercialization of research findings, and income from fee-based education for domestic and international students and from other means of cross-border education delivery. Income generation from the importing and exporting of education programs is expected to increase at a significant rate in the next decade (Larsen, Martin, and Morris 2001). Trade in higher education services is expected to be highly competitive, and new commercial providers are likely to have an impact on public and private nonprofit higher education institutions that are active in this area.

Mobility and Intercultural Awareness

The increasing mobility of the work force is resulting in more temporary and permanent migration. At the same time, growing numbers of students are moving for academic purposes, making campuses and classrooms in many countries more culturally and ethnically diverse. This trend brings new opportunities and new challenges for the teaching/learning process and the development of curriculum, and it increases the need to develop greater intercultural understanding and communication skills. Internationalization is seen as a concrete way to respond to and build on the increasing multicultural nature and intercultural needs of the learning environment.

Other Issues Affecting Education

Other important global issues—related to terrorism, war, health, and the environment—have indirect or direct effects on education. Internationalization is happening at a time of great transformation, if not turbulence. It has never been more important to be cognizant of how internationalization is affected by these changes or is a factor of change itself. It is therefore both prudent and necessary to think about the long-term effects of internationalization, including both intended and unintended consequences.

Meaning and Definitions of Internationalization and Related Terms

This section examines various interpretations and uses of *internationalization* and related terms. It proposes and analyzes an updated definition of *internationalization* that is appropriate for today's realities and challenges.

For more than 20 years, there has been much debate about defining *internationalization*. The term is not a new one. It has been used for centuries in political science and governmental relations, but its popularity in the education sector soared only since the early 1980s. Before then, *international education* and *international cooperation* were the favored terms, as they still are in some countries. In the 1990s the discussion about using the term *international education* centered on differentiating it from *comparative education, global education*, and *multicultural education*. (De Wit 2002 provides a comprehensive and useful overview of the development and use of the terms *internationalization, international education, comparative education*, and other related terms predominantly used in the past 10 years.)

Another set of related terms is emerging, including *transnational education, borderless education, offshore education*, and *cross-border education*. These terms relate to the concepts of border. They differ substantially from the terms *comparative, multicultural*, and *intercultural*.

Transnational education is the term used by UNESCO and the Council of Europe in the Code of Practice on Transnational Education they have developed. The term is defined to mean all types of higher education study in which learners are located in a country different from the one in which the awarding institution is based (UNESCO and Council of Europe 2001). This definition acknowledges the trend in which institutions send programs to students in other countries, but it does not adequately address the trend in which the institution or provider sets up a branch campus or purchases existing institutions in foreign countries.

The term *borderless education* first appeared in an Australian report (Cunningham and others 2000). It then appeared in a similar study in the United Kingdom commissioned by the Committee of Vice-Chancellors and Principals (CVCP). The term refers to the blurring of conceptual, disciplinary, and geographic borders traditionally inherent to higher education (CVCP 2000).

It is interesting to juxtapose the terms *borderless education* and *cross-border education*. The former acknowledges the disappearance of borders, while the latter emphasizes the existence of borders. Both approaches reflect the reality of today. In this period of unprecedented growth in distance education and e-learning, geographic borders seem to be of little consequence. Yet the importance of borders is growing when the focus turns to regulatory responsibility, especially that related to quality assurance, funding, and accreditation.

The term *offshore education* is still used to denote education delivered abroad, but its use is decreasing, due to the more recent introduction of the term *cross-border. Cross-border* activities are one type of internationalization activity.

Yet another related term is the phrase *internationalization at home*, which some believe is a direct response to the current emphasis on mobility and internationalization abroad. It is certainly a sign of the times that *internationalization at home* has entered the lexicon. Wachter (2003) believes that the term has developed from a mature concept of internationalization and the adaptation of intercultural studies to higher education. *Internationalization at home* attempts to forge a closer link between the concepts of international and intercultural in the education domain; it represents an important stage in the development of the international/intercultural dimension of education.

Developing a clear and comprehensive definition for *internationalization* helps clarify the confusion and misunderstanding that currently exists. There will likely never be a true universal definition. But it is important to have a common understanding of the term, so that the phenomenon is clearly understood and there is solidarity when advocating for increased attention and support from policymakers and academic leaders.

Given the many factors affecting internationalization, it is no wonder that *internationalization* is being used in a variety of ways and for different purposes. What is surprising is the small number of academics and policymakers who are studying the nuances and evolution of the term, given the current changes and challenges.

Evolution of the Concept of Internationalization

The definition of *internationalization* evolved over the past decade. In the late 1980s, the term was commonly defined at the institutional level and in terms of a set of activities. Arum and Van de Water (1992) proposed defining *internationalization* as "the multiple activities, programs and services that fall within international studies, international educational exchange and technical cooperation" (p. 202). In 1994 Knight introduced a process, or organizational approach, to capture the notion that internationalization is a process that needs to be integrated and sustainable at the institutional level. She defined *internationalization* as the "process of integrating an international and intercultural dimension into the teaching, research and service functions of the institution" (p. 7). Van der Wende (1997) correctly pointed out that an institutional-based definition had limitations. She therefore proposed a broader definition that includes "any systematic effort aimed at making higher education responsive to the requirements and challenges related to the globalization of societies, economy and labor markets" (p. 18). While this definition includes important elements, it positions the international dimension in terms of only the external environment (specifically, globalization); it does not set internationalization in the context of the education sector and its goals and functions.

More recently, Soderqvist (2002) introduced a definition that focuses on the change process and a holistic view of management at the institutional level. She defines the internationalization of a higher education institution as "a change process from a national higher education institution to an international higher education institution leading to the inclusion of an international dimension in all aspects of its holistic management in order to enhance the quality of teaching and learning and to achieve the desired competencies" (p. 29). This is an example of a definition that has rationales embedded in it and therefore has limited applicability to institutions or countries that see internationalization as broader than teaching, learning, and the development of competencies. It demonstrates an evolution of the definition at the institutional level, but it has limitations as a comprehensive definition. It also begs the question of just what constitutes an international higher education institution.

De Wit (2002, p. 114) concludes:

As the international dimension of higher education gains more attention and recognition, people tend to use it in the way that best suits their purpose. While one can understand this happening, it is not helpful for internationalization to become a catch-all phrase for everything and anything international. A more focused definition is necessary if it is to be understood and treated with the importance that it deserves. Even if there is not agreement on a precise definition, internationalization needs to have parameters if it is to be assessed and to advance higher education. This is why the use of a working definition in combination with a conceptual framework for internationalization of higher education is relevant.

Updated Working Definition of Internationalization

Definitions can shape policy, and practice can influence definitions and policy. Given the changes in the rationales, providers, stakeholders, and activities of internationalization, it is important to revisit the definition in order to ensure that its meaning reflects the realities of today and is able to guide and be relevant to new developments. It is increasingly clear that internationalization needs to be understood both at the national/sectoral level and at the institutional level. Therefore, a new definition is proposed that acknowledges both levels and the need to address the relationship and integrity between them.

A definition must be generic enough to apply to many different countries, cultures, and education systems. Coming up with such a definition is no easy task. While it is not necessarily the intention here to develop a universal definition, it is imperative that the definition be appropriate for use in a broad range of contexts. With this in mind, it is important to ensure that the definition does not specify the rationales, benefits, outcomes, actors, activities, or stakeholders of internationalization, as they vary enormously across countries and institutions. What is critical is that the international dimension relates to all aspects of education and the role it plays in society.

The following working definition is proposed: internationalization at the national, sectoral, and institutional level is "the process of integrating an international, intercultural or global dimension into the purpose, functions or delivery of postsecondary education" (Knight 2003, p. 2). This is intentionally a neutral definition of *internationalization*. Many would argue that the process of internationalization should be described in terms of promoting cooperation and solidarity among nations, improving the quality and relevance of higher education, or contributing to the advancement of research for international issues. While these are noble goals, to which internationalization can contribute, a definition needs to be objective enough that it can be used to describe a phenomenon that is universal but that has different purposes and outcomes depending on the actor or stakeholder.

The terms used in the proposed working definition of *internationalization* were chosen with care. *Process* is used to convey the notion that internationalization is an ongoing and continuing effort. The term denotes an evolutionary or developmental quality to the concept. Process is often thought of in terms of a three-part model of education that includes input, process, and output. The concepts of input and output were not used, even though there is increased emphasis today on accountability and therefore on outcomes. The terms were avoided because if *internationalization* is defined in terms of inputs, outputs, or benefits, it becomes less generic, as it must reflect the particular priorities of a country, institution, or group of stakeholders.

Integrating is used to denote the process of infusing or embedding the international and intercultural dimension into policies and programs in order to ensure that the international dimension is central and sustainable and is not marginalized.

The terms *international, intercultural,* and *global* are used as a triad, as together they reflect the breadth of internationalization. *International* is used in the sense of relationships between nations, cultures, or countries. *Intercultural* is used to address cultural diversity in the home environment. *Global*, often a very controversial and value-laden term, is included to provide the sense of worldwide scope. These three terms complement one another and together give richness in breadth and depth to the process of internationalization.

Purpose refers to the overall role and objectives higher education has for a country or region or the mission or mandate of an individual institution. *Function* refers to the primary elements or tasks that characterize a national higher system and an individual institution. These usually include teaching, training, research, scholarly activities, and service to the society at large. *Delivery* is a narrower concept, which refers to the offering of education courses and programs, domestically or in other countries. This includes delivery by traditional higher education institutions as well as by new providers, such as by companies that are more interested in the global delivery of their programs and services and are not as focused on the international or intercultural dimension of a campus or the teaching, research, and service functions.

Relationship with Previous Definition

Internationalization has been defined as the process of integrating an international or intercultural dimension into the teaching, research, and service functions of the institution. This definition does not conflict with the new definition proposed here. In fact, the two definitions are complementary. The new definition attempts to take account of the realities of today's context, in which the national/sectoral level is extremely important. It covers the growing number and diversity of education providers whose interests and approaches differ from those of traditional institutions in terms of the international, intercultural, and global dimensions. For this reason, the more generic terms *purpose, function*, and *delivery* are used instead of the specific functional terms of *teaching, research*, and service. By using these more general terms, the proposed definition can be relevant for the sectoral level, the institutional level, and the variety of providers—public, private, for-profit, nonprofit, local, international—in the broad field of higher education.

Values and Rationales Driving and Guiding Internationalization

The importance of having clear, well-articulated rationales for internationalization cannot be overstated. Rationales are the driving force pushing a country, sector, or institution to address and invest in internationalization. Rationales are reflected in the policies and programs that are developed and eventually implemented. Rationales dictate the kind of benefits or expected outcomes one would expect from internationalization efforts. Without a clear set of rationales, followed by a set of objectives or policy statements, a plan or set of strategies, and a monitoring and evaluation system, the process of internationalization is often an ad hoc, reactive, and fragmented response to the overwhelming number of new international opportunities available.

This section attempts to look at the shift in rationales. It examines the values that underpin rationales and that may be driving some of the changes in motivations and expectations of internationalization at the country or institutional level.

A clearer articulation of the values guiding internationalization is becoming increasingly important. Why? In these turbulent times of change, there are disconnections and tensions between rationales, policies, and expected outcomes. Values give shape and consistency to the vision, rationales, and expected outcomes that underpin countries' and institutions' drive to internationalize. Values, which are key to this discussion, include cooperation, competition, and the extent to which education is perceived as a public good. These values are especially relevant given the recent growth in the commercial provision and trade of education services across borders. Values are purposely not included in the definition of internationalization, but they have played a critical role in the evolution of the involvement of the postsecondary sector in international activities.

It is important not to place values in opposition to one another. Seldom is there a black and white discussion or an either/or statement of values. More often, values form a continuum. For example, cooperation and competition are neither mutually exclusive nor opposed to each other. It is important not to portray either value in a more positive or negative light than the other. There can be positive spin-offs from increased competition and unintended negative consequences as well. The same is true for cooperation. There are important questions related to the understanding of education as a public or private good. Can one categorically state that education is (as opposed to should be) a totally public or private good? Can education be privately funded or even commercially traded and still be considered a public good? Perhaps education needs to be understood in terms of state responsibilities in response to state priorities and values. If it does, what is the role of education across borders? Clearly, there are important questions to reflect on in terms of the values and rationales underpinning the motivations and benefits of internationalization.

Traditionally, the rationales for internationalization have been presented in four groups that reflect fundamental drivers: social/cultural, political, academic, and economic (table 1.2) (Knight and de Wit, 1997, 1999). In the past several years, much has been written about the changes in rationales both within and between these four groups (Van Vught, Van der Wende, and Westerheijden 2003; de Wit 2002; Gacel-Ávila 2003;

Table 1.2 Rationales Driving Internationalization

Rationales	Existing rationales	Rationales of emerging importance
Social/ cultural	National cultural identity Intercultural understanding Citizenship development Social and community development	*National level* Development of human resources Strategic alliances Income generation/ commercial trade
Political	Foreign policy National security Technical assistance Peace and mutual understanding National identity Regional identity	Nation building/ institution building Social and cultural development and mutual understanding *Institutional level* International branding and profile Quality enhancement, international standards
Economic	Economic growth and competitiveness Labor market Financial incentives	Income generation Student and staff development Strategic alliances
Academic	Extension of academic horizon Institution building Profile and status Enhancement of quality International academic standards International dimension to research and teaching	Knowledge production

Source: Knight (2004).

Knight 2003). These generic categories remain a useful way to analyze rationales, but the blurring of the categories and the significant changes in nature and priority within each category need to be highlighted.

Given the increasing emphasis on competition at the international level, it is tempting to introduce a new category, which recognizes the importance that institutions are giving to branding or developing a strong international reputation. One could say that educational institutions have always competed in trying to achieve high academic standards and more recently an international profile. However, there has been a not so subtle shift toward developing an international reputation in order to successfully compete in a more commercial environment. Institutions and companies are competing for international fee-paying students, for for-profit education and training programs, and for education services, such as language testing and accreditation services. The interest in branding is leading institutions to seek out accreditation or quality assurance services by national and international accrediting bodies, some of which are very reputable and some of which are not. Institutions and providers are trying to create an international reputation and name brand for their institutions or for a network or consortium in order to place themselves in a better competitive position.

The desire for international recognition—for academic, economic, social, or political purposes—is clearly growing. Whether the branding trend should be seen as a separate category of rationales or integrated into the four existing categories is open to discussion. For the purposes of this chapter, the drive for international branding is highlighted as an important motivation as a means to an end, not an end in itself.

The first column in table 1.2 presents the four categories of rationales, as updated by de Wit (2002). These categories remain relevant, but there seems to be more blurring or integration of the rationales across categories. The four categories do not distinguish between national and institutional level rationales, a distinction that is becoming increasingly important (Knight 2004).

Therefore, the third column presents rationales of emerging importance at both the national and institutional levels.

National-Level Rationales for Internationalization

This section highlights some of the new rationales emerging at the national level that cannot be neatly placed in one of the four categories. These cross-cutting rationales are development of human resources, strategic alliances, income generation/commercial trade, nation and institution building, and social and cultural development and mutual understanding. The first four of these emerging rationales are closely linked to the political and economic rationales.

Development of Human Resources

An increasing emphasis on the knowledge economy, demographic shifts, growing labor force mobility, and increased trade in services are driving nations to place more importance on developing and recruiting human capital through international education initiatives. There is increased pressure for and interest in recruiting the brightest students and scholars from other countries in order to increase scientific, technological, and economic competitiveness. Changes in recruitment strategies, incentives, and immigration policies are examples of efforts to attract and retain students and academics with potential for enhancing the human capital of a country. Similarly, more attention is being paid to enhancing the international dimension of teaching and research, so that domestic students and academics can be better equipped to contribute to their countries' international competitiveness. Increased recognition is also being given to the need to further develop intercultural understanding and skills for personal, professional, and citizenship development. The growing importance attached to brain power is directly related to the increasing interest and concern about brain gain/drain and migration.

CREATION OF STRATEGIC ALLIANCES

Strategic alliances can be seen both as a driving rationale and as a means or instrument of internationalization. This section looks at strategic alliances as rationales, for academic, economic, political, or social/cultural purposes. The international mobility of students and academics, as well as collaborative research and education initiatives, are being seen as productive ways to develop closer geopolitical ties and economic relationships. There has been a shift from alliances for cultural purposes to those for economic purposes. This is especially true at the regional level, where countries are trying to achieve stronger economic and political integration with their neighbors by increasing their international education activities on a regional basis. The development of strategic alliances through internationalization of higher education is seen as a way to develop closer bilateral or regional cooperation and to gain a competitive edge.

INCOME GENERATION/COMMERCIAL TRADE

In the past decade, more emphasis has been placed on economic and income-generating opportunities associated with the cross-border delivery of education. New franchise arrangements, foreign or satellite campuses, on-line delivery, and increased recruitment of fee-paying students are examples of a more commercial approach to internationalization. The fact that education is now one of the 12 service sectors in the General Agreement on Trade in Services (GATS) is proof that importing and exporting education and training programs and education services is a potentially lucrative trade area. It is estimated that in 1999 trade in higher education reached $35 billion and the figure is expected to increase significantly (Larsen, Martin, and Morris 2001). Countries are showing increased interest in the potential for exporting education for economic benefit. The development of new international and regional trade agreements is providing regulations that will help decrease barriers to trade, in an attempt to increase the commercial side of international cross-border trade in education (Knight 2002; Sauve 2002).

NATION- AND INSTITUTION-BUILDING

An educated, trained, and knowledgeable citizenry and workforce and the capacity to generate new knowledge are key components of a country's nation-building agenda. But many countries lack the physical and human infrastructure and the financial resources to offer higher education opportunities to their citizens.

Traditionally, international academic projects that developed as part of development and technical assistance work were considered an important contribution to the nation-building efforts of a developing country. International development work, based on mutual benefits for all partners, continues to be a key aspect of the internationalization of postsecondary education. But there has been a discernible shift, which is likely to become more pronounced, from an aid/development approach to international partnerships to one focused on trade for commercial purposes. Some countries are interested in exporting education to generate income, while others are interested in importing education programs and institutions for nation-building.

SOCIAL/CULTURAL DEVELOPMENT AND MUTUAL UNDERSTANDING

The social and cultural rationales, especially those that relate to promotion of intercultural understanding and national cultural identity, remain significant, but their importance does not carry the same weight as the other rationales. Whether, in light of the pressing issues and challenges stemming from culturally based clashes within and between countries, there will be more interest and importance attached to the social/cultural and mutual understanding based rationales remains to be seen. It may be optimistic, but it would be reassuring to think that social/cultural rationales for internationalization will be given equal importance as economic and political ones.

Institutional-Level Rationales for Internationalization

There is a close link between national-level and institutional-level rationales, albeit not always as close as one would expect. The link depends on many factors, one of which is how much the internationalization process is a bottom-up or top-down process. In countries in which internationalization is not given much prominence at the national level—still very much the case in many regions of the world—institutional-level rationales have greater importance and may differ substantially across institutions.

Many factors influence institutional-level rationales. These include mission, student population, faculty profile, geographic location, funding sources and level of resources, and orientation to local, national, and international interests. The four categories presented in table 1.2 apply to institutions, but it appears that the emerging rationales of greater consequence are the following.

ENHANCEMENT OF INTERNATIONAL PROFILE AND REPUTATION

Traditionally, prominence has been given to the importance of achieving international academic standards (however they may be defined). This motivation is still important, but it appears to have been subsumed by the drive to achieve a worldwide reputation as an international high-quality institution. This drive relates to the quest for name recognition internationally in an attempt to attract the brightest scholars and students, a substantial number of international students, and high-profile research and training projects. Academic standards remain important, but there is a perceptible shift from an emphasis on a high-quality academic experience for students and faculty to one in which high academic standards are part of marketing campaigns for branding purposes in order to compete domestically and internationally.

IMPROVEMENT OF QUALITY

For most institutions, internationalization is not an end in itself but a means to an end. The contribution that the international dimension makes to improving the quality and relevance of higher education in relation to international standards is often articulated as a rationale and goal of internationalization. Given the interconnected and interdependent world of today, it is important that higher education, through a strengthened international dimension in teaching and research, contribute to the quality and relevance of its mission to serve the needs of individuals, communities, countries, and society at large. At a more practical level, internationalization is proving to be a useful tool for helping institutions benchmark and come up with innovative solutions to ongoing management, academic, and research-related challenges. This is yet another way in which internationalization can help strengthen the quality of higher education institutions and the primary functions of teaching, learning, and service.

DEVELOPMENT OF HUMAN RESOURCES

There is renewed emphasis on internationalization as a means to enhance international and intercultural understanding and skills for students and staff. A number of factors are contributing to this. The rising number of national, regional, international, and cultural conflicts is pushing academics to help students understand global issues and international/intercultural relationships. The growing emphasis on the knowledge society makes continuous upgrading and a well-developed knowledge and skill base important. The mobility of the labor market and the increase in cultural diversity of communities and the workplace require that both students and academics have a better understanding of and demonstrated abilities to work and live in a culturally diverse environment. At the same time, the increased emphasis on accountability and outcomes-based education is resulting in a substantial effort toward identifying student and staff competencies developed through internationalization initiatives. The development of information and communication technologies, especially the Internet, has highlighted the need for deeper knowledge and understanding of the world and has provided new opportunities for accessing such knowledge. It is interesting to speculate on whether the current attention given to internationalization at home is stimulating or responding to the growing importance of student and staff development.

INCOME GENERATION

More institutions are looking to internationalization activities as a way to generate income. Public institutions are caught in the squeeze of decreased public funding and increased operational costs, all taking place in an environment of increased accountability and probably increased competition.

The purpose or use of the income generated is often questioned, not in terms of where or how the money is being spent but in terms of whether it is generating profits or recovering costs. This is not an issue that has clear answers, as most public institutions would argue that they are by definition not for profit and that therefore any surplus from internationalization activities is used to subsidize other initiatives. Many would suggest that any income generated from internationalization activities should be reinvested to enhance underfunded aspects of internationalization, but this is an institutional matter.

Another factor related to income generation is the emergence of new commercial corporate providers that are in business to generate income. Thus while more importance is being attached to the economic rationale for internationalization at the institution/provider level, the issue is becoming more complicated, as it is part of the larger questions of commercialization and commodification of education, with cross-border delivery of education programs and services playing a major role.

CREATION OF STRATEGIC ALLIANCES

Strategic alliances can be seen as both a rationale for and a means of achieving internationalization. The number of bilateral or multilateral educational agreements has increased exponentially in the past decade. During the early stages of the internationalization process, institutions often react to the multitude of opportunities to establish international institutional linkages. These linkages can be for different purposes (academic mobility, benchmarking, joint curriculum or program development, seminars and conferences, joint research initiatives). Often institutions cannot support a large number of agreements, and thus many are inactive and exist only on paper. As institutions mature in their approach to internationalization, more effort is put into developing strategic alliances in which purposes and outcomes are clearly articulated. An important trend is the development of networks. Networks tend to have clearer and more strategic objectives, but in many cases they are more difficult to manage than bilateral agreements, because of the complexities of working with such different education systems and cultures.

RESEARCH AND KNOWLEDGE PRODUCTION
The role of higher education institutions in the production and distribution of knowledge should not be minimized. Given the increasing interdependence among nations, there are global issues and challenges that cannot be addressed at the national level only. International and interdisciplinary collaboration is key to solving many global problems, such as those related to the environment, health, and crime. Institutions and national governments are therefore making the international dimension of research and knowledge production a primary rationale for the internationalization of higher education, and many institutions are articulating this as a key rationale for internationalization.

All in all, the rationales driving internationalization vary from institution to institution, from government department to government department, from stakeholder to stakeholder, and from country to country. Differing and competing rationales contribute to both the complexity of the international dimension of education and the contribution internationalization makes.

It is very importance for an actor—whether it be an institution, provider, public or private stakeholder, NGO, governmental department or intergovernmental agency—to clearly articulate its motivations for internationalization, as policies, programs, strategies, and outcomes are linked and guided by explicit and even implicit rationales.

Internationalization Strategies, Programs, and Policies

This section looks at internationalization in terms of the strategies, programs, and policies used at the institutional/provider, sectoral, and national level. There is a hierarchical dimension to the use of these three terms. Strategies reflect the most concrete level and include the academic program activities and organizational initiatives at the institutional level. Programs reflect a more comprehensive approach to internationalization and are one of the tools for implementing policy at all three levels. National and institutional values, perspectives, and rationales underpin and frame strategies, policies, and programs.

In the conceptual frameworks for internationalization developed in the past decade (Knight and de Wit 1997, 1999), the term *internationalization strategies* was deliberately used to go beyond the idea of international activities. The term *strategies* referred to both program and organizational initiatives at the institutional level. The notion of a more planned, integrated and strategic approach was implied in the use of the word *strategies*.

Examples of programs and organizational strategies are shown in table 1.3. The table reflects recent changes, especially the growth in the

Table 1.3 Institutional-Level Programs and Organizational Strategies for Internationalization

Type of activity *Program activities*	*Examples*
Academic programs	• Student exchange programs • Foreign language study • Internationalized curricula • Area or thematic studies • Work/study abroad • International students • Teaching/learning process • Joint/double degree programs • Cross-cultural training • Faculty/staff mobility programs • Visiting lecturers and scholars • Links between academic programs and other strategies
Research and scholarly collaboration	• Area and theme centers • Joint research projects and publications • International conferences and seminars • International research agreements • Research exchange programs • International research partners in academic and other sectors
Domestic and cross-border activities	*Domestic* • Community-based partnerships with NGOs or public/private sector groups • Community service and intercultural project work • Customized education and training programs for international partners and clients *Cross-border* • International development assistance projects • Cross-border delivery of education programs (commercial and noncommercial) • International linkages, partnerships, and networks

(continued)

Table 1.3 *(Continued)*

Type of activity *Program activities*	*Examples*
	• Contract-based training and research programs and services • Alumni abroad programs
Extracurricular activities	• Student clubs and associations • International and intercultural campus events • Liaison with community-based cultural and ethnic groups • Peer support groups and programs

Organizational strategies

Governance	• Commitment by senior leaders • Active involvement of faculty and staff • Articulated rationale and goals for internationalization • Recognition of international dimension in institutional mission/mandate statements and in planning, management, and evaluation policy documents
Operations	• Integrated into institution wide and department/college level planning, budgeting and quality review systems • Appropriate organizational structures • Systems (formal and informal) for communicating, liaising, and coordinating • Balance between centralized and decentralized promotion and management of internationalization • Adequate financial support and resource allocation systems
Services	• Support from institution wide service units (student housing, registrar, fund raising, alumni, information technology) • Involvement of academic support units (library, teaching and learning, curriculum development, faculty and staff training, research services) • Support services for incoming and outgoing students (orientation programs, counseling, cross-cultural training, visa advice)
Human resources	• Recruitment and selection procedures that recognize international expertise • Reward and promotion policies to reinforce faculty and staff contributions • Faculty and staff professional development activities • Support for international assignments and sabbaticals

Source: Knight (2004).

commercial aspects of internationalization and the increased interest in "internationalization at home" activities. These programs and strategies are most applicable to traditional public and private higher education institutions. They are less relevant for new providers, which do not focus on research or service to the community or society.

Strategies and a strategic approach are key to the institutional level, but because the national/sectoral level is now covered in the definition, it is necessary to broaden the notion of organizational strategies to the national or sectoral level. Therefore, the terms policies and programs are introduced.

The new frameworks deliberately include policies and programs at all three levels (table 1.4). Programs can be seen in a more macro way than

Table 1.4 Policies and Programs for Internationalization at the National, Sectoral, and Institutional Levels

Level	Policies	Programs
National	Education and other national-level policies relating to the international dimension of higher education (cultural, scientific, immigration, trade, employment policies).	National or subregional programs that promote or facilitate the international dimension of higher education. Can be provided by different government departments or NGOs and be oriented to different international aspects (academic mobility programs, international research initiatives, student recruitment programs).
Sectoral	Policies related to the purpose, functions, funding, and regulation of higher education.	Programs offered by and for the higher education sector. Can be provided by any level of government or by public or private organizations.
Institutional	Policies that address specific aspects of internationalization or policies that integrate and sustain the international dimension into primary mission and functions of institution.	Programs such as student exchange, foreign language study, area or thematic studies, joint and double degrees, and international students.

Source: Knight (2004).

strategies and are used as one of the policy instruments or, more generally, as one of the ways policy is actually translated into action.

At the national sectoral level, all policies that affect or are affected by the international dimension of education are included. This includes policies related to foreign relations, development assistance, trade, immigration, employment, science and technology, culture and heritage, education, social development, and industry and commerce.

At the education sector or system level, all the policies that relate to the purpose, licensing, accreditation, funding, curriculum, teaching, research, and regulation of higher education are included. These policies have direct implications for all kinds of providers—public and private, for-profit and nonprofit institutions, and commercial companies.

Companies offering education programs and services are included, because the growing commercial education industry can be seen as complementing, cooperating with, or competing with the noncommercial sector. The London-based Observatory on Borderless Higher Education has developed a Global Education Index (Garrett 2003), which lists all the companies that provide education and training programs or services and are listed on the stock exchange. There are about 50 at this time, but as trade liberalization of services increases, so will the numbers of for-profit companies. Many policies related to the international dimension of education will affect both public institutions of higher learning and commercial providers. This is why it is imperative that policies at both the national/sectoral and institutional levels be included in a conceptual framework.

At the institutional level, policies can be interpreted in different ways. A narrow interpretation would include statements and directives that refer to priorities and plans related to the international dimension of the institution's mission, purpose, values, and functions. This could include the institutional mission statement or policies on study abroad, student recruitment, international linkages and partnerships, cross-border delivery, international sabbaticals, and other issues.

A broader interpretation of policies at the institution level would include all those statements, directives, or planning documents that address implications for or of internationalization. If the institution has taken an integrative and sustainable approach to internationalization, a very broad range of policy and procedure statements would be implied, including quality assurance, planning, funding, staffing, faculty development, admission, research, curriculum, student support, and contract and project work.

Traditionally, internationalization at the institutional level was thought of as a series of strategies or activities. These strategies have recently been divided into two different streams. The first includes internationalization activities that occur mainly on the home campus. The second relates to activities that occur across borders.

The term *internationalization at home* has been developed to bring attention to aspects of internationalization that occur on a home campus. These include the intercultural and international dimension in research and in the teaching/learning process, extracurricular activities, relationships with local cultural and ethnic community groups, and the integration of foreign students and scholars into campus life and activities. The emergence of this concept can perhaps be seen as a way to counteract the increased emphasis on academic mobility.

The term *cross-border* is starting to be used as a synonym for *internationalization*, thereby neglecting the "at home" components. It is frequently used to describe commercial trade in education. Both of these interpretations are too narrow, which is why it is important to clarify what is meant by the two streams of internationalization. The two streams should be seen as closely linked, interdependent rather than independent. Internationalization abroad has significant implications for internationalization at home and vice versa.

Table 1.5 includes four categories of cross-border education. It takes a comprehensive approach to cross-border education to counterbalance the narrower approach used in trade agreements such as the General Agreement on Trade in Services (GATS). It is important that the four modes used by trade analysts in GATS not be adopted as an education classification system. The four trade modes are restricted primarily to commercially oriented activities; they do not include nonprofit academic partnership activities or international development projects, which are integral parts of internationalization (Knight 2003). The cross-border categories used in table 1.5 include internationalization activities that involve the movement of people, courses and programs, education providers, and projects, whether these activities are provided through virtual or physical movement or through exchange agreements, government or privately funded programs, commercial for-profit ventures, nonprofit initiatives, or a combination of arrangements.

The four categories included in cross-border education are implemented through three primary modes of internationalization: development assistance projects (vertical cooperation); exchanges, linkages, and mutually beneficial initiatives (horizontal cooperation); and commercial and market-driven ventures.

This framework is a work in progress and will continue to develop. It is purposely generic in order to be relevant to the many different countries, jurisdictions, cultures, and education systems; the many institutions, and providers involved in internationalization; to cover the diversity of funding and administrative arrangements; and to include both at home and cross-border activities. The links between the two streams are important; more attention and research is needed to study the nature and implications of this connection.

Table 1.5 Components of Internationalization at Home and Abroad

Internationalization at home (campus based)

Curriculum and programs
- New programs with international theme
- International, cultural, global, or comparative dimension infused into existing courses
- Foreign language study
- Area or regional studies
- Joint or double degrees

Teaching/learning process
- Active involvement of international students, students who have returned from studying abroad, and cultural diversity of classroom in teaching/learning process
- Virtual student mobility for joint courses and research projects
- Use of international scholars and teachers as well as local international/intercultural experts
- Integration of international and intercultural case studies, role playing, and reference materials

Extracurricular activities
- Student clubs and associations
- International and intercultural campus events
- Liaison with community-based cultural and ethnic groups
- Peer support groups and programs

Liaison with local cultural and ethnic groups
- Involvement of students in local cultural and ethnic organizations through internships, placements, and applied research
- Involvement of representatives from local cultural and ethnic groups in teaching/learning activities, research initiatives, and extracurricular events and projects

Research and scholarly activity
- Area and theme centers
- Joint research projects
- International conferences and seminars
- Published articles and papers
- International research agreements
- Research exchange programs
- International research partners in academic and other sectors
- Integration of visiting researchers and scholars into academic activities on campus

Internationalization abroad (cross-border)

Movement of people
- Students study abroad through award-based programs for semester or year long studies, internships, research programs, or full programs abroad.

(continued)

Table 1.5 *(Continued)*

- Professors and experts travel abroad to teach and conduct research, provide technical assistance and consulting, spend sabbaticals, and seek professional development.

Delivery of programs

- Programs and courses, not students, move.
- Educational or training programs offered through linkage or partnership arrangement between foreign and domestic institutions and providers.
- Credit or award normally granted by the receiving institution; in some cases joint or double degrees are offered. (If a foreign degree is involved, the institution or provider has likely moved to the receiving country.)

Mobility of providers

- Institution or provider moves in order to have physical or virtual presence in the receiving country.
- Foreign or international provider has academic responsibility for the program and awards a foreign degree. The provider may or may not have an academic or financial partner in the receiving country. Branch campuses, stand-alone foreign institutions, and some franchise models are examples.

International projects

- Includes a wide diversity of nonaward-based activities, such as joint curriculum development, research, benchmarking, technical assistance, e-learning platforms, professional development, and other capacity-building initiatives.
- Projects and services could be undertaken as part of development aid projects, academic linkages, and commercial contracts.

Approaches to Internationalization

Given the changing, chaotic world in which higher education is functioning, it is important to acknowledge that different countries, educational systems, institutions, and providers face specific challenges and opportunities with respect to the international dimension of higher education. This means that many different approaches are needed to address internationalization.

An approach is different from a definition. Although different countries, and even institutions within a country, may share an interpretation or definition of internationalization, the manner in which they address the task of internationalization may be very different, because of differences in their priorities, culture, history, politics, and resources. An approach to internationalization reflects or characterizes the values, priorities, and actions that a country, the education sector, or an institution is exhibiting as it works toward internationalizing. An approach is not fixed. Approaches change during development. In many cases, countries or institutions use different approaches at the same time. There is no right approach. The notion of approach is introduced to help describe and assess the manner in which internationalization is being conceptualized and implemented at the national, sectoral, or institutional level.

Approaches at the Institutional/Provider Level

The general approaches to internationalization shown in table 1.6 are based on earlier work (Knight and de Wit 1999), but there are three important differences. The "outcome" category was formerly called "competencies." Given the strong emphasis on accountability and results in the higher education sector, it was decided to broaden this category to include a wider interpretation of outcomes.

Table 1.6 Approaches to Internationalization at the Institutional Level

Approach	Description
Activity	Internationalization is described in terms of activities, such as study abroad, curriculum and academic programs, institutional linkages and networks, development projects, and branch campuses.
Outcomes	Internationalization is described in terms of desired outcomes, such as student competencies, increased profile, and more international agreements, partners, or projects.
Rationales	Internationalization is described with respect to the primary motivations or rationales driving it. This can include academic standards, income generation, cultural diversity, and student and staff development.
Process	Internationalization is considered to be a process in which an international dimension is integrated into the teaching, learning, and service functions of the institution through key organizational strategies.
At home/ campus based	Internationalization is interpreted as the creation of a culture or climate on campus that promotes and supports international/ intercultural understanding and focuses on campus-based activities.
Abroad/ cross-border	Internationalization is seen as the delivery of education to other countries through a variety of delivery modes (face to face, distance, e-learning) and through different administrative arrangements (franchises, twinning, branch campuses, and so forth).

Source: Based on Knight and de Wit (1999).

Another important change is the addition of two new categories: "rationales" and "cross-border." The rationales driving internationalization are changing. Policy statements at both the country and the institutional level are becoming more explicit about why there are efforts to internationalize rather than emphasizing simply what needs to be done. To reflect this change, rationales are now included as another approach to internationalization. The other new category—abroad/cross-border—describes institutions and providers that are concentrating their efforts on delivering educational programs across borders and that do not have research or service to society as a major part of their mandate. They are most interested in extending the geographic reach of their teaching, through face to face teaching; distance education, including online learning; or a combination of both. The "ethos" category has been broadened and relabeled "at home/campus based." It remains in this typology because many institutions still concentrate on the intercultural/international dimension of a campus and are not involved in mobility programs or cross-border activities.

The process and at home/campus-based approaches focus on the primary functions and culture of the institution, including curricular, extracurricular, and organizational aspects. The rationales and outcomes approaches can be seen as opposite ends of the same continuum, but they are fundamentally different, as rationales deal with drivers and outcomes attach more weight to the expected results of internationalization. The activity approach, which is still probably the most common approach, emphasizes the actual program initiatives that form part of the internationalization efforts. The abroad/cross-border approach accentuates the linkages with other countries and focuses on all four aspects of academic mobility.

Approaches at the National or Sectoral Level

This section describes four categories of approaches at the national and sectoral levels (table 1.7). These approaches are not mutually exclusive, and they are not meant to exclude other approaches. The purpose of developing these frameworks is to help institutions and policymakers reflect on the dominant features of their current approach to internationalization and to think about what approach they would like to adopt in the future. It is useful and revealing to analyze whether the dominant approach used is consistent with and complementary to the rationales and values driving the efforts to internationalize. An examination of approaches highlights some of the emerging trends, issues, and questions important for internationalization.

Table 1.7 Approaches to Internationalization at the National and Sectoral Levels

Approach	Description
Programs	Internationalization of higher education is seen in terms of providing funded programs that facilitate international activities, such as mobility, research, and linkages.
Rationales	Internationalization of higher education is presented in terms of why it is important that the sector becomes more international. Rationales vary enormously and can include human resource development, strategic alliances, commercial trade, nation-building, and social/cultural development.
Policies	Internationalization of higher education is described in terms of policies that address or emphasize the importance of the international or intercultural dimension in higher education. Policies can come from a variety of sectors, including education, foreign affairs, science and technology, culture, and trade.
Strategies	Internationalization is considered a key element of a national strategy to achieve a country's goals and priorities, both domestically and internationally.

Source: Knight (2004).

Trends, Issues, and Questions

Key words used to study and analyze the international dimension of higher education are *complex, multifaceted, diverse, controversial, changing,* and *challenging*. These adjectives paint a picture of internationalization as a phenomenon that is evolving on many fronts, both as actor and reactor. This evolutionary—some might label it revolutionary—process reveals a number of new issues and raises a number of questions.

Macro trends are affecting higher education. These include the movement to a knowledge society and economy; developments in information and communication technology; a stronger sense of regionalism (trade, economic, cultural); greater mobility of people, capital, ideas, knowledge, and technology; more trade liberalization, through bilateral and multilateral trade agreements; increased emphasis on the market economy; and shifts in locus of governance from national to regional and international.

These trends have the following implications for the international dimension of higher education:

- increased demand for higher education, especially lifelong learning and professional training

- greater diversity of education providers, including commercial companies, private for-profit institutions, for-profit entities of public institutions, and "degree mills"
- innovations in distance/on-line delivery and cross-border provision of higher education
- new types of certifications and qualifications being offered
- new levels and types of quality assurance and accreditation
- more rapid increases in private investment in higher education than in public investment
- new forms of administrative and academic partnerships among different types of providers
- changing forms and purposes of strategic alliances
- increased brain drain and brain gain (physical and virtual)
- new forms of intra- and interregional higher education programs, especially mobility initiatives
- more international competition and innovation in market approach to education
- shift from development aid to partnership exchange to commercial trade in education.

These trends raise important questions. As education and training programs move across borders, what are the implications for quality assurance and accreditation of programs and providers? What role do institutions, national quality assurance, and accreditation agencies play in monitoring incoming and outgoing programs? Is there a need for regional or international mechanisms to augment national/institutional efforts to monitor cross-border delivery?

The emergence of new private sector for-profit companies brings new actors to the world of internationalization. How will these new providers collaborate with, compete with, complement, and change the work of traditional public and private institutions?

How does internationalization deal with the intersection of international and intercultural? Is internationalization a vehicle for increased understanding and appreciation of cultural diversity and fusion, or is it an agent of cultural homogenization? How do curricula, the teaching/learning process, research, extracurricular activities, and academic mobility contribute to intercultural understanding and cultural hybridization/homogenization?

The complexities involved in working in the field of internationalization require additional knowledge, attitudes, skills, and understandings about the international/intercultural/global dimension of higher education. How are these competencies developed and recognized for academics, administrators, and policymakers working in the field of internationalization of higher education?

Is there a shift away from social and cultural rationales toward the economic and commercial interests of internationalization? Is this true in all regions of the world? What are the implications for higher education policy (funding, access, quality, role in society, research, curriculum, regulatory frameworks)?

What are the implications of increased academic mobility for the recognition of academic and professional recognition of credentials? What is the relationship between recognition of credentials and the trend toward validation of competencies? What is the role of the regional UNESCO conventions on credential recognition?

The international dimension of higher education is gaining a higher profile in policy arenas outside of education, such as immigration, trade and commerce, culture, and economic development. How can the education sector work collaboratively with these sectors at the national and regional level to ensure that the internationalization is understood and contributes to human, social, cultural, scientific, and economic development?

How is internationalization contributing to brain drain or brain gain? What mechanisms can help enhance the benefits of increased academic and professional mobility but mitigate the negative impact of the imbalances in the talent flowing out of countries?

What are the connections between academic mobility, labor mobility, and temporary or permanent migration? Are targeted international student recruitment campaigns linked to migration patterns?

How does internationalization facilitate regional integration? How does regional integration affect internationalization?

In 2020 what will the major accomplishments of internationalization of the past 30 years be? Are academic leaders, education policymakers, and politicians taking a long-term perspective on the new opportunities and risks inherent in globalization and its consequences for the internationalization of higher education? What key issues or questions require further evaluation, research, and policy analysis to address and guide the long-term impact and implications of internationalization at the institutional, sectoral, national, regional, and international levels?

If a panel of pundits were to gather in 2020 to reflect on the contributions of internationalization to higher education, what would they conclude? Would they focus on the role of internationalization in the preparation of an elite cadre of internationally talented and mobile scholars, the commercialization and commodification of education as a tradable service, the homogenization or standardization of curriculum and the overuse of English as the language of instruction, the reduction in academic standards and quality as a result of the increase in nonrecognized international degree and accreditation mills, and the inequitable access to higher education opportunities? Or would they conclude that internationalization had contributed to developing students, scholars, professors who are more knowledgeable and analytical about international and global issues and more interculturally aware and skilled; helped address local, national, regional and global issues; improved the quality and relevance of curriculum and the teaching and learning process; used information and communication technology; established new partnerships and delivery methods across borders to increase access to higher education; and demonstrated that the international dimension of higher education augments the indigenous cultural and national characteristics of higher education and contributes to social, economic, and cultural development?

The direction, progress, and contribution of the internationalization of higher education depends on decisions and actions taken today. For this reason, the analysis of opportunities and risks of internationalization at the individual, institutional, sectoral, national, and regional level is important to ensure that policy and political decisions are informed about and aware of the benefits and challenges of the international dimension of education.

References

Adam, S. 2001. *Transnational Education*. Report prepared by the Confederation of European Union Rectors Conference, Geneva.

Altbach, P. 2001. "Higher Education and the WTO: Globalization Run Amok." *International Higher Education* (Boston College) 23: 2–4.

Arnove, R., and C. Torres, eds. 1999. *Comparative Education: The Dialectic of the Global and the Local*. Oxford: Rowman and Littlefield.

Arum, S., and J. Van de Water. 1992. The Need for a Definition of International Education in U.S. Universities. Bridges to the Futures: *Strategies for Internationalizing Higher Education*, C. Klasek, ed. , IL: Association of International Education Administrators.

Bloom, D. 2003. "Mastering Globalization: From Ideas to Action on Higher Education Reform." In *Universities and Globalization: Private Linkages, Public Trust*, ed. G. Breton and M. Lambert, 139–152. Paris: UNESCO/Université Laval/Economica.

Breton, G., and M. Lambert, eds. 2003. *Universities and Globalization: Private Linkages, Public Trust*. Paris: UNESCO/Université Laval/Economica.

Corporate University Xchange. 1999. *Annual Survey of Corporate University Future Directions*. New York: Corporate University Xchange.

Cunningham, S., Y. Ryan, L. Stedman, S. Tapsall, S. Bagdon, T. Flew, and P. Coaldrake. 2000. *The Business of Borderless Education*. Department of Education, Training and Youth Affairs, Canberra, Australia.

CVCP (Committee of Vice-Chancellors and Principals). 2000. *The Business of Borderless Education: UK Perspectives*. London.

Davis, D., A. Olsen, and A. Bohm eds. 2000. *Transnational Education: Providers, Partners and Policy. A Research Study*. IDP Brisbane, Australia.

de Wit, H., ed. 1995. *Strategies or Internationalization of Higher Education: A Comparative Study of Australia, Canada, Europe and the United States*. Amsterdam: European Association for International Education.

————. 2000. "Changing Rationales for the *Internationalization of Higher Education*." In *Internationalization of Higher Education: An Institutional Perspective*. Papers on Higher Education Bucharest, UNESCO/ CEPES. Bucharest.

————. 2002. *Internationalization of Higher Education in the United States of America and Europe: A Historical, Comparative, and Conceptual Analysis*. Westport, CT: Greenwood Press.

Enders, J., and O. Fulton, eds. 2002. *Higher Education in a Globalising World: International Trends and Mutual Observations*. Dordrecht: Kluwer Academic Publishers.

Gacel-Ávila, J. 1999. *Internacionalización de la educación superior en America Latina y el Caribe: reflexiones y lineamientos*. Organisation Universitaire Interamericaine y La Associacion Mexicana para la Educación Internacional, Guadalajara, Mexico.

————. 2003. *La internacionalización de la educación superior: paradigma para la ciudadania global*. Univeridad de Guadalajara, Guadalajara, Mexico.

Garrett, R. 2003. "Mapping the Education Industry. Part 2: Public Companies' Relationships with Higher Education." Observatory on Borderless Higher Education, London.

GATE (Global Alliance for Transnational Education.) 1997. "Certification Manual." Washington, DC, and Wellington, New Zealand.

Kalvermark, T., and M. Van der Wende, eds. 1997. *National Policies for the Internationalisation of Higher Education in Europe*. Hogskoleverket Studies. Stockholm: National Agency for Higher Education.

Knight, J. 1994 *Internationalization: Elements and Checkpoints*. Research Monograph No. 7. Ottawa: Canadian Bureau for International Education.

————. 1999a. "Issues and Trends in Internationalization: A Comparative Perspective." In *A New World of Knowledge: Canadian Universities and Globalization*, ed. S. Bond and J.P. Lemasson, 201–38. Ottawa: International Development Research Centre.

————. 1999b. *A Time of Turbulence and Transformation for Internationalization*. Research Monograph No. 14. Ottawa: Canadian Bureau for International Education.

————. 2002. *Trade in Higher Education Services: The Implications of GATS*. Observatory on Borderless Higher Education, London.

————. 2003. "Updated Internationalization Definition." *International Higher Education* (Boston College) 33: 2–3.

————. 2004. "Internationalization Remodelled: Definitions, Rationales and Approaches." *Journal for Studies in International Education* 8 (1): 5–31.

Knight J., and H. de Wit, eds. 1997. *Internationalization of Higher Education in Asia Pacific Countries*. Amsterdam: European Association for International Education.

————. 1999. *Quality and Internationalisation in Higher Education*. Paris: Organisation for Economic Co-operation and Development.

Larsen, K., J.P. Martin, and R. Morris. 2001. "Trade in Educational Services: Trends and Emerging Issues." Working Paper, Organisation for Economic Co-operation and Development, Paris.

Larsen, K., and S. Vincent-Lancrin. 2002. "International Trade in Educational Services: Good or Bad?" *Higher Education Management and Policy* 14 (3).

Levy, D. 2003. *Expanding Higher Education Capacity through Private Growth: Contributions and Challenges*. Observatory on Borderless Higher Education, London.

Marginson, S. 2000. "Rethinking Academic Work in the Global Era." *Journal of Higher Education Policy and Management* 22 (1).

————. ed. 2001. *Globalization and Higher Education: Views from the South*. Paper No. 46 from the Society for Research into Higher Education Conference in Cape Town, South Africa.

Marquez, A.M. 2002. "The Impact of Globalization on Higher Education: The Latin American Context." In *Globalization and the Market in Higher Education: Quality, Accreditation and Qualifications*. Paris: UNESCO/ Economica.

Nilsson, B. 1999. "Internationalization at Home: Theory and Praxis." *European Association for International Education Forum* 12. Amsterdam.

OECD (Organisation for Economic Co-operation and Development). 2002. "The Growth of Cross-Border Education." *Educational Policy Analysis*. Paris.

Pretelt, C., and M. Lopez, eds. 2002. *Guia para la internacionalizacion de las instituciones de educacion superior de Colombia*. Instituto Colombiano Para el Fomento de la Educacion Superior, Bogotá.

Salmi, J. 2001. "Tertiary Education in the Twenty-First Century: Challenges and Opportunities." *Higher Education Management* 3 (2): 105–30.

Sauve, P. 2002. "Trade, Education and the GATS: What's in, What's Out, What's All the Fuss About?" *Higher Education Management and Policy* 14 (3).

Scott, P. 2000. "Globalisation and Higher Education: Challenges for the Twenty-First Century." *Journal of Studies in International Education* 4 (1): 1–10.

Soderqvist, M. 2002. *Internationalization and Its Management at Higher Education Institutions: Applying Conceptual, Content and Discourse Analysis*. Helsinki School of Economics, Helsinki.

UNESCO (United Nations Educational, Scientific and Cultural Organization). 2002. *Globalization and the Market in Higher Education: Quality, Accreditation and Qualifications*. Paris: UNESCO/Economica.

UNESCO and Council of Europe. 2001. *The UNESCO-CEPES/Council of Europe Code of Good Practice for the Provision of Transnational Education*. Paris: UNESCO.

Van Dalen, Dorrit, ed. 2002. *The Global Higher Education Market for Higher Education*. Netherlands Organization for International Cooperation in Higher Education (NUFFIC), The Hague.

Van Damme, D. 2001. "Higher Education in the Age of Globalization: The Need for a New Regulatory Framework for Recognition, Quality Assurance, and Accreditation." Working Paper, UNESCO, Paris.

————. 2002. *Quality Assurance in an International Environment: National and International Interests and Tensions*. Background paper for the Council for Higher Education Accreditation International Seminar, San Francisco.

Van der Wende, M. 1997. "Missing Links: The Relationship between National Policies for Internationalisation and Those for Higher Education in General." In *National Policies for the Internationalisation of Higher Education in Europe*, ed. T. Kalvermark and M. Van der Wende, pp. 10–31. Hogskoleverket Studies. Stockholm: National Agency for Higher Education.

————. 2002. "Higher Education Globally: Toward New Frameworks for Research and Policy." In CHEPS Inaugurals 2002, pp. 26–69. University of Twente, Netherlands.

Van Vught, F., M. Van der Wende, and D. Westerheijden. 2003. "Globalization and Internationalisation: Policy Agendas Compared." In *Higher Education Dynamics*, ed. J. Enders and O. Fulton, 103–20. Dordrecht: Kluwer Academic Publishers.

Wachter, B. 2003. "An Introduction: Internationalization at Home in Context." *Journal of Studies in International Education* 7 (1): 5–11.

2
Regional and International Challenges to Higher Education in Latin America

Lauritz B. Holm-Nielsen, Kristian Thorn,
José Joaquín Brunner, and Jorge Balán

Mobility of talented individuals, new providers of higher education, and participation in knowledge networks offer many possibilities for countries in Latin America to access state of the art knowledge, transfer technology, and exploit new business opportunities. In open, increasingly knowledge-based economies, advanced education and research are key to remaining competitive. Yet the international dimension of higher education is a double-edged sword for Latin America. Mobility of skilled individuals risks eroding the region's knowledge base and draining scarce resources. Every year emigration claims a significant portion of the region's better-educated population (Wodon 2003).

Countries in Latin America are becoming players in the global market for talent and higher education services. Between 1993 and 2002, the number of Latin American postsecondary students in the United States increased by 50 percent. Foreign providers have also entered the market for higher education in Latin America. European and U.S.-based institutions, such as the University of Bologna, the University of Heidelberg, and New York University, now offer programs or are establishing branches in the region. Within Latin America universities have also begun to operate across borders, such as Mexico's Technological Institute of Monterrey, which offers distance-learning programs over the Internet.

Evidence from Latin America and the OECD suggests that the best strategy for reaching the frontier of new knowledge is to engage in the exchange of people and ideas rather than turn inward. For countries in Latin America, the challenge is to provide learning, research, and job opportunities for talented individuals to ensure a sufficient supply of advanced skills to their national economies. Important steps have already been taken to increase the stock of highly skilled workers. Enrollment in higher education has more than doubled in the past decades and continues to expand, educational opportunities have diversified, and university management has been decentralized to increase responsiveness to students and industry. Nonetheless, the potential for higher education remains unrealized in Latin America. Graduation rates are low, higher education institutions face a multitude of quality problems, inequities are widespread, and there is a mismatch between many specialties offered and the needs of the labor market.

This chapter assesses the extent to which Latin American countries are prepared to meet the challenges and opportunities offered by the knowledge economy and the globalization of higher education. It examines recent trends and reviews the current status of key aspects of higher education in the region. The overview describes the context for the internationalization of higher education, the focus of the rest of this volume.

Expansion and Diversification

Enrollment in higher education increased significantly in Latin America during the past four decades. In 2001, 23 percent of Latin Americans 18–24 were enrolled in postsecondary institutions. This represents an annual growth rate in enrollment of 2.3 percent since 1985. Argentina, Uruguay, and notably Chile are among the regional leaders, with enrollment rates of more than 30 percent (figure 2.1). Despite impressive growth, however, Latin America still lags behind leading economies. Among the OECD countries the average higher education enrollment rate is currently 56 percent (World Bank 2002d).

Figure 2.1 Gross Higher Education Enrollment in Latin America and the OECD, 1965–2000

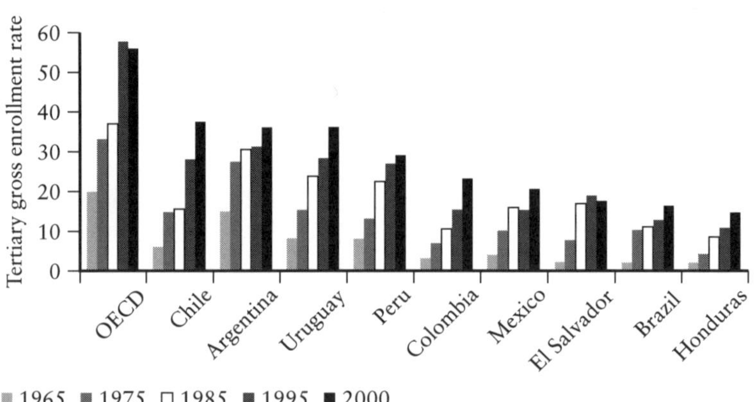

Source: Task Force on Higher Education and Society (2000); World Bank (2002d).

Although less pronounced, expansion has also taken place in graduate education. In 1997 students in MA and PhD programs represented an estimated 2.4 percent of higher education enrollment in Latin America. This figure may understate the actual number, since it does not take into account growth in professions such as law and medicine, which in most Latin American countries do not lead to graduate degrees.

Despite the higher priority given to graduate education in recent years, Latin America produces a small number of PhDs. Every year the OECD countries produce 1 new PhD per 5,000 people (NSF 2002). In contrast, the ratio is 1 PhD per 70,000 people in Brazil, 1 per 140,000 in Chile, and 1 per 700,000 in Colombia (World Bank 2002b).

Approaches to Expansion

Latin American countries have approached the expansion of higher education in different ways. In Argentina, Mexico, Uruguay, and Venezuela, public universities have expanded and diversified, and new public institutions have been created at the regional level to absorb some of the demand. In Brazil, Chile, and Colombia, public education has remained restricted, and private institutions have accounted for most of the increase in opportunities.

Differences notwithstanding, private provision of higher education has grown remarkably across the region in recent decades (table 2.1). Faced with rising demand for advanced learning opportunities, governments in several countries have deregulated the market for higher education, bringing an end to what had been a public sector monopoly. Except in Cuba, private institutions of higher education—for profit and nonprofit—are now found throughout the region, and in most countries the private sector has increased its coverage, complexity, and visibility. Currently, private institutions in Latin America account for more than 40 percent of higher education enrollment.

Nonuniversity Tertiary Education

The growth in private provision has been accompanied by an increase in the number of nonuniversity tertiary institutions. Such institutions comprise technical schools, teacher colleges, and postsecondary vocational training facilities, generally offering programs of a shorter duration than universities. Currently, there are 3,000 nonuniversity tertiary institutions in Latin America, of which roughly 60 percent are private (Schwartzman 2002). A high proportion of postsecondary students in Latin America is enrolled in one of these institutions. The nonuniversity system accounts for 28 percent of total higher education enrollment in Venezuela, 30 percent in Chile, and 32 percent in Brazil (World Bank 2002a, 2002c).

Table 2.1 Private Higher Education in Latin America, 1985–2002

	Percent of total enrollment				
Year	*40–75 percent*	*30–40 percent*	*20–30 percent*	*10–20 percent*	*Less than 10 percent*
1985	Brazil Colombia Dominican Rep.	Chile El Salvador Peru	Argentina Guatemala Paraguay	Costa Rica Ecuador Honduras Mexico Nicaragua Venezuela	Bolivia Cuba Panama Uruguay
2002	Brazil Chile Colombia Dominican Rep. El Salvador Nicaragua Paraguay Peru	Venezuela	Argentina Costa Rica Ecuador Guatemala Mexico	Honduras	Cuba Bolivia Panama Uruguay

Source: Schwartzman (2002); World Bank (2002a and 2003); OECD (2002a); García Guadilla (1998).

The differentiation of higher education has several positive implications. The region features far more learning opportunities today than it did a few decades ago. For this reason, the opportunity to accommodate a diverse student body with different backgrounds, skills, and aspirations has expanded. The impressive growth in higher education coverage could not have occurred had it relied solely on the existing, primarily public, higher education institutions. Diversification is crucial to the region's continual efforts to increase higher education enrollment and accommodate growing demand.

While positive developments in most respects, diversification and increased coverage have come at a price. Diversity of institutional ownership, autonomy, funding, and programs have contributed to a somewhat disjointed and fragmented system, made up of institutions that are only weakly linked. In Colombia, for example, the proliferation of a highly heterogeneous university sector has made it difficult to coordinate efforts and avoid internal inconsistencies (Brunner 2002a). A major difficulty throughout the region is the highly segmented character of nonuniversity tertiary education. These institutions often lack a clear educational policy and strategy, raising many questions about the quality and relevance of the learning offered. Problems are exacerbated by a lack of information on educational content and labor market outcomes that could guide student choice (Brunner 2002a).

Financing Higher Education

Expansion and improvement of higher education require adequate resources. To assess the relative size of investments in higher education in Latin America, figure 2.2 shows total public and private spending on higher education in 1999 relative to the level of income for a sample of 53 countries. The estimated trend line reflects the expected log of total (public and private) investment in higher education per capita when a linear regression is performed on the log of per capita GDP.

While tailing high-income OECD countries, Latin American countries invest close to what is expected based on their level of per capita income. Brazil, Paraguay, and Peru are positioned on the trend line, while Argentina and Mexico invest slightly less than predicted. Colombia and notably Chile perform above what is expected.

Chile and Colombia reveal the advantage of supplementing public subsidies with private contributions. Both are among the Latin American countries that allocate the least public funding to higher education relative to GDP (figure 2.3). But due to sizable private spending, they allocate the highest share of GDP to higher education in the sample. In addition to

Figure 2.2 Total Investment in Higher Education Relative to Income in Selected Countries, 1999

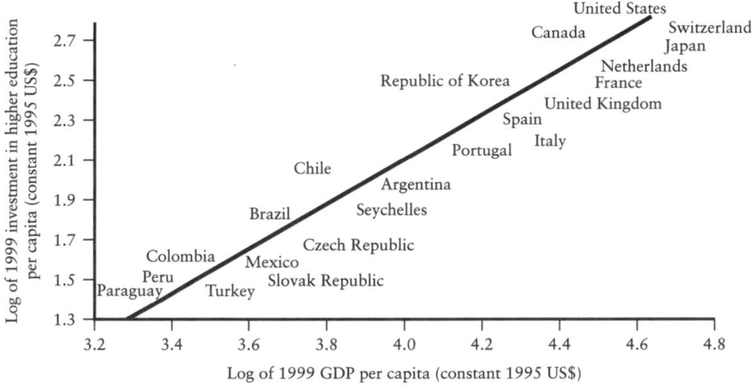

Note: Some countries at the lower range were omitted to make the figure more legible. For the Sub-Saharan African countries in the sample, only 1996 data on public spending on higher education were available.
Source: OECD (2002a); World Bank (2002d); ADEA (1999).

Figure 2.3 Investments in Higher Education in Selected Latin American and Caribbean Countries, 1999 (Percentage of GDP)

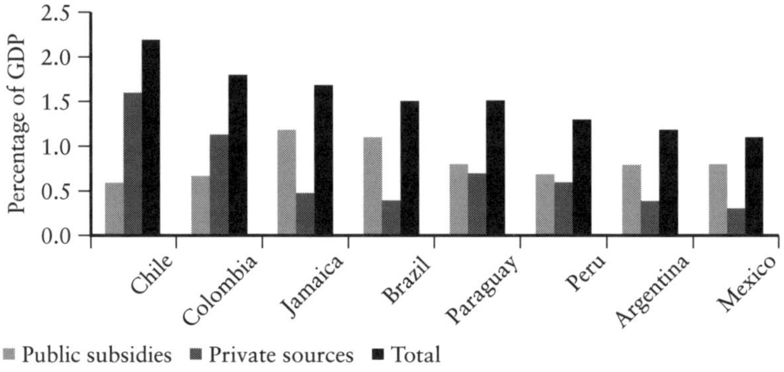

Source: OECD (2002a); World Bank (2002c, 2002d, 2003).

increasing investment, private contributions have the potential to make the higher education system less vulnerable to fluctuations in the public sector's ability to invest in education.

Public universities in Latin America are financed primarily through taxes. Reforms to increase reliance on cost recovery through student payment in one form or another are often politically contentious and are in many cases met with resistance. In 1999, for example, a move to raise tuition at Mexico's largest university, the National Autonomous University of Mexico, was abandoned following a student strike that closed down the university for several months.

Nonetheless, the tendency in recent years has been to rely increasingly on cost sharing in Latin America. Charging tuition to students who can afford to pay or have access to credit may be beneficial, since it provides additional resources for higher education and eases the strain on state budgets. In addition, it ensures that the costs of higher education are borne by those who reap the benefits.

The fraction of costs borne by students at public universities varies across countries (figure 2.4). In Chile, Colombia, Costa Rica, Ecuador, and Jamaica, the level of student financing is similar to that in Ireland, the Republic of Korea, and Spain. In other countries in the region, such as Bolivia, Guatemala, and Honduras, cost recovery is very low. In Argentina and Brazil, which charge no tuition for undergraduate studies at public universities, financial contributions from students are insignificant.

To prevent reducing quality as higher education expands, increasing reliance on cost recovery may be a viable option. Since charging tuition shifts

Figure 2.4 Cost Recovery at Public Universities in Selected Countries in Latin America and the Caribbean

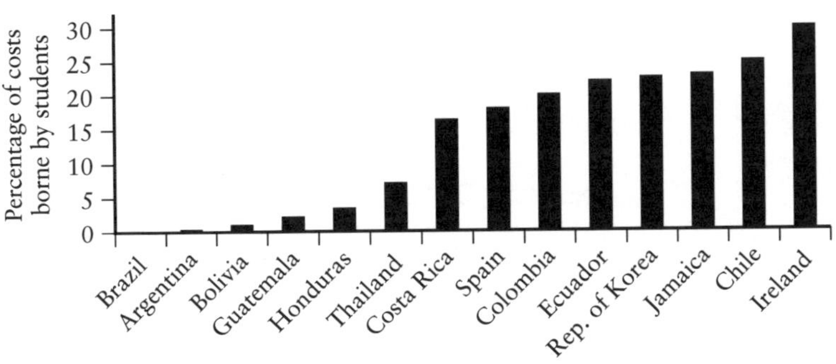

Source: Schwartzman (2002); World Bank (2002b); De Ferranti and others (2003).

influence from the institution and the government to the student and the family, such a measure would pave the way for a more demand-driven system. However, cost recovery is no panacea. Tuition-financed higher education may imply greater inequities. In Argentina, for example, students from the richest 20 percent of the population constitute 29 percent of the student body in free public higher education institutions, whereas the corresponding ratio in fee-charging private institutions is more than 60 percent (Del Bello 2002). The composition of the student body in Brazilian universities is similar (Schwartzman 2002). Consequently, reliance on cost recovery must be tied closely to financial assistance to needy students to maintain accessibility for low-income families.

In several Latin American countries, public universities are developing new ways of raising revenue. Many universities recognize that public subsidies will not grow in the near future. For that reason, they must be entrepreneurial. Some universities have begun generating income by selling services, contracting research, and renting out facilities. In Argentina, for example, resources generated by universities increased from 7 percent of the total budget in 1991 to 11 percent in 2001 (Becerra and others 2003). Exploring new sources of revenue can increase the universities' ability to be innovative and improve quality. It may also increase their relevance, since the sale of services requires universities to be responsive to the needs of society.

Addressing problems of low internal efficiency could ease budgetary constraints and provide the basis for improving quality and increasing coverage. Throughout the region, graduation rates are very low, and they have deteriorated in recent decades. Internal inefficiencies are particularly

Figure 2.5 Annual Number of Students Admitted to and Graduated from Universities in Argentina and Colombia, 1982–2001

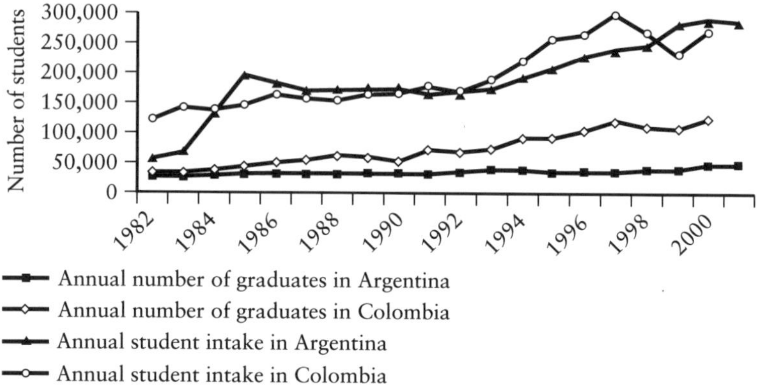

Note: Figures for Argentina are for national universities, which account for about 85 percent of enrollment in higher education.
Source: Ministerio de Educación, Ciencia y Tecnología de Argentina (2002); ICFES (2000).

prevalent in countries with open access to universities. In Argentina, for example, 40 percent of university students drop out the first year (Marquis 2003). Assuming that it takes five years to complete higher education, only one in four admitted students graduates in Argentina; the figure is one in three in Chile and one in two in Colombia (figure 2.5).

The efficiency of higher education institutions varies across countries. While figure 2.6 arguably does not reflect differences in quality, it is noteworthy that Brazil, Colombia, and Venezuela have similar levels of enrollment as Malaysia, Mexico, Peru, and Thailand but spend a much higher percentage of GDP on higher education. Similarly, Argentina, Portugal, and Spain have higher enrollment rates than Chile but spend 1 percentage point of GDP less on higher education.

Low student-teacher ratios are a source of inefficiency in several Latin American countries. In federal universities in Brazil, for example, there are only 9 students per teacher, compared with 15.9 in Spain, 16.7 in the OECD, and 17.4 in Ireland (OECD 2002a). Combined expenditures on current and retired faculty members represent 80 of the total budget in Argentina and 90 percent in Brazil, leaving only limited resources for nonsalary expenditures (Marquis 2003). In comparison, the Republic of Korea spends less than half of its budget on teacher compensation (OECD 2002a).

Figure 2.6 Gross Higher Education Enrollment Rate and Expenditure on Higher Education as a Percentage of GDP in Selected Countries, 2002

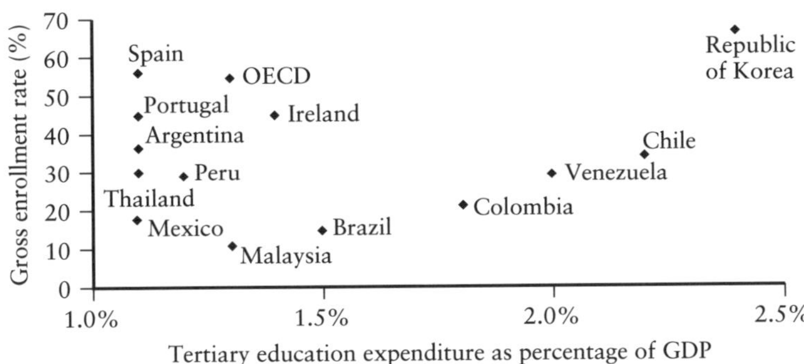

Source: OECD (2002a); World Bank (2002d).

Teaching, Quality, and Relevance

The quality and relevance of human capital and knowledge generated by higher education institutions is critical to Latin America's social and economic development. While high-income countries are raising the stakes, Latin America is still dealing with longstanding problems, such as underdeveloped curricula, lack of teaching materials, underqualified faculty, and labor market imbalances.

Adopting New Pedagogical Approaches

The significant expansion of higher education in Latin America has increased the diversity of interests, skills, and aspirations of admitted students. However, universities have not made sufficient provisions to accommodate such diversity by developing curricula that include a mix of teaching methods, learning content, and programs. High regional dropout rates and delays in graduation are testimony to this fact.

Most Latin American countries have yet to fully adopt a pedagogical model that involves student participation and an emphasis on "learning to learn" methodologies. Reproduction of content and sole reliance on classroom instruction are still widespread, and inadequate focus is often placed on cultivating skills such as creativity, reflection, and entrepreneurship. Adoption of a more problem-based mode of knowledge formation is made difficult by weak ties between university departments and the lack of a multidisciplinary approach among instructors (Altbach 2003). In addition, students are usually required to specialize at the beginning of their studies. This system generates rigidities in the learning process. It goes against the international tendency of more general and module-based undergraduate education and specialization at the graduate level, and it complicates the delivery of short-term courses to an international audience.

A reason for concern is the loose ties between scholars and universities in Latin America. Roughly 60 percent of teachers at public and 86 percent of teachers at private universities work part time, and many of them hold more than one job (World Bank 2002b). While mobility brings some benefits, part-time employment often goes against attempts to establish a critical mass of professional instructors and researchers and efforts to create attractive learning environments in which teachers and students have time to interact.

Processes to adjust pedagogical methods to changing circumstances in Latin America are slowed by deep-rooted practices and compensation structures that emphasize seniority rather than performance (Altbach 2003). To overcome such obstacles, teaching awards have been established in a number of countries to increase the visibility of good practices and encourage excellence in teaching and research. Mexico, for example, has a program that gives national recognition to outstanding members of academia. In addition to improving the quality of teaching, the program has been successful in reducing brain drain by providing opportunities and higher salaries to talented scholars (El-Khawas 1998).

Improving the Quality of Higher Education

Latin American countries face a multitude of quality problems in higher education. These include overcrowded universities, deteriorating physical facilities, lack of equipment, obsolete instruction material, and outdated curricula. Provision of high-quality education is also hampered by weak learning outcomes in primary and secondary education. Universities in Latin America must often devote significant time and resources to upgrading the skills of secondary graduates who are ill-prepared for higher education (Brunner 2002a).

Insufficient qualifications of teaching staff are another concern. Few university professors in the region hold doctoral degrees (figure 2.7). Less than 4 percent of professors in Colombia and Mexico have PhDs; among the regional leaders in higher education, only 1 in 10 professors has a PhD, except in Brazil, where 30 percent of professors hold doctorates. For Latin America as a whole, less than 26 percent of professors hold master's degrees (García Guadilla 1998).

Figure 2.7 Percentage of Professors with Doctoral Degrees in Selected Countries, 2001

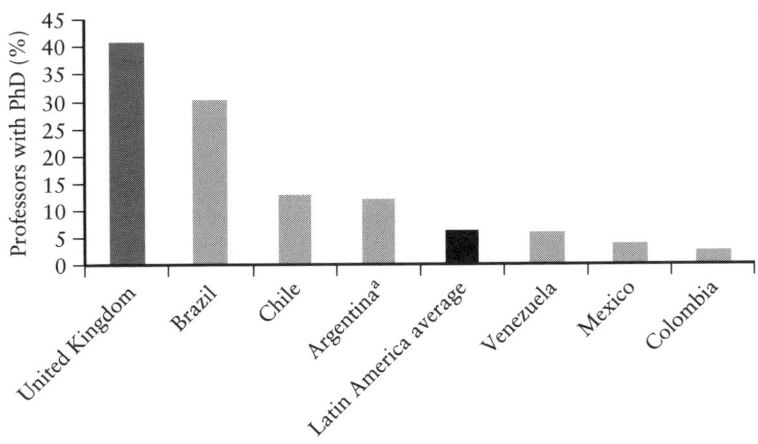

a. Includes public universities only.
Source: World Bank (2002a)

Assuring Quality

Concerns about quality, deregulation of higher education, and growth in private provision have sharpened the focus on academic standards and quality assurance mechanisms throughout Latin America. Governments increasingly want to make sure that students receive value when investing time and resources in higher education (Balán 1996). Quality assurance is also recognized as a vital element in ensuring that the entrance of foreign providers does not reduce quality.

A tangible sign of the priority given to upholding quality standards is the establishment of independent national accreditation agencies and committees. Such systematic modes of quality control generally involve the certification of new higher education institutions and the accreditation of existing programs based on established standards and expectations.

In recent years accreditation agencies for undergraduate programs have been created in Argentina, Belize, Bolivia, Chile, Colombia, Costa Rica, El Salvador, Mexico, and Nicaragua. One example is Argentina's National Commission for Evaluation and University Accreditation (CONEAU). Created in 1995, CONEAU represents an attempt to establish a centralized and uniform system for monitoring the quality of universities (Hansen and Holm-Nielsen 2002). CONEAU plays a key role in granting legal status to new institutions, both public and private, and it monitors private institutions for a number of years. While the most common arrangement is a single national agency, countries such as Colombia and Mexico have taken a more pluralist approach by establishing separate agencies for different regions, purposes, and types of undergraduate programs.

Accreditation of graduate education is also expanding in the region. The prime example is Brazil, which has a long-standing tradition of quality assurance of its graduate programs through the Coordination for the Improvement of Higher Education Personnel (CAPES) (Balbachevsky and Quinteiro 2003).

Methods of quality assurance used throughout the region include external peer review, quantitative performance indicators, and student assessment. In addition, institutional self-assessment focusing on strengths and weaknesses is a key ingredient in efforts to improve quality (DePietro-Jurand and Lemaitre 2002). There is also a trend toward emphasizing learning outcomes and acquired competencies of students rather than inputs and process aspects of education. Making good use of collected information and self-assessment processes requires universities to have the skills and resources to examine their programs critically and know how to improve them. For some institutions in Latin America, this entails strengthening the administrative capacity and nurturing a culture of improvement to ensure that quality assurance initiatives result in the desired change (El-Khawas, DePietro-Jurand, and Holm-Nielsen 1998).

Where governments in Latin America have neither the resources nor the means to manage the higher education system from above, indirect measures of quality assurance are sometimes used. One possibility is making public and private higher education institutions compete for high-scoring students with access to information on the quality and relevance of programs offered. In Chile, for example, incentives for quality improvement have been created by tying a fraction of public subsidies to each student admitted whose score in the national university entrance exam is among the top 27,000 (Araneda and Marín 2002). Another, not yet very widespread, option is limiting public financial aid to students attending accredited institutions (Hauptman 2002).

Improving Information on Labor Market Responses

Effective labor market feedback systems, such as tracer surveys and regular consultations with employers and recent graduates, are indispensable for adjusting curricula and programs to meet the needs of society. Yet few governments or institutions in Latin America collect such information on a regular basis. Very few data are available on career paths of

Figure 2.8 Degree to Which University Education Is Perceived to Meet the Needs of a Competitive Economy

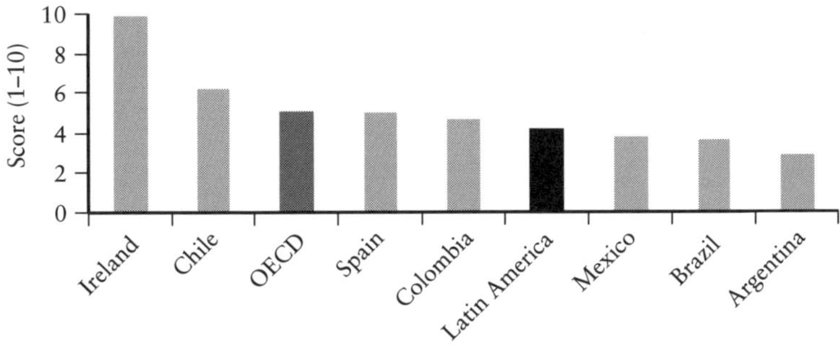

Note: Variables are normalized on a scale of 0 (lowest) to 10 (highest).
Source: IMD (2002).

higher education graduates, making it difficult to uncover potential discrepancies between supply and demand of highly skilled labor. Despite increased labor market responsiveness due to the rise of private higher education, programs in Latin America are still offered primarily on the basis of tradition or scholar preferences (Levy 2002).

Increasing the Relevance of Higher Education

Higher education is not perceived as meeting the needs of a competitive economy in Latin America. Surveys conducted in 49 countries by the Institute for Management Development show that—with the exception of Chile—every country in the region falls short of the OECD average (figure 2.8). Mexico, Argentina, and Venezuela fare worst, while Colombia and Brazil receive marginally better evaluations. While cross-national surveys should be interpreted with caution, the data suggest that higher education in Latin America lags behind high-income nations in terms of relevance for industry.

The relative wages of higher education graduates are on the rise in Latin America (see figure 2.12). Still, clear evidence of labor market imbalances remains. In Argentina, for example, the proportion of highly educated people among the pool of unemployed workers rose from 29 percent in 1990 to 38 percent in 1999 (EIU 2001). Some fields turn out large numbers of graduates despite the lack of demand in the economy. Argentina has more physicians per 1,000 people than the United States. By contrast, other careers, such as engineering, are undersupplied (Hansen and Holm-Nielsen 2002).

Recognizing the need to improve the relevance of higher education and to address imbalances, some countries have established labor market monitoring programs. Chile and Colombia recently set up labor market "observatories" to monitor and analyze the occupational performance of university graduates (Brunner and Meller 2004). Better information on labor market responses and experiences of graduates in their early careers can guide human resource policy, curricular adjustments, and investments in higher education. Across the region, countries are also trying to boost labor mobility between higher education institutions and the productive sector.

Equity and Financial Aid

Expansion of higher education in Latin America has paved the way for better access to advanced training for less privileged groups. However, as enrollment of students from low-income families has increased, so has enrollment of groups already overrepresented in the system. The end result appears to be a distribution of students that is very much the same as before the expansion. Higher education in Latin America remains largely elitist, with the majority of students coming from the wealthier segments of society (figure 2.9).

Figure 2.9 Distribution of University Students in Selected Countries, by Income Quintile, 2001

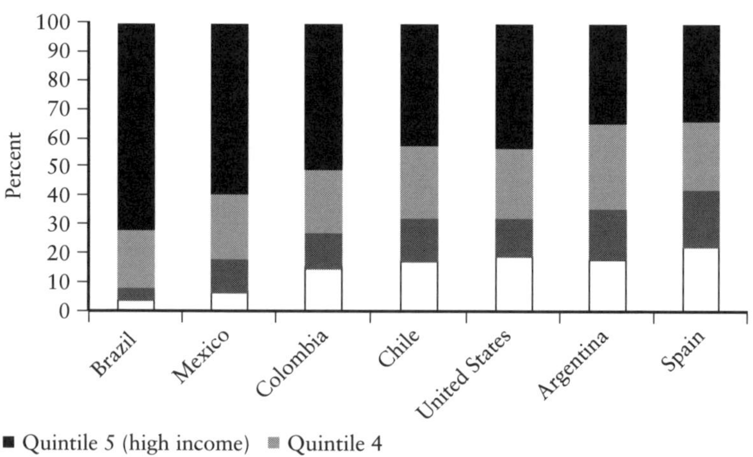

Note: Data for the United States are based on first-year students at four-year colleges in fall 2002.
Source: World Bank (2002b); U.S. Census Bureau (2002); Chronicle of Higher Education (2003).

In Brazil students from the richest 20 percent of the population make up more than 70 percent of enrolled students, whereas the poorest 40 percent make up just 3 percent of the student body. In Mexico the least affluent 60 percent of the population accounts for only 18 percent of enrollment in higher education. Colombia, Chile, and particularly Argentina fare somewhat better, but access to higher education remains highly unequal.

In many cases regressive patterns in higher education stem from inequities in basic education. Students who can afford to pay for high-quality private primary and secondary education are often much better prepared for university entrance exams. Quality differences in basic education and tough admission policies lead to the situation in which affluent students are overrepresented in free public higher education institutions. Ill-prepared students from poor families are left with fewer choices, usually involving paying for education in private institutions that place less emphasis on test scores or forgoing higher education altogether. In countries where tuition is charged in public as well as private higher education institutions, less privileged students generally have few options for paying for schooling, let alone living expenses. As rates of return of higher education have risen relative to primary and secondary education, regressive enrollment patterns in higher education translate into higher returns on educational investment for richer families—a recipe for mounting inequalities in already unequal societies.

An effective response to income inequities is targeting financial aid to the most vulnerable. Such aid can be provided in the form of loans or scholarships. Experience from Latin America shows that a financial aid system that relies exclusively on loans can be an obstacle to increasing access to the neediest students (Schwartzman 2002). Poor families are often incapable of providing collateral and are generally reluctant to put themselves in debt. An approach that has proven effective is to make grants available to students with high need and merit and to provide loans to students with some need and excellent academic records (Hauptman 2002). Another option, applied with success in Australia, is providing loans with income-contingent repayment (Chapman 1997).

Despite its positive implications, the supply of financial assistance for higher education does not come close to meeting demand in Latin America. Student aid is generally scarce, and the availability of scholarships remains low. In Venezuela, for example, only 8 percent of students in higher education receive some form of aid. Financial assistance has a value of about one-fifth of the minimum wage, and no aid is available for nonuniversity institutions, where most needy students are enrolled (World Bank 2002a). Moreover, the little financial aid available in Latin America is not always targeted to students from low-income families. In Mexico, for instance, the likelihood of receiving a scholarship for university studies rises with the level of income (De Ferranti and others 2003).

Expanding access to higher education for academically qualified but financially needy students is critical to realizing the full potential of talented individuals in Latin America. Financial aid can, however, be a serious drain on public resources, since real interest and repayment rates are usually low (Hauptman 2002). A promising example of a financially sustainable student aid program is Mexico's Society for the Promotion of Higher Education (SOFES). Participating private universities buy shares in the designated student loan company, which is capitalized by the government and the World Bank. Interaction with students is the responsibility of universities that on-lend funds to students on unsubsidized terms. To date, the program has had single-digit default rates (Canton and Blom 2004). This is partly due to a provision under which a university has to replenish SOFES or become ineligible for additional funds if more than 10 percent of its portfolio is nonperforming. Although this and other initiatives in the region hold considerable promise, they operate on a relatively small scale. Much more remains to be done.

Income inequality does not translate into gender differences in higher education enrollment: in the region as a whole, there are few differences in enrollment rates between men and women, and in Argentina, Brazil, Colombia, El Salvador, Honduras, and Uruguay, women students are in the majority (figure 2.10). This is in contrast to the Republic of Korea, which enrolls a higher percentage of men. Not only do women in Latin America enroll in large numbers, they also perform better than their male counterparts and graduate at higher rates. In Colombia, for example, of the cohort that matriculated in 1995, 53 percent of the women and just 43 percent of the men graduated (World Bank 2003).

Figure 2.10 Gender Distribution of University Enrollment in Selected Countries, 2001

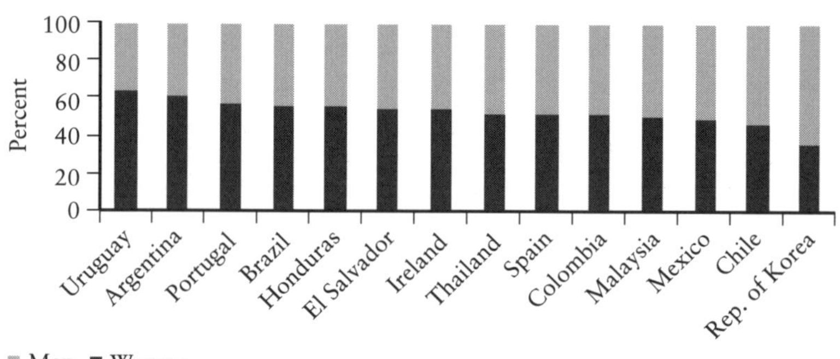

Source: UNESCO (2003); World Bank (2002a, 2002b, 2003).

The majority of Latin American women—like their counterparts around the globe—study traditional fields. Women are overrepresented in education, social sciences, and fine arts and underrepresented in engineering and the hard sciences. They make up a significant proportion of students in law and medicine.

The proportion of women among higher education faculty is generally high throughout Latin America. In Argentina, for example, women outnumber men in full-time university positions (Marquis 2003).

Management of Higher Education

Historically, central and federal governments in Latin America played a significant role in planning and controlling higher education. Regulations and systemwide procedures left limited room for institutional innovation and differentiation. In many Latin American countries, the Ministry of Education determined budget allocations, student admission policies, and the content of offered programs. Institutions had little influence on the number of staff positions, the level of salaries, or promotions (Schwartzman 2002).

As educational opportunities and private sector provision of higher education expand, the rising complexity of the sector has made the model of top-down state control difficult to uphold. Most central and federal governments in Latin America have responded by transferring some powers to the regional or state level. Provinces now manage nonuniversity tertiary education in Argentina, states have a central role in university education in Mexico, and municipalities and states provide a significant part of postsecondary education in Brazil. As a result, funding for higher education has become more geographically dispersed, and the number of postsecondary institutions outside major metropolitan areas is on the rise.

In parallel with the process of decentralization, higher education institutions have been granted greater autonomy. In Venezuela the 1999 constitution guarantees the largest universities autonomy, giving universities there greater freedom to plan and organize programs, appoint their own authorities, designate personnel, and administer the budget (World Bank 2002a). Behind this and similar reforms in the region is the general assumption that those closest to the daily management of higher education institutions are in the best position to make and carry out decisions. In line with international trends in higher education, governing boards and managers are therefore given more leeway to make changes and transform institutions.

Improving Accountability and Incentives

Autonomy, deregulation, privatization, and the arrival of foreign providers of education are not incompatible with continuing quality control and maintaining a steering role for government. In parallel with deregulation and the delegation of authority, supervising ministries in Latin America increasingly rely on establishing a framework that provides incentives for desirable behavior in all areas of the higher education system (Thompson 1998). Such efforts entail holding institutions accountable for their use of public resources and creating systems that reward efficiency and quality. The aforementioned accreditation agencies are testimony to the importance attributed to performance and learning outcomes by governments in the region.

In keeping with these trends, the budget reform agenda in Latin America has moved away from negotiated budgets in which resources are allocated in accordance with tradition or political influence. Such allocation principles are deemed undesirable, since they do not reward high-performing institutions or foster efficiency. Instead, a number of Latin American countries are attempting to establish a direct link between performance and the disbursement of public subsidies. Some of the mechanisms used or being considered are competitive funds, performance-based funding formulas, and institutional performance contracts (Thorn, Holm-Nielsen, and Jeppesen 2004). The competitive fund under the Higher Education Improvement Project in Chile is an example of an innovative approach to university funding. Designed to accelerate processes of institutional modernization, the fund supports projects developed and proposed by higher education institutions. Committees of peers review and select proposals based on transparent procedures and criteria. To date, selected projects have targeted the need for reforming curricula, updating equipment, and strengthening graduate programs (Marquis 2000).

Improving Governance Structures

Important differences exist between public and private universities with regard to internal management. Most private institutions have a centralized, profit-oriented management structure similar to that of a private enterprise. There are generally few mechanisms for internal consultation, and faculties often have limited influence on overall planning and management. While such arrangements are efficient and simplify processes of change, they do little to nurture a feeling of ownership among scholars, and they tend to reduce the flow of information and ideas from below.

By contrast, most public higher education institutions are governed by internally elected academic leaders represented in academic councils. In Brazil, for example, federal universities rely on collegial decisionmaking processes and elected leadership in each department or institution (Schwartzman 1998). Such an arrangement is a central component of a vital and creative academic community. It does, however, run the risk of politicizing and decelerating necessary management decisions. In addition, internal elections do not provide a solid basis for professional leadership, as academic leaders are rarely trained in the management of large, complex institutions (Altbach 2003). For these reasons, public higher education institutions are generally in a weak position to take advantage of the opportunities arising from decentralization.

Strong links between universities and society in the management of higher education institutions can be an effective way to improve the relevance of programs and strengthen national innovation systems. However, universities in Latin America do not have strong traditions of involving and consulting stakeholders. In contrast to OECD countries, few higher education institutions in the region have a governance structure allowing for participation by representatives of industry and civil society (World Bank 2002b). This inward orientation of faculty and management is reflected in the perception of knowledge transfer between universities and industry (figure 2.11). With the exception of Chile, every sampled country in Latin America falls below the OECD average and significantly behind the best performers.

The lack of openness of higher education institutions comes at the expense of taking account of broad societal interests and realizing the full potential of cross-sector synergies and cooperation.

Increasing Flexibility

An issue of rising importance in the management of higher education institutions is the ease with which students can move between different

Figure 2.11 Perception of Knowledge Transfer between Universities and Industry in Selected Countries, 2001

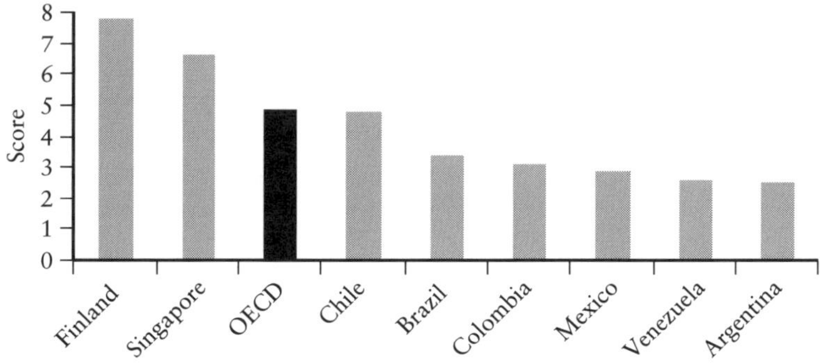

Source: IMD (2002).

learning settings. In most Latin American countries it is difficult to transfer credits from one program to another, let alone between institutions or between programs in different countries. In Venezuela, for instance, almost no agreements exist between universities to allow for the transfer of students or exchange of professors. Students who transfer rarely receive credits for previously completed coursework and often must take supplementary courses, even if the transfer is for the same degree program (World Bank 2002a). Despite relatively few language barriers, no attempt has been made to establish cross-national transfer systems, such as the European Credit Transfer System (ECTS). Strengthening vertical and horizontal linkages between institutions and programs in Latin America would reduce transactions costs, improve efficiency, promote competition between providers of education, and facilitate a focus on student demand for learning opportunities rather than the supply of predefined programs. It would also facilitate the return of students completing part of their education abroad and open the formal postsecondary education system up for lifelong learning opportunities.

Productivity and Innovation

In recent years countries in Latin America have opened their economies by liberalizing trade and encouraging foreign investment. Integration into the world market has improved the region's access to technology and amplified the importance of knowledge as a factor of production.

Productivity and competitiveness gains associated with the use of new technologies have increased the demand for advanced human capital. As a result, the relative wages of workers with higher education are on the rise everywhere in Latin America. In Brazil, for example, returns to higher education rose 23 percent between 1982 and 1998, while returns to primary and secondary education decreased (figure 2.12).

The payoffs to higher education are high in most Latin American countries. The rate of return is twice as high as the return to secondary education in Argentina, Chile, and Colombia and more than five percentage points higher in Brazil, Bolivia, and Mexico (table 2.2). A striking feature of Latin America is the fact that the rise in relative wages has taken place in parallel with increases in the relative supply of workers with higher education. Observed wage changes may therefore not fully reflect the increase in demand for higher education graduates.

Innovation as a Driver of Economic Growth

Access to advanced human capital is not only crucial in the productive sector, it is also a central component of national innovation systems. Evidence shows that the ability of public institutions and private firms to interact in a concerted way to generate and adopt knowledge, technology, and prod-

Figure 2.12 Returns to Education in Brazil, by Level of Education, 1982–98

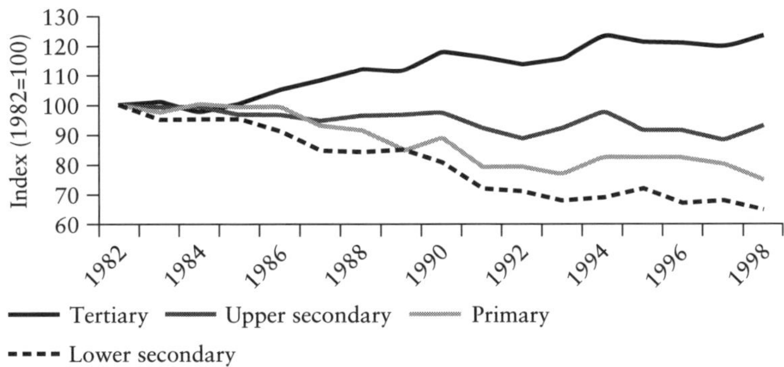

Source: Blom, Holm-Nielsen, and Verner (2001).

ucts is a primary driver of economic growth (Lundvall 1992; De Ferranti and others 2003). Countries in Latin America have unrealized potential for improving their innovative capacity (figure 2.13). The number of scientific publications and patents is low, and ties between universities and the private sector are weak.

Low Investment and Private Sector Involvement in Research and Development

Total investment in research and development (R&D) almost doubled in Latin America between 1990 and 2001. Increases in spending were particularly large in Mexico, Chile, and notably Brazil, which has traditionally

Table 2.2 Rates of Return to Secondary School and University Education in Selected Latin American Countries, 2001

(percent)

Country	Secondary school graduates	University graduates
Argentina	8	16
Bolivia	8	14
Brazil	15	22
Chile	12	24
Colombia	5	18
Mexico	10	16

Source: De Ferranti and others (2003); Duryea, Jaramillo, and Pagés (2001).

Figure 2.13 Indicators of National Innovation Systems in Latin America

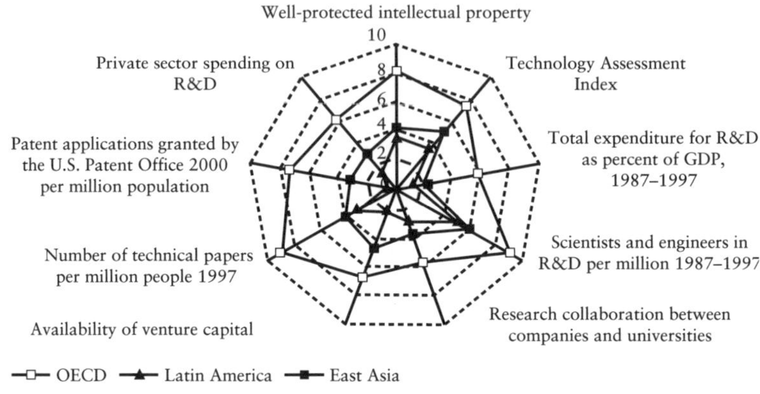

Note: Variables are normalized on a scale of 0 (lowest) to 10 (highest).
Source: World Economic Forum (2000); World Bank (2002d).

given high priority to research at federal universities (World Bank 2002c). The region, however, still falls considerably behind world leaders in the field. In 2000 Latin American countries as a whole allocated 0.54 percent of GDP to R&D, while the average for the OECD was 2.24 percent (OECD 2002b). Ireland allocated 1.54 percent and the Republic of Korea 2.70 percent of GDP to R&D (World Bank 2002d).

Large structural differences exist between Latin America and the OECD with regard to the financing and execution of research. In OECD countries private industry is the main investor in R&D. In Latin America, by contrast, the bulk of research is financed by the government and carried out by public research institutes and universities. In Chile, for example, industry accounts for only 15 percent of research; in Peru the figure is just 10 (Hansen and others 2002). Research activities at private universities are also very limited in Latin America because of a focus on instruction and the low availability of qualified researchers among the faculty. In addition, the high percentage of part-time faculty places private institutions in a weak position to carry out research. Complementing public resources by encouraging private sector investment in R&D would provide Latin America with a much stronger basis for research and commercialization of innovations.

Inadequate Stock of Researchers

In addition to being centers of research, higher education institutions play an important role as suppliers of researchers. Universities in Latin America have not been effective in producing doctoral graduates and postdocs beyond their own need for qualified staff. In 1999 the region had only 0.32 researchers per 1,000 inhabitants, an alarmingly low figure given the OECD average of 5.51 (OECD 2002a). This gap can be explained partly by the low priority given to graduate and postgraduate programs, which translates into low annual PhD production in Latin America. The gap also stems from a lack of career opportunities for young researchers (Mullin and others 2000). In an environment of increasing internationalization of research and education, talented young researchers from Latin America often go abroad to make a better life for themselves and to progress in their fields.

International Connectivity of Higher Education

The internationalization of higher education provides new opportunities for Latin America to access new knowledge, attract talented individuals, and learn from practices in higher education abroad. International connectivity in advanced education and research also holds considerable potential for strengthening national innovations systems in Latin America. For these reasons, Latin American countries are increasingly engaging in the global market for talent and higher education services.

Latin America has more students at U.S. universities relative to the proportion enrolled at home than any other region in the world (figure 2.14). Europe—particularly Spain, Italy, and France—also hosts a significant number of students from Latin America (OECD 2002b).

Figure 2.14 Foreign Students at U.S. Universities Relative to Proportion Enrolled in their Region of Origin, 1993 and 1998

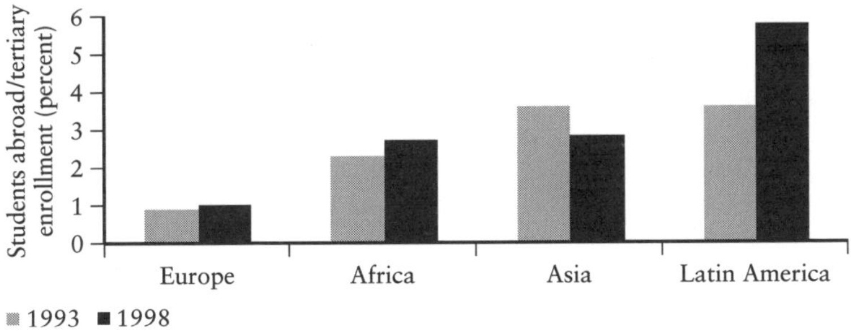

Source: De Ferranti and others (2003).

Figure 2.15 Emigration by Educated Nationals in Selected Countries in Latin America and the Caribbean, 2000

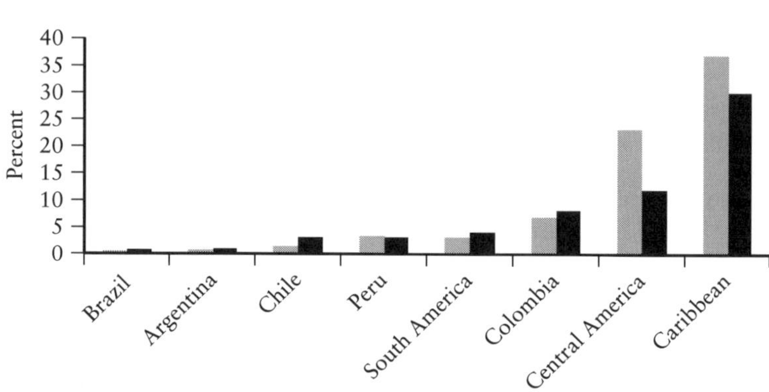

Source: Wodon (2003).

Moreover, a rising number of scholars from Latin America are teaching or conducting research abroad. In 2002 the number of visiting scholars in the United States from Argentina, Brazil, Colombia, and Mexico grew 20 percent (Chin 2003).

Temporary international mobility of skilled labor has positive implications for access to new knowledge. Permanent migration, however, erodes the human capital base and drains scarce resources. Every year emigration from Latin America to the United States claims a significant number of the region's better educated population. This is especially the case for countries in the Caribbean, among which 30 percent of graduates leave the country, and Central America, which loses 10 percent of its graduates to emigration. Estimated rates for South America are lower, with a high of 8 percent for Colombia (figure 2.15).

For Latin American countries, the challenge is to provide quality education and adequate opportunities for employment and merit-based career progression in order to retain talented individuals. To do so, Mexico runs a program targeted at researchers who have recently completed their PhDs abroad. The program provides incentives to return by establishing research positions, paying higher salaries, and covering repatriation expenditures. Between 1991 and 2000 the program funded the repatriation of more than 2,000 Mexican researchers living in 33 countries (Wodon 2003). Chile has established centers of excellence to raise the quality of research and to lure back highly skilled nationals. Reinforcing such initiatives will place the region in a better position to profit from internationalization by harnessing feedback effects and drawing on the experience and skills of returnees.

Forming Partnerships with Foreign Institutions

In recent years foreign providers have entered the market for higher education in Latin America. European and U.S.-based institutions provide learning opportunities or are setting up institutions in Latin America, and universities in the region are developing strategic alliances with sister institutions abroad. Within the region a number of universities have also launched programs targeted at students in neighboring counties and remote areas. Brazil, Colombia, Costa Rica, and Mexico, among others, have established distance learning programs. Mexico's Technological Institute of Monterrey (ITESM) operates a virtual university that provides distance education to more than 12,000 students throughout the Americas. To overcome cross-national inconsistencies and provide the means for certification of skills, ITESM has formed partnerships with local universities, such as the Universidad Católica in Chile and the Instituto Tecnológico de Buenos Aires in Argentina (UNESCO 2002; Burkle 2002).

Inadequate Strategies for Trade in Higher Education Services

Latin American countries are sending students abroad in great numbers. However, they have been less successful in attracting skilled foreigners to the region. Governments in Australia, the United Kingdom, and a number of smaller OECD countries have developed active international recruitment strategies and provided the necessary resources to cater to foreign students. These countries now have above 10 foreign students per 100 national students. For Uruguay, Chile, Argentina, and Mexico, foreign students constitute less than 1 percent of enrollees in higher education (figure 2.16).

Trade in higher education services is a reality, and its future growth has significant implications for Latin America. The OECD estimates the current monetary value of trade in higher education services at about 3 percent of total trade in services in its member countries (Larsen, Morris, and Martin 2002). Due to a high outflow of students and a limited inflow, Latin American countries are facing a growing deficit in the trade of higher educational services. Brazil, for example, spent an estimated $78 million on nationals studying abroad in 2000. The same year, revenues generated by foreign student flows into Brazil amounted to only $4 million. In contrast, Australia had a surplus in the trade of higher education services of almost $1.8 billion in 2000 (OECD 2002b).

Figure 2.16 Foreign Students as a Percentage of All Students Enrolled in Host Country, in Selected Countries, 2000

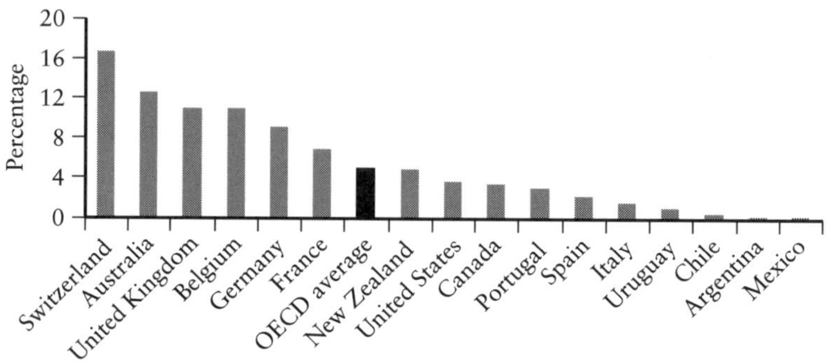

Note: Data for Argentina, Chile, and Uruguay are from 1999.
Source: OECD (2002a).

Latin American strategies for reaping greater benefits from trade in educational services are still in their nascent stages. It remains to be seen how the Global Agreement on Trade in Services (GATS) will influence the global market for higher education and what role Latin America will play in this market (Knight 2003).

The Way Ahead

This chapter overviews developments in higher education in Latin America in order to assess the readiness of the region to realize the potential of the knowledge economy and the globalization of higher education. Considerable progress has been made in recent years. Enrollment in higher education has risen to almost one-third of the 18–24 age cohort, and growth of private provision and nonuniversity tertiary education have expanded learning opportunities. Quality assurance mechanisms are being established in the region, and institutions are increasingly being held accountable for their performance. Latin American countries offer many possibilities for students wishing to enroll in advanced education, and recent advancements hold considerable promise for bringing the region closer to the international knowledge frontier.

Important progress notwithstanding, many problems persist, and there is a need to give priority to higher education. Programs are often of low quality and relevance, and talent is underused, due to considerable inequities. Widespread inefficiencies reduce the return on the use of scarce resources, the lack of credit transfer mechanisms impedes national and international mobility, and the region falls far short of building a critical mass of researchers of international repute.

The process of internationalization has important implications for Latin America, especially with regard to gaining access to the rapidly increasing pool of knowledge and know-how. The internationalization of education appears not yet to have reached a sufficient level of importance on the political agenda. A large number of Latin American students study outside Latin America, and many university graduates emigrate to the north. Latin American countries have not been able to develop adequate strategies to attract foreign students or skilled nationals from abroad. It is therefore likely that Latin America in general will not reap the full benefits of the GATS.

Adopting a proactive approach to higher education and research by setting strategies for the medium and long term would help the region shape the agenda for the future rather than reacting to changes introduced by other stakeholders in the international educational community. In this regard, it is critical that Latin American countries strengthen their capacity to generate and analyze data on the performance of their higher education sectors. Filling information gaps in learning and labor market outcomes would provide a strong basis for long-term policy decisions, which, in turn, would improve the prospects of reaping the full benefits of internationalization.

Recent reforms of higher education in Latin America are broadly consistent with international trends. While Latin American countries appear to be on track to develop modern higher education systems, they may not be moving at a fast enough pace, as high-income nations continue to advance rapidly. Latin America should not only create learning opportunities at the current rate of the OECD countries but also aim at closing the gap. Boldly welcoming this challenge by applying creative and innovative approaches to higher education will be key to the success of Latin America in the global market for knowledge and talent.

References

ADEA (Association for the Development of Education in Africa). 1999. *Statistical Profile of Education in Sub-Saharan Africa.* Paris.

Altbach, Philip G. 2003. *The Decline of the Guru: The Academic Profession in Developing and Middle-Income Countries.* New York: Palgrave MacMillan.

Araneda, Hernán, and Cristóbal Marín. 2002. *Meeting the Challenge of the Knowledge Economy: Lifelong Learning in Chile.* World Bank, Washington, DC.

Balán, Jorge 1996. "Quality and Quality Assurance as Policy Issues in Higher Education." Paper presented at the Conference on Higher Education Reform in Latin America, Harvard University, Cambridge, MA.

Balbachevsky, Elizabeth, and Maria da Conceição Quinteiro 2003. "The Changing Academic Workplace in Brazil." In *The Decline of the Guru: The Academic Profession in Developing and Middle-Income Countries*, ed. Philip G. Altbach, 75–106. New York: Palgrave MacMillan.

Becerra, Marcelo, Oscar Cetrángolo, Javier Curcio, and Juan Pablo Jiménez. 2003. "Expenditure on University in Argentina." Working paper, World Bank Office for Argentina, Chile, Paraguay, and Uruguay, Buenos Aires.

Bernasconi, Andrés. 2003. "Private Higher Education with an Academic Focus: Chile's New Exceptionalism." *International Higher Education* (Boston College) (Summer): 18–19.

Blom, Andreas, Lauritz Holm-Nielsen, and Dorte Verner. 2001. *Education, Earnings and Inequality in Brazil 1982–98: Implications for Education Policy.* World Bank, Washington, DC.

Brunner, José Joaquín. 2002a. *Aseguramiento de la calidad y nuevas demandas sobre la educación superior en América Latina.* Consejo Nacional de Acreditación, Cartagena.

———. 2002b. *The Colombian Higher Education System: Problems and Challenges.* LC-SHD Paper Series, No. 71, World Bank, Washington, DC.

Brunner, José Joaquín, and Patricio Meller, eds. 2004. *Oferta y demanda de profesionales y técnicos en Chile: el rol de la información pública.* Santiago: Editorial Ril.

Burkle, Martha. 2002. "Virtual Learning in Higher Education in Mexico and South Africa: Prospects and Possibilities." Paper presented at the Virtual Learning and Higher Education Conference, September 10–11, Oxford.

Canton, Erik, and Andreas Blom. 2004. "Can Student Loans Improve Accessibility to Higher Education and Student Performance? An Impact Study of the Case of SOFES, Mexico." Policy Research Working Paper No. 3425, World Bank, Washington, DC.

Carrington, William J., and Enrica Detragiache 1998. *How Big Is the Brain Drain?* IMF Working Paper, International Monetary Fund, Washington, DC.

Castro, Claudio de Moura, and Daniel C. Levy. 2000. *Myth, Reality, and Reform: Higher Education Policy in Latin America.* Inter-American Development Bank, Washington, DC.

Chapman, B.J. 1997. "Conceptual Issues and the Australian Experience with Income Contingent Charges for Higher Education." *Economic Journal* 107 (442): 738–51.

Chin, Hey-Kyung Koh. 2003. *Open Doors: Report on International Education Exchange.* New York: Institute of International Education.

Chronicle of Higher Education. 2003. "Attitudes and Characteristics of Freshmen at 4-Year Colleges." Almanac Issue 2003–04, 50 (1).

Courard, Hernán ed. 1993. *Políticas comparadas de educación superior en América Latina.* Latin American Faculty of Social Sciences (FLACSO), Santiago.

De Ferranti, David, Guillermo E. Perry, Indermit Gill, J. Luis Guasch, William E. Maloney, Carolina Sánchez-Páramo, and Norbert Schandy. 2003. *Closing the Gap in Education and Technology.* World Bank Latin American and Caribbean Studies, Washington, DC.

Del Bello, Juan Carlos. 2002. *Desafíos se la política se la educación superior en América Latina: reflexiones a partir del caso Argentino con énfasis sobre la evaluación para el mejoramiento de la calidad.* LCSHD Paper Series, No. 70, World Bank, Washington, DC.

Delannoy, Françoise. 2000. *Education Reforms in Chile, 1980–1998: A Lesson in Pragmatism.* Education Reform and Management Publication Series 1 (1). World Bank, Human Development Network, Washington, DC.

DePietro-Jurand, Robin, and Maria-José Lemaitre 2002. "Quality Assurance in Colombia." In *Colombia: Tertiary Education Paving the Way for Reform*, 99–120. Washington, DC: World Bank.

Duryea, S., O. Jaramillo, and C. Pagés. 2001. *Latin American Labor Markets in the 1990s: Deciphering the Decade.* Inter-American Development Bank, Washington, DC.

Economist. 2002. "Making the Most of an Exodus: Emigration from Latin America." February 21.

EIU (Economist Intelligence Unit). 2001. *Country Profile 2001: Argentina.* London.

El-Khawas, Elaine. 1998. "Developing Internal Support for Quality and Relevance." LCSHD Paper Series, No. 29, World Bank, Washington, DC.

El-Khawas, Elaine, Robin DePietro-Jurand, and Lauritz Holm-Nielsen. 1998. "Quality Assurance in Higher Education: Recent Progress, Challenges Ahead." LCSHD Paper Series, No. 23, World Bank, Washington, DC.

European Commission. 2003. "Third European Report on S&T Indicators." Directorate-General for Research, Brussels.

Figueroa, Carlos Pallán, Joan M. Claffey, and Alan Adelman, eds. 1995. *Relevancia de la educación superior en el desarrollo.* Asociación Nacional de Universidades e Instituciones de Educación Superior, Mexico City.

García Guadilla, Carmen. 1998. *Situación y principales dinámicas de transformación de la educación superior en América Latina.* CRESALC/ UNESCO, Caracas.

———. 2000. "The Institutional Basis of Higher Education Research in Latin America with Special Emphasis on the Role Played by International and Regional Organizations." In *The Institutional Basis of Higher Education Research: Experiences and Perspectives*, ed. Stefanie Schwarz and Ulrich Teichler. Dordrecht: Kluwer Academic Publishers.

Gil-Antón, Manuel. 2003. "Big City Love: The Academic Workplace in Mexico." In *The Decline of the Guru: The Academic Profession in Developing and Middle-Income Countries*, ed. Philip G. Altbach, 23–50. New York: Palgrave MacMillan.

Hansen, Thomas Nikolaj, and Lauritz Holm-Nielsen. 2002. "Education and Skills in Argentina: Assessing Argentina's Stock of Human Capital." Working paper, World Bank Office for Argentina, Chile, Paraguay, and Uruguay, Buenos Aires.

Hansen, Thomas Nikolaj, Natalia Agapitova, Lauritz Holm-Nielsen, and Ognjenka Goga Vukmirovic. 2002. *The Evolution of Science and Technology: Latin America and the Caribbean in Comparative Perspective.* LCSHD Paper Series, No. 80, World Bank, Washington, DC.

Hauptman, Arthur. 2002. *Reforming Student Financial Aid: Issues and Alternatives.* LCSHD Paper Series, No. 76, World Bank, Washington, DC.

Holm-Nielsen, Lauritz, and Natalia Agapitova. 2002. *Chile: Science, Technology, and Innovation.* LCSHD Paper Series, No. 79, World Bank, Washington, DC.

ICFES (Colombian Institute for the Development of Higher Education). 2000. *Estadísticas de la educación superior 2000: resumen anual.* Bogotá.

IMD (Institute for Management Development). 2002. *World Competitiveness Yearbook 2001/02.* Lausanne: IMD.

IOM (International Organization for Migration). 2003. *World Migration 2003: Managing Migration.* Geneva: IOM.

Johnstone, Bruce. 1998. *Institutional Differentiation and the Accommodation of Enrollment Expansion in Brazil.* LCSHD Paper Series, No. 29, World Bank, Washington, DC.

Knight, Jane. 2003. "Trade Talk: The Four Modes." *International Higher Education* (Boston College) 31: 3–4.

Larsen, Kurt, Rosemary Morris, and John P. Martin. 2002. *Trade in Educational Services: Trends and Emerging Issues.* Paris: Organisation for Economic Co-operation and Development.

Levy, Daniel C. 2002. *Latin America's Tertiary Education: Accelerating Pluralism.* Washington, DC: Inter-American Development Bank.

Lundvall, Bengt-Åke, ed. 1992. *National Systems of Innovation: Towards a Theory of Innovation and Interactive Learning.* London: Pinter Publishers.

Marquis, Carlos. 2000. *Innovation Funds for Universities.* Washington, DC: World Bank.

————. 2003. "Universities and Professors in Argentina: Changes and Challenges." In *The Decline of the Guru: The Academic Profession in Developing and Middle-Income Countries,* ed. Philip G. Altbach, 51–74. New York: Palgrave MacMillan.

Ministerio de Educación, Ciencia y Tecnología de Argentina. 2002. *Comisión nacional para el mejoramiento de la educación superior.* Buenos Aires.

Mullin, James, Robert M. Adam, Janet E. Halliwell, and Larry P. Milligan. 2000. *Science, Technology and Innovation in Chile.* International Development Research Center, Ottawa.

NSF (National Science Foundation). 2002. *Science and Engineering Indicators 2002.* Washington, DC: NSF.

OECD (Organisation for Economic Co-operation and Development). 2000. *Science, Technology and Industry Outlook 2000.* Paris: OECD.

————. 2001. *Education at a Glance: OECD Indicators 2001.* Paris: OECD.

————. 2002a. *Education at a Glance: OECD Indicators 2002.* Paris: OECD.

————. 2002b. *Indicators on Internationalisation and Trade of Post-Secondary Education.* OECD/U.S. Forum on Trade in Educational Services. Paris: OECD.

————. 2002c. *Main Science and Technology Indicators.* Vol. 2. Paris: OECD.

RICYT (Latin American Network of Science and Technology Indicators). 2003. *Indicadores de ciencia y tecnología.* Buenos Aires.

Schwartzman, Simon. 1998. *Higher Education in Brazil: The Stakeholders*. LCSHD Paper Series, No. 28, World Bank, Washington, DC.

———. 2002. "Higher Education and the Demands of the New Economy in Latin America." Background paper for the 2003 LAC Flagship Report, World Bank, Washington, DC.

Schwartzman, Simon, and Elizabeth Balbachevsky. 1996. "The Academic Profession in Brazil." In *The International Academic Profession: Portraits of Fourteen Countries*, ed. Philip G. Altbach, 231–80. Princeton, NJ: Princeton University Press.

Task Force on Higher Education and Society. 2000. *Higher Education in Developing Countries: Peril and Promise*. Washington, DC: World Bank.

Thompson, Quentin. 1998. *Trends in Governance and Management of Higher Education*. LCSHD Paper Series, No. 33, World Bank, Washington, DC.

Thorn, Kristian, Lauritz B. Holm-Nielsen, and Jette Samuel Jeppesen. 2004. "Approaches to Results-Based Funding in Tertiary Education: Identifying Finance Reform Options for Chile." Policy Research Working Paper, No. 3436, World Bank, Washington, DC.

UNESCO (United Nations Educational, Scientific and Cultural Organization). 2002. *Open and Distance Learning: Trends, Policy and Strategy Considerations*. Paris: UNESCO.

———. 2003. *Enrollment in Tertiary Education by Country*. Caracas: UNESCO Institute for Statistics.

U.S. Census Bureau. 2002. *United States Census 2002*. Washington, DC: U.S. Census Bureau.

Wagner, Alan 1998. *From Higher to Tertiary Education: Evolving Responses in OECD Countries to Large Volume Participation*. LCSHD Paper Series, No. 34, World Bank, Washington, DC.

Wesley, Yin, and Andreas Blom 2002. *Unmet Demand in a Segmented Market*. World Bank, Washington, DC.

Winkler, Donald R. 1994. *La educación superior en América Latina: cuestiones sobre eficiencia y equidad*. World Bank, Washington, DC.

Wodon, Quentin, ed. 2003. *International Migration in Latin America: Brain Drain, Remittances, and Development*. Washington, DC: World Bank.

World Bank. 2002a. *Bolivarian Republic of Venezuela: Higher Education Sector Profile*. Washington, DC.

———. 2002b. *Constructing Knowledge Societies: New Challenges for Tertiary Education*. Washington, DC.

———. 2002c. *Higher Education in Brazil: Challenges and Options*. Washington, DC.

———. 2002d. *World Development Indicators 2002*. Washington, DC.

———. 2003. *Tertiary Education in Colombia: Paving the Way for Reform*. Washington, DC.

World Economic Forum. 2000. *World Competitiveness Report*. Geneva, Switzerland: Center for International Development.

3

Internationalization of Higher Education in Argentina

Julio César Theiler

This chapter describes and analyzes the international dimension of higher education in Argentina. It examines current conditions, government policies and programs, and the priorities, strategies, and activities implemented by universities. It also briefly describes the Argentine higher education system and outlines some of the trends that have characterized the internationalization of higher education in Argentina.

The internationalization of higher education can be defined as "the development and implementation process of policy and programs to include the international, intercultural and global dimensions for the purposes and functions of higher education" (Knight 2003, p. 2). The process has just started to appear on the agendas of universities as well as in recent government policy.

Internationalization has not been considered a subject for analysis until recently. For this reason, compiling information on the subject has not been easy. The information available is very limited and fragmented, and a bibliography on the subject has not yet been developed.[1]

The Network of Heads of International Cooperation of the National Universities (RedCIUN), which falls under the National Inter-University Council, recently conducted a survey on internationalization at public universities. The survey provides information on 20 of the 37 public universities in Argentina (Theiler 2003a).[2] A similar survey conducted among private institutions, with the collaboration of the Council of Presidents of

---

[1] The Ministry of Education, Science and Technology has information on the activities it carries out directly, but it does not have data on activities by public or private universities. In general, the higher education institutions themselves possess no system for providing or disseminating information on their international activities.

[2] The 20 universities include the University of Buenos Aires, one of Latin America's largest universities; other large universities (Córdoba, La Plata, and Tucumán Universities and the National Technological University); medium-size universities (Cuyo, Litoral, Nordeste, Río Cuarto, Salta, and Sur); and small universities (Catamarca, Centro de la Provincia de Buenos Aires, Entre Ríos, General Sarmiento Tres de Febrero, La Pampa, Luján, San Luis, and Santiago del Estero).

Private Universities (CRUP), provides information on nine private institutions (Theiler 2003b).[3] The data from these surveys are the main sources of information for this chapter. While the sample covers a small number of universities, inclusion of universities of different sizes makes it possible to draw general conclusions from the results.

The Higher Education System in Argentina

Higher education at the university level began in Argentina in the mid-seventeenth century, with the establishment of the University of Córdoba. The development of higher education since then has been determined by political and institutional ups and downs that Argentine society has been forced to face at all levels over the years. During the late nineteenth and early twentieth century, the number of universities increased as a result of the policies of liberal governments to accept the participation and contribution of European professors living in Argentina.

The indisputable significance of university autonomy to the development of education in Argentina began with the University of Córdoba reform process in 1918. For more than 85 years, asserting this autonomy has been one of the central themes of national policies on university-related issues. This has led to the forging of a special model based on such concepts as free higher education, access to teaching positions through public selection processes, and unrestricted access to higher education by all citizens. During periods in which higher education was undermined for various reasons, university students demanded reestablishment of these principles, especially during military dictatorships.

The university reform process has had a strong influence on several countries in Latin America that also adopted reforms that remain in place today. Argentina was at the forefront of the development of higher education throughout much of South America during the twentieth century. Argentina's scientific development, its regional leadership in production of scientific publications, and its acceptance of a large number of foreign students, especially during the 1950s and 1960s, all attest to this.

The recurrent crises faced by the country as a result of the continuing interruptions of democracy led to the collapse of the Argentine university model between 1966 and 1983, the mass exodus of talented people, and a strong decline in the quality of higher education. After 1983 universities recovered their autonomy and began a sluggish recovery process that has been hampered by ongoing economic decline and the lack of appropriate

---

[3] The study covers Aconcagua University, Austral University, Belgrano University, Buenos Aires Technological Institute, Córdoba Catholic University, Maimónides University, Salvador University, Santa Fe Catholic University, and the University of Business and Social Sciences.

development policies in Latin America in general and Argentina in particular.

Structure of the Higher Education System

Since 1995 higher education has been governed by a new legal framework. The Higher Education Law No. 24521 declares that "university institutions shall have academic and institutional autonomy," including the right to establish their own statutes, elect their own authorities, create undergraduate and graduate degree courses, manage their economic resources, and grant university degrees and diplomas.

The organizational structure of the system consists of two subsystems: university institutions and nonuniversity institutions, also known as tertiary institutions. University institutions include establishments created or recognized as such, even if they do not bear the name "university." Nonuniversity institutions include teacher training institutions (*institutos superiors de formacion docente*), technical training (*institutos de formacion tecnica*), art education schools, and various "short courses" (courses lasting one to four years) (Dahlman and Scherer 2002; UNESCO 2001). Historically, there has been almost no coordination between the two subsystems. Law No. 24521 led to significant progress regarding coordinating regulatory and academic issues, especially in faculty training.

UNIVERSITY AND NONUNIVERSITY INSTITUTIONS
The Higher Education Law defines the functions of universities as including training people and promoting, developing, and extending scientific and technological research. It distinguishes between universities, which pursue activities in a variety of disciplines, and university institutes, which are confined to a single discipline. Universities offer predegree programs; undergraduate programs; and graduate programs (specializations, master's, and doctorates).

Universities and university institutes can be public or private (table 3.1). Private universities are more numerous than public universities. The

Table 3.1 Universities and University Institutes in Argentina, 2000

Type of institution	Universities	University institutes	Total
Public	36	5	41
Private	42	10	52
Provincial	1	0	1
Total	79	15	94

Source: MECYT 2000.

regulation governing the creation and functioning of such institutions re-quires that they be constituted as nonprofit institutions, that they have the authorization of the executive branch of government, and that the quality and relevance of their educational services be subject to the evaluation of the National Commission for Evaluation and University Accreditation (CONEAU). The activities and operations of private universities are not subsidized by the state.

Nonuniversity tertiary institutions may be divided into those offering faculty training and those providing technical and professional training. Such institutions are under the authority of provincial educational au-thorities. Their operations may be subsidized by the state.

Federal law (1993) provides for university colleges, a type of institution that serves as a link between universities and training institutes. Their or-ganizational approach is similar to that of colleges in the United States and Canada.

Coordinating Bodies for Higher Education

The coordination structure of higher education involves several bodies.

NATIONAL INTER-UNIVERSITY COUNCIL

Created in 1985, the National Inter-University Council is made up of uni-versity presidents of national and provincial universities. It is responsible for developing coordination-related activities, holding consultations with local higher education authorities, promoting programs of common interest, and establishing relations with other local and foreign public and private institutions. The Network of Supervisors for International Cooperation of National Universities (RedCIUN) comes under its authority.

COUNCIL OF PRIVATE UNIVERSITY PRESIDENTS

Created in 1967, the Council of Presidents of Private Universities (CRUP) is made up of all private universities in Argentina. It performs functions in the areas of representation, coordination between its members and other public and private institutions, and cooperation and exchange. Its board of directors includes representatives from different regions of the country.

REGIONAL PLANNING COUNCILS FOR HIGHER EDUCATION

The Regional Planning Councils for Higher Education (CEPRES) are re-sponsible for coordinating the functioning and academic opportunities of university and nonuniversity institutions in every region in Argentina. Six CEPRES are in operation. With varying degrees of effectiveness, they over-see the complex relationships between universities and the provincial au-thorities that regulate nonuniversity higher education institutes.

UNIVERSITY COUNCIL

The University Council is the supreme coordinating and advisory body for federal authorities in higher education. Its functions include proposing policies and strategies in the areas of development, cooperation, and interinstitutional coordination and setting rules governing the accreditation of undergraduate, graduate, and other programs. It is made up of representatives of the National Inter-University Council, the CRUP, the CEPRES, and the Federal Council of Culture and Education, an organization consisting of ministers of education from all provinces.

To date the ability of the state to coordinate the university system has remained weak. The autonomy of universities is so strong that it has often inhibited regional and national coordination of the system. Universities devise their own development plans, and only a very limited number of activities are designed to include several universities in joint projects. In practice, there is consensus among all actors in the higher education system on the need to enhance coordination within the system, and in recent years greater efforts have been made to do so.

Enrollment in Higher Education Programs

In 2000, 1.3 million students were enrolled in higher education programs in Argentina (table 3.2). Over the past decade, national universities grew at an annual rate of 5.2 percent, while private universities grew at 4.4 percent a year.

Argentina has one of the highest access rates to higher education in Latin America, at almost 40 percent. Forty-four percent of students study social sciences, 25 percent applied sciences, 14 percent health-related sciences, 14 percent human sciences, and 3 percent basic sciences.

On average, Argentine students take 60 percent longer than they should to complete their studies (MECYT 2000). Law students spend 1.35 times as long as required, and civil engineering students spend about 1.9 times as

Table 3.2 University Enrollment in Argentina, by Type of Institution, 1990 and 2000

Type of institution	1990	2000
Public universities	679,403	1,124,044
Private universities	100,000[a]	166,539
National university institutes	0	17,364
Total	779,403	1,307,947

a. Estimate
Source: MECYT 2000.

long. Combined with a drop-out rate of more than 40 percent among first-year students, these figures contribute to very low completion rates. In 1999 public universities had 280,000 incoming students and graduated 38,400 (14 percent), while private universities had 51,400 incoming students and graduated 13,500 (26 percent) (MECYT 2000). The problem is a constant topic of analysis by the Ministry of Education and among the universities themselves.

Another problem facing higher education in Argentina is the fact that most faculty members are employed on a part-time basis. Only 14 percent of professors at public universities work full time, 21 percent work part time (24 hours a week), and 65 percent work on an hourly basis (12 hours a week).

Argentina has traditionally promoted profession-oriented university training. While it was the first Latin American country to begin developing its scientific research base, it started to offer graduate education only in the 1980s. Growth has been explosive, and since 1966 it has been accompanied by a mandatory evaluation and accreditation plan implemented by CONEAU (table 3.3).

The disciplines with the highest number of accredited doctorate programs are chemistry, physics, philosophy, the earth sciences, and the biological sciences. The highest number of accredited master's programs are in engineering, medicine, agronomy, administration, economics, arts, educational sciences, and social sciences. Careers such as law, dentistry, architecture, medicine, and engineering are traditionally pursued through specialized programs; agronomy, economics, and management sciences

Table 3.3 CONEAU–Accredited Graduate Courses in Argentina, 1999 and 2003

Accreditation ranking	1999		2003	
	Master's degrees	Doctorates	Master's degrees	Doctorates
A	13	39	31	62
B	27	20	72	40
C	12	8	69	22
An	8	4	11	2
Bn	16	4	30	10
Cn	20	1	42	6
Total	96	76	255	142

Note: A = excellent, B = very good, C = good. The subindex "n" refers to new careers and courses in which graduate students were not enrolled at the time of ranking.
Source: MECYT 2000 and CONEAU Web site (www.coneau.edu.ar).

are pursued through master's studies; and the exact and natural sciences and humanities through doctorate programs.

The data on the number and characteristics of graduate students in Argentina are very limited, and not even the Ministry of Education possesses reliable information. According to the 1999–2000 *University Statistics Yearbook*, about 30,000 graduate students were enrolled in public universities in 1999 (no information is available on the total figure for all universities). About 30 percent of these students were enrolled at the University of Buenos Aires. At the large universities, there are only 4 graduate students for every 100 undergraduate students; the ratio is even lower at smaller universities.

Access to Higher Education

Unrestricted access to public education is one of the most distinctive features of Argentina's higher education system. Unlike many other Latin American and European countries, Argentina does not have a common national evaluation system for all incoming students. Access is regulated by the universities themselves. While the regulations vary, most public universities have unrestricted admission, except for preadmission, support, and remedial courses. For medical studies, entry is determined on the basis of the number of positions available in the profession. Unrestricted entry among public universities is one of a number of factors that has contributed to the rapid expansion of higher education in Argentina but also to the high drop-out levels and low completion levels.

Accreditation and Evaluation

In the late 1980s—and in line with the explosive increase in the number of students enrolling in universities—a debate was initiated regarding the quality of higher education. The Law on Higher Education led to the creation of the National Commission for Evaluation and University Accreditation (CONEAU), whose multiple functions distinguish it from similar institutions in other countries. Its responsibilities include carrying out periodic external evaluations of universities, accrediting degree and graduate programs, determining the relevance of opening new national universities, and preparing reports in order to accredit private universities.[4]

CONEAU was constituted as a very strict control body, intended to curtail the opening of private universities as well as the opening up

---

[4] To date CONEAU has carried out significant work in all the areas in which it is involved. It has conducted more than 25 external evaluations of higher education institutions; it has fully implemented an obligatory accreditation system for graduate courses and it has initiated an accreditation process for degree studies in medicine and engineering. Only those courses considered by the University Council to be of general public importance need be accredited.

in Argentina of branches of foreign universities (which are treated in the same way as private universities). Since its creation, CONEAU has approved only 9 of 79 applications received. To date the University of Bologna is the only foreign university authorized to operate in Argentina.

CONEAU participates actively in Mercosur's plan for recognizing programs and skills based on common program evaluation and accreditation frameworks. It also participates actively in the Iberoamerican Network for the Accreditation and Quality of Higher Education (RIACES). Created in 2002, RIACES seeks to broaden opportunities for exchanging knowledge, technical cooperation, and human resources across university systems by reinforcing the common objectives governing evaluation and accreditation agencies and units in each member country. It serves as a medium for educational integration of countries in Latin America by designing joint, common, and coordinated responses to the challenges posed by the current globalization process in higher education. Other participants include CONEAU's sister agencies in Chile, Colombia, Cuba, Mexico, Spain, and the Central American Higher University Council (CSUCA).

Argentina's Scientific and Technological System

Argentina is no different from the rest of Latin America in terms of its science and technology system. The system is characterized by "its limited scope in terms of number of researchers and investment made in relation to GDP; its low impact in relation to global scientific production; and the largely elementary nature of research" (Guarga Ferro 2002, p. 8).

According to the Latin American Network of Science and Technology Indicators (RICYT) (www.ricyt.org), investment in research and development in Latin America has grown slowly in recent years, reaching 0.39 percent of GDP in 2002. This places Argentina below the regional average of 0.64 percent of GDP.[5] The number of researchers in Argentina is equivalent to 25,656 full-time researchers, about 0.5 percent of the world's researchers. By contrast, the United States accounts for 26 percent, Latin America 3 percent, and Spain 2 percent.

The Science Citation Index indicates an almost threefold increase in the participation of Latin Americans in the 1990s, when the figure jumped to 3 percent of the global total. In 2000 Argentina's share was equivalent to a little more than 0.5 percent of the total, with the major contributions coming from chemistry, biology, and agriculture. In 2000 Argentina published

---

[5] Japan spends 3 percent of GDP, the United States 2.65 percent, Brazil 1.05 percent, and Spain 0.98 percent.

1.9 articles for every 10 full-time researchers. This figure was almost identical to that of Brazil, which produced four publications for every $1 million invested in research and development, a level of productivity that is far higher than the average for Latin America (2.5 publications per every $1 million invested). These figures indicate that Argentine researchers were able to maintain an acceptable level of publications despite the decline in financing.

The major organization for scientific development is the National Council of Scientific and Technological Research (CONICET). Created in 1958, it coordinates with the universities with which it shares most of its institutes and faculty.

In the 1990s the National Agency for Scientific and Technological Promotion was created. The agency is responsible for administering most of the funds used to subsidize scientific and technological activity in Argentina.

Financing Higher Education

According to Coraggio and Vispo (2001, p. 51), "In most Latin American countries today, there is a general perception that, for several years, higher education has been faced with a severe crisis of growth and adaptation to the new development-related conditions of the different countries," a situation that has generated great tension regarding the financing of higher education. While the United States invests about 2.3 percent of its GDP in higher education, Argentina invested only 1.1 percent of GDP in 1999 (OECD 2002). This percentage has grown slightly over the past 15 years, but it has been accompanied by an explosive increase in the number of students entering public universities. The funding problem has led to various structural problems, such as the lack of investment in infrastructure and equipment, very low salaries, and a low percentage of full-time faculty. The issue of financing has led to ongoing conflict between universities and the national government.

Argentina spends $1,618 per student, a very low figure compared with developed countries (Germany: $3,976; Canada: $5,208; the United States $8,724) but higher than in some other Latin America countries (Mexico: $682; Chile $1,215) (Coraggio and Vispo 2001). After the 2002 devaluation of the Argentine peso, annual investment per student fell to about a third of its previous value.

Financing for national universities is provided mainly from public funds. Although other sources of financing exist (tuition for graduate programs, revenues from consultancy work and contract research), they account for less than 20 percent of university financing.

Reforms and Trends in Higher Education

Some of the most significant reforms and trends that have taken place in higher education in Argentina in the past 10 years include the following (Fernández Lamarra 2002):

- adoption of Higher Education Law No. 24521 in 1995
- creation and implementation of system coordination and consultation bodies
- implementation of a university evaluation system through the creation and launching of CONEAU
- application of the norms and guidelines governing the recognition of private universities and foreign universities.
- increase in the number of national universities, distance learning programs, and continuing education programs
- significant rise in graduate degrees offered
- growth in the number of careers requiring nonuniversity tertiary education
- development of the Fund for Enhancement of Educational Quality (FOMEC), designed to promote improvements in the quality of higher education
- progress in adding flexibility to curricula and strengthening the link between basic contents
- consolidation of regional educational integration activities by means of the Regional Coordinating Committee for Higher Education of Mercosur
- stronger links between tertiary nonuniversity and university systems
- ongoing conflict of financing for the system
- establishment of the economic and financial independence of national universities
- consolidation of university autonomy achieved in 1983
- significant rise in enrollments at public universities
- establishment of national agreements on common minimum training contents for medicine, engineering, agronomy, law, veterinary science, and other programs
- growth in higher education activities in technology transfer
- increased research activities at universities on the basis of policies implemented by universities and the national government.

It is widely believed that significant changes in the university system are long overdue and vital, given the very difficult socioeconomic conditions facing Argentina. The chronic problems besetting the system—including the instability of educational policies, the insufficiency of economic resources, the resistance of the university system to change and modernization, the obsolescence of its installations, the lack of an appropriate administrative structure and a scientific environment, the meager investment in research and development, and the low percentage of full-time university professors must be solved.

The International Dimension of Argentine Higher Education

The international dimension of Argentine higher education was not viewed as a priority for university policies and activities. Some isolated activities took place: Argentine university graduates pursued graduate studies in Europe and North America, students from other countries in Latin America attended institutions in Argentina, and relations between certain local and foreign scientific groups were forged, beginning mainly in the 1960s.

In the early 1990s universities neither viewed internationalization as part of their mission and objectives nor possessed specific administrative structures for international activities. No government policies promoted the internationalization of higher education, and institutional relations existed between only a few universities and foreign universities. Ties had been forged between Argentine researchers and their foreign counterparts, but they were limited to elite groups. Meanwhile, economic and political crises in Argentina were causing a brain drain toward North America and Europe.

In light of the globalization process, which started taking shape in the early 1990s, the internationalization of higher education has been promoted and strengthened worldwide. Many countries devised internationalization promotion strategies, and a large number of universities developed institutional efforts. Interest by Argentina's universities in the internationalization process began only in the late 1990s.

One of the most important factors behind this interest was the creation of the Latin American opening for university cooperation by means of cooperation-related activities between Latin America and Spain through the Spanish Agency for International Cooperation (AECI) and the establishment of the Mutis scholarship program at the Ibero-American Summit of Heads of States and of Government. It was through the implementation of the AECI programs, particularly the Inter-University Cooperation Program (PCI) program, that many of Argentina's universities first began to undertake institutionally planned international activities.[6]

In view of the need to organize these activities and the lack of specific administrative structures, most universities were forced to create structures

---

[6] Between 1994 and 2002 the PCI program promoted the mobility of thousands of university students (without recognition of studies) and faculty from Spain and Latin America.

for administering their international relations. In doing so, they were able to join student, faculty, and promotion exchange networks with Spanish universities and to participate in educational and research networks. As financing for student and faculty exchange activities was provided on a bilateral basis, for the first time universities in Argentina had to earmark budgets for international activities. The AECI programs helped present the idea of internationalization to Argentina's universities. For the most part, university offices of international relations were created through implementation of the PCI program. One indication of the impact of this program is the high percentage of relations and activities in which Argentine universities currently engage with Spanish universities.

Another important motive is the regional integration process involving Argentina, Brazil, Paraguay, Uruguay, and, more recently, Chile and Bolivia. Mercosur is involved in a process that, though riddled with obstacles to its implementation and with limited achievements, has encouraged universities to address this situation and pursue schemes and relations to promote regional integration, even outside Mercosur. Networks, such as the Montevideo Group University Association (AUGM), an association of 15 universities in Argentina, Brazil, Chile, Paraguay, and Uruguay; the Council of University Presidents for the Integration of the West-Central Sub-Region of South America (CRISCO); and ARCAM, a network of universities from Mercosur, are examples of the efforts that have been made.

Another major reason for promoting international relations may be the need to form alliances with foreign institutions with the aim of offering high-quality degree programs in Argentina. International cooperation could help diversify course offerings, particularly at the graduate level.

External conditions must be borne in mind. Globalization exerted a very strong impact on Argentina in the 1990s, when the country adopted neoliberal policies. Despite the failure of these policies, which mired the country in an unprecedented economic crisis, they have provided the framework for the promotion of the universities' international relations. Moreover, the implementation of external programs designed to promote international activities in Latin America, whether through specific countries or multilateral organizations, has enabled Argentine universities to participate actively in these activities and initiatives. Since the 2001 devaluation, the national economic framework has been shifting significantly for universities, changing from one in which importing educational services was highly favored to one that favors their export.

Some of the internationalization trends that have characterized higher education in Argentina led to the following developments:

* establishment of branches of European universities (Bologna University), courses provided by U.S. universities in Argentina (New York

University and Harvard University), and research and development centers (New York University, Harvard University, Salamanca University, and others)

- an increase in academic training opportunities in the form of distance learning and on-site programs offered by foreign universities granting credentials that are not recognized in Argentina (examples include the Autonomous University of Barcelona, UNED (the National University for Distance Learning), the Madrid Polytechnic, and Seville University)
- establishment of joint undergraduate or graduate qualifications granted on the basis of academic cooperation agreements between Argentine and foreign universities (Belgrano, Blas Pascal, Salvador, San Martin, and Tres de Febrero Universities, among others)
- consolidation of interuniversity institutional networks on the basis of research projects (the ALFA project of the European Union) or strategic objectives
- a rise in the number of exchange programs for faculty and undergraduate and graduate students (examples include the Fulbright Scholar Program and various programs sponsored by the European Union, Spain, Canada, and other countries), as well as the use of visiting professors from foreign universities in mainly graduate courses.

The Impact of Transnational Education on Argentina

According to Salmi (2002), "Higher education is already facing unparalleled challenges at the beginning of the twenty-first century, as a result of the impact of globalization, of knowledge-based economic growth, and of the information and communications revolution. These momentous changes taking place around us are spreading to the traditional frontiers of higher education. The time dimension appears to have been affected by the need for continued learning while the new technology is completely erasing space-related barriers."

If transnational education is used to mean any teaching or learning activity in which students are in a country other than that of the institution, the inclusion of higher education in services protocols as an item to be negotiated by the World Trade Organization (WTO) is a cause for deep concern within the Argentine university community. Transnational education is viewed as inimical to national education, its market, and its culture. It is also believed to cause major adverse reactions between public universities and specific areas of government. Nevertheless, international educational cooperation is highly valued as a sign of vitality and as a source for strengthening the institutions. The new concept espoused by UNESCO, in which higher education should be considered a "highly global social good" has led to deep concern in the university community. This concern is due to the implicit risk of national borders disappearing.

The impact of transnational education on Argentina is not high. While there is no specific regulation governing it, the law seems to be restraining this form of higher education. Argentine institutions possess practically no experience in providing transnational education, and very few have any explicit strategic objective to develop it in the near future. No public university in Argentina has opened a branch abroad or granted a franchise. While several institutions are developing distance learning education programs, their target market is highly local. Meanwhile, the number of programs offered by foreign institutions in Argentina is growing.

In other countries in Latin America—especially those in Central America and northern South America—a large number of foreign institutions has sprung up. These institutions are not regulated by the government, they possess questionable institutional backgrounds, and they offer educational services of dubious quality. The institutions responsible for supervising higher education in these countries are overwhelmed by the appearance of foreign academic programs offering distance education, institutional franchises, and correspondence courses.

In Argentina actions by the CONEAU have helped curtail the appearance of foreign institutions and the external academic programs they offer directly or through agreement with local universities by applying the same regulations that govern private universities. To date, one foreign university, the University of Bologna, has an authorized branch in Argentina, and it has had to deal with the complex authorization mechanism laid down by the higher education law. In 1999 the CONEAU rejected the application submitted by the International University Lynn of the United States, which sought to set up a branch in Argentina.

The experience of foreign universities with branches or programs in Argentina has varied (Banfi 2000). Since 1998 the University of Bologna has offered graduate studies, such as the master's in international relations with emphasis on the European Union and Latin America, which includes studies in both Buenos Aires and Bologna; the master's in methodology of social research, taught jointly with the Tres de Febrero National University; and the master's in innovation engineering (http://www.unibo.edu.ar).

Through an agreement with the Marplatense Association of Criminal Law Studies, the University of Salamanca organized the master's in criminal law in Mar del Plata. In November 2001 the university set up a branch in Buenos Aires and presented a series of graduate qualifications. The program has been put on hold because of the economic situation in Argentina.

New York University (NYU) runs a Buenos Aires branch of the New York University Centre, which offers courses for NYU students studying abroad. The grave political, social, and economic situation that Argentina went through in 2002 led to the suspension of NYU's activities.

Under an agreement with the Ortega y Gasset Foundation, the University of Chicago offers its students the opportunity to attend its Buenos Aires branch. Under an agreement with the University of San Andrés, the University of Pennsylvania offers its students the opportunity to take courses in Spanish, Latin American culture, and contemporary Argentine literature in Argentina. The university also has two exchange programs, one offered by the COPA Consortium with the Universities of Torcuato Di Tella, Salvador, and Buenos Aires, the other with the University of San Andrés. Under an agreement with the University of Belgrano, Pepperdine University offers an exchange program through which its students may study certain subjects at the University of Belgrano.

Company-run universities are another form of competition faced by Argentine universities, especially in continuing education. This kind of academic option has begun to appear more and more, mainly through strategies undertaken jointly with existing universities. An example is the association between the National Technological University and the international company CISCO Academy, which offers continuing education in different parts of the country.

The number of public universities offering distance learning education programs rose 62 percent between 2000 and 2002. About 85 percent of public universities in Argentina offer some form of distance education activity. Only about 26 percent of private university institutions offer distance education (Martín 2002).

Distance learning remains insufficiently developed in Argentina, with most programs supplementing programs that require attendance on campus. Given their importance, two examples warrant highlighting. In 1998 Quilmes University of Buenos Aires and the Catalunya Open University agreed to undertake a joint distance learning initiative. Inaugurated in 1999, the Quilmes Virtual University Program currently has more than 3,000 students and offers seven undergraduate and five graduate courses. The courses are offered in Spanish, and most of the students are Argentines.

Since 1999 Litoral National University has been creating educational schemes based on satellite technology accessed through 70 remote classrooms. The experience has been very successful, although, for the time being, the institution is trying to ensure that it remains regional in scope and does not expand beyond Argentina's borders.

Distance education programs have been designed exclusively for the Argentine market, with little or no international impact. Programs offered by institutions elsewhere in Latin America are numerous and varied. A significant number of Argentine students now have access to a wide range of programs being offered, the most important of which are offered by the Autonomous University of Barcelona, the National University for

Distance Learning (Spain), the Polytechnic University of Madrid, the University of Salamanca, Harvard University, New York University, and Pacific Western University (García Guadilla, Didou Aupetit, and Marquís 2002). Undergraduate degree programs are practically nonexistent, because foreign degree programs are not recognized in Argentina.

Joint programs have spread extensively throughout Argentina, by means of graduate (and sometimes undergraduate) courses taught jointly by an Argentine and a foreign higher education institution.

Brain Drain

The emigration of Latin American professionals, scientists, and technologists is a severe problem that undermines development of the region. Argentina has not been exempt from this trend, especially in recent years.

Emigration by mature researchers does not appear to be a serious problem in Argentina (Albornoz, Luchillo, and others 2002). The situation is very different among young researchers and those undergoing training. More than 55 percent of Argentine students pursuing graduate studies in the United States show a willingness to stay there. Among the economically active population, the percentage of Argentine professionals and technicians residing in the United States is the highest in Latin America. Argentine researchers are much more inclined than Brazilian researchers, for example, to remain in the United States, as reflected by the type of visa they usually possess when obtaining doctorates. Between 1991 and 2000, 136 of 638 Argentine doctoral students (21 percent) had permanent visas. In contrast, only 116 of 1,481 Brazilian doctoral students (8 percent) had permanent visas. During the same period, of 4,048 Latin American doctoral students in the United States, 37 percent were Brazilian and 16 percent Argentine (Albornoz, Polcuch, and Claudio 2002).

According to Albornoz, Luchillo, and others (2002, p. 32), "The seriousness of the problem surrounding the migration of trained individuals does not lie in the fact that this trend is adversely affecting the foundations of Argentine scientific institutions in a way that is radically different from in previous years, but rather in the obviously disproportionate rise in the procedures for legalizing academic qualifications. Based on this, it may therefore be inferred that there is, indeed, a significant rise in the desire of a considerable number of individuals to leave the country." This trend leads one to believe that "the impact on the local scientific system will be felt in the medium term, not so much because of the direct loss of researchers, but because of a significant loss of the country's best young graduates."

The Integration Process in Mercosur

On March 26, 1991, Argentina, Brazil, Paraguay, and Uruguay signed the Treaty of Asunción, creating the Common Market of the South, or Mercosur. With the subsequent incorporation of Bolivia and Chile, and based on agreements relating to the consolidation of democracy, the defense of fundamental freedoms, human rights, and environmental protection and sustainable development, the partners now seek to expand the scope of their national markets through integration.

The Educational Sector of Mercosur (SEM) has been proposed as a regional space to foster the integration of educational sectors of member countries. The SEM was created in 1991 with the signing of the Protocol of Intent by the Ministers of Education of the region, made up of member countries and associates (Bolivia and Chile). Although the SEM has moved forward with great caution, its activities and meetings have exhibited a high level of continuity.

In December 2000 the Ministers of Education adopted the Gramado Agreement, with an action plan for 2001–05. The agreement covers internships and student and faculty mobility; accreditation of degrees offered throughout Mercosur (the three study programs chosen to initiate the accreditation process are agronomy, engineering, and medicine); and interinstitutional cooperation at the level of graduate programs, faculty training, and scientific research.

The most significant progress made has been in the area of joint accreditation of university programs. This progress led to agreement on the implementation of an experimental Mechanism for the Accreditation of University Programs (MEXA), which has been implemented for agronomy-related careers. This process is currently in full operation and is being implemented in Argentina by the CONEAU in line with the quality guidelines established by the MEXA.

In the near future, the Mercosur integration process must enter a definitive stage. Either it will make progress on the regional integration process as a strategic necessity and in an attempt to balance forces in order to be able to relate more appropriately to other blocs, such as the European Union and NAFTA, or it will disintegrate and be absorbed by different integration schemes, such as the Free Trade Area of the Americas, which is being promoted by the United States.

National Policies and Structures for Internationalization

This section describes the Argentine government's policies for addressing and promoting the internationalization of higher education system. The ministries involved are the Ministry of International Relations,

International Trade and Worship and the Ministry of Education, Science and Technology.

Ministry of International Relations, International Trade and Worship

The relationship between the university system and the Ministry of International Relations, International Trade and Worship is developed mainly through its General Cooperation Office. That office is responsible for coordinating the international provision of cooperation with the needs of the universities by strengthening ties between institutions in Argentina and international organizations and cooperation-related agencies in other countries.

In the official development aid arena, twice in a single decade the macroeconomic indicators used by international organizations have led to changes in Argentina's rating status for numerous cooperation programs.[7] For this reason, it has kept its status as a cooperation-recipient country while, since 1992, committing to becoming a donor country.

ARGENTINA AS A COOPERATION-RECIPIENT COUNTRY

Multilateral cooperation includes cooperation-based relations with the multilateral agencies of the United Nations, regional organizations, and other schemes, such as the Latin American Summit of Heads of State and Government and the European Union. Although Argentina is a recipient of cooperation from numerous international sources (the European Union, the United Nations Development Programme, the United Nations Industrial Development Organization, the Food and Agricultural Organization, the World Environment Fund, the Organization of Iberian States, the Organization of American States (OAS), and the Latin American Summit), Argentine universities do not generally participate in this kind of international cooperation.

In bilateral cooperation, there are two fields of action: scientific and technological cooperation, whose executing authority is the Secretariat for Science, Technology and Productive Innovation of the Ministry of Education, Science and Technology, and technical cooperation, negotiated by the Ministry of International Relations, International Trade and Worship.

As a recipient of bilateral cooperation, Argentina receives support from Germany, Italy, Japan, and Spain. Japanese bilateral cooperation, administered by the Japanese International Cooperation Agency (JICA) has had a

---

[7] During the first half of the 1990s, Argentina's macroeconomic indicators placed it among the group of cooperation-donating countries. The economic collapse of 1997 reclassified it as a cooperation-recipient country.

significant impact on Argentina's university system. Between 1989 and 1998, the JICA sponsored 937 Argentines, who pursued training activities in Japan. A high percentage of these scholarship holders are from the university system. The JICA has also donated research equipment to Argentine universities as part of two projects, Research Cooperation for the Faculty of Veterinary Sciences of the La Plata National University[8] and the development of the National Catalysis Center of the Litoral National University.[9]

Germany does not offer institutional support for higher education, but German organizations offer scholarships for specialized training for Argentine faculty. The German Academic Exchange Service (DAAD) has initiated a support program to foster faculty exchange between German and Argentine institutions, through agreements signed by several universities, which jointly finance faculty flows in both directions.

Bilateral cooperation with Italy is handled through the Italian-Argentine Joint Fund, which finances 24 projects in environmental studies, physics, chemistry, agriculture, health, and communications. The Joint Fund is negotiated by the Department for Science, Technology and Productive Innovation (SECYT).

Cooperation with Spain is handled through the Hispanic-Argentine Joint Fund, negotiated by the Ministry of International Relations, International Trade and Worship. The fund has financed 56 projects, in 10 of which local Argentine universities served as counterparts.

The General Cooperation Office has a dissemination and consultation system for external scholarship programs and provides information on the administration of the Organization of American States' Fellowship Programs scholarships. In conjunction with the International Migration Organization, it also offers discount airfares to individuals going on study trips or missions abroad.

ARGENTINA AS A COOPERATION-DONATING COUNTRY

In 1992 the Ministry of International Relations, International Trade and Worship created the Argentine Fund for Horizontal Cooperation (FO-AR). In doing so, the country became both a donor and recipient of cooperation projects.

There are two types of FO-AR cooperation: the sending of Argentine experts overseas and the hosting of foreign professionals in Argentine

---

[8] This project led universities to develop studies on epidemiology and on the improvement of techniques for diagnosing and preventing major livestock diseases. The $2.5 million project sent 30 Argentinean faculty to Japan and 49 Japanese experts to La Plata. The Faculty of Veterinary Sciences is considered a key participant in the first action undertaken by the Partnership Programme for Joint Cooperation between Japan and Argentina.

[9] The National Council for Scientific and Technical Research and the University of Litoral received $1.5 million for providing scholarships, sending experts abroad, and purchasing equipment.

institutions. Since its creation, the FO-AR has sent about 3,000 experts abroad to work on 1,900 projects. The experts participating in the program are chosen mainly from universities, the CONICET, and government.

The projects are concentrated in Central America (58 percent), South America (36 percent), Eastern Europe (2 percent), Africa (3 percent), and Asia and Oceania (1 percent). The projects are jointly financed by the organization employing the experts and the Ministry of International Relations, International Trade and Worship. The main thematic areas for FO-AR–based technical assistance are livestock breeding, agriculture, forestry and fisheries, regional development, health, industry, education, and natural resources.

The FO-AR is a prime example of South-South cooperation. While this cooperation is limited in terms of resources and range of actions, it allows vital cooperation projects to be implemented, especially in Latin America.

In 2001 the FO-AR signed an agreement with the JICA that led to the launching of the Partnership Programme for Joint Cooperation between Japan and Argentina. The objective of this agreement was to enable the JICA to use its broad experience in development cooperation to support the South-South cooperation efforts undertaken by Argentina.[10]

Ministry of Education, Science and Technology

The Ministry of Education, Science and Technology includes two highly differentiated international relations units: the Secretariat of Science, Technology and Productive Innovation, which includes the Office of International Relations, and the Secretariat of University Policies. Within the Ministry is also the Office of International Cooperation, which reports directly to the Minister.

The fragmented structure impedes the development of a global and structured internationalization policy. Nevertheless, in 2003 the Secretariat of University Policies and the Office of International Cooperation created a joint unit for international cooperation. The unit coordinates its functions and activities with the universities, with a view to promoting the internationalization of higher education throughout the country.

SECRETARIAT OF SCIENCE, TECHNOLOGY AND PRODUCTIVE INNOVATION

For many years Argentina has promoted international scientific activities. The Secretariat of Science, Technology and Productive Innovation

---

[10] The most valuable experience undertaken to date involves the Faculty of Veterinary Sciences of the National University (UNLP). The project, financed within the framework of the FO-AR-JICA Program, finances the teaching of 5 training courses on animal health to 74 Latin American scholarship holders and the provision of 14 experts.

administers several agreements geared toward implementing joint activities of investigation with similar organizations in other countries.

The joint research activities can be divided into activities of bilateral and multilateral cooperation. With regard to bilateral cooperation, the framework is determined by the signing of specific agreements between the Secretariat of Science, Technology and Productive Innovation and its counterparts in other countries. Argentina has active agreements with Germany (58), France (49), Italy (45), Brazil (26), Cuba (9), Chile (7), Mexico (7), Hungary (5), Slovenia (5), and Belgium (4). Agreements with Australia, China, Finland, Malaysia, and Portugal are also in the pipeline. Argentina signed a bilateral science and technology agreement with the United States in 1972, but the agreement was never implemented.

In 1987 Argentina and Brazil established the Argentine-Brazilian Center of Biotechnology (CABBIO). Over the past 15 years, CABBIO has implemented 64 joint projects and developed a significant number of specialization courses through the Argentinean-Brazilian Biotechnology Institute (EABBIO) (see www.secyt.gov.ar).

With regard to multilateral cooperation, the Secretariat of Science, Technology and Productive Innovation participates in the OAS, the Latin-American Program for Science and Technology (CYTED), the European Union (through the participation of numerous Argentine groups in the European Union's R&D framework programs), and UNESCO. Through the Secretariat of Science, Technology and Productive Innovation, and in its capacity as a member state, Argentina makes financial contributions to the Inter-American Institute for Research on Global Change (IAI); the International Center of Genetic Engineering and Biotechnology (ICGB); the Third World Academy of Sciences (TWAS); and the Latin American Network of Biological Sciences (RELAB). The Secretariat of Science, Technology and Productive Innovation recently created the Program for the Promotion of the Technological Internationalization for Competitiveness, with the aim of linking bilateral and multilateral scientific and technological cooperation programs to international in-company innovation development programs.

Within Mercosur, the Specialized Meeting for Science and Technology in the Mercosur (RECYT) was created in 1993, with the purpose of linking the science and technology policies of member states. As in Mercosur's other technical areas, annual meetings have been held on an ongoing basis, but only limited achievements have been made toward coordinating government policies.

Activities that promote joint actions have been developed and implemented for decades, despite changes of government. These activities lack a clear definition of thematic priorities of strategic interest to the country, however, thus undermining the potential impact of the results of joint research. In recent years, the annual science and technology projects have set guidelines to ensure that, thanks to international cooperation, R&D activities contribute to the search for solutions to the problems of competitiveness of production structures and to the social problems affecting Argentina.

OFFICE OF INTERNATIONAL COOPERATION OF THE MINISTRY
OF EDUCATION, SCIENCE AND TECHNOLOGY
The Office of International Cooperation of the Ministry of Education, Science and Technology is responsible directly to the Minister and acts in coordination with the Secretariat for University Policies with regard to the Mercosur Educativo program. It also administers two overseas residences, the Argentina Foundation in the International University City of Paris and the Nuestra Señora de Luján Argentine residence hall in Madrid. These residences provide accommodation for Argentine students pursuing graduate studies in Paris and Madrid. They were built at a time when there were almost no graduate programs offered in Argentina, and when Paris and Madrid were common destinations for students seeking advanced training. As graduate education has developed extensively in Argentina, the residences have largely lost their value. It is now considered necessary to reassess the objectives of these residences and to seek ways to broaden their missions, in order to convert them into vital tools for the internationalization of the country's higher education system.

The Office of International Cooperation of the Ministry of Education, Science and Technology also provides information on overseas scholarships. Its information complements that provided by the International Cooperation Office of the Argentine Ministry of Foreign Affairs (www.me. gov.ar/becas/index.html).

SECRETARIAT OF UNIVERSITY POLICY
The Secretariat of University Policy is the government division responsible for setting higher education policies in Argentina, within the framework of university autonomy. In 2003 the Secretariat formally included an international relations area within its functional structure; before then it had not developed policies for internationalization. This lack of government action had a significant impact on universities, since internationalization depended almost exclusively on the institutions' own objectives and priorities. The same year, the Secretariat of University Policy and the National Bureau of International Accounts (DNCI) created an Area of International University Cooperation, which seeks to promote and support the internationalization of universities.

The Secretariat of University Policy has also developed the Program of Graduate Associated Centers. This program, developed within the framework of the Educational Cooperation Agreement between Brazil and Argentina, supports academic exchange between universities in both countries. The objective of the program is to encourage international associations between master's and doctorate degree programs. By mid-2003 the first 15 projects, in which numerous Argentine universities are participating, had been set in motion. The program also promotes faculty and graduate student exchanges, seeks to ensure recognition of the credits granted through joint provision of guidance in the preparation of theses and the issuing of joint academic degrees, and encourages the exchange of integration-related teaching and research experiences.

Within the framework of the Organization of American States' Inter-American Council for Integral Development (CIDI), a multilateral project, adopted in 2002, aims to provide enterprising young people with university training in order to strengthen the link with the productive and technological sector. Other countries participating in this project, which is coordinated by Argentina through its Secretariat of University Policy are Brazil (Ministry of Education), Chile (Santiago de Chile University), and Uruguay (the Kolping Institute). When the project is completed, efforts will be made to form a technical regional network among institutions responsible for coordination in each country.

Network of Heads of International Cooperation of the National Universities (RedCIUN) and the Italian-Argentine University Consortium

Established in 1999, the Network of Heads of International Cooperation of the National Universities (RedCIUN) is a network of directors of international relations offices at public universities. The network seeks to create a forum for the internationalization of public universities, promote synergy between universities, circulate strategic information, advise the National Inter-University Council on specific issues, maintain relations with other similar associations in other countries, and enhance the training of staff at university international relations offices.

The operations and actions carried out by the RedCIUN have helped address the lack of importance that universities and the government attach to internationalization. The network is currently developing important projects, such as an integrated system providing information on international scholarships, courses, and activities; its own Web site (www. redciun.edu.ar); and a meeting newsletter. One of its most important functions has been to standardize practices among universities, something that is very important for universities that are not engaged in much international activity. In 2003 the RedCIUN agreed to work jointly with the Ministry of Science and Technology, MECYT's Area of

International University Cooperation, and the Council of Private University Presidents (CRUP), with the purpose of conducting forums and projects that promote and develop internationalization within the university system.

The RedCIUN plays an active role in establishing relations with similar networks in other countries (mainly in Latin America) or run by international organizations. It supports the idea of forming a Latin America international relations network at the university level, an idea that is still at an embryonic stage.

One of the RedCIUN's major achievements was convincing the government to change the visa requirements for foreign exchange students pursuing approved studies in Argentina. Before 2002 such students had to obtain temporary resident visas, which were very costly and involved lengthy bureaucratic procedures. Today students can enter Argentina on a student visa, which can be issued within 10 days.

In 2002 the Italian-Argentine University Consortium was created. This agreement brings together a large number of Italian universities and Argentine public universities by means of the National Inter-University Council. To date the Consortium has not conducted any significant activities. However, in 2000 the National Inter-University Council signed a cooperation agreement with the Council of University Presidents of Spanish Universities (CRUE). The Council of Private University Presidents (CRUP) does not yet possess a similar structure, although initiatives to create one are underway.

International Organizations Active in Argentina

Argentine universities participate in several programs and projects financed by international organizations engaged in promotion and cooperation. The organizations whose programs produce the greatest impact are the European Union; the AECI; UNESCO (although it has been less active in Argentine universities in recent years); the Organization of Ibero-American States for Education, Science and Culture (OEI); the JICA; and the OAS (Theiler 2003a).

The OEI is redoubling its efforts to increase cooperation-related activities in higher learning, as demonstrated by the creation of the student exchange, Academic Exchange and Mobility Program (PIMA) described below. In 2001 the OEI promoted the creation of an Argentine-Uruguayan Department of Science, Technology, Society and Innovation, which brings together Argentine universities; the Secretariat of University Policies; the Secretariat of Science, Technology and Productive Innovation; and the University of the Republic of Uruguay.

The European Union has increased its presence in the Argentine university system, and there are signs that it will increase the number of activities it promotes. Over the past few years, it has developed new cooperation-related programs with Latin America and increased the economic resources allocated for such programs. Examples are the Latin America Academic Training (ALFA) program, which provides cooperation between higher education institutions in the European Union and Latin America; the High Level Latin-American Scholarship (AlßAN) program, which supports Latin American students wanting to study in Europe; @ LIS, a distance learning program; and Argentina's participation in the Sixth Framework Program of Science and Technology. Despite the high number of ALFA networks with Argentine participation, the program has not had a significant impact in Argentina, because ties were not maintained after European Union financing ceased.

Throughout Latin America, there has been a dramatic increase in student mobility, facilitated by such programs as the Mutis programs of the Latin-American Summit of Heads of State and Government, the Inter-University Cooperation Program of the AECI (which modified its arrangements in 2003), and the PIMA program of the Organization of Ibero-American States for Education, Science and Culture.

Organizational and Administrative Structures in Universities

For many years, universities gave no systematic priority to internationalization; those activities that did exist were initiated by individual faculty or groups of faculty. Only in the late 1990s did universities begin to declare internationalization a strategic objective and start to make it a part of the objectives of their strategic development plans, although in most cases this was not matched with concrete actions or budgetary allocations for pursuing such an objective.

Public universities are governed by a university statute that defines their institutional objectives, structure, and organization. Most universities also possess strategic development plans that are generally related to the institutional evaluations conducted by the CONEAU.

In 15 percent of public universities and 33 percent of private universities, the statutes make little reference to certain aspects of internationalization (Theiler 2003a, b). This is understandable if one bears in mind that statutes were approved at the time the university was created, which in most cases was before 1990. In more than 75 percent of public universities and 100 percent of private ones, the international dimension is included in the development plans as an area that should be developed.

Organizational Structures

Ninety percent of public universities and two-thirds of private universities have an ad hoc structure for administering international activities. Argentine universities are usually organized and structured hierarchically, with the secretariats at the top of the hierarchy. The status of about half of the international relations offices at both public and private universities is that of offices (Theiler 2003a, b), while some 20 percent enjoy the status of secretariat. The remaining 30 percent are low in the hierarchy.

The staff engaged in the development of activities at international relations offices in both public and private universities are limited, and most lack special training. The average office has about four people. About 55 percent are university professionals, while the others are assistants or student interns. Given that the management of international relations requires the specialized knowledge of supervisory staff and that experience is vital to the success of management activities, it is salient that staff generally lack specialized training and the officials in charge (university secretaries, undersecretaries, or directors) usually spend a relatively short time in their posts, leaving whenever there is a change in institutional authorities (which is often at public universities). This does not allow the staff time to acquire sufficient experience in the activities they perform, and it inhibits the maintenance of internationalization policies over time.

The small size and lack of international relations offices seriously restrict the number of activities they can perform, limiting these to the administration of extramural programs, the management of international agreements, and protocol-related activities. Only rarely do these offices serve as the administrators of specific higher education institution internationalization programs, which may include the management of designated financial resources.

Allocation of Resources

International relations offices in public institutions operate mainly with economic resources provided by the institution's official budget; very few of these entities earns revenues through international activities (Theiler 2003a). About 60 percent of the international relations offices in public institutions are not specifically assigned budgetary resources and are therefore dependent on higher administrative areas. While the remaining 40 percent do have their own budgets, the amount is very low (about $17,500 a year, excluding staff salaries). The money allocated to international activities represents no more than 0.3 percent of the annual budget of public universities. The same may be said about private universities, only 44 percent of which report having financial allocations for international relations offices.

One common function of international relations offices is the search for revenues for the institutions through the financing of specific projects by international organizations or cooperation agencies in certain developed countries. In only a limited number of cases do they develop any other kind of revenue-producing action. Such activities include offering Spanish language courses for foreigners (Buenos Aires, Córdoba, Litoral, and Belgrano Universities, among others); receiving foreign students on contracts with intermediary enterprises (Cuyo National University and Salvador University, among others); and offering graduate courses designed for foreigners wishing to take advantage of the low cost of living in Argentina.

Planning and Evaluation of Internationalization-Related Processes and Actions

Of the cases examined, only one private university had any systematic activities for evaluating international activities. Records are kept of only activities and projects that have been implemented (Theiler 2003b).

In the case of institutional evaluations undertaken by the CONEAU, the international dimension is not specifically analyzed, since it is not viewed as important enough to deserve evaluation. In spite of this, the evaluation commissions frequently make proposals to the universities in their reports. In accrediting programs, CONEAU requests and evaluates information on international agreements.

Programming Strategies of Universities

This section describes the main international activities conducted by universities. It also evaluates the level of dissemination of such activities among the institutions and analyzes their impact.

Student Mobility

International student mobility has been developed in Argentina since the mid-1990s. Since 2000 it has grown significantly, through the implementation of student exchange programs by multilateral organizations (the Organization of Ibero-American States for Education, Science and Culture), bilateral agencies (AECI), bilateral agreements between foreign universities and institutions in Argentina, and university networks (AUGM, CRISCO, and the Latin American Universities Union [UDUAL])

Public universities do not give priority to student exchange, and their involvement in external programs of multilateral organizations and university networks is very weak. About 15 percent have no history of mobility. The value and importance of this activity is clearly on the rise, however, and institutions are beginning to understand that it adds significant value to the training of their students. Some of the most successful programs are described below.

THE INTER-UNIVERSITY COOPERATION PROGRAM

The Agency for International Cooperation's Inter-University Cooperation Program (PCI) has played an important role in the consolidation of international activities in Argentine universities, especially public universities. It is the first activity undertaken in the area of student exchange for most universities. Implemented in 1994, the PCI has enabled about 1,800 students from 41 Argentine universities (29 public and 12 private) to study at Spanish universities and about 2,200 Spanish students to study at Argentine universities. Of all the universities participating in the PCI, the ones most actively involved are the Nordeste, Rosario, and Córdoba National Universities. Financing for the program is shared by the AECI and the Argentine universities, which have made considerable effort to increase the number of exchanges conducted.

CRISCO STUDENT MOBILITY PROGRAM

In 1998 the Council of University Presidents for the Integration of the West-Central Sub-Region of South America (CRISCO) created the first program of this type. It was developed among the countries of Latin America and included the recognition of studies by the universities forming part of the network. Between 1998 and 2002, it allowed 313 students to study in other countries. The resources to finance the program are provided by the universities. Mobility is organized into five networks based on the following subject areas: historical and cultural heritage, management of technological innovation, water resources, regional economies, and university-company relations.

THE ESCALA PROGRAM OF THE MONTEVIDEO GROUP UNIVERSITY ASSOCIATION

With experience in faculty exchange, the Montevideo Group University Association (AUGM) decided in 2000 to create the ESCALA program. The program provides reciprocity by associated universities, semester-long visits by students, and recognition of studies pursued. Financing for the program is provided by participating universities and is complemented by some additional funding from the OEI.[11] The ESCALA program currently allows 100–150 students per semester to study abroad. Six Argentine universities take part in these exchanges.[12]

---

[11] The AUGM and the OEI have signed an agreement with the ESCALA and PIMA programs.
[12] The participating universities are the Córdoba, Entre Ríos, Litoral, La Plata, Buenos Aires, and Rosario National Universities.

ACADEMIC EXCHANGE AND MOBILITY PROGRAM OF THE ORGANIZATION OF
IBERO-AMERICAN STATES FOR EDUCATION, SCIENCE AND CULTURE
Created in 2000, the Academic Exchange and Mobility Program (PIMA) of
the OEI is the first program that had widespread impact throughout Latin
America and that included recognition of the studies pursued. Twenty-
four PIMA exchange networks are being developed, in which 10 Argentine
public universities participate.[13] University networks created under PIMA
are coordinated by one of these networks, one of which is coordinated by
an Argentine university (the Litoral National University).

ACADEMIC STUDENT MOBILITY PROGRAM OF THE LATIN AMERICAN
UNIVERSITIES UNION
During 2002 the Latin American Universities Union (UDUAL) launched a
student exchange program in which pairs of universities engage in mutual
student exchange activities and recognize each other's studies. In 2003, 24
Latin American universities, including 4 Argentine institutions (the Cuyo,
Entre Ríos, Litoral, and Mar del Plata National Universities), participated
in the program.

Significant activities are taking place regionally to promote student mobility. Almost no initiatives have been set up with North America, Europe,
or the rest of the world, however. One exception is the European Union's
ALFA program, some of whose networks include student mobility, although mobility has generally not been reciprocal (flows are from Latin
America toward the European Union, not vice versa).

The only example of a student mobility–related program involving
public universities is the International Student Mobility (PROINMES) program of the Litoral National University. This program allocates budgetary
resources for this activity and has an appropriate infrastructure for managing the program (ad hoc office, student welcome system, residence hall
for exchange students, internal system for recognizing courses). The program currently includes more than 120 students, all of whose courses are
recognized.

More than 80 percent of public universities in Argentina participate in
student mobility programs in which the studies pursued are not recognized (Theiler 2003a). In 2001 and 2002 the average number of students involved in exchanges was 25 per university (including those sent and those
received). Only 58 percent of universities have experience in developing
exchanges in which studies are recognized, and the average number of
students per university in such programs is just nine.

---

[13] The participating universities are the Buenos Aires, Córdoba, Catamarca, Entre Ríos,
General San Martín, La Plata, Litoral, Lomas de Zamora, Rosario, and San Juan National
Universities.

Two-thirds of private universities undertake mobility activities without recognition of studies, with an average of about 10 students per university; 89 percent engage in mobility with recognition of studies, with an average of about 20 students per university. The destinations are North America, Europe, and Latin America.

One major limitation to the mobility of Argentine students is their inadequate command of foreign languages. Failure to learn a second language is widespread, both in secondary school and in the higher education system, where it is often not a curricular requirement or an accreditation standard.

Another serious limitation to mobility is the absence of an official system of credits similar to the European Union's (European Credit Transfer System) system. In Argentina courses are usually measured on an hourly basis, which impedes recognition by other institutions.

Another facet of student mobility is the opening up of universities to students from countries outside interuniversity agreements. European and North American institutions often encourage their students to pursue part of their studies at a foreign university. Although the bulk of these exchanges take place within the Northern Hemisphere, Argentina is becoming a common destination, because of its low costs, the beauty of the country, and its highly developed university system. There has been a clear rise in the number of foreign exchange students (MECYT 2000). But most Argentine universities, especially public universities, do not have strategies or appropriate structures for managing this kind of arrangement. This has led to the paradoxical situation in which foreign students who pay exorbitant university fees in their own country receive free tuition at an Argentine university.

A special case is that of the Buenos Aires, Cuyo, Salvador, and Torcuato Di Tella National Universities. These universities are part of the Cooperation Program in the Americas (COPA) Project, made up of Butler University and the Universities of North Carolina, Illinois, and Texas. Under the project, U.S. students take courses at Argentinean universities, which offer cultural activities, Spanish language courses, and special courses on regional development.

Faculty and Researcher Mobility

University faculty in Argentina include two well-defined groups. The first are research faculty, many of whom perform scientific work through subsidized projects. Most of these professors are full-time faculty. Many belong to the CONICET's scientific researcher network. Research professors frequently participate in exchanges with other foreign institutions, attend conferences abroad, and maintain relations with foreign researchers. The second group includes part-time faculty, who engage in little international mobility and have few international academic relationships.

Most universities possess mobility support mechanisms for their faculty, but only a few have created the facilities needed to receive faculty from abroad (such as residences for visiting professors). During 2001 each public university sent and received an average of about 65 faculty (Theiler 2003a). At some universities, such as the University of Buenos Aires and the La Plata National University, more than 100 faculty members are involved in mobility programs; other universities have no mobility support systems.[14]

Spain is the most important exchange partner. Flows of faculty within Latin America are not significant. Researchers tend to interact more with North American or European universities than with Latin American universities. One major exception is the Montevideo Group University Association. It possesses a faculty mobility program that facilitated the mobilization of hundreds of its faculty members with the support of UNESCO. (This activity has decreased significantly since 2001, because UNESCO suspended financing.) Faculty mobility to and from universities in Asia, Africa, and Oceania is very limited, and the few cases that exist are mainly with Australia.

There is a rich tradition of programs that facilitate human resources training programs in foreign institutions (table 3.4). Scholarships are financed by the universities or by other institutions in host countries. One interesting case is the agreement reached between the University of Belgrano and Fulbright Foundation, under which 150 faculty from the University of Belgrano have received training in the United States.

Regional and International Networks

In recent years the importance and value of functional multilateralism has grown significantly, owing especially to the growth of networks and strategic alliances among universities. Latin America has not escaped this trend, as a significant number of regional and international interinstitutional associations have been formed. Most of these associations are forums in which different aspects of higher education are analyzed and technical assistance fostered in such areas as organization and university administration. A huge effort is put into promoting student and faculty mobility, joint research projects, and standardization of undergraduate and graduate courses.

---

[14] The information presented here is incomplete, as it includes only the mobility flows recorded by the universities' central authorities and fails to includes the flows financed by research subsidies, funds derived from specialized work carried out by scientific groups, and other sources.

Table 3.4 Overseas Scholarships Granted to Argentines, 1997–2002

Scholarship	1997	1998	1999	2000	2001	2002
Antorchas Foundation	24	24	23	21	0	0
Fulbright Commission	80	123	97	100	90	84
Fund for the Enhancement of Educational Quality (FOMEC)	132	152	146	36	16	0
National Council for Scientific and Technological Research (CONICET)	60	60	60	60	80	0
France	10	10	18	22	19	12
Spanish Agency for International Cooperation (AECI)	161	176	99	168	100	0
Total	467	545	443	407	305	96

Source: Albornoz, Luchilo, and others (2002); Network Center (www.centroredes.org.ar).

The high level of participation of Argentine university institutions in different networks should be highlighted, and it should be recognized that the impact and levels of involvement of such institutions are very different. Virtually all of the universities on which information is available participate in university networks. The main international networks in which they participate are the Montevideo Group University Association; the Universities in Mercosur network; the Council of University Presidents for the Integration of the Central West Sub-Region of South America; the Union of Latin American Universities; the Latin-American University Association of Graduate Education; the Columbus Association; the Inter-American University Organization; and the Latin-American Network for the Accreditation of Higher Education Quality (Siufi 2003).

Argentine universities also participate in other networks. These include the Argentina, Brazil and Paraguay Regional University Integration Association; the Latin-American Educational Television Association; the Distance Education Network Consortium; the Association of Jesuit Universities in Latin America; the Latin American University Cooperation Network; the International University Association; and the Latin American University Association.

Argentine universities participate mainly in Latin American networks. Paradoxically, bilateral relations of Argentine institutions are developed primarily with universities in other continents, mainly Europe.

There are two different types of networks. Macro-networks are composed of a large number of universities, including many Argentine universities. Examples of these networks are the Inter-American University Organization and the Union of Latin American Universities. Participation by Argentine institutions tends to be merely formal, with some exceptions. In general, these networks are only slightly noticeable inside Argentine university communities.

Regional networks are formed by a limited number of universities within a region. Networks of this kind usually promote activities in the areas of faculty and student exchange (with affordable costs for universities). They frequently sponsor academic conferences, with a high level of member participation.

Joint Courses with Foreign Institutions

The teaching of undergraduate and graduate degree programs in conjunction with foreign institutions has spread throughout Argentina, with about half of universities offering such programs (Theiler 2003a, b). Most of the programs offered by public universities are for graduate students; a few (offered at the Cuyo and Entre Ríos National Universities) are undergraduate programs. Virtually all of these joint programs are designed for the Argentine market; there are no records of joint degree courses involving Argentine and foreign universities that have been designed and offered to the international market. The programs generally require attendance at classes taught by faculty from the foreign university counterpart and thus involve the exchange of both faculty and students.[15] These courses are recognized "as the universities are autonomous, such degrees have the same validity as the others they issue" (García de Fanelli 1999, p. 47).

International Interinstitutional Agreements

Public universities in Argentina have signed an average of 85 cooperation agreements with foreign universities, although the number varies with the size of the institution. Despite the high number of signed agreements, the

---

[15] The Universities of Belgrano and Salvador, both of which are private, offer many joint programs. Belgrano University offers 31 joint courses, with Alcalá de Henares University, the Lyon Management School, the Marcile-Luminy School of Architecture, the University of Barcelona, the Polytecnica University of Madrid, the University of Illinois, the University of Rome La Sapienza, and the University of Toronto. Salvador University offers joint courses in conjunction with Carlos III University, Georgetown University, Deusto-Bilbao University, Paris I University, Paris X University, the State University of New York-Albany, and the Universitá degli Studi di Pisa, among others.

Table 3.5 Countries and Regions of Institutions with Which Argentine Public Universities Have Signed Agreements

Region	Percentage of agreements in force
Latin America:	
Mercosur	45
Rest of Latin America	20
United States and Canada	26
Europe:	
Spain	53
Rest of European Union	45
Europe outside European Union	33
Asia, Oceania, and Africa	53

Source: RedCIUN 2003.

number of agreements currently in force is quite low, with only 55 percent materializing into some kind of activity.

About half of the cooperation agreements signed are with universities in Europe, and about 50 percent of these remain in force (table 3.5). Only 9 percent of agreements are with North American institutions, and only 26 percent of those agreements are in force. Agreements with Latin America represent 41 percent of all agreements, with a predominance of Mercosur countries. Relations with universities in Africa, Asia, and Oceania are very limited.

Private universities signed an average of 59 cooperation agreements with foreign universities, 26 of which (44 percent) are in force. The largest number of agreements were signed with institutions in the European Union.

Joint Research with Foreign Institutions

All public universities on which there are data and two-thirds of private universities pursue joint research activities with foreign institutions. The partner institutions are located mainly in the European Union, especially Spain, France, Germany, Italy, and the United Kingdom, and to a smaller degree, the United States and Canada. Within Latin America, Argentine researchers work mainly with partners from Brazil, Chile, and Uruguay. Sixty-three percent of joint research activities are carried out with institutions located in the European Union, 21 percent with institutions in Latin America, 14 percent with institutions in North America, and 2 percent with Asian institutions (Theiler 2003a, b).

Funding for joint research comes mainly from the agreements that the Secretariat of Science, Technology and Productive Innovation holds with several countries and from the subsidies granted by such organizations as France's National Scientific Research Center (CNRS), the United States' National Science Foundation (NSF), Brazil's National Council for Scientific Development (CNPq), and other foundations, such as the European Union's Sixth Framework program. Only 20 percent of public universities and no private universities have received or are applying for joint patents with foreign institutions.

Spanish Language and Argentine Culture Programs

Spanish language and Argentine culture programs are growing steadily at both public and private universities in Argentina. The Buenos Aires, Córdoba, Cuyo, and Litoral National Universities; the Universities of Belgrano and El Salvador; and other institutions offer courses in Spanish as a foreign language. The University of Buenos Aires has a record of considerable experience in this activity. The University of Litoral and the University of Cuyo have designed programs in Argentine studies for foreigners, in which the teaching of Spanish is complemented by courses on Argentine culture.

Participation in Development Cooperation

Argentina undertakes development cooperation–related activities mainly through the Argentine Fund for Horizontal Cooperation (FO-AR), administered by the Ministry of International Relations, International Trade and Worship. A number of public universities participate in these activities by providing experts. About half of public universities currently undertake, or have undertaken, development cooperation activities funded by the FO-AR. Institutions frequently contributing experts include the Buenos Aires, Cuyo, Litoral, Luján, and Río Cuarto Universities. As the FO-AR normally approaches public organizations, private universities show no record of having carried out such activities.

The La Plata National University is the headquarters of a joint program between the FO-AR and the JICA that is being developed through the Partnership Programme for Joint Cooperation between Japan and Argentina. The initiative involves South-South cooperation from Argentina in the area of animal health, with Japanese support channeled through the JICA.

The Internationalization of Curricula

According to the OECD, an internationalized curriculum may be defined as "an internationally oriented curriculum in content and/or form which is aimed at preparing students to perform professionally and socially within an international and multicultural context and which is designed for both local and foreign students" (Van der Wende 1996, p. 45). Argentine students receive significant international basic educational training, since the elementary and secondary stages of the educational system include content of Latin American and global interest in history, geography, economics, and other areas. Lack of adequate second language learning during early education is a problem, however.

Argentine universities have generally not acknowledged the need to train graduates to have an international profile or be suited to a global market. Universities are in the early stages of developing internationalization strategies for the courses they offer. With a few exceptions, public universities have not designed curricula that include international courses (such as international relations and international law), courses that promote the study of certain subjects from an international perspective, or courses that include a period of study abroad—that is, courses that have the stated objective of training students for an international market.

In recent years, however, a large number of graduate courses have sprung up that have been designed to train professionals for the international market. This has led to the creation of numerous—and successful—MBA programs at both private and public universities, for which there is strong demand.

Conclusions

The internationalization of higher education in Argentina is still in its early stages and has attracted relatively little attention. It still goes unnoticed in the university community, and its impact remains weak.

Argentina's universities have begun to expand their international activities and, in a few cases, to pursue a regional and global framework for their activities. In general, they still do not have a clear idea of the benefits that this change may yield for the institutions, their faculty, and their students, however. In most institutions internationalization is included in development plans and strategic planning as an objective to be pursued, but is usually insufficient to develop it. A clear conviction that an important objective of internationalization should be to boost the quality of university services appears to be lacking.

If internationalization is to become a priority on the agenda of universities, there must be a change in policies. Its promoters must be supported, and internationalization must be fostered in all of the universities' core functions.

Government programs for internationalization are insignificant. Effective policies need to be implemented to promote and guide universities in their quest for the international dimension of their missions and activities. The Report of the National Commission for the Improvement of Higher

Education in the Republic of Argentina (2002) notes that "there is a lack of properly coordinated policies and strategies among Argentine universities, with regard to international cooperation. As a result, some of the actions undertaken may have adverse consequences, such as producing a brain drain, especially among scientists and engineers, even though scholarship programs that do not effectively contemplate the availability of opportunities are intended to encourage the return of scholarship holders to the country."

A number of developments suggest that Argentine higher education may be able to engage in the internationalization process successfully. The most important of these are the following:

- advances in regional educational integration within Mercosur
- inclusion of internationalization-related objectives in the strategic plans of universities
- consolidation of RedCIUN and the National Inter-University Council
- growth in the number of educational programs offered through transnational education, particularly through distance education
- creation of joint graduate courses by Argentine and foreign universities
- the increase in joint research activities between Argentina and foreign institutions
- the increase in, and growing institutional acknowledgment of, student exchanges in which studies are recognized
- the growing participation of universities in international networks
- valuable experiences obtained through the technical cooperation for development provided through the FO-AR
- the large number of cooperation agreements signed by Argentine and foreign institutions of higher education
- the actions taken by the CONEAU.

Despite these strengths, certain issues may become serious obstacles to the internationalization process:

- the lack of adequate funding for higher education
- the low priority given by government policy to the promotion of the internationalization of higher education
- the small size and lack of power of offices of international relations in most institutions
- the grudging attitude toward innovation and the promotion of specific actions in the area of internationalization
- the lack of institutional interest in promoting educational programs beyond the country's borders
- the lack of evaluation-related activities for international actions
- the meager budgets allocated by universities to internationalize.

Higher education in Argentina is firmly founded on the principle of social justice, which has characterized it since the beginning of the twentieth century. Indeed, at more than 40 percent, access to higher education is higher than in any other country in Latin America, close to that of the OECD. Argentina is the Latin American country whose system grants access to the highest percentage of citizens from lower income groups. The significant rise in the demand for higher education over the past 20 years has been addressed largely by the public higher education system, through the creation of new universities and the increase in enrollment in existing institutions. At the same time, per capita investment in higher education in Argentina, including both private and state investment, represents a relatively small percentage of GDP. This unresolved conflict will undoubtedly set the conditions for future development of the country's higher education system and its internationalization process.

At the beginning of the third millennium, Argentina suffered one of the most serious crises to shake the social structure of the country. The higher education system has not remained unscathed by this situation. While the university system is alive and possesses both a tradition that supports it and a scientific and educational heritage of outstanding merit, it is widely believed that the time has come for important changes, many of them long overdue. Will the internationalization of Argentina's higher education be influenced by this situation? Of course it will. Will its development be set back by the efforts made to overcome the crisis and by the changes taking place? Or far from becoming an obstacle, do these efforts have the potential of becoming important promoters and engines for this development? Time will show, but the international dimension of higher education must undoubtedly be approached as a priority area to be attended to within the context of the transformations promoted.

Higher education can no longer be conceived of only on the basis of national conditions and criteria. The crucial question is therefore what the priority geographical framework for the internationalization of Argentine higher education will be.

The Latin American educational system exhibits characteristics quite similar to those of the European system: a highly heterogeneous integration framework, in which the challenges of coordinating higher education are addressed. At the same time, the possibility of integrating Latin America's higher education systems is affected by the inclusion of higher education in the services protocol as an item to be negotiated within the context of the World Trade Organization (WTO). This action fails to take the opinion of the educational communities into account and promotes the globalization of higher education in the expectation that states will give up their political function of providing guidance, supervision, and administration in their areas of social responsibility. As Barsky and Dávila (2002,

p. 28) note, "This scenario justifies an acceleration of the debate on, and changes to, Latin America's higher education systems, in the sense that their relative isolation and backwardness with regard to global processes may aggravate an already unfavorable situation by placing them at a disadvantage in an increasingly interconnected global educational system."

References

Albornoz, Mario, Ernesto Fernández Polcuch, and Alfaraz, Claudio. 2002. *Hacia una nueva estimación de la "fuga de cerebros."* Centro Redes, Buenos Aires. www.centroredes.org.ar.

Albornoz, Mario, Lucas Luchilo, Gustavo Arber, Rodolfo Barrere, and Julio Raffo. 2002. *El talento que se pierde: aproximación al estudio de la emigración de profesionales, investigadores y tecnólogos argentinos.* Centro Redes, Buenos Aires. www.centroredes.org.ar.

Banfi, Cristina. 2002. *El fenómeno de la educación superior transnacional: su impacto en Argentina.* Centro ESSARP, Buenos Aires.

Barsky, Osvaldo, and Mabel Dávila, 2002. *Las transformaciones del sistema internacional de educación superior.* Working paper, University of Belgrano, Buenos Aires.

Comisión Nacional para el Mejoramiento de la Educación Superior. 2002. *Informe de la Comisión Nacional para el Mejoramiento de la Educación Superior.* Ministerio de Educación, Ciencia y Tecnología de la República Argentina, Buenos Aires.

Coraggio, José Luis, and Adolfo Vispo, coordinators. 2001. *Contribución al estudio del sistema universitario Argentino.* Buenos Aires: Consejo Interuniversitario Nacional-Editorial Miño y Dávila Editores.

Dahlman, Carl, and Peter Scherer. 2002. *Beyond the Crisis: From the Old to the New Economy in Argentina.* Washington, DC: World Bank Institute.

Del Bello, Juan Carlos, and Eduardo Mundet. 2001. *Alternativas para facilitar la movilidad de estudiantes, egresados y docentes en el sistema universitario de América Latina.* Working paper, University of Belgrano, Buenos Aires.

Fernández Lamarra, Norberto. 2002. *La educación superior en la Argentina en debate: situación, problemas y perspectivas.* Buenos Aires: Instituto Internacional para la Educación Superior en América Latina y el Caribe–Editorial Universitaria de Buenos Aires.

García de Fanelli, Ana. 1999. *La educación trasnacional: la experiencia extranjera y lecciones para el diseño de una política de regulación en la Argentina.* Serie Estudios n° 1, CONEAU, Buenos Aires.

García Guadilla, Carmen, Silvie Didou Aupetit, and Carlos Marquís. 2002. *New Providers, Transnational Education and Accreditation of Higher Education in Latin America.* Report prepared for Institute for Higher Education in Latin America and the Caribbean/UNESCO.

Guarga Ferro, Rafael. 2002. *La investigación científica en las universidades de América Latina: características y oportunidades.* Mexico: Publicaciones UDUAL.

Knight, Jane, and Hans de Wit, eds. 1997. *Internationalisation of Higher Education in Asia Pacific Countries.* European Association for International Education, Amsterdam.

Knight, J. 2003. "Updated Internationalization Definition." *International Higher Education* (Boston College) 33L 2.

Martín, José F. 2002. *La educación superior a distancia en el sistema universitario Argentino.* Boletín nº 8 del Consejo Interuniversitario Nacional, Buenos Aires.

MECYT. 2000. *1999–2000 Yearly Report of University Statistics.* Department of University Policy, Secretariat of University Policies, Buenos Aires.

Nagata, Javier. 1998. *Las universidades extranjeras en el derecho Argentino.* Ministerio de Cultura y Educación de la Nación, Buenos Aires.

OECD (Organisation for Economic Co-operation and Development). 2002. *Education at a Glance: OECD Indicators 2002.* Paris: OECD.

Programa de Mejoramiento del Sistema de Información Universitaria de la Secretaría de Políticas Universitarias. 2001. *Anuario 1999–2000 de estadísticas universitarias.* Ministerio de Educación, Ciencia y Tecnología, Buenos Aires.

RedCIUN. 2003. *Survey.* University of Cordoba, Argentina.

RICyT (Red Iberoamericana de Indicadores de Ciencia y Tecnología). 2003. *Indicators.* www.ricyt.org.

Salmi, Jamil. 2002. *La educación superior en un punto decisivo.* World Bank, Washington D.C.

Secretaría de Ciencia, Tecnología e Innovación Productiva. 2002. *Plan Nacional de Ciencia, Tecnología e Innovación 2003.* Buenos Aires.

———. 2003. www.secyt.gov.ar.

Secretaría de Políticas Universitarias. 1999. *Guía de posgrado 1999.* Ministerio de Cultura y Educación de la Nación, Buenos Aires.

Siufi, Gabriela. 2003. "La cooperación internacional y educación superior: experiencias, tendencias y perspectivas." In *Políticas de estado para la universidad Argentina: balance de una gestión en el nuevo contexto nacional e internacional,* ed. Juan Carlos Pugliese. Secretaría de Políticas Universitarias del Ministerio de Educación, Ciencia y Tecnología de la República Argentina, Buenos Aires.

Theiler, Julio. 2003a. *Relevamiento de actividades de cooperación internacional de las universidades nacionales Argentinas.* Working paper, Red de Cooperación Internacional de las Universidades Nacionales (RedCIUN), University of Cordoba, Argentina.

———. 2003b. *Relevamiento de actividades de cooperación internacional de las universidades privadas Argentinas.* Working paper, Universidad Nacional del Litoral, Argentina.

UNESCO (United Nations Educational, Scientific and Cultural Organization). 2001. *Argentina: Education System.* Paris: UNESCO

Van der Wende, M.C. 1996. *Internationalising the Curriculum in Dutch Higher Education: An International Comparative Perspective.* OECD. The Hague: Organisation for Economic Co-operation and Development.

4
Internationalization of Higher Education in Brazil

Sonia Pereira Laus and Marilia Costa Morosini

This chapter describes and evaluates the internationalization of higher education in Brazil. It begins by reviewing the history of education in Brazil, describing the characteristics of the higher education system, and examining the Mercosur region and transnational viewpoints. It then addresses the international dimension of higher education in Brazil and the actors in university internationalization. It identifies internationalization programs (national, multilateral, and academic networks) and describes the new modes of higher education and their suppliers.[1]

The chapter raises questions about trends identified in this new international scenario. It identifies the factors that have given rise to internationalization in Brazil, including those that regard internationalization as a driving force for national development, those that attempt to modify institutions and bring them in line with progress in a contemporary world in order to provide global training for their graduates, and those that try to add value to the product they offer in the higher educational market.

The Higher Education System in Brazil

Brazil was one of the last countries in Latin America to establish universities. Since its leading classes were educated in Europe during the colonial period (1500–1822), the first university faculties emerged only at the beginning of the nineteenth century, following the Napoleonic model for professional training in engineering, medicine, and law, in isolated schools in certain capital cities. In 1907 Brazil had 25 universities, with 5,795 students (Leite and Cunha 1992).

History of Higher Education in Brazil

The first Brazilian university, the University of Rio de Janeiro, was founded in 1920, marking a new era in higher education in Brazil. The

---

[1] Systematic data on the international activities of institutions of higher learning are not available. Some activities may therefore not be covered in this chapter.

Statute of Brazilian Universities of 1931, which gave more emphasis to teaching than to research, was essentially elitist and maintained a professional orientation toward programs and the autonomy of university faculties (Oliven 2002).

In this period the establishment of public universities increased, with the foundation of universities such as the University of São Paulo, founded in 1934, with the hiring of many professors and researchers from Europe. Between 1930 (which marked the consolidation of the urban-industrial society and the increasing opening of the job market in public and private sectors) and 1964 (when the military government took power), 22 federal universities were founded in Brazil. These were located in the capital cities of states and became part of the structure of the federal system of public universities, which expanded greatly from the 1960s onward. This same period saw the creation of nine religious universities (eight Catholic and one Presbyterian) (Oliven 2002).

A third era in higher education began with the university reforms of 1968, which were based on administrative efficiency, departmental structure, and the indivisible triad of teaching, research, and extension. These reforms were accompanied by the development of graduate education and the tendency to send Brazilians abroad for advanced training. A Humboldtian model of a university based on research, in line with the principles of American universities, was established. This phase of development was characterized by internationalization as a fragmentary process, developed in isolated niches in universities, especially in graduate studies.

A fourth phase in the development of higher education began in the early 1990s and reflected tensions that existed in the 1988 Constitution and appeared in the Law of Regulation and Norms for National Education 9394/96. This phase followed international tendencies. Higher education needed to become more flexible in its policies, as reflected in the various modes in which it was offered; the role of the central government needed to be reduced; the system needed to be expanded; and the way in which university quality was evaluated needed to be improved. University internationalization became a key factor in higher education in Brazil.

Features of Higher Education in Brazil

Brazil is the tenth-largest economy in the world. It has dimensions of continental proportions (8.5 million square kilometers) and a population of 177.8 million inhabitants, growing at an annual rate of 1.31 percent. Its annual rate of inflation was 15.7 percent between January and October 2003, and its GDP was $440.5 billion in 2002, with annual growth of 1.6 percent (World Bank 2004).

Brazil suffers from serious social inequalities: 33.6 million people are at the official poverty level (family income of two to five times the minimum wage); the rate of unemployment is 9–10 percent (2002); 12.4 percent of the population is illiterate; and only a third of the population is enrolled in secondary level education (www.mre.gov.br).

MAGNITUDE, COMPLEXITY, AND DIVERSIFICATION
The higher education system in Brazil is the largest in Latin America: there are 1,637 higher education institutions (88 percent of them private) and 3,482,069 face to face undergraduates (INEP 2004). Social exclusion is reflected in the gross rate of enrollment in higher education by young adults 18–24, which at 17 percent is less than half that in other Latin American countries and far below the 50 percent in the developed nations of the world (World Bank 2002b).

Academic Organization of the Higher Education System

Brazil's higher education system is divided into universities, university centers, integrated faculties, faculties, higher institutes or schools, and technological centers (Morosini 2003). *Universities* are multidisciplinary institutions for training of professionals, research, extension, mastery, and cultivation of human knowledge, exemplified by intellectual, scientific, and cultural production, institutionalized at both the national and regional levels. At least one-third of the teaching staff of universities possess master's degrees or doctorates, and at least a third of the teaching staff are full-time, tenured members of the faculty. Universities have scientific and didactic autonomy, as well as autonomy of administration and management of financial resources and property. They are bound by the principle that teaching and research are inseparable.

University centers are multicurricular institutions that offer education of excellence and have autonomy in their higher education courses and programs. *Integrated faculties* are multicurricular institutions organized to act in a common way and under a unified regime. *Faculties* are single-curriculum institutions directly under the control of the central government. *Higher institutes of education* are institutions for training teachers. Finally, *federal centers for technological education* are autonomous federal institutions that offer education at the basic, technical, or technological level at the middle school level and pedagogical training for teachers and specialists.

Based on the concept of research as a defining criterion of academic organization, it is the convention to classify the higher education system into universities and nonuniversities (university centers, integrated faculties, faculties, higher institutes, and federal centers for technological education). The first category is based on research as its principal core activity,

Table 4.1 Higher Education Institutions in Brazil, by Administrative Type and Academic Organization, 2002

		Nonuniversities				
Type of institution	*Universities*	*University centers*	*Integrated faculties*	*Faculties, schools, and institutes*	*Technical education centers*	*Total*
Public	78	3	3	80	31	195
Federal	43	1	0	7	22	73
State	31	0	0	25	9	65
Municipal	4	2	3	48	0	57
Private	84	74	102	1,160	22	1,442
Privately owned	28	47	85	943	22	1,125
Confessional, community, and philanthropic	56	27	17	217	0	317
Total	162	77	105	1,240	53	1,637

Source: http://www.inep.gov.br.

whereas the second is dedicated to teaching. Defined in this way, Brazil has 162 universities and 1,475 nonuniversities (table 4.1).

Universities and university centers are considered as autonomous institutions; all other institutions of higher learning are considered nonautonomous. Brazil has 239 autonomous higher education institutions and 1,398 nonautonomous ones.

Types of Higher Education Institutions

Brazil has 195 higher education institutions that were created or incorporated, financed, and administered by the public sector. This figure includes 73 federal institutions, 65 state schools, and 57 institutions maintained and administered by municipal authorities.

Public provision is complemented by 1,442 privately financed and administered institutions. These may be profit or nonprofit institutions. Nonprofit institutions include community institutions, which are financed by members of the community; confessional institutions, which have a specific religious or ideological orientation; and philanthropic institutions, which provide services to society in general by complementing government services without charging for them.

Brazil's institutions of higher education are unevenly distributed across the country. More than half are in the more developed region (the southeast), while just 5 percent are in the less developed north). In the southeast there are more private universities than public ones—50 private universities and 23 public ones. In the north, there is only one private university and 10 public ones.

Table 4.2 Number of Students Enrolled in Face to Face Undergraduate Programs in Brazil, by Administrative and Academic Organization, 2002

Type of institution	Total number of students	Universities		Nonuniversities	
		Number of students	Percentage of total	Number of students	Percentage of total
Public	1,051,655	915,902	87	135,753	13
Federal	531,634	500,455	94	31,175	6
State	415,565	380,957	91	34,612	8
Municipal	104,452	34,486	33	69,966	67
Private	2,428,258	1,237,757	51	1,193,501	49
Privately owned	1,261,901	354,323	28	867,578	69
Confessional, community, and philanthropic	1,166,357	840,434	78	325,923	28
Total	3,479,913	2,153,659	62	1,329,254	38

Source: http://www.inep.gov.br.

Levels of Education and Programs

The higher education system is divided into undergraduate programs, technological programs, continuing education programs, extension programs, and graduate programs.[2] About 3.5 million students were enrolled in face to face undergraduate programs in 2002 (table 4.2).

Graduate studies in Brazil are considered to be the most developed in Latin America (Morosini 2003). In 2000 2,367 programs offered master's and doctorate programs. These programs had 96,595 students, of which 63,591 were in master's programs and 33,004 in doctorate programs (table 4.3). Between 1987 and 2000, 35,194 students completed doctorate programs and 121,861 completed master's programs in Brazil (CNPq 2004).

Graduate programs, specifically master's and doctorate programs, have been at the heart of university internationalization. The international

---

[2] *Undergraduate programs* provide education in a wide variety of subjects in face to face, distance, or mixed modes. Upon completion of their studies, students receive baccalaureate; *licenciatura* (full, short, or first grade); or professional degrees. *Continuing education* programs are offered in various fields at different levels. Candidates need to have finished middle school. Some continuing education programs require authorization and recognition by the Ministry of Education and lead to diplomas or certificates. *Extension programs* are open to candidates who fulfill the requirements established by the teaching institution. These programs lead to certificates and can be offered at initial, upgrading, qualifying, and other levels. *Graduate programs and courses* are open to holders of undergraduate degrees. They include specialization, master's degree, and doctoral programs, offered face to face or in mixed mode (distance and face to face).

Table 4.3 Number of Students in Master's and Doctorate Programs in Brazil, 1987–2000

Year	Matriculating students		Graduating students	
	Master's degree	Doctorate	Master's degrees	Doctorate
1987	30,337	8,309	3,866	1,005
1988	31,575	8,515	3,965	990
1989	33,273	9,398	4,797	1,139
1990	36,502	10,923	5,579	1,410
1991	37,205	12,015	6,772	1,750
1992	37,412	13,682	7,272	1,769
1993	38,265	15,569	4,557	1,876
1994	40,027	17,361	7,550	2,031
1995	43,121	19,492	8,982	2,497
1996	44,925	22,004	10,356	2,972
1997	47,271	24,250	11,925	3,604
1998	50,844	26,797	12,510	3,945
1999	67,031	29,985	15,356	4,862
2000	63,591	33,004	18,374	5,344
Total	601,379	251,304	121,861	35,194

Source: http://www.dc.mre.gov.br/brasil/textos/cienetecno.pdf.

nature of these programs is the feature most highly appreciated in the evaluation of graduate programs conducted by the Coordinating Agency for Graduate Education (CAPES) and the Ministry of Education.

Academic Functions of the Higher Education System
The diversity of the higher education system is most clearly demonstrated by the relationship between teaching and research. Higher education institutions defined as universities are distinguished from other types of institutions because they conduct research. Teaching is a feature of undergraduate programs, whereas teaching and research are more characteristic of graduate programs.

These functions determine the degree of internationalization in an institution. Institutions involved in research as a core activity tend to have a higher level of potential for internationalization than those that are involved only in teaching. Teaching is heavily dependent on the central government, and parameters for the accreditation of courses are strictly evaluated by the Ministry of Education, which only recently accepted the inclusion of international activities in undergraduate curricula. In the teaching of graduate programs (master's and doctorate), although the central government, through CAPES, maintains control of evaluation of reaccreditation, internationalization is strongly encouraged, and research has always enjoyed a high degree of freedom from government control.

The academic qualifications of the faculty are another example of institutional diversification. In 2002, 62 percent of instructors with master's degrees and 65 percent of instructors with doctorates worked at public institutions.

The importance of research for the development of internationalization is reflected in the growth in the number of articles published in international indexed scientific journals between 1995 and 2000. In five years Brazil nearly doubled its production of publications in international journals, from 5,508 in 1995 to 9,511 in 2000. Between 1993 and 2000, the number of research groups increased from 4,404 to 11,760, and the number of researchers rose from 21,541 to 48,781 (CNPq 2004).

Expansion and Privatization of the Higher Education System

The increase in the number of private institutions marked a turning point in higher education in Brazil in the past few years: in 2002, 88 percent of higher education institutions were private. These institutions accounted for 63 percent of all courses, 70 percent of matriculation, 63 percent of the teaching staff (38 percent with master's and 12 percent with doctorates), 53 percent of the administrative staff, 46 percent of applicants, and 77 percent of entering students (INEP 2004).

The trend in Brazil reflects the worldwide tendency toward increases in private provision (World Bank 2002a). The growth of private institutions in Brazil is found in the south-eastern, central-western, and southern regions, where private institutions outnumber public institutions. In the less developed northern and northeastern regions of Brazil, public institutions outnumber private institutions. In these regions the economy is not sufficiently robust to ensure the successful development of good-quality private institutions.

Accreditation

Higher education in Brazil is under the regime of Law 9394/1996, which establishes the regulating principles and bases for national education and is subject to the decisions of the National Education Council. The law has been modified by numerous legislative additions, of which Decree No. 3860/2001 is a notable example.

By means of this legislation, and continuing in a long-established tradition of central control of higher education, the federal government is responsible for coordinating different levels and systems of education and regulating, redistributing, and substituting elements in other educational bodies, such as organizing and financing the federal teaching system and promoting higher education. Evaluation represents one of the most obvious ways in which the government exercises control over higher education, at both the undergraduate and graduate level.

Undergraduate and graduate education is subject to control in terms of authorization, recognition, and renewal of recognition given for a fixed period of time, as established by the Chamber of Higher Education of the National Education Council. The final classification of graduate programs is based on the results of evaluation conducted by CAPES and incorporated by the Ministry of Education.

Based on criteria of internationalization, master's and doctorate programs are evaluated on their scientific, cultural, artistic, or technological production; their competitiveness with similar programs of quality abroad; and clear evidence that the teaching staff has a leadership role and representation in the community.

In 2001 the National Education Council extended government control to graduate courses taught at a distance. These programs can be offered exclusively by institutions accredited for this purpose and are subject to control in terms of authorization, recognition, and renewal of recognition.

The Ministry of Education is responsible for providing the legal framework for the recognition of courses offered by foreign institutions and the validation of degrees, diplomas, and certificates obtained abroad. Law 9394/1996 establishes that degrees awarded by foreign universities "will be validated by public universities that offer courses of the same level and content, or equivalent, respecting international agreements of reciprocity or equivalence. The same applies to master's or doctorate degrees."

To control the quality of programs offered by foreign institutions in Brazil, Regulation No. 228 of the Ministry of Education (1996) and Resolution No. 1 of the National Education Council (1997) establish the norms for recognizing and validating undergraduate and graduate courses operated by foreign institutions in Brazil, whether or not they are associated with a Brazilian institution. According to the law, "[those courses] taught . . . principally by distance or mixed mode, directly or through whatever form of association with Brazilian institutions [. . .] will not be validated or recognized, for whatsoever legal purpose, without the due authorization of the Government in terms established by Article 209, I and II, of the Federal Constitution."

In 2001, Resolution No. 2 from the Chamber of Higher Education regulated graduate courses offered in Brazil by foreign institutions, directly or through an agreement with Brazilian institutions. Under the law, the Ministry of Education has the power to sanction violations by immediately halting the registration of new students.

Such norms have put the brakes on the boom of graduate programs organized through agreements with foreign institutions, most of which began in the 1990s, outside the boundaries of the laws and regulations controlling quality. This boom has been spurred by some institutions' search for international prestige and their desire to penetrate the market for graduate courses in some regions and upgrade staff in line with Law 9394/1996, which requires that one-third of staff in all institutions have master's or doctorate degrees in order to qualify for recognition as a university.

Regional Integration of Higher Education

The search for the building of a Latin American economic and political presence is not new. There have been a number of unsuccessful attempts to develop regional integration, (Laredo 1994). As a result of globalization, the pressure for regionalization has been very strong.

The Common Market of the South (Mercosur) came into being March 26, 1991, when Argentina, Brazil, Paraguay, and Uruguay signed the Treaty of Asuncion. To give impetus to the economies of the region, especially in terms of their commercial potential, Mercosur has facilitated the integration of education, through the Educational Sector of Mercosur (SEM), created in 1991.

Subregional accords have expanded Mercosur. Chile became an associate member in 1996, and Bolivia joined as an associate member in 1997. In 1998 the Framework Agreement for the Creation of the Zone of Free Commerce between Mercosur and the Andean Community (Bolivia, Colombia, Ecuador, Peru, and Venezuela) was signed.

At the First Summit Meeting of the Americas, in 1994 in Miami, there was a proposal for the establishment by 2005 of the largest commercial and economic block in the world, the Free Trade Area of the Americas (FTAA), involving 34 of the 35 countries of the Americas (all but Cuba), with 800 million inhabitants and a GDP of $13 trillion. Even greater integration is envisaged with new blocs, such as that created by the Academic Common Area between the European Union, Latin America, and the Caribbean (UEALC). An association with the European Union would constitute the greatest free trade area on the planet between nonneighboring countries.

Other alliances are being sought between Mercosur and developing nations. In September 2003 a protocol was signed with the Cuban government for the analysis of conditions to register diplomas in healthcare, and studies are being conducted under pressure from 6,000 students of medicine at higher education institutions in Latin America.

Brazil's president, Lula da Silva, has proposed the adoption of a new geographical perspective for commercial organizations with the creation of a G3, made up of Brazil, India, and South Africa, and the strengthening of the G20, composed of emerging countries led by Brazil, China, and India. Brazil's support of strengthening regionalization does not imply a retreat from multilateral accords but rather an attempt to create a new forum for managing the impact of globalization.

History of the Internationalization of Higher Education in Brazil

In a system of education that is heavily regulated and centralized, the process of internationalization began as the result of deliberate action in response to the priorities of the government. It was put into action by a concerted effort by the government and the higher education institutions to reach critical mass to develop the nation.

Internationalization was first an attempt to revolutionize the institutions and later, more effectively, to strengthen graduate education. Only in the past few decades has the process become a joining of forces and actions to try to bring an international character to academic functions in a wider sphere of action.

At the beginning of the twentieth century, universities were committed to international development programs that later turned into joint research projects and efforts to strengthen institutions. These programs were directed at strengthening the knowledge base and educating leaders that would develop the country. They sought to adopt "systematic policy . . . that regards cooperation as a pattern that might enable [Brazil] to establish and consolidate political and cultural influence over elites from other countries" (Lessa 2002, p. 105).

This traditional model of cooperation—in many cases not symmetrical, without opportunities for any possibility of mature institutional collaboration—was one of the first formal instruments for internationalization. It dominated the process from the 1930s until the late 1960s, when the experts that emerged from this process began to play a fundamental role in the development of thought and scientific development in Brazil, particularly in the social sciences and humanities. After World War II, the process of formalizing accords with foreign countries began. During the 1960s, this process evolved into bilateral agreements for scientific and technological cooperation.[3]

This process of internationalization achieved more significant proportions in the 1970s. International agencies with a presence in Brazil began offering joint programs (ranging from scholarships for graduate training abroad to support for joint research), and national programs were established to support the same activities in order to strengthen graduate studies and create an exchange of information and experts. These actions demonstrate that the government and the universities had an interest in working together to define the strategic priorities of the country by signing cooperation agreements and creating structures for management and internal negotiation.

---

[3] Agreements were signed with the Federal Republic of Germany (1963), Denmark (1966), France (1967), Portugal (1967), Switzerland (1969), Japan (1971), and the Netherlands (1971) (Lessa 2002).

The process of globalization and the massive increase in access to information has still not enabled significant portions of the academic sector in Brazil to join the rest of the academic world. But in the past few decades, the process has begun to take on a life of its own and imprint itself on the academic world at the national level. This in turn has produced reactions from institutions. Programs in foreign languages, joint research, and the widespread use of information technology for teleconferencing and distance education are all now offered by most institutions, public and private.

The process of internationalization derives from many different sources, ranging from a concerted effort by government and institutions to develop the country to the search for prestige on the part of institutions. Some institutions have made bad choices in the selection of their partners and methods of joint action.

Joint action with international institutions has grown in a disorganized fashion, with low standards of quality, often as a result of market trends rather than deliberate institutional strategic planning. But the truth is that it is increasingly difficult for academic systems to orientate themselves independently in a world that is increasingly competitive, constantly changing, and dominated by universities in industrial countries (Altbach 2001). The strongest universities are those in English-speaking countries (the United States, the United Kingdom, Canada, and Australia) as well as the largest countries in the European Union (notably France and Germany, followed by Italy and Spain).

Spanish institutions are leaders in providing interinstitutional programs and collaborating in networks and mobility programs with Brazilian universities. The principal drive for this relationship may be found in the linguistic proximity of the two countries' languages and the proactive policies of Spanish institutions, spurred by decisions at recent summit meetings of Ibero-American heads of state.

The General Agreement on Trade and Services (GATS) has fueled debate in Brazil over the risks associated with including higher education as a service regulated by the WTO. As a result of the debate, government and public institutions in Brazil have reaffirmed their position that education belongs to the public and knowledge is the property of society (Dias 2002).

Internationalization is attracting considerable attention from private institutions and is discussed at national seminars and meetings organized by the National Association of Private Universities (http://www.anup.br). According to experts, the opening of educational services will primarily affect graduate programs, principally those considered to be leaders in the country. These institutions enroll about 400,000 of the 3.2 million students enrolled in higher education. They attract people who value international standards highly and who might leave Brazil if high-quality programs are not available (MRE 2004b).

Principal Actors in the Internationalization of Higher Education in Brazil

The principal actors in the internationalization of higher education in Brazil are the Ministry of Education, the Ministry of Science and Technology, and the Ministry of Foreign Relations. Many minor actors also play important roles.

Federal Government

The Ministry of Education, the Ministry of Science and Technology, and the Ministry of Foreign Relations are the principal agents of internationalization in education, science, and technology in Brazil. The process of internationalization of higher education began in public universities and institutes for training and research of the Ministry of Agriculture and the Army, as well as in the fields of aerospace, science, and technology. As a result of action by the Ministry of Education and the Ministry of Science and Technology, the process has expanded throughout the higher education system since the late 1990s.

MINISTRY OF EDUCATION
The Ministry of Education is the principal actor in the process of internationalization and the main agent for its regulation. Its actions are directed by Law 9394/1996, Law for the Regulation and Bases of National Education. That law defines education, the principles and goals of national education, rights to education, the obligation to educate, the organization of national education, levels and modes of education and teaching, and professional standards in education and its financial sources, among other things. The law promotes decentralization of and autonomy for schools and universities, provides a standard process of evaluation of teaching, and defines the organization of systems of teaching by means of collaboration between different levels of government (federal, state, and municipal).

The Ministry of Education is responsible for formulating and evaluating national educational policy, maintaining quality, and enforcing observation of the law and other normative regulations. To carry out its responsibilities, the Ministry of Education relies on CAPES and the National Institute of Educational Planning and Research (INEP), as well as a number of secretariats, including the Secretariat of Higher Education, which is responsible for the coordination of the country's higher education system.

The Secretariat of Higher Education is in charge of supervisory and fiscal tasks and evaluation of all Brazilian higher education institutions, as well as the regulations and finances of the Federal Institutions of Public Higher Education.

CAPES promotes graduate studies and provides consultancy on the formulation of policy for graduate studies. It was created in 1951 and made into a foundation in 1992. CAPES awards scholarships for master's degrees and doctorates directly to institutions that receive a certain grade in their evaluations.

Foreign studies complement graduate courses in Brazil, training teachers and researchers of a high academic level for university teaching and research. CAPES has funded more than 1,400 scholarships for study abroad.

Three departments within the Ministry of Education are responsible for international relations: the International Advisory Office of the Secretariat of Higher Education; the Advisory Office for International Affairs, which is responsible for the Undergraduate Student Program Agreement (PEC-G), described below; and the General Coordination of International Cooperation of CAPES, which is responsible for graduate study activities in Brazil in a global context.

MINISTRY OF SCIENCE AND TECHNOLOGY

Created in 1985, the Ministry of Science and Technology is the federal ministry responsible for coordinating and deploying the National Complex of Science, Technology and Innovation and developing policy in this area. The National Council for Scientific and Technological Development (CNPq) is its principal agency. The ministry operates in two major areas, research funding and training of advanced human capital. It awards grants for initial scientific training, technical support, researcher productivity, master's and doctoral degrees, and postdoctoral studies, and it finances research projects.

The CNPq promotes scientific and technological research in Brazil and contributes to the formulation of national policies for science and technology. It contributes directly to the training of researchers (master's and doctorate level) by funding scholarships. Since its creation in 1951, it has been one of the most important public bodies for the support of science, technology, and innovation.

The internationalization of universities is directly related to the development of research and the production of knowledge. Brazil's National Innovation System involves many institutions, both federal and state, that promote research and training, as well as universities and research institutes, public and private, that produce scientific and technological knowledge. The Ministry of Science and Technology and the Ministry of Education play key roles in strengthening the system. They work closely with the Financing of Studies and Projects (FINEP), the CNPq, CAPES, and the Ministries of Agriculture and Livestock, Health, Environment, Development, Industry, and Foreign Trade. At the state level, the system includes the Secretariats of Science and Technology and the promotion agencies, called State Foundations for the Support of Research.

MINISTRY OF FOREIGN RELATIONS
The Ministry of Foreign Relations works in three integrated areas: received technical cooperation, both bilateral and multilateral; technical cooperation between developing countries; and scientific and technical cooperation. The Brazilian Agency for Cooperation of the Ministry of Foreign Relations is responsible for bilateral and multilateral technical cooperation in all spheres of knowledge.

DIVISION OF EDUCATIONAL MATTERS
In July 2003 the government created the Division of Educational Matters, which acts in three different areas of educational cooperation: given cooperation, for the training and education of foreign students in Brazil; received cooperation, for the training and education of Brazilian students abroad; and support and treatment of educational matters in the international agenda, at both the bilateral and multilateral level. The Division of Educational Matters participates in a number of mixed commissions and work groups, such as the Work Group on Education (with Germany) and the Neighborhood Commission (with Colombia). It also works with many different countries on the negotiation of accords and memoranda of agreements on educational cooperation. It deals with matters relating to the Latin American Faculty of Social Sciences (FLACSO), the Fulbright Commission, the educational services of the WTO, Mercosur, FTAA, and the Permanent Commission of Authors' Rights (Ministry of Foreign Relations 2004a).

Networks and Offices of International Relations

Regulation of Brazil's higher education system is highly centralized. However, institutions of higher education enjoy a significant degree of autonomy with respect to internationalization. For this reason, significant interinstitutional differences exist in the levels of internationalization.

NETWORKS OF UNIVERSITY AUTHORITIES
With the increasing expansion and diversification of the educational system, new groupings of university authorities have emerged that have developed parallel or complementary actions. These include the Council of Brazilian University Rectors, the National Association of Federal Higher Education Authorities, the Brazilian Association of Rectors of State

and Municipal Universities, the Brazilian Association of Rectors of Community Universities, and the National Association of Private Universities.

The Council of Brazilian University Rectors has been prominent in promoting the development of international activities by creating the Ibero-American University Council and by signing agreements with the Council of Rectors of Portuguese Universities and the Congress of Rectors of Germany, the Congress of Rectors and University Authorities in Quebec, and the University System of Florida.

- An agreement with the Council of Rectors of Portuguese Universities and the Congress of Rectors of Germany provides for general training, teaching, and research. It has made it easier for graduates of Brazilian universities to pursue advanced staff training programs, mainly in Germany.
- The 1966 agreement with the Congress of Rectors and University Authorities in Quebec established a student exchange program.
- The 1992 agreement with the University System of Florida established the Florida-Brazil Institute. The institute strengthens academic, cultural, and scientific ties and provides for the development of human resources, information exchange, teaching, cooperative research, joint scientific publications, staff and student exchange, conferences, seminars, exhibitions, and other activities of mutual interest.
- The Ibero-American University Council is a network of networks made up of the National Associations of Universities and the Councils of Rectors in Latin America. At their annual meeting in Brazil in November 2003, the network chose the following themes for priority action in 2004: quality and accreditation, involvement with the community, Ibero-American cooperation, and the linking of Latin America to European higher education. In the guise of a new mechanism for multilateral cooperative action in the region, the Latin American University Council (CUIB) insisted on the need to maintain the agreements made at the World Conference on Higher Education of UNESCO in Paris in 1998, which emphasized the fact that higher education is an entity that belongs to the community.

The Council of Brazilian University Rectors also encourages its members to become affiliated with international university organizations. Of these, the Inter-American University Organization is particularly important, since the largest number of its members come from Brazil.

Although other associations of authorities of higher education institutions have not made explicit in their policies the need to internationalize their member institutions, all are members of international associations of universities. This demonstrates the multilateral character of their interaction with the international academic community.

Forum of Brazilian University Offices for International Affairs
Offices of international relations are important institutional actors in the process of internationalization. In the early 1990s, these offices were "in theory a real part of 82 percent of the higher education institutions, although in barely 60 percent of these was there an authority specifically dedicated to internationalization, since in at least 64 percent of the cases surveyed the authority in charge also handled other institutional responsibilities" (Schlindwein 1990, p. 48).

In 1988 the Forum of Brazilian University Offices for International Affairs was created. It has attempted to bring into the open the matters and activities relating to internationalization in higher education. It has encouraged the creation of offices of international relations at institutions that did not possess them. It has also promoted the training of staff working in this area through seminars, workshops, and annual meetings. It has begun to promote Brazil's higher education institutions to national and international agencies that work with Brazil (embassies, consulates, international organizations).

In 2003 the Forum of Brazilian University Offices for International Affairs had 119 member institutions: 65 public institutions (39 federal, 24 state, and 2 municipal); 29 community institutions; and 25 private institutions. Of these, 88 percent already included an office of international relations in their official organization charts.

While the increase in these offices indicates progress, in Brazilian institutions as a whole there is no evidence of institutional policies for training staff in international affairs. Brazilian universities have still not given strategic importance to the process of internationalization. Their institutional management is almost always in the hands of a professor, researcher, or administrator with an academic background who happens to master one or more foreign languages (Laus 1998b) and who has some experience working in the international academic sector but no specific training in this work and minimal administrative support.

As long as the internal conceptualization of the process remains unchanged, there are limited possibilities for progress. Clear institutional policies that envisage a longer term process are needed. Permanent structures need to be established, and high-level staff needs to be trained to manage this area.

Types of Studies

Large differences exist in the degree of internationalization between graduate and undergraduate studies in Brazil. Graduate education has been a key driver in the process, whereas undergraduate education just recently began to internationalize.

Graduate Studies

Graduate studies in Brazil have always been linked to research. Researchers develop networks of colleagues, nationally and internationally; carry out projects; participate in or direct research; and contribute to scientific knowledge with minimal institutional control. Research is coordinated by the Ministry of Science and Technology and supported by the CNPq. In addition to a salary for teaching, researchers receive financial support (support for research productivity, for their projects, and for participation in scientific events) and research team support, over which the university has little or no control. Research is clearly at the center of the process of the internationalization of higher education.

Graduate studies are strictly controlled by CAPES, which evaluates graduate courses. Since 1998 it has used a model based on external evaluation and focused on productivity. This evaluation rates institutions on a scale of 1 to 7, with rankings of 6 and 7 considered to be of "international level".

One hundred forty-seven institutions have received grades of 6 or 7 (CAPES 2002a). Among programs receiving a grade 6, 64 are based in São Paulo and 39 are based in Rio de Janeiro. Forty institutions receiving a grade of 7 are in the south-eastern region, 27 of them being in São Paulo. The international-level programs are predominantly in public universities. In the private higher education institutions, 15 programs received a grade of 6 and 2 a grade of 7 (1 in Rio Grande do Sul and 1 in Rio de Janeiro).

Undergraduate Studies

In all education, but especially in undergraduate education, there is strong control from the central government. The university has relatively little autonomy over the most important decisions, such as the curriculum and the issuance and recognition of degrees. Curricula are determined by the Ministry of Education and by curricular directives. These directives ensure higher education institutions full liberty as to the timing of course offerings and study modules. They promote independent study; encourage study, skills, and competences acquired outside the institution; and strengthen the linking of theory with practice, giving weight to individual and group research and to practice and extension activities (National Education Council 2004).

Internationalization can be included in undergraduate studies—if the institution wants to internationalize. Examples of internationalization in undergraduate studies include undergraduate sandwich programs and double degrees. Sandwich programs give credit for study or internships performed during two semesters at foreign institutions. A protocol drawn up by the Brazilian institution and the foreign one or a specific agreement is used that must be approved by the legal department of the Brazilian institution, its highest organ of government (usually the university council), and the rector. Under a double degree program, students receive their degrees from both the Brazilian and the foreign institution.

Despite advances, the internationalization of Brazilian undergraduate education remains an unfinished agenda. According to Neves (2002, p. 12):

> Graduate studies were successful, without doubt, because they were internationalized from the start. . . . Our undergraduate studies were not, in part because legislation prohibited the possibility of more flexible curricula; the whole process of undergraduate internationalization was blocked, held in a bureaucratic straitjacket, and did not allow the possibility of student mobility. . . . The [law] began a change in this regime when it lifted the ban on undergraduate education without the minimal curriculum, but it needs to do more. It is necessary to internationalize the debate and renew visions of undergraduate studies.

Participation in Knowledge Networks

Some universities have encouraged their faculty to participate in international congresses, visit foreign institutions, and publish jointly with foreign scholars. Academics have worked with other institutions on a bilateral basis as well as with networks of researchers. The growth in spontaneous efforts has motivated some public institutions to offer new modes of education that are different from those promoted by government policy. Under pressure to generate income, and in the face of inadequate government investment in education, they have increased their supply of programs, almost always in association with a foreign institution.

Most programs of academic mobility are promoted by foreign or national organizations or agencies. A survey of members of the Forum of Brazilian University Offices for International Affairs (FAUBAI 2003), which represents all types of institutions in the system, reveals that a significant number of institutions maintain these programs within the framework of academic cooperation agreements: 92 percent of institutions have programs for academic staff mobility, and 70 percent have programs for student mobility. Forty percent of public and private institutions offer double graduation programs with foreign higher education institutions, almost always with financing of the programs by participating institutions. Eighty percent of these institutions offer programs that teach foreign languages.

Almost all international mobility in public universities receives support from one of the programs mentioned earlier. Nevertheless, private and community institutions have much greater latitude than public institutions. They seek not only to achieve international characteristics but also to attract students, through efforts that range from providing residences at foreign universities to offering short stays at Disney World, under the guise of work experience. The academic benefit of such programs is questionable, but in the eyes of the institutions involved these programs add value to the product they are marketing, and they enable participants to acquire a second language and gain intercultural experience.

An evaluation conducted by the Latin America Academic Training (ALFA) network international relations office (1998), is based on data from the Universidade Federal do Rio Grande do Sul and the Universidade Federal de Minas Gerais. It finds that the institutions studied had explicit planning strategies for internationalization. These strategies are developed at the highest levels of the institution and sometimes by the international relations office, which participates in defining the strategy.

The ALFA study reveals that the goals of internationalization programs are to promote participation in networks and international associations; to develop existing international relations and broaden contacts with institutions in Europe and the United States; to promote and support bilateral exchanges, with emphasis on new modes of interaction; to promote student and staff exchange; to seek, in collaboration with the productive sector and the government, the establishment of relationships with respected Asian universities and organizations in science and technology; to stimulate approaches to other Mercosur countries; and to open channels for attracting foreign resources.

Resources for internationalization come from a variety of sources, including the regular budget; UNESCO, for academic exchange within Mercosur related to participation in the Association of Universities of the Montevideo Group; international foundations, such as the Ford Foundation and the Vitae Foundation, for the development of human resources abroad and participation in scientific activities; and the private sector, for the support of scientific activities and studies.

The conception, design, negotiation, and execution of academic programs of research are the responsibility of academic departments and the academic staff themselves. The offices of international relations have a role in promoting and finding resources, facilitating exchanges, organizing international seminars, and cooperating with businesses.

The ALFA study identifies several challenges facing the internationalization process at the institutional level:

- A clear university strategy for internationalization is lacking. According to Guia IRO-NET (1998, p. 82), "There are no clear and precise strategies on the course to take for international activity in each institution, but only a series of general principles, that are somewhat vague and fail to define a series of clear lines of action or priorities for international activity." A clear strategy and priorities are essential for allocating limited resources, both material and human. The report proposes convening university officials, representatives of the university community involved in internationalization, and representatives of universities in developed countries in order to establish these strategies.

- Participation in international activities by academics is limited, "normally due to the lack of previous experience on the part of the teaching staff, whether because of the quality of the participants or the quality of the coordinators of international projects or programs" (Guia IRO-NET (1998, p. 83). Possible solutions to this problem include setting up an administrative group to support faculty and simplify bureaucratic procedures.
- Foreign students are inadequately integrated into university life in Brazil, because of "lack of adequate mastery of the language, very little previous knowledge of the community in which they find themselves, the welcome given by the family with which they are placed, and so forth" (Guia IRO-NET 1998, p. 84). Greater integration with Brazilian students and their associates is suggested, as well as greater use of e-mail and provision of good health services.
- Other challenges mentioned include the need for real co-financing of projects; the need for transnational elements in projects; the difficulty of finding ideal partners; the need to provide services to people who take part in staff or student mobility; lack of affordable housing for visiting students; tension between international relations offices, still in an embryonic state, and international activities that have become traditional; and the lack of the flexibility needed to provide specific services associated with international programs.

World events since September 11 may have increased foreign demand for higher education in Brazil, which is perceived as less vulnerable to the risks of world terrorism than many other countries. More and more Canadian and American students are studying Portuguese, a factor that can be exploited by universities and the government to attract foreign students to Brazil.

Programs for the Internationalization of Higher Education

Several programs have been developed to support the internationalization of higher education in Brazil.

National Programs

Although student exchange has existed in Brazil since the early 1900s, the numbers of students involved were small and the efforts largely reflected individual initiatives. In 1917 Brazilian students were studying in

Uruguay; in 1919 Argentineans, Chileans, Paraguayans, and Uruguayans were studying in Brazil, at the Military Academy, the Naval School, and elsewhere. In 1941, as a result of the increase in cultural exchange between Brazil and Bolivia, the first wave of Bolivian students arrived in Brazil. After World War II, Brazil strengthened relations with other Latin American countries, seeking common interests and promoting greater student exchange (Laus 2002).

BILATERAL CULTURAL COOPERATION AGREEMENTS
Promotion of international cooperation is the responsibility of the Ministry of Foreign Relations, the Ministry of Education, and the Ministry of Science and Technology at the federal level and certain Secretariats of Science and Technology at the state level. This section describes the principal agreements.

Bilateral Received Technical Cooperation
The Council for Technical Cooperation (CTRB), of the Ministry of Foreign Relations, is the principal instrument for promoting structural changes in Brazil. It facilitates the transfer of technology and the acquisition of knowledge that contribute to socioeconomic development in Brazil by conducting high-level consultancies, training and upgrading the skills of Brazilian technicians, and in some cases donating high-tech equipment to Brazilian institutions. The principal cooperation partners are Japan (52 percent), Germany (18 percent), the United Kingdom (13 percent), France (9 percent), Canada (5 percent), Spain (2 percent), the Netherlands (2 percent), and Italy (1 percent). Active projects are mainly in the areas of the environment, agriculture, industry, health, social development, public administration, energy, transport, education, and town planning (http://www.mre.gov.br).

Foreign Student Agreements
The Undergraduate Student Program Agreement (PEC-G) is being developed on the basis of joint protocols with indefinite duration. The two ministries involved are the Ministry of Education, with the participation of higher education institutions, and the Ministry of Foreign Relations, with the collaboration of diplomatic missions and Brazilian consular offices. Through PEC-G, more than 600 foreign students enter Brazil each year. In order to participate in this program, candidates have to possess the Certificate of Knowledge of Portuguese and be from one of the following countries: Algeria, Angola, Benin, Cameroon, Cape Verde, China, Democratic Republic of Congo, the Republic of Congo, Côte d'Ivoire, East Timor, Gabon, Ghana, Guinea-Bissau, India, Mali, Morocco, Mozambique, Namibia, Nigeria, Kenya, São Tomé and Principe, Senegal, South Africa, or

Tunisia. In Latin America and the Caribbean, students from the following countries are eligible to study in Brazil: Antigua, Argentina, Barbados, Bolivia, Chile, Colombia, Costa Rica, Cuba, the Dominican Republic, Ecuador, El Salvador, Guatemala, Guyana, Haiti, Honduras, Jamaica, Mexico, Nicaragua, Panama, Paraguay, Peru, Surinam, Trinidad and Tobago, and Uruguay (Ministry of Education 2004).

The Graduate Student Program Agreement is similar to the PEC-G. Students from the same countries with which Brazil maintains agreements for cultural, scientific, and technological cooperation are eligible.

Student and Faculty Mobility

The internationalization of higher education is concentrated in the area of research and developed mainly at the level of graduate studies. While graduate studies are predominantly represented by public universities, the system of higher education is centralized and supported by a process of evaluation carried out by the Ministry of Education. Institutional internationalization actions depend on the approval of the government. CAPES and the CNPq provide data indicating the scale of international mobility financed by the government.

CAPES promotes and supports internationalization by consolidating research and graduate studies centers and increasing opportunities for training master's and doctorate students. It grants scholarships for doctoral studies abroad. It also supports researchers who participate in international events and exchanges or who study or conduct research abroad.

CNPq support is given predominantly to scholarship holders carrying out a full or sandwich doctorate, followed by support to postdoctorate research studies and sandwich undergraduate programs (table 4.4).

The CNPq has invested mainly in the exact sciences, earth sciences, and engineering (46 percent), followed by life sciences (34 percent), and the

Table 4.4 Brazilian Scholarships for Study Abroad, by Mode of Study, 2003

Mode	Number of scholarships	Percent of total
Sandwich undergraduate	115	7.7
Specialization	18	1.2
Master's	3	0.2
Sandwich doctorate	426	28.4
Doctorate	719	47.9
Postdoctorate	219	14.6
Total	1,500	100.0

Source: http://www.capes.gov.br.

humanities (23 percent). CAPES has awarded 615 scholarships in the humanities; 583 in the exact sciences, earth sciences, and engineering; and 332 in life sciences. The single area with most support is engineering and computing science.

Most CNPq support goes to a small number of higher education institutions in Brazil: 14 higher education institutions received $8.2 million, while the remaining $6.8 million went to 653 higher education institutions. Seven public universities receive the most support. These include five federal universities (the Federal University of Rio de Janeiro, the Federal University of Rio Grande do Sul, the Federal University of Minas Gerais, the Federal University of Santa Catarina, and the University of Brasilia) and two state universities (the University of Campinas and the University of São Paulo). Thirty percent of these scholarships are for studies abroad (CNPq 2002a). Scholarships for studies abroad give preference to applicants from the southeastern regions (40 percent of total funding) and the State of São Paulo (17 percent). In 2002 the leading recipients of students from Brazil were the United States (738), France (520), and the United Kingdom (293) (table 4.5).

CAPES supports PhD–level researchers who participate in international events. During 1995–2002, it received nearly 11,000 requests for support. A total of 3,546 scholarships were awarded. The fields that received the most

Table 4.5 Brazilian Scholarships Abroad, by Country, 2002

	CNPq		CAPES		Total	
Country	Number	Percent	Number	Percent	Number	Percent
United States	280	38	458	31	738	33
United Kingdom	130	18	163	11	293	13
France	101	14	419	28	520	23
Canada	54	7	67	4	121	5
Spain	43	6	78	5	121	5
Germany	28	4	152	10	180	8
Australia	20	3	26	2	46	2
Italy	18	2	33	2	51	2
Portugal	15	2	68	5	83	4
Netherlands	14	2	25	2	39	2
Switzerland	3	0	11	1	14	1
Other[a]	33	4	0	0	33	1
Total	739	100	1500	100	2239	100

[a.] Includes Argentina, Austria, Belgium, Chile, Costa Rica, Côte d'Ivoire, Denmark, the Dominican Republic, Finland, India, Israel, Mexico, New Zealand, Northern Ireland (United Kingdom), Japan, Sweden, and Uruguay. The CNPq does not include short-duration scholarships in these figures.

Table 4.6 CAPES–Sponsored Student Exchanges, Joint Research Activities, and Joint Research Projects, by Brazilian and Foreign Institutions

Partner/Country	Number of study exchanges	Number of research missions	Number of active joint projects
COFECUB (France)	183	207	112
PROBRAL (Germany)	68	82	57
DFG (Germany)	0	4	3
Fachhochschulen (Germany)[a]	22	25	20
ICTTI (Portugal)	7	88	43
British Council (United Kingdom)	4	68	34
MES (Cuba)	6	4	3
SETCIP (Argentina)	50	43	26
ANTORCHAS (Argentina)	1	3	2
Total	341	524	300

a. Partnership is with the Federal Center of Technological Education (CEFET).
Source: CAPES (2003).

scholarships were engineering (721); human sciences (698); exact sciences (675); health sciences (362); biological sciences (338); applied social sciences (274); astronomy and physics (268); electrical and biomedical engineering (235); literature and linguistics (228); education (151); physiology, pharmacology, morphology, biochemistry, and biophysics (140); agrarian sciences (186); agronomy (106); medicine (93); economics (65); and the arts and music (69) (Nunes Sobrinho 2002).

An evaluation of academic training in CAPES international programs concludes that "the Brazilian government continues to invest in the training of human resources abroad so that a state of excellence of the Brazil academic community might be assured; the training of researchers in the best foreign universities is essential to maintain an academic elite in the Brazilian context that might operate as a means of regulating quality" (Neddermeyer 2002, p. 12).

Joint Research Projects and University Partnerships

CAPES promotes and supports joint research projects, student exchange, and research activities (table 4.6).[4] Brazilian research groups must be associated with graduate programs recognized by the Ministry of Education, preferably with a grade of 5 or more.

[4] For a description of CAPES's principal international programs, see http://www.capes. gov.br.

In addition to joint research projects and scholarships for master's and doctoral studies, CAPES supports binational university partnership programs. Begun in 2001, these programs aim to increase exchanges by undergraduate students and to promote exchanges by graduate students and faculty. The partnerships are between Brazilian and foreign universities. Credits are recognized by both partners, and courses and curricula are aligned.

Graduate program partnerships aim "not only to establish temporary partnerships between the groups, but also to stimulate directly the joint development of national graduate programs with other programs of excellence so that it might be possible to create a training network for cadres of graduates that is highly internationalized" (Baeta Neves 2002, p. 11).

The two principal financing bodies for science and technology in Brazil are the CNPq and CAPES. State foundations, such as the State Fund for Support to Research in the State of São Paulo, also promote and support such activities.

Scientific exchange with foreign countries takes four different forms: presentation of work at scientific events, visiting researchers, doctoral scholarships, and research grants. In 2001 scientific exchange involved 1,317 grants for scholarships and support in all four areas. The largest number of applications approved (946) was for participation in scientific events. Two hundred and eight (208) grants supported visiting researchers. The United States received most approved applications for scholarships and support (391), followed by France (105), Canada (70), and Spain and Portugal (68 each). Agreements signed with the German Academic Exchange Service, the Portuguese National Science and Technology Council, and the British Council yielded 11 scholarships, 8 of them for foreign researchers for the purpose of developing research in São Paulo and 3 for Brazilians studying abroad. Investment in scholarships in 2001 was $2.46 million, $1.57 million of which was awarded to researchers with institutional links to the University of São Paulo, the State University of São Paulo, or the University of Campinas (CNPq 2001).

The support that the State Fund for Support to Research in the State of São Paulo offers researchers is not representative of the country as a whole. There is a large variance in the degree to which state research foundations have matured, and eight states are outside the scheme altogether, since "none of them achieved the same degree of autonomy, the stability of financing and the gains made in the state of São Paulo. Many of them suffered from a total lack of support from their state governments and stability in carrying out their programs" (Bampi 2003, p. 6).

NEW POLICIES

Management of the process of internationalization demands new policies in various fields of cooperation.

Science and Technology
The growth in graduate studies has been based on the development of
policies that support international academic cooperation. But the lack of
continuity in financial support to maintain the quality of laboratories and
national research centers has caused setbacks and inefficiency in exploiting investments made. In some cases, lack of resources has resulted in
brain drain: just 51 percent of researchers who received scholarships during the 1990s were working in Brazil (Freire 2003).

Through the CNPq and CAPES, the government has adopted policies
to encourage the repatriation of students completing their studies abroad.
The Program to Promote the Retention of Doctorate Qualified Staff
(PROFIX) was created in 2001. It provides "incentives so that researchers
at the doctorate level remain in the country or that those without work
links to Brazilian higher education institutions return home" (CNPq
2002a). Beneficiaries can receive a monthly salary, support for the installa-
tion of infrastructure, airline tickets, support for participation in international events (one per year), medical insurance, and supplementary grants
for technical support and initiating scientific research. Both programs
have been widely criticized for the shortness of the duration of the work
link (18–36 months) and the fact that grant recipients tend to be concentrated in the southern and southeastern regions, which have more needs
for better infrastructure than for human resources.

The Program to Stimulate Retention of Human Resources of Interest
provides services to technically trained people and people with MAs and
PhDs who lack work links with their country. Its principal purpose is to
facilitate the integration of trained workers in regions of the country that
most need them (Freire 2003). Another iniative is the Program for the
Temporary Absorption of Doctorate Qualified Staff. This program promotes the hiring of PhDs under the age of 41 by graduate programs evaluated by CAPES. State Foundations for the Support of Research perform
similar functions at certain state research foundations.

By strengthening institutions, all of these efforts help to reduce Brazil's
brain drain. The policy of retaining PhDs is essential, since, in contrast to
China and India, which lose almost 80 percent of their PhDs to the United
States, almost 80 percent of Brazilian graduate students return home after
completing their studies (MRE 2003a).

The lack of job opportunities for PhDs in Brazil is caused by lack of
public competition for positions in universities and research institutes.
Together with the limited absorption of the productive sector, it has forced
recent PhDs to work abroad.

Scientific and Technological Cooperation to Achieve Economic Goals
From the point of view of the Ministry of Foreign Relations, scientific and
technological cooperation is directed at providing universities, research

centers, and private enterprise with the sophistication, specialization, and competitiveness required by the new world economy. Research centers and commercial enterprises are striving to gain access to the most advanced technology in order to maintain their competitive position (MRE 2003a).

Orienting science and technology toward economic goals reflects Brazilian foreign policy in two lines of action. The first is state of the art technological transformation, including distance education through computer technology and automation, biotechnology, new materials, space technology, and precision engineering. The second is improvement of technology that has a direct impact on education, public health, basic sanitation, urban and regional development, security, hunger, nutrition, the environment, energy, and transportation (MRE 2003a).

Development of Graduate Studies

Studies carried out at the instigation of the CNPq, CAPES, and the State Foundations for Support to Research have focused on revising concepts and making structural modifications to the Development of Graduate Studies, Science and Technology program. The report that emerged in December 2003 (CAPES/CNPq 2003) makes several recommendations for training Brazilians at home and abroad and cooperating internationally:

- Support training of PhDs abroad in strategic areas; give incentives to begin postdoctoral work or studies in Brazil shortly after completion of studies.
- Promote agreements for cooperation between Brazilian and foreign institutions, with emphasis on commitment by foreign institutions.
- Promote evaluation of international cooperation by ensuring equal participation by partner institutions, strengthening institutions and the regions in which they are located, giving priority to projects that have more than one research group, and stimulating researchers to seek international resources.
- Link scholarships provided by the Brazilian government with bilateral and multilateral agreements that focus on priority areas and programs.
- Reinforce bilateral exchanges that send students and researchers to and receive students from cooperating institutions; provide cofinancing that requires the participation of all parties involved in the exchange; support joint teaching, which implies the orientation and supervision of teaching staff from all institutions involved; and support the granting of double degrees that are recognized by all institutions.
- Promote equal participation in scientific research by participating parties, strengthen institutions and regions by expanding the base for science and technology in Brazil, promote research in priority areas, strengthen international agreements with foreign partners, promote cooperation in multilateral forums, reduce dependency on national

resources, and encourage researchers to seek international resources for exchange in priority areas, including international cooperation actions in sector funding.

- Promote evaluation of international cooperation and its expansion guided by such action, making modifications wherever indicated by this process.
- Maintain agreements with the Ministry of Foreign Relations so that the Brazilian Cooperation Agency promotes consultancy with scientific experts and national promoting agencies when it prepares international agreements that include research activities, technological development, and graduate training.
- Develop strategic joint programs for international cooperation that are coordinated regionally and linked to the State Foundations for the Support of Research, CAPES, and the CNPq.

RELATIONS WITH OTHER COUNTRIES

Brazil's relations with other countries traditionally focused on Europe and the United States. However, in response to the new direction of foreign policy since 2003, priority has been placed on developing cooperation with developing countries, including China, India, South Africa, and countries in Latin America.

Ibero-America

As a result of the actions of different ministries, academic relations with Ibero-America have begun in some areas. Bilateral and multilateral academic programs are in place, and networks have been formed. Moreover, sporadic and spontaneous relations have been established between groups and institutions. Ibero-American relations have also intensified as a result of the new programs established by the Ibero-American Summit Meetings, UNESCO, and the European Union.

European Union

The European Union is very active in internationalizing higher education, through support of the ALFA and AlßAN Programs. Between 2000 and 2005, 62 Brazilian projects, involving 75 Brazilian institutions, were approved. Five of these projects were coordinated by a Brazilian institution (ALFA n.d.)

The AlßAN program, created in 2002, has awarded 63 grants to Brazil, to carry out studies in the United Kingdom (23), Spain (15), Portugal (10), France (9), Italy (3), the Netherlands (2), and Germany (1). The total number of grants for Latin America was 251 (ALFA/AlßAN 2004).

Asia and Africa

The search to identify academic partners in Asia and Africa has led to a series of actions:

- The Mixed Commission, Brazil-India (http://www.universiabrasil.net) met in New Delhi in October 2003 to discuss graduate education, the eradication of illiteracy, and distance education.
- Agreement for scientific cooperation was reached between India's Council of Scientific and Industrial Research and the CNPq. The agreement foresees the exchange of researchers and the establishment of joint research and development projects. Established in 1942, the Council of Scientific and Industrial Research is the principal institution for the promotion of research in India. An autonomous body linked to the federal government, it has a network of 40 laboratories and 81 research centers all over the country (FAPESP 2004).
- In 2003 Brazil and China established the Sino-Brazilian Program for Satellites for Terrestrial Resources, one of the most important high-tech bilateral projects in Brazil. Brazil is involved in a diversified program of cooperation with China, which has been its principal commercial partner since 2003 and is now the second-largest importer of Brazilian goods and services after the United States. The government plans to enhance relations with China.
- Scientific and technological cooperation agreements were signed with Angola and Mozambique in 2003. The agreements cover research in science and technology and mobility of students, principally from Portuguese-speaking African countries.
- The Milton Santos University Foundation was established in 2003. The foundation includes a network of Brazilian public institutions, in multicampus systems, that will host African students (not only those that speak Portuguese) who receive scholarships for undergraduate and graduate studies.
- The Technical Cooperation between Developing Countries agreement is based on policies and guidelines issued by the Ministry of Foreign Relations and the demands of countries with which Brazil has cooperation agreements. Activities are supported with financing by the Brazilian Cooperation Agency, with additional funding from Brazilian institutions participating in the projects and activities and the Brazilian Cooperation Fund, through resources provided by international bodies, including the Food and Agricultural Organization, the Organization of American States, and the Inter-American Development Bank. Most activities involve cooperation with Latin American and Caribbean nations and Portuguese-speaking African countries. Within Mercosur, participation is implemented through the Technical Cooperation Committee, the Programming and Evaluation Committee of the Inter-American Development Bank /Mercosur, and the Joint Consultative Committee with the European Union. The principal sectors benefiting are agriculture, agricultural development, and agro-industry; health; urban transportation; forestry development; mining; public

administration; professional training; the environment; civil aviation; small and medium-size enterprises; the energy industry; planning and technological development; sanitation; and education (MRE 2003b).

Multilateral Programs and Academic Networks

The Ministry of Foreign Relations includes among its programs the Multilateral Received Technical Cooperation Program developed between Brazil and international bodies that implement technical cooperation activities.[5] The purpose of this program is to transfer technical knowledge and experience that may contribute to the socioeconomic development of the country. It sponsors seminars, meetings, lectures, short-duration missions, and preparatory projects.

Implementation of multilateral cooperation projects and other activities involves contributing technical and financial support (provided by international bodies and national institutions, in differing proportions). Projects being carried out are in the fields of the environment, public administration, education, health, energy, telecommunications and information technology, agriculture, industry, services, social development, foreign trade, civil aviation, and regional development. These projects are operating nationally (33 percent), in the north-east (22 percent), the south-east (22 percent), the north (7 percent), the south (6 percent), the central west (4 percent), and in Latin America in general (6 percent). Foreign sources of funding are the United Nations Development Programme (41 percent), UNICEF (18 percent), the United Nations (14 percent), UNESCO (12 percent), the Inter-American Institute for Cooperation in Agriculture (6 percent), the Food and Agricultural Organization (4 percent), the Inter-American Development Bank (3 percent), the International Tropical Wood Organization (3 percent), and other institutions (13 percent). Multilateral cooperation has supported 400 active projects (half of them small-scale projects worth less than $66,666); another 200 projects are

---

[5] The principal partners are the Latin American Integration Association; the Inter-American Development Bank; the Economic Commission for Latin America and the Caribbean; the Food and Agriculture Organization; the Latin American Faculty of Social Sciences; the UN Population Fund; the UN Center for Human Settlement (HABITAT); the Inter-American Institute for Cooperation for Agriculture; the International Civil Aviation Organization; the Organization of American States; the International Labor Organization; the International Tropical Wood Organization; the World Meteorological Organization; the World Organization for Intellectual Property; the UN Development Programne (UNDP); the International Telecommunications Union; the UN Program for the Control of Drugs and the Prevention of Crime; the UN Educational, Scientific and Cultural Organization (UNESCO); the UN Children's Fund (UNICEF); the UN Development Fund for Women; the UN Organization for Industrial Development; the UN Volunteers; and the Universal Postal Union.

being negotiated or are under evaluation. The resources invested in 1995 were $58.4 million, 32 percent of which were obtained from abroad and were nonreimbursable and 68 percent of which were matching funds from the Brazilian government (MRE 2003a).

Some multilateral programs can serve as examples of national policy on academic cooperation (Neves 2002; Morosini 1998). These include the Ibero-American Program for Science and Technology Development; the Association of Universities of the Amazon Region; the Network for Integration and Academic Mobility; the University Twinning and Networking Scheme (UNITWIN/UNESCO); and the Ibero-American Program for Inter-University Mobility in Advanced Branches of Professional Training.

Mercosur has made advances in harmonizing educational systems and processes. The 1999 Protocol for Acceptance of University Degrees for the Exercise of Academic Activities in Member Countries is in the process of being approved. It is expected that undergraduate degrees obtained from programs that include at least four years or 2,700 hours of study and graduate degrees (specializations that include at least 360 hours of face to face instruction and all master's and doctorate degrees) will receive accreditation exclusively for the purpose of teaching and conducting research in higher education.

The Protocol for Educational Integration for the Continuation of Graduate Studies in Mercosur Universities has been in effect since June 7, 1999. It allows recognition of degree certificates obtained from programs that include at least four years or 2,700 hours of study, exclusively for entry into graduate courses.

These agreements were followed by other protocols, in addition to those for cultural cooperation between Brazil and Mercosur countries. Among them are protocols that strengthen graduate studies and cooperation in science and technology, signed with Argentina and Chile in 1996. Under this agreement, the Antorchas Foundation of Argentina provides five grants for each member country for researchers in science or the humanities.

The focus on integration is currently directed at recognizing undergraduate degrees in certain areas of knowledge, with the objective of incorporating the Mercosur seal, which allows for the recognition of diplomas in all member states. Studies of an experimental mechanism for the accreditation of undergraduate degrees have begun in agronomy, medicine, and engineering. An Action Plan for 2001–05 was agreed to in 2002. The plan included the following priority areas: assistantships for short stays, teacher and student mobility, accreditation of degree programs throughout Mercosur, interinstitutional cooperation in graduate studies, teacher training, and scientific research. The objective is to make Mercosur more than a custom-free zone between Brazil and neighboring countries. Rather, it should create the conditions to reach a level of development that is similar in all countries, through cooperation and the transfer of technology (MRE 2003b).

New Modes of Higher Education and New Suppliers

New suppliers of higher education have emerged in Brazil, principally in the form of virtual education or mixed mode (semidistance) education from corporate universities, franchises, and transnational corporations.

DISTANCE EDUCATION PROVIDED BY FOREIGN UNIVERSITIES

Despite the rigid system of control by the government to maintain the quality of the higher education system, in recent years there has been a large increase in the supply of distance learning programs in Brazil. A notable example is the American World University, which offers more than 200 undergraduate and graduate programs in 14 areas through a modern distance education delivery system. This university is based in Iowa and Hawaii in the United States, where Brazilian students are formally matriculated. The degree certificates awarded, like all others of the same type, have to be authenticated by the consular service of the Brazilian Embassy in the United States before being processed for recognition in Brazil, as regulated by Law 9394/1996 and resolutions of the National Education Council.

Semidistance education reached its peak at the end of the 1990s, with the proliferation of graduate programs, including master's and doctorate programs, offered jointly with foreign institutions, some of which had great prestige in Europe. The lack of adherence of these programs to the regulations established by national legislation provoked a reaction from CAPES, which produced a report denouncing all of the foreign institutions involved. This situation, which arose out of the need to maintain the quality of higher education in Brazil and protect Brazilians against the proliferation of diploma mills, has created conflict between CAPES and some foreign institutions.

At the same time, the increasing demand for continuing education, together with the appeal of foreign or "international" degree certificates, has opened the way for numerous MBA programs. These programs are offered by international institutions that are either based in Brazil or operate in virtual or semidistance mode. Although these institutions are agents in the process of internationalization, some of them are of poor quality and operate without the backing of national legislation. To deal with this situation, the government has released a list of institutions authorized to offer courses in association with foreign institutions. This list is published on the Web sites of the Ministry of Education and CAPES.

Some MBA programs offered by foreign institutions are now operating in Brazil. An example of the way international programs can diversify educational supply and satisfy market demand is the University of Pittsburg's program. In the 2004 ranking of the best executive MBA programs, its international executive MBA ranked first among the programs available in Brazil. Following the model adopted in the United States, it offers 8- to 10-day classes. Between sessions, students receive tutorial assistance over the Internet, by video-conference, or by telephone. They also spend three weeks on a campus in the United States before finishing the program.

Commercial universities are also operating in Brazil. The Apollo International Company, operated by the Apollo Group, owners of the University of Phoenix, has a large presence. Associated with the Pythagoras Group, owners of the third-largest chain of private schools in Brazil, Apollo has established the Pythagoras Faculties in Belo Horizonte, one of the largest cities in Brazil. Using an exemplary educational model dedicated to preparing students for the job market, the Pythagoras Faculties offer undergraduate programs in administration and industrial engineering for 1,100 students in Belo Horizonte and 200 more in Curitiba and Ipatinga (Burton 2003). Two-thirds of the students are adults with an average age of 24, attend evening classes while working full time.

INTERNATIONAL CAPITAL IN PRIVATE HIGHER EDUCATION INSTITUTIONS
U.S., Canadian, and European investment groups negotiate with universities and faculties in Brazil to buy and manage institutions, with the aim of selling them at a profit. This type of business operation arises from new interpretations of Law 9394/1996, which permits higher education to make a profit. The new interpretation is attracting both foreign and domestic investors, including the Patria Group.

These enterprises raise new questions, challenge time-honored traditions, and change the status quo in the academic sphere. A nationwide debate is needed to establish guidelines that offer a wide range of choices without affecting the fairness, relevance, and quality of education. It is the government's responsibility to regulate this explosion of educational supply (through CAPES and the National Education Council) and to analyze its implications. University and scientific associations need to study the situation and analyze the positive and negative consequences for education and society in general.

Conclusions

The internationalization of higher education in Brazil has expanded since the 1990s. The process is far from completed, however.

In an effort to promote national development, the government has supported international academic cooperation in order to raise its graduate programs and research centers to international levels. Its policies have increased mobility for researchers, professors, and students, both between Brazilian institutions and with foreign ones. This mobility has had a significant impact on the internationalization of the academic sphere. It has increased mastery of foreign languages and introduced new customs, technology, academic practices, and standards of quality into Brazilian institutions.

Too little has been done, however. At most higher education institutions, the culture of internationalization is only just beginning. It remains highly dependent on the type of institution, the institutional authorities in charge, and the faculty involved.

Public educational policies are needed that promote and regulate internationalization in teaching, support the official recognition of degrees and diplomas earned at approved institutions outside Brazil, and provide more flexibility and academic freedom to researchers. Research must be sustained by networks of researchers and promoted by the development of distance technology.

The internalization of higher education exists at different levels, depending on the institution involved. There are higher education institutions in Brazil in which internationalization may be linked to the roots of the institution, others at which it is limited to certain niches, and yet others where it is nonexistent or hardly beginning.

Because of the high degree of government control, university functions related to undergraduate studies are only recently permitting internationalization. In the case of graduate education, internationalization is considered to be the model to be followed, and this is reflected in patterns of government spending. The strategy of forming international partner universities is seen as a way of consolidating graduate study programs and thus forming cadres of academics for the future.

Enhancing internationalization is key to strengthening education at the national, institutional, individual, and professional level. Public and institutional policies promote internationalization by diversifying and strengthening the scientific and technological basis of sustainable development while preserving national interests and incentives to implement networks for excellence in scientific and technological research. Revitalizing Mercosur broadens Brazil's participation in the international market while preserving its national interests.

It is critical to generate discussion in academic and government circles about the theoretical foundations, the underlying motivation, and the results hoped for from internationalization. The whys and wherefores need to be analyzed and linked to mechanisms for managing internationalization and specifying policies in the face of changes in society. Are institutions preparing themselves for a strategic alliance with the government in order to reap the benefits from this process? Is the Brazilian higher education system preparing itself strategically to compete in a highly competitive market? The answer to these questions may provide the key to the crafting of government and institutional policies that support the process of internationalization of higher education on the basis of national values.

References

Alß AN. n.d. *A High-Level Scholarship Programme Specifically Addressed to Latin America.* http://www.programalban.org/.

ALFA (América Latina Formação Acadêmica). n.d. http://europa.eu.int/comm/ europeaid/projects/alfa/index_en.htm.

————. (n.d.) http://europa.eu.int/comm/europeaid/projects/alfa/information/ statistics/brazil1_6.pdf

Altbach, Philip G. 2001. "Higher Education and the WTO. Globalization Run Amok." *International Higher Education* 23 (Spring).

Baeta Neves. 2002. "Infocapes." *Boletim Informativo CAPES* 10 (4): 5–15. Brasilia.

Bampi, S. 2003. "A atuação das FAPs eo fortalecimento do sistema nacional de C&T." *Jornal da ADUFRGS* 1191 (August 15).

Burton, B. 2003. "Apollo International Builds on a Local Network to Create Colleges in Brazil." *Chronicle of Higher Education.* 49(42):A24

CAPES (Coordinating agency for graduate Education). 2002a. www.capes.gov.br.

————. 2002b. *Programas de postgrado strito sensu.* www.capes.gov.br./capes/ portal/.

CAPES/CNPq. 2003. *Relatório final. Sumário executivo.* Interministerial Ministry of Science and Technology, Ministry of Education, Nº 270 de 22/05/2003. http:// www.capes.gov.br./capes/portal/.

CNPq. 2001. *Relatorio de atividades.* http://www.cnpq.br.

————. 2002a. *Relatorio de atividades.* http://www.cnpq.br.

————. 2002b. *Relatório de gestão institucional.* http://www.cnpq.br/sobrecnpq/ informacoesinstitucionais/relat_gestao_institucional.pdf._

————. 2003. www.CNPq.br

————. 2004. *Ciência e tecnologia no Brasil. Apoio a núcleos de excelência.* http://www. dc.mre.gov.br/brasil/textos/cienetecno.pdf

Cooperação Técnica Recebida Multilateral.

http://www.mre.gov.br/portugues/politica_externa/temas_agenda/cooperacao _inter/cooperacao.asp.

Dias, M. 2002. "Educação superior: bem público ou serviço comercial regulamentado pela OMC?" In *Universidade: um lugar fora do poder,* ed. Wrana Maria Panizzi. Porto Alegre: Ed. da UFRGS.

Diretórios de Grupos de Pesquisa. n.d. http://lattes. cnpq.br/diretorio.

FAPESP (State of São Paulo Research Foundation). 2001. *Relatorio e atividades 2001.* www.fapesp.br.

———. 2004. *Parceiros em desenvolvimento*. Agência de Notícias da Fundação de Amparo à Pesquisa do Estado de São Paulo. www.fapesp.br.

FAUBAI (Fórum de Assessorias das Universidades Brasileiras para Assuntos Internacionais). 2003. *The Assesorial Bodies of Brazilian Universities for International Matters*. Brazil.

Freire, J.D. 2003. *A formação de recursos humanos de alto nível no exterior e sua inserção profissional no Brasil*. Master's dissertation University of Brasilia.

Gatti, B., M. André, O. Favero, and V. Candau. 2003. "O modelo de avaliação da CAPES." *Revista Brasileira de Educação* ANPED, Autores Associados 22 (January–April): 137–44.

Guia IRO-NET. 1998. *Guia comparativo de gestion de oficinas de relaciones internacionales*. ALFA/IRO-NET, Salamanca.

INEP (National Institute of Educational Planning and Research). 2004. www.inep. gov.br

Laredo, Íris. 1994. *Lo transfondo político del proceso de integracion*. Universidade no Mercosul. Cortez/CNPq, São Paulo.

Laredo, Íris. 1994. *Lo transfondo político del proceso de integracion*. MOROSINI, M. C. Universidade no Mercosul. São Paulo: Cortez/CNPq. 44–72.

Laus, Sonia. 1997. "La internacionalización de las universidades: realidades y perspectivas." In *Educación global*. Jalisco, Mexico: Doble Luna Editores.

———. 1998. *El estado actual de las políticas educacionales en el ámbito del Mercosur y las redes regionales de cooperación*. Mexico: Doble Luna Editores.

———. 1998. "A gestão da cooperação acadêmica internacional nas universidades de língua portuguesa: o caso Brasileiro." In *Anais do viii encontro da associação das universidades de língua Portuguesa*. Macau, China.

———. 2001. "La formación de pregrado y postgrado: algunas experiencias de Brasil en la cooperación con Ibero América." In *La universidad como espacio para la cooperación iberoamericana: cursos de estío 2000. La universidad, las universidades: perspectivas*. Universidad de Valladolid, Spain.

———. 2002. "El proceso de internacionalización de las universidades brasileñas." Paper presented at the international seminar Desafios de la Internacionalización del Sistema Universitario Boliviano, Santa Cruz de la Sierra, Bolivia.

Leite, D., and M. Cunha. 1992. *Universidade e ensino de graduação no Brasil*. EdUFPEL, Pelotas, Brazil.

Lessa, Antônio Carlos. 2002. "Ciência e tecnologia nas relações Brasil-França (1964–2001)." In *Anuário Brasil-Europa: relações de cooperação em ciência & tecnologia*, ed. Wilhelm Hofmeister and Franklin Trein. Rio de Janeiro: Fundação Konrad Adenauer.

Luce, M.B., and M.C. Morosini. 2003. *A educação superior no Brasil: políticas de avaliação e credenciamento*. Texto elaborado para la red ALFA-ACRO: acreditación y reconocimiento oficiales entre universidades de Mercosur y la UE. Porto Alegre.

Mercosur. n.d. http://www.mre.gov.br/portugues/politica_externa/temas_agenda/ciencia_tecnologia/cooperacao.asp.

Ministry of Education. 2004. www.mec.gov.br. Brasilia, Brazil.

Morosini, M.C. 1994. *Universidade no Mercosul*. Cortez/CNPq, São Paulo.

————. 1997. "Academic Networks and the Consolidation of Mercosul/European Union." Paper presented at the 19th Annual European Association of Institutional Researchers Forum, European Higher Education Society, Coventry, United Kingdom.

————. 1998. *Mercosul/Mercosur: políticas e ações universitárias*. Porto Alegre: Autores Associados/EdUFRGS.

————. 2003. *Enciclopédia de pedagogia universitária*. Porto Alegre: RIES/FAPERGS.

MRE (Ministry of Foreign Relations). 2003a. *Cooperação científica e tecnológica*. Brasilia.

————. 2003b. *Cooperação técnica com países em desenvolvimento*. Brasilia.

————. 2004a. *Divisão de temas educacionais*. Brasilia.

————. 2004b. *Escola tipo exportação*. Brasilia.

National Education Council. 2004. *Diretrizes curriculares*. Brasilia.

Neddermeyer, D. 2002. "A política de formação de recursos humanos no exterior da CAPES: a visão de quem entende do assunto." *INFOCAPES* 10 (3). CAPES, Brasilia.

Neves, C.E.B. 2002. "Ciência e tecnologia no Brasil." In *Educação superior no Brasil*, ed. S. Soares, 205–41. CAPES, Brasilia.

Neves, C.E.B., and M. Morosini. 1995. "Cooperação universitária no Mercosul." *Aberto* 15 (68): 16–35. Ministry of Education, Brasilia.

Nunes Sobrinho, G. 2002. "Infocapes." *Boletim Informativo CAPES* 10 (4): 37–41. CAPES, Brasilia.

Oliven, Arabela Campos. 2002. "A história da educação superior no Brasil." In *Educação superior no Brasil*, ed. S. Soares, CAPES, Brasilia.

Panizzi, Wrana Maria. 2002. *Universidade. Um lugar fora do poder*. Porto Alegre: Ed. da UFRGS.

Ristoff, D. 2003. *"Fortalecimento do sistema público é a única esperança." Jornal da Universidade* 6 (67): 6–7. Porto Alegre, Brazil.

Schlindwein, P. 1990. "Diagnóstico da cooperação internacional nas instituições brasileiras." In *Anais do iii encontro nacional do fórum das assessorias das universidades brasileiras para assuntos internacionais*. Fortaleza.

World Bank. 2002a. *Constructing Knowledge Societies: New Challenges for Tertiary Education*. Washington, DC.

World Bank. 2002b. *Higher Education in Brazil: Challenges and Options*. Washington, DC: World Bank.

World Bank. 2004. *Brazil at a Glance*. World Bank, Washington DC.

5

Internationalization of Higher Education in Chile

Carlos Ramírez Sanchez

Internationalization is a strategic process that embraces all sectors of higher education. This chapter examines the challenges and actions policymakers need to address if Chile is to successfully internationalize its institutions of higher learning. It draws on survey data from 40 Chilean institutions of higher education.

The Higher Education System in Chile

The historical evolution of higher education in Chile is similar to that of the rest of Latin America. The first university, created in 1738, was San Felipe, which in 1843 became the University of Chile. In 1898 the Pontifical Catholic University of Chile was founded.

Development of new universities remained limited until the late 1980s, when a structural change to the system was initiated that led to a series of profound transformations. This reform process encouraged greater diversity and opened the way for the creation of new institutions. The government decided to "give maximum support to the establishment of private higher education institutions as a method of meeting and channeling the demand for higher education without cost to the State" (Brunner and Bricall 2000, p. 49).[1] This reform reduced the flow of state funds to higher education, passing on part of the cost to the private sector, on the assumption that dissemination of information and the transparency of the market would be necessary and sufficient conditions to regulate academic demands and those of the workplace.

As of 2002, there were 229 institutions of higher education in Chile. Four types of institutions are recognized under Chilean law: universities; professional institutes; centers for technical training; military academies, polytechnics, schools of the armed forces, the technical Aeronautical

---

[1] The number of universities in Chile grew at one of the fastest rates in Latin America, reducing the number of students per university. Fifty-four percent of students are enrolled at private institutions.

School of the General Civil Aviation Authority, and the Higher Institute of Police Science of the Carabineers of Chile. Of these institutions, 63 are universities, including 38 private universities; 51 professional institutes; and 115 technical training institutes.

Universities are often classified as traditional or nontraditional. Traditional universities include the 25 council of rectors' universities (16 public and 9 private), which existed before 1981, when the reforms to higher education were made.

The 16 state universities have public legal status. They are autonomous and have ownership rights over their property. Among the universities that do not belong to the state are six universities of the Catholic Church and three universities created by the private sector that received official status in 1980. Sixty-four percent of traditional and private universities are located in the areas of Chile where most economic activity is concentrated: the Metropolitan Region, Valparaiso, and Concepcion. There are no state professional institutes or centers for technical training. The last two that existed were converted into two new state universities in 1993.

Higher education institutions in Chile have 486 campuses, including 145 university campuses (56 traditional and 89 private). There are 136 professional institute campuses and 205 technical training center campuses. Among students enrolled in undergraduate and graduate programs, 49 percent are in the Metropolitan Region, 13 percent in Valparaiso, and 12 percent in Concepcion. The cities of Santiago, Valparaiso, and Concepcion account for 71 percent of all students enrolled in professional institutes and 66 percent of those in centers for technical training. In terms of subject area, 30 percent of all students are studying technology, 16 percent social sciences, 13 percent commerce and administration, and 12 percent education.

Chile allocates about 3.5 percent of its GDP to education. Public sector spending on higher education accounts for 0.6 percent of GDP, or 18 percent of total public education spending (MINEDUC 2005). Adding financing from the private sector raises this figure to 2.2 percent of GDP.

In the mid-1990s, 12 percent of professors at traditional universities held doctorates, 18 percent held master's degrees, and 70 percent held only bachelor's degrees. The proportion of scientists and engineers in research and development (R&D) was low. In 1998 there were 459 scientists and engineers for every 1 million inhabitants, yielding an investment in R&D (both public and private) of about 0.54 percent of GDP (UNESCO 2005).

Most graduate programs in Chile are offered by traditional universities. In 2003 there were 364 master's programs and 75 doctorate programs. Graduate students represent about 4 percent of the student body (MINEDUC 2005).

Since 1998 the government has invested in several projects aimed at improving the quality of higher education in Chile. More than 300 projects have been implemented at the technical, undergraduate, and graduate level, targeting such areas as staff training, teaching facilities, curricular redesign, student support services, and incorporation of information technology into learning processes. There was also significant investment in bringing 23 university libraries up to state of the art levels (MINEDUC 2005).

One important agreement reached between basic and higher education was to link a new university entrance exam directly to the school curriculum. This was a watershed reform, which replaced a system that had been in place for more than 30 years. More than 4,000 primary and secondary school teachers with international experience contributed to this process through networks of teachers, helping develop a system that can also be used in an international context.

National Policies Toward Internationalization

In 1994 support for new programs was increased significantly, with the aim of modernizing and improving the quality and consistency of higher education. In 1997 a new framework of policies for higher education was established. The Ministry of Education established four principal strategies for this process, one of which was internationalization.

Despite this commitment, 81 percent of higher education institutions believe that the government has not concentrated sufficiently on this area of development (Ramírez and others 2004). All of the traditional universities agree that there is a lack of explicit policies and coherent actions by government departments in internationalization. Policy has been more implicit than explicit, more responsive than deliberate, and more partial than global.

Rationale for Internationalization

The rationale for internationalization was mostly political in the 1990s, as the government sought to reestablish bilateral and multilateral relations. Chile's return to the international arena while slowly and gradually restoring a state of democracy should be attributed to the systematic efforts of the governments of Presidents Aylwin, Frei, and Lagos. The government has encouraged higher education institutions to establish links with institutions in other countries. Genuine support—in the form of new programs and funds to enable these institutions to participate effectively within the framework of new cooperative agreements—remains lacking, however.

Another motive that appears to cause the government to act in this sphere is the question of security. Maintaining peaceful relations with neighboring countries strengthens Chile's integration with them. This item on the agenda is more political than academic, given that Chilean institutions have not shown a preference for forming links with neighboring countries.

One of the most relevant aspects of the process of internationalization is the fact that Chile's geopolitical position has changed. A few decades ago, Chile was perceived as a remote country surrounded by an impassable mountain chain. Isolation from the rest of the world was considered normal. The experience of recent decades and the economic and political development of Chile toward democracy and economic stability has opened up a window of opportunity. The rest of the world now perceives Chile as a potential commercial and scientific partner. The most recently signed treaties, such as the Free Trade Agreement with the United States, the agreement with the European Union, and the treaty with the Republic of Korea, provide evidence of this.

One of the most important factors accounting for this transformation has been Chile's stability and economic growth in comparison with the rest of Latin America. Trade has been the principal motive for linking Chile to the rest of the world. This development has also challenged the higher education institutions. In the words of Gonzalez (2003, p. 10), national policies for internationalization "have become justified by the need to relate to other cultures, in order to better compete in international markets so that our graduates might work better in international environments. Moreover, they have become justified by the need to confront the questions of competence and competitiveness."

Principal Actors

A number of different actors are involved in the process of national development of internationalizing higher education. The following sections describe the most important ones.

MINISTRY OF EDUCATION
Although the Ministry of Education is the principal actor and has its own Department of International Relations, it has left the task of internationalization in the hands of other government departments and of the higher education institutions themselves. According to the Ministry's own statement, it is not capable of coordinating, orienting, or directing other government departments and the higher education institutions in this area.

MINISTRY OF FOREIGN RELATIONS
The Directorate of Promotion of Exports Pro-Chile falls under the Directorate of International Economic Relations of the Ministry of Foreign Relations. Its

mission is to support the development of exports and the internationalization of Chilean companies. The Directorate concentrates on diversifying and stimulating exports of products and services, particularly nonconventional ones, by providing information to the exporting sector and supporting it with contacts for potential foreign buyers. One important aspect of its work has been the *International Program of Economic and Commercial Positioning of Chile Abroad*, which aims to create a favorable image of what Chile offers in a wide range of goods and services of excellent quality. Since 1997 these services have included educational services.

Ministry of The Interior

In 2003 the Under-Secretariat of Regional Development, which falls under the Ministry of the Interior, began strengthening regional areas in international matters. In joint action with the Ministry of the Interior, the Ministry of Planning and the Ministry of Foreign Relations have begun a plan to strengthen the international presence of each of Chile's 13 regions by appointing a regional director of international relations in each. The initiative aims to strengthen the standing and capacity of regional governments in the international sphere. It includes three lines of action: Regional strengthening of institutional and professional capacity; incorporation of more efficient and better coordinated structures for action between institutional, national, and regional actors; and support to the management of cooperation and links between the regions and international commerce.

Chilean International Cooperation Agency

In 1990 Chile established the Chilean International Cooperation Agency (AGCI), a public organization that defines cooperation policies and programs in line with national development objectives and priorities, in order to support them with international cooperation funding. When it began, its fundamental task was to restore Chile's international presence in a world that had distanced itself from Chile. It now focuses on international programs that reduce poverty, promote equality, encourage the transfer and adaptation of technology, decentralize regional and local administration, conserve the environment, modernize public administration, and train Chileans abroad.

The AGCI has strengthened the slogan "Chile, a country for cooperation" by means of bilateral international cooperation. This cooperation includes technical assistance programs, graduate scholarships for study in Chile, and technical and professional training.

Higher Education Council

The Higher Education Council is an autonomous public body responsible for accrediting private higher education institutions. Its most important function is accrediting private universities and professional institutes. In this capacity, it has the power to evaluate, approve, or reject proposed institutional projects; establish and administer the system of accreditation; evaluate, approve, or reject proposals for new degree programs; establish selection examinations; design and apply mechanisms for supervision or evaluation; and recommend to the Ministry of Education the application of sanctions to institutions in the process of accreditation. Its strategic objectives include building public trust in higher education institutions, ensuring conformity with quality standards, promoting institutions' global development, and protecting consumers.

NATIONAL ACCREDITATION COMMISSION

The National Accreditation Commission certifies the quality of study programs in various subjects offered by autonomous higher education institutions. It works through two commissions, the Commission for the Undergraduate Accreditation and the Commission for Graduate Accreditation. The process of accreditation, which is voluntary, aims to ensure and promote quality in higher education programs. In 2004 a project of institutional accreditation was begun. The objective is to ensure that higher education institutions have reliable internal systems for regulating quality.

A law is currently under review in the legislature to establish a National System for the Assurance of Quality in Higher Education. The proposal includes the possibility of working with private, public, national, and international accreditation agencies—supervised by the national system, which would determine the requirements for these agencies to operate in Chile—to establish the regulations for educational institutions' operation in Chile.

NATIONAL COMMISSION FOR SCIENTIFIC AND TECHNOLOGICAL RESEARCH

The National Commission for Scientific and Technological Research (CONICYT) was created in 1967 to advise the government on science and technology. Its actions promote and coordinate scientific and academic research, training for human resources, and development in new areas of knowledge. It also manages the resources available for these purposes.

Among its fundamental objectives are promoting research in science and technology as an instrument for national development; developing a National Information System in science and technology; providing coherence and planning for the development of human resources in research and development of science and technology, with an emphasis on increasing the number of researchers above the bare minimum in emerging or deficient areas of research that are essential for Chile's development; promoting exchanges of researchers at an international level and establishing an international presence; and strengthening cooperation programs with countries in North America, Latin America, and the European Union. Among the resources most important for this purpose are the National Fund for Scientific and Technological Development, the Fund for Advanced Research in Priority Areas, the Program for Publicizing and Promoting Science and Technology, and the Regional Program for Promoting Research and Reaching Critical Mass in the Regions.

No less important is the work carried out by the Department of Human Resources and Graduate Scholarships, which supports the training of professionals who already have graduate qualifications, and the Department of Information, which administers programs that compile and publish scientific and technological research findings and develops programs that provide access to national and international information required by scientific inquiry.

The Department of International Relations is responsible for integrating the national scientific community with its counterparts all over the world. It links the work of CONICYT with national and international institutions in science and technology. The department coordinates its work with that of international counterparts in Argentina, Brazil, Colombia, Cuba, France, Germany, Italy, Japan, the Republic of Korea, Mexico, Peru, Portugal, Spain, the United Kingdom, the United States, Venezuela, and other countries.

INTERNATIONAL RELATIONS COMMISSION OF THE COUNCIL OF RECTORS
The Council of Rectors was created in 1954. The council coordinates the work of 25 traditional universities. In 1997 it created the Commission for International Cooperation, a network of the coordinators of cooperation and international relations at the 25 universities. From the moment of its creation this commission has provided a forum for encounter, debate, analysis, and training in order to promote and stimulate internationalization in its member universities. Currently, this is the only university network for internationalization in Chile. It carries out work in three key areas: training in the management of international cooperation, promotion of the work carried out, and dissemination of relevant information abroad and promotion of exportable educational services.

INTERNATIONAL ORGANIZATIONS AND FOUNDATIONS
Other actors in the internationalization of higher education in Chile include international organizations and sources of cooperation, some of which have delegates in Chile. Among those that have supported projects of different kinds in the higher education institutions, especially the universities, are the World Bank, the Inter-American Development Bank, the Japanese International Cooperation Agency, the Spanish Agency for International Cooperation, the UN Economic Commission for Latin America and the Caribbean, the Ford Foundation, the Konrad Adenauer Foundation,

the Rockefeller Foundation, the Humboldt Foundation, the National Science Foundation, the Guggenheim Foundation, the Andes Foundation, the Adveniat Foundation, the Volkswagen Foundation, the Kellogg Foundation, the German Society for Technical Cooperation, the International Organization for Migration, the British Council, the Fulbright Commission, the German Academic Exchange Office, the Goethe Institute, the UN Development Programme, the UN Food and Agricultural Organization, the UN Educational, Scientific and Culture Organization (UNESCO), Science and Culture, and the Inter-American Institute for Cooperation in Agriculture. A wide range of scholarships for training abroad are channeled through the Chilean International Cooperation Agency (17 sources) or provided directly by international agencies (29 sources).

International Dimension of Higher Education

Two instruments were designed to investigate the international dimension of higher education in Chile: an open response questionnaire and a closed response questionnaire (Ramírez and others 2004). The research population was a group of 40 Chilean institutions of higher education. Interviews were conducted with representatives of these institutions.[2]

The majority of higher education institutions have been influenced, some under pressure from outside, others internally, to implement a planned policy of action toward internationalization in order to face the challenges globalization has produced. For this reason they have developed and increased international actions, especially since the 1990s, that have enabled them to take on the challenge of internationalization. This has been made evident in explicit institutional policies, some clearer than others, to consolidate and promote this process within the institutions.

All the traditional universities claim to be carrying out international activities and encouraging their academic staff to be involved internationally. Seventy-two percent of the institutions surveyed report providing some type of stimulus for this activity. Eighty-one percent of the traditional

---

[2] Interviews were conducted with representatives of the Andrés Bello Diplomatic Academy, the Chilean Agency for International Cooperation, the Directors of International Relations of the Council of Rectors, the Directors of International Relations in Private Universities, the Directors of International Relations in Technical-Professional Institutes, the Directors of Research of the Higher Education Institutions, the Division of Higher Education of the Ministry of Education, the International Cooperation Commission of the Council of Rectors, the Ministry of Foreign Relations, the National Accreditation Commission, the National Commission for Science and Technology, the Office of International Relations of the Ministry of Education, the Pro-Chile Program of the Ministry of Foreign Relations, the Regional Directors of International Relations, the University Program Regional Government of the Under-Secretariat of Regional Development, and others, as well as with rectors and former rectors of selected Chilean universities.

universities affirm that an international dimension is incorporated into the institution's educational plan, as expressed by the university's mission statement. Before the 1990s, less than 5 percent of the institutions had clearly stated institutional objectives for internationalization (Ramírez and others 2004).

The presence of international policies can be noted at higher education institutions, especially the universities. Some professional institutes in the Metropolitan Region have expressed their intentions to introduce internationalization as a substantive part of their work. In many cases, this intention is more in word than in deed and lacks a coherent vision incorporated into institutional policy, lacking goals, means of evaluation, and indeed genuine understanding of the matter by top authorities. Such institutions focus on internationalization on the fringe of the university agenda, carrying out international actions in a patchy and disconnected fashion, in many cases responding to supply and demand in international matters without engaging in adequate examination and planning before beginning the process.

Before the 1990s higher education institutions did not incorporate the concept of institutional internationalization. For this reason, and despite the advances made in the past 10 years, a significant proportion of higher education institutions (perhaps more than 30 percent) have not fully realized that incorporating the international dimension is a real and substantial part of their responsibilities.

One of the first challenges that higher education institutions should take on in the next few years is to find a means to make their communities assume a global conscience. This involves ensuring that everyone shares a common language in dealing with such a complex process of change. The lack of conceptualization has caused the internationalization process to be viewed as marginal in institutional development policies, as it is in national educational policy.

Institutional Rationale

In nearly all the institutions surveyed the principal reasons for strengthening the internationalization process are academic and economic (Ramírez and others 2004). Academics are interested in widening their horizons by means of international recognition and appreciation, which would enable research and training programs, especially at the graduate level, to achieve international standards. This would allow the institutions to acquire international recognition.

The economic reasons for strengthening internationalization are that it is a powerful tool to improve the revenues of higher education institutions by offering educational programs and educational services to both Chilean students and students from abroad.

In this respect, it is important to distinguish between two types of higher education institutions in Chile. Some are committed to redesigning organizational strategies to embrace internationalization. Others regard the international dimension as a marketing tool rather than a genuine way to achieve institutional growth. These institutions are interested in developing their international links through publicity, in order to attract a new market of students rather than to achieve an in-depth internationalization process that genuinely will become part of institutional development in the long term.

Planning

Although many institutions in Chile underline the importance of internationalization, few have effective plans for introducing this process. Most institutions, especially the universities, have developed a growing and heterogeneous range of international activities, based on mobility of students or faculty and scientific exchanges. All of the traditional universities claim to carry out international activities, but these activities have not been taken on as a part of a deeper process that results from a model to enable the design and application of internationalization strategies in the institutions themselves. The policies of nearly 60 percent of these institutions do not contain specific attention or reference to internationalization in their core institutional development plans.

In almost 70 percent of the universities surveyed, planning in the offices responsible for international relations is carried out independently, without connections to the rest of the university agenda. Only a few universities have defined their international strategic policies clearly as part of a general institutional strategy. Doing so would enable them to coordinate, prioritize, and evaluate the wide range of international activities they carry out (Ramírez and others 2004).

More than 80 percent of the highest authorities at Chilean institutions, especially the universities, have begun to develop leadership in these matters. This represents a fundamental breakthrough in implementing internationalization policies. University faculty appears to fully appreciate and understand this process. At more than 40 percent of the universities surveyed, the rector has a profound impact on internationalization. The process thus depends very much on who is in charge. In many cases, the change of rector has resulted in significant slippage in the process of making internationalization an institutional priority (Ramírez and others 2004).

At 54 percent of the universities surveyed, internationalization has not been successfully implemented in a strategic sense into the mid-level administration (Ramírez and others 2004). As a result, internationalization is maintained in a restricted area of the institution and does not permeate the university agenda in all departments and areas. Strategic planning is thus not integrated into all areas of university action.

One of the major challenges facing higher education institutions in Chile is to include all high-ranking administrators in this process. New academic and administrative paradigms need to be adopted, in which flexibility plays a key role. In some cases, dramatic changes will be needed. Convincing everyone in a position of authority to work on internationalization strategies in a coordinated fashion is critical.

Management of International Relations

Eighty-one percent of universities surveyed have institutional organizations with their own budgets for dealing with internationalization. This process has occurred over the past 10 years, when 40 percent of the traditional universities formed their international offices. In contrast, the trend has been more recent at private universities, no more than 30 percent of which have created formal administrative structures (Ramírez and others 2004).

These administrative structures are under the central university administration. They have various titles and functions, including providing orientation for setting up and facilitating international links, distributing information on sources of international cooperation, collaborating in drawing up interinstitutional agreements, coordinating the international agendas of university authorities, receiving foreign delegations, and implementing institutional representation and student mobility. They fail to pay attention to more central issues of internationalization.

These offices are located in different departments, at different levels, and under different authorities. The offices are called departments of foreign affairs in about 90 percent of traditional universities. In most cases these offices report directly to the university president, which makes decisionmaking easier and faster and ensures deeper institutional commitment. In other institutions, the offices are located at a lower level in the hierarchy. In these cases, internationalization tends not to be a core institutional strategy.

Only 45 percent of the universities surveyed have internationalization committees as part of their organizational structure, incorporating the active presence and participation of strategic elements in their institutions (Ramírez and others 2004).

HUMAN RESOURCES IN INTERNATIONAL AFFAIRS OFFICES

Two to four people manage international affairs offices at institutions of higher education in Chile. In more than 30 percent of the universities surveyed, the strategic force of the work to be carried out has been inadequately defined, partly because the institutions failed to define the characteristics and qualifications of staff responsible for internationalization (Ramírez and others 2004).

Staff turnover is high, because these positions are considered political appointments and therefore change when a new university president takes over. In the most recent changes of administration, turnover at traditional universities exceeded 65 percent.

High turnover makes progress difficult. Other factors impeding progress include lack of experience in managing internationalization, lack of links and acquaintance with foreign actors, lack of training, and the need to combine these functions with other activities. If institutions genuinely want to act in a manner that is consistent with their policies and principles, they should employ staff that are well qualified and up to date. Duties should be assigned to professionals who can carry out their duties regardless of political changes higher up in the institution.

BUDGET

Only a small percentage of an institution's budgets is assigned to internationalization, but the budget has increased in recent years. Measuring the budget is difficult, because of the wide range of international activities involved. Eighty-one percent of the traditional universities surveyed have their own central budget for the international affairs offices; 18 percent obtain financing from NGOs to carry out their activities. No institution receives government funds (Ramírez and others 2004).

The bulk of resources for international activities still goes toward scientific and technological research and graduate training. There is little funding for undergraduate internationalization and less for management of the process. Higher education institutions generate funding through consultancy services and receive funding from external cooperation partners to finance the internationalization process.

Traditional universities have increased their support of international activities. Recent actions—technical missions, presidential tours, scientific and technological agreements, and new approaches to international relations between participating governments, businesses, and universities—have increased in both quantity and quality in recent years.

Too little is still being done, however. To spur internationalization, the government will need to provide funds that institutions can compete for. This kind of funding would help institutions prioritize, develop, promote, and strengthen deficient areas of internationalization. The provision of funds for improving the quality of higher education could be considered an opportunity to steer funds into internationalization, especially at traditional universities.

EVALUATION MECHANISMS

Few institutions have procedures or criteria for planning and evaluation that take internationalization into account. Since they do not appear to consider internationalization an important indicator of academic production or a factor that can improve the quality of education in procedures for institutional evaluation, it is very unlikely that government supported programs will make available funding to institutionalize the process of internationalization.

The internationalization process is beginning to assume greater importance, because it obliges the institutions to reconsider their work and functions. Only a few years ago, these functions were strictly dictated by government regulations and norms, giving institutions very little flexibility to consider other alternatives, including new providers of educational services.

Growing international activity, innovations by the higher education institutions themselves, and an increasing variety of educational services with different content, pedagogical processes, and methodology are creating a new scenario, a scenario for which the higher education system is not prepared. To accommodate these changes, new evaluation procedures that include criteria that incorporate the international dimension are needed. Procedures to bring Chile in line with other countries must be analyzed. Chile needs to cooperate with other institutions to design and implement joint evaluations and international accreditation, at least within Latin America.

All of the universities surveyed affirm that it is practically impossible to carry out the planning process for something as complex as internationalization without a system that ensures its quality and enables the institution to detect failings and weaknesses in their actions in order to guarantee international standards in this area in the future. Seventy-three percent of the universities report facing serious difficulty in carrying out such a process, because of the lack of parameters for measuring progress and the almost complete absence of instruments and mechanisms to evaluate it. Thirty-six percent of universities report having designed evaluation processes and follow-up procedures to improve the quality of internationalization (Ramírez and others 2004).

Analysis of the evaluation instruments used by higher education institutions reveals certain elements that could serve as indicators for evaluating the internationalization process. These include the number of cooperation agreements in force, the number of Chilean students studying abroad, the number of foreign students studying in Chile, faculty mobility, and the number of international joint research projects. These are only limited indicators of a complex process.

The evaluation of internationalization is still absent in higher education institutions in Chile. It is essential to incorporate this element into all self-evaluation and accreditation processes, with the help of international experts in international education.

Internationalization Efforts

International agreements are facilitating the internationalization process.

Institutional Networks and Agreements

The 25 traditional universities surveyed in 2003 had signed 1,729 agreements with 61 different countries (Table 5.1). Europe participates in the greatest number of them, with 41 percent (715 agreements with 29 countries). South America follows, with 27 percent (472 agreements with 9 countries); followed by North America, with 15 percent (260 agreements with 2 countries); and Central America and the Caribbean, with 12 percent (211 agreements with 11 countries) (Ramírez and others 2004).

The eight private institutions surveyed had 210 agreements, with universities in Europe (38 percent), South America (24 percent), North America (23 percent), Central America (12 percent) (Ramírez and others 2004).

No evaluation has been conducted of the impact of participation in international networks or of the effectiveness of these networks. Smaller, more focused networks appear to have the greatest impact, however.

More than 800 networks were approved in the first phase of the Latin America Academic Training (ALFA) program of the European Union. Chile participated actively in some of these networks. The University of Chile belongs to 80 networks in ALFA I and 16 in ALFA II. Ten of the ALFA

Table 5.1 Cooperation Agreements between Traditional Chilean Universities and Foreign Universities, by Region

Region	Number of countries	Number of agreements	Percentage of agreements
Europe	29	715	41.4
South America	9	472	27.3
North America	2	260	15.0
Central America and the Caribbean	11	211	12.2
Asia	6	48	2.8
Oceania	2	21	1.2
Africa	2	2	0.1

Source: (Ramírez and others 2004)

II networks are coordinated by public and private universities in Chile. Among the principal international networks in which Chilean institutions participate are those promoted by intergovernmental organizations, such as the Organization of Ibero-American States, the Andrés Bello Agreement, UNESCO, and the Organization of American States.

International networks are playing an increasingly important role in Chile. Traditionally focused on research, in recent years networks have become linked to undergraduate and graduate work and to university management. The change reflects the growing importance of internationalizing these activities in order to strengthen strategic international alliances and associated projects in order to acquire institutional capacity by cooperating with foreign partners.

Student Mobility

Student mobility is one of the most obvious aspects of the process of internationalization in Chile's higher education institutions, despite the fact that there has been no strategy to eliminate barriers.

INTERNATIONAL STUDENTS IN CHILE

The number of international students in Chile has grown over the past 10 years, mainly as a result of increases in foreign student enrollment at universities. In 2000 higher education institutions received 3,477 foreign students. The principal countries of origin of these students were the United States (612), Peru (517), Argentina (354), Bolivia (317), Brazil (156), Colombia (130), Germany (97), Spain (85), Mexico (80), and France (58). The large number of students from other Latin American countries (41 percent of all foreign students in Chile) reflects growing interest in Chile's graduate programs.

In 2001 the number of foreign students in Chile rose by 5.6 percent to 3,675. The United States accounted for 23 percent of these students. Germany, France, and Spain accounted for 9 percent of the total. Traditional universities received 62 percent of all foreign students. The main recipients were the Pontifical Catholic University of Chile, the University of Chile, the Austral University, the Pontifical Catholic University of Valparaiso, and the University of Tarapaca. In the private sector, the Adolfo Ibañez University had the largest number of foreign students.

Foreign students represent a significant source of revenue. Institutions have created business units in response to this growing demand to study in Chile in order to promote key advantages of studying in Chile. These include the quality and wide variety of educational programs as well as Chile's good climate, geographical diversity, and tourist attractions.

Only a small number of universities have designed, implemented, and marketed short-term (two-week to six-month) programs on a wide variety of subject areas. More universities could be tapping this market. Regional universities in particular could offer intercultural programs, including programs that would attract students from Argentina and Bolivia.

To operate these programs, a wide range of options is available, from direct implementation by the universities themselves to operation through intermediary institutions (especially for the reception of North American students). The main agencies that specialize in recruiting foreign students in Chile are Cooperating Programs; the Council for International Educational Exchange; the Institute for Studies Abroad Butler Programs; International Education Students; International Studies Abroad; Plattsburgh State University of New York; Student International Training; and the University Enrollment Division, Chile. The agencies recruit students, charging $6,500–$12,500 per semester, of which $2,500–$3,000 goes to the Chilean university. In addition, some universities, including American University, Notre Dame University, Stanford University, Trinity College, the University of California, the University of Heidelberg, have offices in Santiago.

This process has been developed gradually over the past 10 years as a result of demand from abroad. It does not reflect a clear and coherent offer of services by Chile, as part of government policy to strengthen the process of internationalization of Chile's higher education institutions.

CHILEAN STUDENTS ABROAD

The number of Chilean students enrolled in university programs in other countries is estimated at 4,115 in 2000, 1.4 percent of the total number of students in Chile. Thirty-eight percent study in the United States, 19 percent in Spain, and 11 percent in Germany; 48 percent are in English-speaking countries (Davis 2003). Chileans are less proficient in English than other Latin Americans, making mobility of students within Latin America more common.

The Agency for International Cooperation (AGCI) plays an important role in providing information and scholarships. In 2001, 680 students were accepted into international programs on the basis of information provided by AGCI (Gonzalez 2003).

Staff Mobility

The process of internationalization of higher education is cemented by international relations established by university researchers. Over the past 30 years, Chilean researchers have done much to establish connections with their colleagues in other continents. Researchers upgrading their skills abroad through postdoctoral fellowships have contributed to international networks.

An important milestone for Chile was the exodus in 1973 of many intellectuals who were forced to emigrate. The majority of these scholars settled in Australia, France, Italy, Mexico, Spain, Sweden, the United States, and Venezuela. Some of these academics returned to Chile in the 1990s, while others remain abroad. Ties with these expatriates, many of whom wish to develop links between Chile and their second homelands, could be drawn on to enhance and internationalize higher education in Chile.

Less than 40 percent of academics have international experience (studying abroad, working abroad, publishing in international journals, attending international conferences, belonging to international networks). The processes of self-evaluation and institutional accreditation of the international dimension of teaching and research would constitute a valuable mechanism for more involvement in international work.

Internationalization of the Curriculum

Since the early 1990s, more than 80 percent of Chilean universities have modified their curricula. New networks and syllabuses have been developed in line with the new world Chile is facing. To ensure that they incorporate an international dimension, the new curricula should incorporate the following elements: knowledge of what is happening in the world, international relations, the geography of international politics, comparative international education, bilingualism, literacy in new information technology, and study abroad. All these elements should be incorporated in the plans and syllabuses of Chile's higher education institutions.

Few institutions offer programs or courses that emphasize the comparative or intercultural point of view or allow students to specialize in cultural studies and foreign languages. This leaves students from less internationally advanced institutions at the margin of internationalization.

Double or Joint Degree Programs

Double or joint degree programs are one of the strategies most adopted by higher education institutions, especially universities, in the past five years, and their number is growing. It is still too early to evaluate results, but there is evidence that most universities will eventually offer these programs.

The main problems facing Chilean students wishing to study abroad are lack of finances and lack of proficiency in a foreign language. For this reason, Chilean institutions should promote the double degree scheme with other universities in Latin America. This is a realistic and valid option, at least in the short term.

Despite the advantages of partnering with Latin American countries, the majority of double degree schemes are with European and North American institutions. Some of the universities involved include Pierre and Marie Curie University, Sup de Co Montpellier, the University of Avignon, the University of Montpellier, and the University of Paris 5 (France); the Fachhochschule (Germany); Turin Polytechnic (Italy); Santiago de Compostela University (Spain); and San Diego State, Tulane, and Yale Universities (United States).

Academic Programs and the Study of Languages

Chile has given insufficient priority to the study of foreign languages. Increasing access of the student population to new information technology is making the mastery of other languages a must.

Forty-five percent of traditional universities report that their faculty do not have spoken or written mastery of a foreign language. This problem slows the scope of international relations, making it impossible, for example, for unilingual professors to attend lectures that are not in Spanish, spend time at non-Spanish-speaking universities, or participate in a wide variety of international projects and networks.

To help combat the problem, 45 percent of the traditional universities surveyed report that mastery of a second language is mandatory before graduation. Eighty percent of traditional universities report that they have centers or standard programs for teaching languages. The Arturo Prat de Iquique University has implemented an institutional project for the obligatory learning of languages by all its students (Ramírez and others 2004).

The government has initiated a plan at the primary and secondary level to make bilingualism a core strategy in the next few years. Higher education institutions also need to include the study of languages as part of their mission statement in order to give their graduates a competitive advantage.

Centers for the Teaching of Spanish and Chilean Culture

Despite the importance of and growing demand for the study of Spanish in higher education institutions in Chile, especially the universities, few centers are formally designed to do so. Programs for the teaching of Spanish and local culture are generally integrated into student mobility offices and related to the language departments of each university, which are promoted by the agencies for the recruitment of foreign students that operate in Chile. Among universities that operate programs in Spanish are the Border University, the Pontifical Catholic University of Chile, the Pontifical Catholic University of Valparaiso, the University of Chile, and the University of Valparaiso, all of which offer a wide range of flexible programs for studying the Spanish language and Chilean culture.

Research and Development

Internationalization of scientific and technological research in Chile has achieved some level of success. During the 1960s and the early 1970s, an initiative to develop Chile's scientific and technological capacity helped create programs to upgrade scientists and develop research in universities. It also led to the creation of research institutes and corporations.

Chilean researchers have conducted research for the past 50 years. More than 6,000 Chileans are actively carrying out research, 2,000 of them leading researchers. The number of scientific publications from Chile rose from 754 in 1982 to 1,752 in 2000. Nevertheless, between 1981 and 2000, just 24,147 articles were published (0.16 percent of the total) and 163,953 were cited (0.09 percent). This is lower than Mexico, which accounted for 0.31 percent of all publication and 0.14 percent of all citations and Argentina, which accounted for 0.32 percent of all publications and 0.15 percent of all citations. Chile's contribution is similar to that of Portugal and a long way from countries such as the United States, the United Kingdom, and Japan.

Significant international experience has been acquired in recent years in university-enterprise relations. Sixty-five percent of Chile's scientific and technological capacity is still performed at its universities. The application and exploitation of the results of R&D is still not effective despite progress, especially at universities, in connecting the institutions with international partners through exchanges and information sharing, consultancy and technical assistance, advisory studies, hiring of staff, joint R&D, mixed R&D centers, technological consortia, internal or autonomous offices for the transfer of technology, incubation centers for businesses and derived businesses, and joint businesses.

In 2002 resources worth $25.2 million were provided to finance 818 traditional projects, 199 projects to promote international cooperation, 102 doctoral projects, 52 postdoctoral projects, and 19 projects in complementary lines of research.

In 1990 there was no fund to support research projects related to the productive sector. In 2002 nearly $17.5 million was provided for such projects, through the National Fund for the Development of Science and Technology (FONDEF). In international scientific cooperation, CONICYT financed 455 initiatives, strengthening cooperation programs with North America, Latin America, and the European Union (CONICYT 2005).

In 2002 the Program for Scientific Cooperation submitted for evaluation 138 projects with international counterparts, 33 of which were approved. Of these projects, 17 were approved by the Committee of Evaluation and Direction of the Scientific Cooperation (ECOS) and 16 by the National Center for Scientific Research (CNRS). Ten of these projects were developed with the Higher Council of Scientific Research in Spain, five were prepared with the German Academic Exchange Service, one with the

National Council for Research in Italy, and one with the Institute of International Scientific and Technological Cooperation in Portugal. All but one of these projects involved traditional universities.

International Extension Programs

In recent years there has been an increase in international extension activities in Chile. In addition to academics, business people and government authorities from other countries participate in these activities, an indication of growing interest in promoting international links between government and the business world. Despite the opportunities these activities offer, the events are presented rather randomly and promoted directly by the organizing institutions. There is no national policy to provide information about or promote these programs abroad in a systematic way.

International cultural extension is conducted largely by the traditional universities, which work with cooperation agencies, embassies, and private companies to attract international culture to Chile. To a lesser extent the higher education institutions have promoted Chilean culture abroad. Such international experiences are few and are rather sporadic actions that do not result from a specific strategy, however.

Technical Assistance and International Cooperation

Technical assistance and international cooperation have been among the most relevant actions in the process of internationalization. Technical assistance aims at strengthening institutions in Chile in managing and coordinating international cooperation, reinforcing and expanding the presence of Chile on the international scene, taking advantage of and managing cooperation scholarships, promoting Chile's technical capacity abroad through cooperation projects with peer institutions, and widening and developing actions with countries at lower levels of development.

International cooperation has been incorporated into government programs as an instrument for reintroducing Chile to the rest of the world, designing strategies to direct resources toward projects in priority areas, promoting the capacity of Chilean experts to the outside world, and tightening Chile's bonds with sources of multilateral and bilateral cooperation.

Universities have received the greatest share of the resources provided through technical cooperation. These resources have enabled them to improve their capabilities by bringing faculty up to date, promoting links between the university and commercial sectors, and promoting R&D. In recent years, higher education institutions have evaluated offers of cooperation with greater rigor in order to determine whether they really respond to and are consistent with their own policies and development plans.

Distance Education

Higher education institutions have made great progress in incorporating new information technology, enabling them to become a part of international networks and develop new forms of teaching, such as distance education. Chile's geography makes distance education particularly important.

Some universities have created virtual campuses, which enable students to have contact with experts from other parts of the world. The Pontifical Catholic University of Chile and the University of Chile have made particular progress in this area, as have the Pontifical Catholic University of Valparaiso, Technical University Federico Santa Maria, the University of Los Lagos, and the University of Playa Ancha, to cite just a few examples.

Almost 80 percent of the universities surveyed offer some type of distance education, and some offer undergraduate degrees by distance education. Distance education represents an important source of income for these institutions (Ramírez and others 2004).

Most distance learning programs in Chile are provided by international institutions. Spanish institutions, including the National University of Distance Education and the Open University of Catalonia, dominate, but other institutions, including the Technological Institute of Higher Studies of Monterrey (Mexico), the Open University of Israel, and the Teleuniversité of Quebec, also offer distance learning programs. Universities and international institutes, such as the European School of Management, the Institute for Executive Development, the University Institute of Graduate Studies, and the University of Miami, offer many on-line courses and programs. The quality of these programs has not been evaluated.

Transnational Campuses

The most important Chilean campus abroad is the Federico Santa Maria Technical University in Ecuador. Founded in 1996, the university has enrollment of 400 undergraduate and graduate students. Other examples of this type of institutional structure are the Corporation International University Exchange, Inc. of the University of Chile, in the United States; the representative office of the Technology Transfer Center of the Pontifical Catholic University of Valparaiso, in Spain; and the representative institutional office of the University of Valparaiso, in Argentina.

Commercialization of Educational Services Abroad

Chilean educational services, especially those offered by traditional universities, have a competitive edge in the region because of their prestige, tradition, and efficacy. A wide range of programs is provided. Notable are the diploma and MBA programs offered in Argentina, Bolivia, Ecuador, and Guatemala.

A survey of Chilean executives carried out by *América Economía* reveals that 59 percent of them would prefer to study in Chile, while 41 percent would prefer that the university form a partnerships with business schools in Chilean universities. In the *América Economía* ratings, of the top 34 MBA programs in Latin America, 9 Chilean programs are featured, with the Pontifical Catholic University of Chile and the Adolfo Ibañez University ranking among the 10 best programs.

An interesting initiative was begun in 1997 with PROCHILE through the Exportation of University Services Committee, in which more than 30 universities participate. This has been an innovative element in the selling of educational services abroad, providing a marketable service in four major areas: formal education, research, extension, and university management. The initiative has helped give Chilean universities a more visible presence abroad. The strategic objectives of this committee are to strengthen the image of Chile as an exporter of university services, help position Chilean universities as providers of services to government and the private sector abroad, and promote the university system in Chile. It fosters collaboration and exchange, quality, diversity and variety, and the provision of clear and reliable information. It has supported missions to prospective markets, commercial missions, market analyses, seminars in Chile and abroad, training, and participation in trade fairs in Bolivia, Costa Rica, Ecuador, El Salvador, Guatemala, Panama, Paraguay, Peru, and the United States.

Exporters of educational services have still not resolved issues of administration, accounting, and flexibility. Especially at public universities, the high degree of rigidity and bureaucracy makes it difficult to adopt innovative approaches to exporting services. The administrative apparatus of these institutions is not prepared for such challenges. These institutions are governed by laws and regulations that are more than three decades old. This reduces their competitiveness with institutions of other countries.

International Providers of Educational Services

Foreign educational services are operating in Chile in growing numbers, offering face to face, distance, and mixed mode programs. Forty-five percent of institutions surveyed regard this phenomenon as a positive development that will contribute in the long run to establishing international standards by a natural process of competition. But the majority of institutions regards these institutions as unregulated and possibly damaging to the assurance of quality (Ramírez and others 2004).

Some Chilean universities have formed strategic alliances with foreign partners to have their programs recognized abroad and vice versa. Foreign institutions are looking for partners in order to make their programs official in Chile and provide them with legal recognition. To date, only one foreign program—SEK University, which obtained official status in Chile in 1988—is able to award degrees that are officially recognized on their own.

In 2000 Sylvan Learning acquired 60 percent of the shares of the University of the Americas. In 2003 it invested $51 million in this venture and committed to invest another $17 million, transforming the university into the largest foreign university in Chile. It has a strong presence in the market for international education. Foreign languages and information technology are required elements in their programs.

Spanish and Brazilian institutions are the main providers of face to face programs. There were 193 programs of this kind in 2000, 60 percent of them in the humanities and social sciences and 24 percent in engineering and technology. Spain accounts for 20 percent of the programs, with 38 programs from 22 Spanish universities. Polytechnic Universities of Madrid has six programs, and the Universities of Valladolid and Lleida have five each. By the end of the 1990s, the University of Chile had 347 academic interinstitutional programs with foreign universities and the University of Santiago had 71, mostly with Spanish universities but also with universities in the United States. Chile also has connections with foreign institutions such as the Tec de Monterrey of Mexico and Latin Australia Education, which represents a number of Australian universities.

The use of distance education and the practice of sending foreign academics to teach in Chile for short periods are the most common delivery systems used in the national market. These strategies are strongly influenced by commercial interests.

Conclusion

The internationalization of higher education has made progress in Chile, especially in the past 10 years. Most of this progress has been the result of actions by institutions themselves rather than national or government policy. This progress notwithstanding, Chile lacks strategic policies and clear plans for the future. It lacks specialized staff, permanent forums to debate the issue, evaluation instruments, and funds for evaluation. The lack of conceptualization of internationalization and vague notions about what it is have caused widespread failure to make greater progress or consolidate the progress that has been made.

It will be a challenge to sustain educational internationalization in the future by maintaining certain fundamental principles and common interests among higher education institutions. The government should assume a more active role as a promoter of policies and mechanisms that promote internationalization, and it should provide greater coordination to promote internationalization. "The complexity that higher education systems have acquired, their enormous growth, the growing private sector with market orientation, its relevance for development programs, and its shortcomings in facing the challenges of competitiveness that comes from an emerging global information society and an economy based on knowledge, push governments to assume a more clearly defined attitude toward this scenario and seek new policies to enable its expansion and find a context that might stimulate change at institutional level" (Brunner and Bricall 2000, p. 40).

All stakeholders in Chile need to grasp the idea that strengthening national and regional networks is a key factor to competing in the global economy. Internationalized higher education institutions can make a significant contribution to the social and economic development of Chile.

Public sector institutions should have the same administrative machinery as the private sector if they are to strengthen their international presence by commercializing their services. The private and public sectors should increase their efforts to level the playing field between the two sectors. The tendency to sign too many bilateral and multilateral agreements should be replaced by a tendency to deepen international relations rather than simply increase the number of links between institutions.

Adequate regulations to guarantee this process are already in force in Chile. "The evaluation and accreditation of programs and institutions constitutes a typical mechanism to regulate higher education programs by distance mode, which in turn reinforces the influence of the government in this area and gradually produces a more competitive environment, while it stimulates competition for institutions' reputations" (Brunner and Bricall 2000, p. 48). Evaluation and accreditation will assure transnational quality by providing information that is clear and honest and helps protect consumers. This process requires the higher education system and its institutions to develop mechanisms to compile, analyze, and retrieve information needed to create a national data bank on the subject.

New means and mechanisms have to be established to export university services. The government should play a fundamental role in this process to ensure a more systematic presence and participation of Chile's universities abroad. Foreign students should be encouraged to come, and barriers to their entries should be reduced.

References

America Economia. 2005. www.americaeconomia.com.

Brunner, José Joaquín. 2000. "América Latina: políticas de educación superior durante los años 90: dinámicas y efectos." Discussion paper, Corporación de Promoción Universitaria, Santiago.

Brunner, José Joaquín, and Joseph M. Bricall. 2000. "Universidad siglo XXI: regulación y financiamiento." Columbus document on University Management, Paris.

Brunner, José Joaquín, and Gregory Jose Y Elacqua. 2003. "Human Capital in Chile." Adolfo Ibanez University, Chile.

Brunner, José Joaquín, and Jefrey M. Puryear. 1995. "Educación, equidad y competitividad económica en las Américas: un proyecto del diálogo interamericano." General Secretariat of the Organization of American States, Department of Educational Affairs, Washington DC.

CONICYT (National Commission for Scientific and Technological Research). 2005. www.conicyt.cl

Davis, Todd M. 2003. *Atlas of Student Mobility.* Institute of International Education, Washington DC.

García Guadilla, Carmen. 2002. "GATS, educación superior y América Latina: algunas ideas para contribuir a la discusión." Columbus, Paris.

González, Luis Eduardo. 2003. "Los nuevos proveedores externos de educación superior en Chile." Instituto de Educación Superior para América Latina y el Caribe, Caracas.

IMD (Institute for Management Development). 2002. *Informe de la competitividad mundial.* Davos, Switzerland.

MINEDUC (Ministerio de Educación). 2005. *Chile: compendio de educación superior.* Santiago.

Ramírez Sanchez, Carlos, Ximena Pedrosa, Marisa Nash, and Cecilia Letelier. 2004. "Survey of Chilean Tertiary Institutions and their Stakeholders on the International Dimension of Higher Education." Directorate of Links and International Cooperation, University of Valparaiso.

UNESCO. 2005. "UNITWIN Networks Established in 2003 at the University of Chile." portal.unesco.org.

6
Internationalization of Higher Education in Colombia

Isabel Cristina Jaramillo

The creation of an international culture for higher education in Colombia is a vital step into the world of knowledge and the advancement of science. In Colombia the internationalization of higher education is a recent phenomenon, although the international dimension has been a constant element since the universities were founded by Europeans some hundred years ago. Internationalization has evolved, especially since the beginning of the 1990s, when the country experienced a process of opening up to the world economy never before seen in its history.

The Colombian university has traditionally looked inward rather than explore new ways of working in an academic world without borders. Despite this, since the 1990s, the internationalization process has expressed itself in diverse ways. A series of poorly structured activities have taken place that have not been guided by a planning process or by government or institutional policies, as internationalization of higher education has received very little attention from the government. As a result, efforts have been inadequate and uneven. Colombia's higher education system has not been fully integrated into the global context, and its actors have not internationalized the nature of the process.

The scant literature on the internationalization of institutions and their programs, services, academic products, experiences, faculty and researchers, and administrative systems has made it difficult to propose guidelines for internationalizing in Colombia. No one knows for certain what has been done so far or where institutions are heading in the global context.

This chapter presents the national picture of internationalization. It identifies its evolution, characteristics, and the impact it has had on Colombian higher education institutions since the 1990s. The discussion is intended to serve as a starting point to strengthen the national vision of internationalization with adequate and sustainable policies, not only at the central level but at the regional and institutional levels as well.

The information presented is the result of a 2002 study conducted by the author. The study included surveys of and interviews with people in charge of international relations at 40 universities, both public and private, selected on the basis of their legal status, location, and number of academic programs and registered students. Ninety-five percent of the universities responded and provided specific information regarding advances in internationalization in Colombia. Neither technical nor technological institutions were included because of their limited international activity. All participating institutions are part of the Association of Colombian Universities (ASCUN) and the Colombian Network for the Internationalization of Higher Education (RCI).

The interviews—with national and international experts from governmental and multilateral organizations, as well as private associations for higher education—dealt with issues, perceptions, and opinions regarding state and governmental policies of internationalization as well as the importance of this process for Colombian higher education. The results allowed the author to interpret and compare the evolution of the internationalization of higher education across universities, identify the characteristics of the process, establish its limitations and advantages, and propose a series of measures that serve as a basis for alternatives for both the central government and higher education institutions. This analysis constitutes the beginning of a permanent reflection process that seeks a better understanding of the characteristics of internationalization in order to better understand the achievements of this new dimension for Colombian higher education, which ASCUN (2002) has identified as scant.

The Higher Education System in Colombia

The origin of Colombian universities goes back to the colonial period. Toward the end of the sixteenth century, the first universities were founded. The models for these first universities were largely copied from those in force in Spain.

Teaching was carried out predominantly in Latin. The introduction of Spanish in the classroom toward the end of the eighteen century, initiated at the University of Villa de Mompox, represented an important turning point. In 1826 the Napoleonic model for Colombian universities was adopted (Yarce, Lopera, and Pacheco 2002). Once again an external model influenced the development of higher education, suggesting the importance these models had on nascent nations.

Almost two centuries later, Colombia's higher education system has received recognition in Latin America. Since the 1990s the sector has experienced fundamental transformations in response to the need to increase access to education, diversify its system, and modernize it to meet the challenges imposed by today's world.

Figure 6.1 Colombian Higher Education Organizational Chart

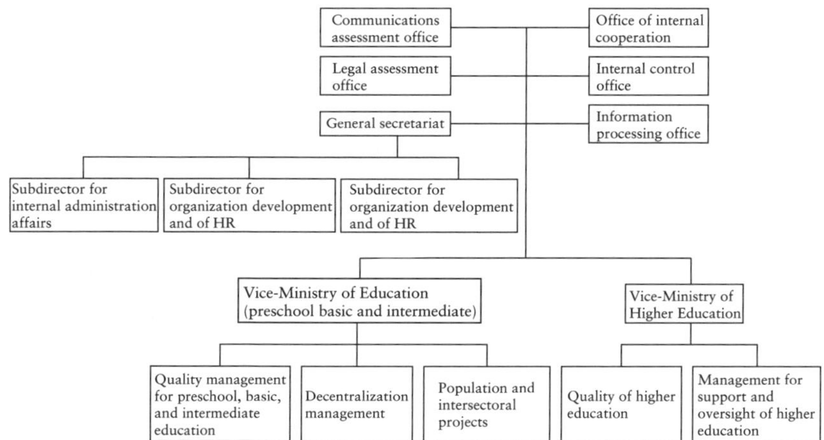

Source: Ministerio de Educación Nacional (2004).

Colombian higher education is defined by Law 30 of Higher Education of 1992. The law is complemented by regulatory decrees and constitutional court rulings, which have allowed higher education to be offered by both public and private institutions.

Various actors are involved in higher education (figure 6.1). The President of the Republic is the top administrative authority. He delegates to the Ministry of Education the design of policies, plans, programs, and projects. He also coordinates international cooperation, based on guidelines proposed by the Ministry of Foreign Affairs.

Under the umbrella of the Ministry of Education, other bodies have been active in the internationalization of the country's higher education. These include the Colombian Institute for the Development of Higher Education (ICFES), responsible for evaluating the Colombian educational system at all levels and the Colombian Institute for Educational Loans and Technical Studies Abroad (ICETEX).

The recently created Vice-Ministry of Higher Education features a Quality Assurance Office for Higher Education, responsible for proposing criteria for the internationalization of higher education, in close relation with the International Cooperation Office, which depends directly on the Ministry of Education. The Quality Assurance Office is also responsible for the certification of documents issued by Colombian higher education institutions in order to be accredited abroad and for certificating studies and degrees obtained abroad.

The growth of higher education institutions in Colombia, which has been led by private institutions, has been much more rapid than in Latin America as a whole. In 2003 there were 320 higher education institutions in Colombia (271 central institutions and 49 branches), the large majority created in the decade since the passage of Law 30 in 1992. They are located in all regions of the country, with a dense concentration in the capital and the four main cities of the country. Law 30 classifies higher education institutions into four categories: technical training institutions (51 institutions), technological institutions (63), university institutions (99), and universities (105), which can be state owned (32 percent) or private (68 percent). In 2003, 82 percent of all students enrolled in higher education attended universities or university institutions; the remaining 18 percent attended technical and technological institutions (Ministerio de Educación Nacional 2002).

Despite the 68 percent increase in enrollment during the 1990s, access to higher education remains low, with only 20 percent of the population 17–24 enrolled. This low rate of access is caused partly by the social conflict and economic recession, which has fostered a high drop-out rate and prevented students from the poorest families from gaining access to, much less remaining in, higher education institutions.

Entering students enroll mainly in programs in engineering, architecture, economics, administration and accounting, social sciences, and law and political science. There is very little demand for mathematics and natural science. Enrollment in all higher education institutions reached 981,458 undergraduate students and 63,245 graduate students in 2001, of which 6,775 are enrolled in master's degree programs and 350 in doctoral programs (SNIES 2002). The government has set the objective of increasing total enrollment by 400,000 students by 2006.

Colombia has 259 specialization programs, 323 master's degree programs, and 47 doctoral programs. Every year Colombia graduates 1 PhD per every 1 million residents—one of the lowest rates among the large countries of Latin America (SNIES 2002). The majority of these students are in the social sciences.

Most specializations are offered by private institutions, which enjoy autonomy but must nevertheless propose them to the state for evaluation and registration. Master's degrees and doctorates are offered exclusively by universities, which must be evaluated by the National Council for Quality Assurance of Higher Education (CONACES) before being approved.

Too few graduate programs are available in the exact sciences. These programs are needed to increase Colombia's research and innovative capacity, so that it can respond to the scientific and technological challenges of a globalized world (Yarce, Lopera, and Pacheco 2002).

Teaching is performed by 97,522 professors. Twenty-three percent of them work full time, 10.6 percent work part time, and 66.4 percent work on an hourly basis.

Public universities account for 77 percent of the country's research (Perilla Santamaría 2003). In 2002 there were 13,095 researchers and 2,118 research groups. At 0.6 percent of GDP, investment in science and technology in Colombia is very low, even compared with other countries in the region.

The Development of Internationalization in Higher Education

Three stages mark the internationalization of higher education in Colombia. As mentioned, the first began with the establishment of the Colombian university, which was modeled after universities in Europe (Henao and Bustos 2002).

A second stage began in the 1950s, when some internationalization processes were carried out, responding mostly to individual needs rather than clear institutional policies. These efforts had little impact and were responses to international cooperation offers from abroad that did not take the country's needs into account. The process during this time had very limited support from the state. The first higher education institutions that began to associate themselves with international technical cooperation processes were state institutions (Ochoa 1998).

Since the 1950s Colombian students have pursued graduate studies abroad. Many have done so through scholarships offered by the Colombian Institute for Educational Loans and Technical Studies Abroad.

During the 1960s, many Latin American leaders, especially from Panama and Venezuela, studied in Colombian universities, and many Colombian institutions received visits from professors and some students from other countries. The University of the Andes was founded on a U.S. model. Since its founding, it has engaged in exchanges with foreign universities, especially universities in the United States.

During the Cold War, education began to be seen as an instrument of development. Cooperation intensified during the 1960s and 1970s, and much of the aid given to Colombia by industrial countries was to improve human resources. This explains in part the flow of academic cooperation toward developing countries from the United States and the Soviet Union. During this period Europe did not offer many scholarships, and it was a less attractive destination for study abroad than it is today. The United States constituted at that time a natural destination for Colombians who wished to pursue graduate studies, which practically did not exist in Colombia. Both the United States and the Soviet Union offered full scholarships to

Colombian students at their most prestigious universities during this time. Internationalization was characterized as exogenous, unilateral, and with a strong emphasis on North-South cooperation, which helped increase the exodus from the South toward the North. Students who returned from abroad, constituted a seed for internationalization in the future. They were particularly important given the lack of large flows of immigrants into Colombia and its parochialism and conservative tendencies, both politically and socially.

The 1980s, known as the "lost decade," saw the diminishing of opportunities for international cooperation. Some of the reasons for this lack of opportunities included high tuition costs in the United States and Europe, the high cost of living in these regions given Colombia's devalued national currency, the new focus of internationalization policies of certain countries that affected the flow of nationals to traditional destinations, and the limited capacity of government organizations to continue supporting international programs that had been so fruitful to the country.

A new type of internationalization began in the 1990s. The most important driving forces came from the educational sector, mainly from outside Colombia. This process was directed from abroad, delivered in a context of change and globalization that facilitated and sometimes demanded the internationalization of higher education.

The 1990s displayed a rupture of traditional schemes and triggered the opening up of Colombian universities. The new global context, the Constitution of 1991, and Law 30 of Higher Education of 1992, which provided the legal framework for higher education, produced a new internationalization. In addition to the work done by the ICETEX, the country saw the emergence of other organizations, mixed or private in nature. The organizations included the Foundation for the Future of Colombia (COLFUTURO), the Caldas Network, and the Colombian Agency for International Cooperation, which, since the early 1990s has allowed a significant number of Colombians to study abroad through its lending program. Later the implementation of Ibero-American academic integration programs—through Intercampus, the declarations issued by UNESCO, and the integration processes carried out by the European Union—inspired the promotion of Colombian academic communities internationally and stimulated the creation of international relations offices in most higher education institutions in Colombia.

The opening up of the sector influenced its development in a number of significant ways. Some negative situations began to develop as well, with worrisome consequences. For example, the quality of some foreign university programs offered in Colombia was found to be questionable, reinforcing a very conservative attitude of some state bodies, which were reluctant to provide a better and a more flexible opening to the foreign education market.[1] Since the quality of foreign supply has not been systematically evaluated and its effects and consequences have not been weighed or measured, this aspect remains of concern.

In 1996 the Network for the Internationalization of Higher Education (RCI) was created as an initiative of the Association of Colombian Universities. This network includes most of the offices of international relations of higher education institutions in Colombia. Its main objective is to stimulate, promote, and strengthen the culture of international cooperation among Colombian higher education institutions.

A clear and organized initiative on the part of the central and regional governments would have given impetus to this process in a very significant way. However, leadership by the government has been and remains the missing element in some initiatives. Resources and a well-defined framework are needed to allow institutions to participate in international academic life. Recognition must be given to the efforts and support provided by the Colombian Institute for Educational Loans and Technical Studies Abroad; by the Colombian Institute for the Development of Science and Technology (COLCIENCIAS), in stimulating excellence in research to the point that it can compete in the international market of knowledge; and by ICFES, which, together with the national export promoting agency (Proexport), has tried to promote Colombian higher education abroad.

New decrees that modified the structure of both the Ministry of Education and ICFES established new arrangements for internationalization, assigning responsibility to the new Quality Assurance Division for Higher Education in the Ministry of Education. These decrees constitute the most systematic and coherent official initiative for the internationalization of higher education, although this is not sufficient to guarantee its sustainability.

The International Market for Services: New Actors, New Tendencies

At the beginning of the twenty-first century, the scenario has become unpredictable and uncertain, in a world in which knowledge has become a tradable commodity and the university a negotiator of this knowledge. Free trade agreements, such as the General Agreement on Trade in Services (GATS) and the Free Trade Area of the Americas, and negotiations

---

[1] Decree 916 of 2001, by which the requisites and procedures for master's degree and doctoral programs are unified, allows Colombian universities to make agreements with foreign educational institutions to get their academic support. Only Colombian institutions can issue degrees, however.

with other parts of Latin America and the world have turned out to be a difficult issue, given the impact that the introduction of these agreements has on higher education.

Low and uneven access to higher education, the limited number of faculty members holding graduate degrees, and scant state financial resources allocated to higher education make Colombia a favorable setting for international suppliers of educational services. Opportunities also appear for Colombian institutions abroad, given the wide range of academic programs they offer and the recognition they have in Latin America.

Countries such as Cuba, Spain, and Australia have competed for Colombian students. Recently, Colombia has seen an increase in the presence of foreign higher education institutions offering formal courses and programs as well as nonformal courses. Institutions such as the Atlantic International University of Honolulu, which offers distance learning services, and Oracle University, which provides continuing education in many Latin American countries, are now operating in Colombia (García Guadilla, Didou-Aupetit, and Marquis 2002). More and more foreign institutions are providing services through formal and nonformal programs as well as distance and virtual programs, for which there is no special regulation in Colombia.

New providers are competing with traditional institutions in Colombia. Unfortunately, this tendency has not been taken into consideration by the government. Its impact has therefore not been measured or quantified. Moreover, it has polarized those who defend the traditional universities as the sole centers of knowledge and those who see new providers as an opportunity for the educational sector.

Colombia is regarded as an attractive market by providers of educational services. Only 3 percent of students registered in higher education come from the poorest 20 percent of the population (quintile one), 6 percent from quintile two, and 12 from quintile three, indicating that only 21 percent of students registered in higher education come from the lowest socioeconomic levels. In contrast, 27 percent of students come from quintile four and 52 percent from quintile five (richest). Colombia also has few master's and doctorate programs, which limits its potential in terms of research and development. Given the limited number of PhD programs, future staffing needs are unlikely to be filled with faculty holding PhDs. The system could face a crisis in terms of meeting its staffing needs with adequately qualified academics, which in turn may reduce the quality of teaching and research (World Bank 2003).

Colombian institutions have begun to transnationalize their programs and services, based on interinstitutional agreements, particularly with companies that require tailored academic programs. Colombia has a wide supply of programs available for export. However, the experience of Colombian higher education institutions is varied, and trade in academic services is still not fully recognized as a potential line of business (I. Jaramillo 2003).

The Legal Framework

The dawn of the 1990s brought a legal reordering without precedent in Colombia. This was achieved by the National Constitution of 1991 and the promulgation of Law 30, which addresses and governs the academic and administrative life of the educational sector. Together the Constitution, Law 30, and the national development plans promulgate a new planning system in Colombia that supports and offers a legal framework under which the recent internationalization of higher education has evolved.

The National Constitution of 1991

The National Constitution of 1991 was fundamental to internationalization of Colombian higher education. Through this reform, Colombia's educational legislation has been nourished by the development of the rights, principles, and values incorporated into this political Magna Carta. Under the Constitution, the government is responsible for "promoting the internationalization of political, economic, social and ecological relations based on equity, reciprocity and national interest." The values, principles, and rights established in the Constitution have been the basis for ensuring profound changes in education.

Law 30 for Higher Education of 1992

Since there was a need for a special regime for public universities after the Constitution of 1991, the first step was to issue Law 30 for Higher Education in 1992, through which the public service of higher education was organized. Law 30 introduces internationalization as one of the sector's principal challenges. Under the law, higher education institutions are responsible for stimulating training, strengthening academic communities, and coordinating with other bodies at an international level. The law assigns to ICFES the promotion of training, the strengthening of international academic communities, and the recognition of prior experience and degree equivalencies for studies undertaken abroad.

The National Accreditation System was created as a voluntary process for institutions. It is carried out by the National Accreditation Council, which issues Guidelines for Accreditation of Programs and Institutions. It stimulates knowledge by applying international standards, assessed by national and international peers and establishing networks for academic exchange of information, discussion groups, internationally indexed publications, and dialogue with other international entities, so that the academic community may transcend national boundaries. As of June 2004, it had accredited 234 programs from 105 public and private institutions. By January 2004 only four universities, three private and one public, had received institutional accreditation from the Ministry of National Education, the maximum recognition for quality.

Law 30 created other governmental bodies that support the incorporation of Colombian universities into the international arena, such as the International Cooperation Office at the Ministry of Education, through which it plans to organize the international relations system.

National Development Plans

Since the adoption of the Constitution of 1991, National Development Plans have been prepared for four-year periods. In a participative way, these plans strengthen national actions with the central government, territorial bodies, and the private sector (Saavedra and others 2001).

Official policies have been expressed in these development plans. These include the Pacific Revolution (1990), the Social Leap (1994), the Change to Construct Peace (1998), and the democratic manifesto elaborated and presented by President Alvaro Uribe Velez known as the Education Revolution. These plans have not been translated into coordinated actions, however. Government policies expressed by administrative acts or mechanisms of financial support are insufficient to provide the incentives needed to stimulate adequate internationalization of Colombian higher education, and these policies have not led to a coherent coordinated plan.

Main Actors and Actions

The Colombian Education system is characterized by a large number of government agencies with overlapping functions. It is of critical importance that the agencies cooperate and coordinate their work.

National Governmental Organizations

In lieu of a framework of coherent public policies, a series of activities from the central state has emerged. State organizations involved include ICETEX, ICFES, COLCIENCIAS, and, more recently, the Ministry of Trade, Industry and Tourism and its export promoting agency, Proexport.

COLOMBIAN INSTITUTE FOR EDUCATIONAL LOANS AND TECHNICAL
STUDIES ABROAD
The Colombian Institute for Educational Loans and Technical Studies Abroad (ICETEX) is the national body in charge of administering scholar-

ships for international cooperation. Since 1952 it has enabled access to the best educational programs in the world in order to contribute to Colombia's economic and social development. Such cooperation is the result of agreements between Colombia and several foreign governments and multilateral organizations. International scholarships are a special type of financial support intended to cover, partly or fully, educational expenses abroad.

ICETEX also administers scholarships provided by the Organization of American States (OAS). It supports student loans from the Rowe Fund of the OAS, created specifically for Colombians pursuing undergraduate or graduate studies at prestigious universities in the United States.

Although loans for studying abroad have been increasing since 1995, they are scarce in relation to demand. The number of students that have benefited grew 4.6 percent between 2000 and 2003. Demand nevertheless exceeds supply. Spain and the United States are the destinations most in demand (table 6.1). In 2000 scholarships allowed 551 students to study abroad, the majority of them to pursue master's programs in administration and health. By 2003 about 22,000 Colombian professionals had been trained at excellent universities abroad.

Table 6.1 Colombian Students Studying Abroad with Scholarships from ICETEX, by Destination, 2000

Destination	Number of students	Percentage of total
Latin America	110	20.6
Mexico	28	5.2
Brazil	16	3.0
Argentina	14	2.6
Cuba	13	2.4
Costa Rica	12	2.3
Chile	10	1.9
Venezuela	9	1.7
Other countries in Latin America	8	1.5
United States and Canada	112	21.0
United States	92	17.2
Canada	20	3.8
Europe	312	58.4
Spain	220	41.2
France	34	6.3
United Kingdom	24	4.5
Netherlands	10	1.9
Other countries in Europe	24	4.5
Total	534	100.0

Source: ICETEX 2001.

ICETEX has awarded scholarships to about 4,800 foreigners who have come to Colombia to pursue graduate studies, carry out research, and pursue continuing education cofinanced by OAS and the education centers. ICETEX also supports higher education institutions by subsidizing the presence of international professors and language assistants from France, Jamaica, and the United Kingdom.

COLOMBIAN INSTITUTE FOR THE DEVELOPMENT OF HIGHER EDUCATION
Law 30 for Higher Education of 1992 gives ICFES responsibility for developing the internationalization of higher education in Colombia. Noteworthy is its Educational Diplomacy Program, created in 1999, supported by Proexport, the lead agency for the promotion of nontraditional exports. This program stimulated internationalization of high-quality programs. Its main objective was to position Colombian higher education within the national and international diplomatic and educational community. It intended to benefit academic exchange that might improve the quality of education, expand Colombia's international relations, and generate new sources of income through academic cooperation. Some of the most important development strategies for the Educational Diplomacy Program were training, participation in international events and fairs, academic missions and visits to and from Colombia, a reliable information system, promotional activities, research, dissemination of information about Colombian higher education institutions and their internationalization processes, and expansion of the Spanish language internationally. Through this program, various missions were carried out in Central America, the Caribbean, and the Andean region, with the objective of assessing the potential of these geographic areas for the services and programs offered by the institutions. Opportunities for graduate programs, continuing education programs, and Spanish language programs were identified. Unfortunately, despite its important contributions, this program was shelved, after the government modified the structure of ICFES in 2003 and transformed it into the public establishment responsible for the evaluation of the Colombian educational system as a whole.

COLOMBIAN INSTITUTE FOR THE DEVELOPMENT OF SCIENCE AND TECHNOLOGY
The Colombian Institute for the Development of Science and Technology (COLCIENCIAS) is the leading organization for fostering, promoting, and developing activities related to science and technology in Colombia. It is the only governmental organization that works with the academic, industrial, and official sectors to promote technological and scientific development. One of its units, the Internationalization Science Division, which is part of the Sub-Direction of Strategic Programs, is responsible for improving human capital, exchange, mobility, association with research networks, and project development among national and international scientific communities.

COLCIENCIAS provides scholarships to Colombian students wishing to pursue their master's or doctorate degrees abroad, although the lack of budget, as a result of reduced funding by the government for these programs, has impeded the program's continuity and sustainability. During 1997, the program provided funding for 151 doctoral students and 42 master's degree students. These scholarships were financed by part of a loan offered by the Inter-American Development Bank. This number has now dropped substantially: in 2000 only six students received support for doctoral and two for master's programs abroad (World Bank 2003).

COLCIENCIAS participates in several Latin American networks. It has established agreements with national science and technology councils in Mexico, Peru, and Venezuela; with the National Science Foundation of the United States; with international development banks, such as the World Bank and Inter-American Development Bank; and with international organizations and universities in Latin America, Europe, and Asia.

MINISTRY OF TRADE, INDUSTRY AND TOURISM
The Ministry of Trade, Industry and Tourism recently emerged as a new actor in the internationalization of higher education, committing itself to the strengthening of a new culture for exports by the country's academic bodies and the productive sector. In 2001 it created the International Business Program in order to "strengthen the integral training of higher education students in professional programs, as well as technical and technological programs, other than foreign trade, international business or related areas, in order to internationalize and direct their education toward a more oriented entrepreneurial exporting vision." The program was created to internationalize higher education programs, create a more global vision among higher education institutions, and stimulate team work with a long-term strategic vision.

By 2003 the program had been developed in 97 institutions, and about 6,000 students had benefited from it. The Ministry has developed seminars for professors in Colombia's main cities in which 145 instructors from 33 cities and 23 departments of Colombia have participated.

With the support of Proexport, the Ministry of Trade, Industry and Tourism has been strengthening the availability of Spanish language studies to the Anglo-Saxon countries of the Caribbean region. This two-way alliance also favors the development of English as a second language in the seven universities that participate in this project, three of which are public universities.[2]

---

[2] The participating universities are the Antioquia University, the Industrial University of Santander, La Sabana University, the National University of Colombia, the Northern University, and the Pontificia Javeriana University (Bogotá and Cali).

MINISTRY OF FOREIGN AFFAIRS
Colombian foreign policy aims to maintain national interests and effect changes in the international system that could take the nation to a higher level of interdependence. The President of the Republic determines the course of policy. The Ministry of Foreign Affairs develops and proposes methods that allow a fair internationalization of public, economic, social, and ecological relations as well as integration with other nations, especially countries in Latin America, that is not limited to trade. The Ministry of Foreign Affairs develops a policy that facilitates the entry and stay of foreigners in Colombia. With the collaboration of the Colombian Network for the Internationalization of Higher Education, the visa system was reformed to support academic activity. The Ministry of Foreign Affairs also seeks to stimulate the active involvement of Colombian communities abroad through ColombiaNosUne (Colombia Unites Us), which represents an enormous potential for the social development of the country (Ministry of Foreign Affairs 2004).

MINISTRY OF NATIONAL EDUCATION
ICFES's responsibilities for internationalization have recently been transferred to the Ministry of Education. The ministry has assigned this responsibility to the new Higher Education Quality Management Division, in collaboration with the International Cooperation Office, according to a decree issued in August 2003.

National Nongovernmental Associations, Foundations, and Networks

Government agencies cooperate with a large number of national nongovernmental associations, foundations, and networks.

ASSOCIATION OF COLOMBIAN UNIVERSITIES
The Association of Colombian Universities (ASCUN), founded in 1957, is a private, nongovernment association that includes 74 public and private universities. Its main objective is to serve as a meeting point and a space for permanent reflection on the state and future of higher education, to establish ties between universities and different government organizations nationwide, and to maintain interinstitutional and international relations of cooperation.

The association has collaborated with and promoted higher education internationalization through the implementation of various strategies, since "Colombian universities cannot or should not continue developing themselves in an isolated manner in relation to world events" (ASCUN 2002, p. 24). In its *Agenda of Policies and Strategies for Higher Education in Colombia 2002–2006: From Exclusion to Equity*, the scant presence and articulation of internationalization are presented as critical challenges. The association has initiated various actions intended to increase basic understanding of internationalization by executing programs that allow universities and the government to incorporate internationalization into institutions' main functions, in the hope of converting the international dimension into a strategic element that raises the quality, relevance, and competitiveness of education.

The association promotes the establishment of agreements between organizations such as the Association for Higher Education Institutions and Universities in Mexico, the German Universities Presidents' Conference, the Higher Education National Council in Ecuador, the Spanish Universities Presidents' Conference, the Association of Canadian Colleges and Universities, and the Venezuelan University Presidents' Association. It also works with international organizations and associations, such as IESALC/UNESCO, the Latin American Graduate University Association, and the Quebec University Presidents Conference, which promotes the exchange of undergraduate students. It is part of the Ibero-American University Council, which brings together university associations and the Ibero-American Presidents' councils in order to strengthen the cooperation between the associated universities and others from different parts of the world. It maintains close ties with international organizations, such as the American Council for Education, the Inter-American University Organization, the International Association of Universities, and the Latin American University Union, as well as with the Inter-American Development Bank and the World Bank. Since 1996 it has supported and coordinated the Colombian Network for the Internationalization of Higher Education, which brings together the international relations offices of Colombia's higher education institutions for the purpose of developing interinstitutional work in order to strengthen international culture in the institutions.

COLFUTURO

The Foundation for the Future of Colombia (COLFUTURO) was founded in 1991 as a nonprofit organization. It is a joint initiative by the private and public sectors and some higher education institutions to offer financial aid to students who wish to pursue graduate degrees abroad or to improve their English.

Between 1992 and 2002, COLFUTURO financed 873 students, 81 percent for master's programs, 13 percent for doctorate programs, and 6 percent for specializations (table 6.2). Most of the requests were related

Table 6.2 Degree Programs Supported by COLFUTURO, 1992–2003

Year	Master's	Doctorate	Specialization	Total
1992	31	8	7	46
1993	37	9	6	52
1994	32	15	4	51
1995	34	13	1	48
1996	68	6	10	84
1997	141	20	8	169
1998	120	14	3	137
1999	88	11	4	103
2000	63	8	4	75
2001	89	18	2	109
2002	115	24	2	141
2003	143	27	0	170
Total	961	173	51	1,185
Percent of total	81	15	4	100

Source: COLFUTURO internal document.

to administration, followed by engineering, law, and political science (table 6.3).

Between 1992 and 2003, the countries most in demand for studies abroad were the United States and the United Kingdom, followed by Spain, France, Canada, and the Netherlands. Almost 50 percent of these scholarships were granted to students from Bogota.

Table 6.3 Distribution of Educational Loans Granted by COLFUTURO, by Field, 2003

Field	Requests	Beneficiaries
Administration	1,035	325
Engineering	580	181
Law and political science	351	153
Social sciences	443	115
Health sciences	609	86
Economy	225	64
Architecture	278	74
Agriculture	218	50
Arts	180	58
Basic sciences	190	50
Education	76	29
Total	4,185	1,185
Percent of total	100	28

Source: COLFUTURO internal document.

BOGOTÁ CHAMBER OF COMMERCE
The Bogotá Chamber of Commerce has combined business principles
with academic motivation in an innovative project called Bogotá University
Alliance. Eleven prestigious institutions in the capital belong to the alliance,
which seeks to facilitate the processes of internationalization, cooperation,
and international and interinstitutional relations to increase the competitiveness of the Bogotá area. Other organizations supporting this program
are the Ministry of National Education; the Ministry of Trade, Industry and
Tourism; the municipality of Bogotá; and the Association of Colombian
Universities.

UNIVERSIA.NET
Founded in 2000 by the Grupo Santander Central Hispano of Spain, Uni-
versia.net is the largest university portal in the world. Its main office is in
Spain, with branches in Portugal and eight countries in Latin America. The
portal provides information, services, and teaching of academic, scientific,
and technological content at associated universities. Universia.net/Colom-
bia has created an international network of 51 public and private higher
education institutions. The participating universities have produced 600
articles, 395 other publications, and 3,810 programs and courses, which
are complemented with on-line libraries and electronic data bases.

COLOMBIAN NETWORK FOR THE INTERNATIONALIZATION OF HIGHER EDUCATION
In 1994 the need to interrelate and complement, not substitute for, the
efforts carried out by higher education institutions in relation to internationalization stimulated the creation of the Colombian Network for
the Internationalization of Higher Education (RCI) (Revelo 1994). The
Association of Colombian Universities has coordinated and strengthened
the actions of RCI since its foundation in 1996. With more than 100 member institutions from all regions of the country, RCI is the only organization that includes most of the offices of international relations of higher
education institutions, in order to stimulate, promote, and strengthen the
culture of international cooperation. It also serves as the focal point for cooperation with other international networks worldwide (Baeyens, Corpas,
and Jaramillo 1998).

Five main lines of work characterize this network: training in international cooperation, information and dissemination of international opportunities, policies, quality of internationalization, and integration. Some of
its projects have been published and have become the point of reference
in Colombia for information about student opportunities abroad, scholarships, credits, and so forth. Since its creation, RCI has maintained a continuing education program in different parts of the country through
workshops, meetings, congresses, and seminars to assist institutions in their

internationalization efforts. It works with public and private national and international organizations in promoting and exporting teaching services. Academic mobility has been developed through the Academic, Technical and Scientific Exchange Program, through which RCI has organized exchanges with 27 regional universities.

MUTIS UNIVERSITY NETWORK

The Mutis University Network is made up of higher education institutions and other bodies that seek to strengthen interinstitutional and international relations. This network dates back to the 1990s, when it was begun by the Technological Institute of Monterrey. It is a private university network that promotes the exchange of students, faculty, and researchers based on its excellent relations and cooperation with national and international institutions. The basic strategy of its programs is the intensive use of information and communication technologies.

CALDAS NETWORK

COLCIENCIAS created and coordinates the Caldas Network, established in 1992 as a communication instrument for the exchange of scientific and technological knowledge among Colombian researchers working abroad and the national scientific community. The Caldas Network is included in the science internationalization policies defined by the National Science and Technological System. The network's objectives are to facilitate the establishment of a virtual community of knowledge, led by Colombian scientists and researchers both inside and outside the country and to launch a program for scientific and technological knowledge in Colombia. The importance and impact of its work in the development of science and technology has been highly recognized.

SCIENTI NETWORK

Aware of the need to improve the country's productivity and competitiveness, COLCIENCIAS manages the International Network of Information and Knowledge Sources for Science, Technology and Innovation Management (Scienti Network). This network consists of a data base of all activities developed by those carrying out technological research, innovation, and development in Latin America and the Caribbean. The network was developed in order to establish a presence in the world and to raise national technological and scientific capacity to the international level. It also promotes the Latin American Program for Advanced Scientific Exchange. Its strategy is to strengthen cooperation among Latin American and Caribbean countries based on regional capacity to upgrade professional staff to doctoral and postdoctoral levels. This program seeks to promote scientific capacity in the region in all areas of knowledge, stimulate work on research issues of high regional relevance, and strengthen research groups and regional doctoral programs (COLCIENCIAS 2004).

International Governmental Organizations and Agencies

UNESCO, the World Bank, the Inter-American Development Bank, and the Organization for Economic Cooperation and Development (OECD) have committed themselves to promoting reforms in Colombia that will improve the country's capacity in human and international terms (I. Jaramillo 2003). UNESCO; IESALC/UNESCO, as an autonomous body attached to UNESCO; and other bodies recognized by UNESCO, such as the International Association of Universities and the International Organization for Migration, have had a significant impact on strengthening international university cooperation. Equally important is the philanthropic work carried out by private foundations, such as the Ford and Rockefeller Foundations, which have been essential in developing international scientific research in Colombia.

Transformation processes proposed by some financial organizations, such as the Inter-American Development Bank and the World Bank, have created conditions that enable the sector to respond in a more appropriate way to the country's needs and to the challenges they must overcome in the globalization era. The assessment of the state of higher education carried out by the World Bank at the instigation of the government included several studies and made recommendations on how the funding, governance, structure, and scope of higher education could be reformed to better meet the country's needs and the challenges it will face in a global market economy (World Bank 2003). After analyzing the Colombian situation, the World Bank approved a $200 million loan to improve the quality and equity of higher education in Colombia.

At the regional and subregional levels, the Organization of Ibero-American States for Education, Science and Culture (OEI) is a government organization that supports mobility programs in education, science, technology, and culture across Latin American countries and the Iberian Peninsula. The Andres Bello Treaty promotes integration in the region and carries out efforts to benefit education, science, and technology. Its attempt to implement a more harmonious higher education system in the Ibero-American region has been largely unfruitful and has not facilitated mobility among the institutions that form part of the treaty.

Mobility programs have received financial support from the government and from higher education institutions themselves (Jaramillo, García, and Blom 2003), but most of the support has come through the bilateral cooperation programs that support international scholarships to Colombian professionals. Traditionally, this support has been provided by granting scholarships that cover all or part of the cost of training abroad. This cooperation has allowed the exchange of experiences and the mobility of experts in issues of common interest. The educational sector participates in meetings held by the International Cooperation Office of the Ministry of Education, where agreements and matters related to the sector are addressed.

SCHOLARSHIP PROGRAMS

On behalf of the countries in the European Union, the European Commission negotiates cooperation agreements with developing countries. Two programs proposed by the Commission, the High-Level Scholarships for Latin America (AlßAN) program and the Latin America Academic Training (ALFA) program, have become the main contributors to Colombia's human and academic development.

During the first call for applications, Colombia received 37 of the 251 scholarships granted, the second-highest number in the region. About 43 percent of Colombian students went to Spain, while another 5 percent went to the United Kingdom. AlßAN scholars also studied in Austria, France, Germany, the Netherlands, and Portugal. Nine scholarships granted were in engineering and technology and six in the natural sciences. During the second call for AlßAN scholarship applications (2004–05), 113 Colombians were among the 779 students funded. Most went to Spain, the United Kingdom, France, and Germany.

ALFA is a decentralized regional cooperation program between the European Union and Latin America. Colombia is participating in the program's second stage, with 24 approved projects and one coordinated project. Of the five Andean Community countries, Colombia has the highest level of participation in ALFA.

INTERNATIONAL COOPERATION AGENCIES

The Spanish Agency for International Cooperation (AECI) promotes university exchange programs aimed at building human capacity in order to strengthen university research as well as graduate and doctoral training. In Colombia it has contributed to the development of educational projects for Colombian students and professors who wish to study at Spanish universities. Its scholarships and Inter-University Cooperation (PCI) program have become efficient instruments for promoting exchange of university students and professors.

Other international agencies are the German Service of Academic Exchange (DAAD); the Japanese International Cooperation Agency (JICA), whose scholarship program has allowed more than 1,600 Colombians to study in Japan; and the British Council, established in Colombia in 1940, which administers a variety of scholarships on behalf of British and Colombian institutions.

BILATERAL RELATIONS

Colombia has signed bilateral agreements with various Latin American countries; Canada and the United Status; Belgium, France, Greece, Italy, Spain, the United Kingdom; and China, Egypt, Israel, and Japan. Some efforts have also been financed by embassies in Colombia, many of which support the academic community through agreements established with national bodies, both governmental and private.

Since 1996 the French Embassy, and its International Cooperation Program for Researchers through the Ecos Nord program, has promoted high-level scientific exchanges between French and Colombian research centers. It has had several calls for proposals, in which more than 50 projects have been financed. More than 100 laboratories and researchers participated in these projects.

Another bilateral cooperation program between France and Colombia is the Fund for Studies in France, created in 1998, in which 25 universities in Colombia participate. This fund provides scholarship programs in order to develop exchanges between the two countries. One hundred ninety-six Colombian students have received one-year scholarships to study in France. Forty students were selected for 2003–04.

Scholarship programs offered by the Alliance Française Institutes in Colombia support improvement of the teaching of French in Colombia and of Spanish in France. This program, administered by ICETEX, also aims to increase knowledge of the cultural, linguistic, and academic aspects of the two countries. In the 2003–04 call for applications, 80 Colombians and 12 French nationals were selected.

Relations between Colombia and Mexico have traditionally been cordial. Recently, they have taken on a new dynamism. Through the Foreign Relations Ministry, Mexico offers scholarships to Colombian citizens to pursue graduate studies in Mexico. In June 1979 both governments signed the Basic Agreement of Technical and Scientific Cooperation, which has been in force since March 6, 1981. These and other programs have played an important leadership function over the years, but in recent years collaboration has been reoriented to other areas of greater impact.

ASSOCIATIONS AND NETWORKS

Colombian universities actively participate in international organizations. This interaction allows the strengthening of university networks that provide communication mechanisms within institutions. The following are notable examples:

- COLUMBUS's was established for the purpose of strengthening interinstitutional collaboration between Latin America and Europe. Ten major Colombian universities are members. COLUMBUS's actions center on six priority areas: quality, reforms in higher education, managerial training, information and communication technology, internationalization, and regional development. COLUMBUS is currently collaborating with the National Accreditation Council in Colombia in identifying academic reviewers for institutional and program evaluation and accreditation of COLUMBUS member universities.

- The Graduate Latin American University Association is an international NGO recognized by UNESCO. It is dedicated to developing graduate and doctorate programs in Latin America. Regional coordination for the Andean countries is the responsibility of the Universidad del Valle in Colombia.
- The Inter-American Organization for Higher Education promotes cooperation among universities in its 34 member countries. Colombia is the Counselor of the Andean Region, which jointly adopts and puts into practice the yearly activity program. Twenty-two institutions in Colombia are members, including the Association of Colombian Universities.

Other regional associations and networks in Colombia also support and stimulate internationalization of higher education and regional integration, including the following:

- the Latin American University Union, which has 17 affiliated institutions participating actively in all programs.
- the Inter-University Development Center, a network of prestigious Latin American and European universities that promotes university integration with national development. Its Board of Presidents is currently directed by a Colombian rector.
- the Association for the Integration of Latin American and Caribbean Universities, with 25 affiliated institutions.
- the Latin American Network for University Cooperation, created in 1997, an interuniversity collaboration project of private universities in the region that encourages maximum efficiency in cooperation involving human and technical resources.

LASPAU

Academic and Professional Programs for the Americas (LASPAU) was created in 1964, in response to an initiative by the Colombian government through which outstanding high school students could study in the United States. Today LASPAU, together with COLCIENCIAS, promotes research, advanced scientific training, and dissemination of technological information. The Human Resource Training Program for Strengthening the Scientific Community, financed by the Inter-American Development Bank, allowed 400 Colombians to pursue graduate studies abroad in engineering, the social sciences, and the natural sciences. LASPAU monitored, assessed, and supported 100 students who studied in the United States and 300 in other parts of the world.

INTERNATIONAL PROGRAMS FOR ACADEMIC EXCHANGE
The International Association for the Exchange of Students for Technical Experience enables undergraduates to study and conduct research in more than 80 countries. Since 1996, 226 Colombian students have participated in this program, and Colombian institutions and organizations have received 108 international students. Thirty-two Colombians began studies abroad in 2003, and 30 foreign students began their studies in Colombia. AIESEC (an international work exchange organization dedicated to increasing cultural understanding) has been serving Colombian students since 1948. More than 120 students a year pursue an international experience in one of the 85 countries in the network.

INTER-UNIVERSITY COOPERATION PROGRAM
The Inter-University Cooperation Program (PCI), established in 1994 and formally known as Intercampus, has been one of the initiatives with greatest impact in the development of internationalization. Funded by the Spanish Agency for International Cooperation (AECI) and Spanish and Latin American universities, the program has mobilized university students and professors in the Ibero-American region, and it has yielded fruitful academic cooperation programs. Between 1994 and 1999, Colombia received 1,023 Spanish students, making it the second most visited destination in Latin America. During this period 717 Colombians went to Spain to study. The high degree of reciprocity sustains the program and has guaranteed its continuity. AECI also supports graduate studies in Spain, through scholarships offered by the Carolina Foundation and by the Mae and Mutis programs.

OTHER SCHOLARSHIP PROGRAMS
Colombian institutions actively participate in other scholarship programs, such as the Alexander Von Humboldt Foundation in Germany and networks that have been established over the past decade, such as the Academic Program for Student Mobility of the Latin American University Union, the Exchange and Academic Mobility Program of the OEI, and the Student Mobility Program of the Inter-University Development Center. Some of these programs are still small and relatively new. Various factors, such as legislation, curricular rigidity, lack of financial aid, and immigration restrictions, threaten their sustainability and limit their performance. These networks have gained recognition in Colombia and are one of the most effective ways of working collectively.

Since 1957 the Fulbright Commission of the United States has provided 2,800 Colombians with full or partial scholarships for graduate studies in the United States. In addition, about 800 American citizens have come to Colombia as visiting professors or students. Before the 1990s most demands for fellowships were in the social sciences and humanities. Since the 1990s engineering and environmental sciences have been in greater demand, as have finance, political science, and basic sciences.

Organizational and Planning Strategies

Institutions committed to strengthening the internationalization process have adopted various organizational and planning strategies.

Organizational Strategies

Organizational strategies involve the management of, leadership of, and institutional commitment to internationalization; the implementation of programs; the establishment of support systems; and the building of human capacity.

Twenty-two public and private institutions in Colombia have developed internationalization processes (42 percent of public universities and 50 percent of private universities). Many of these institutions conduct their internationalization activities in an ad hoc and marginal way rather than as part of the university's core functions. Few have international programs, and the number of participating students is small. Although 37 percent say they have institutional policies for internationalization, many activities are the result of unplanned activities that, in the end, do not have an impact on the main functions and, consequently, on the quality of higher education. Nevertheless, 58 percent of the institutions claim that they are developing internationalization processes through activities, programs, and plans that have an impact on the academic, social, and cultural life of the university as a whole.

Almost 89 percent of the institutions' internationalization efforts are led by the rector. In other institutions, the process is led by the research vice-rector's office or the general secretariat. At all institutions the process has the support of the schools, the deans, and the academic vice-rector's office, demonstrating commitment by senior leaders.

About two-thirds of the universities internationalize in order to achieve high academic standards in teaching and research. About two-thirds internationalize in order to generate revenues. Seventy-one percent do not justify their internationalization on political grounds.

Half of the institutions explicitly incorporate the international dimension into their mission, vision, and institutional policies, thereby preventing the activities from being carried out in an arbitrary way, which would not strengthen the institution's academic quality.

About half of the universities think the government has not oriented the internationalization process in terms of financing, regulations, norms, and so forth. The guidance and resources provided have not been sufficient, given the need for clear policies to help Colombia overcome the isolation of its higher education institutions.

Eighty-four percent of the institutions have formally established offices for international relations, most of which were created more than seven years ago. Most of the offices are very small: 68 percent have one or two people, 27 percent employ three to five people, and only 5 percent have more than six people including the person in charge of the office. Most of the offices are made up of a director and an assistant.

Fifty-five percent of the universities call the office the international relations office, while 23 percent call it the interinstitutional and international relations office; the rest call it the international relations department or center. None of these offices is at the level of a vice-rectorship. Some offices combine their international activities with other responsibilities, creating ambiguity about their functions.

The main services offered by these units are assessing and supporting the university academic community, keeping in contact with the international community, disseminating information about and promoting the institution's international activities and achievements, coordinating the implementation of international policies, establishing and following up on agreements, and organizing services for academics and foreign students. Very few are responsible for managing, evaluating, and following up the process itself.

Twenty-one percent of the institutions are assigned a specific budget, determined by the institution. Half do not enjoy financial autonomy and operate under very centralized structures. The annual budget allocation is generally $2,000–$4,000. Thirteen percent receive a yearly budget of $4,000–$8,000. Fifteen percent fall into the $8,000–$20,000 range, and 18 percent have budgets of more than $20,000 a year (Jaramillo 2003). Those that receive resources from outside the institution's regular budget usually get them from the government or from selling services; only a small number receive resources from international agencies and foundations or from the private sector.

Internationalization requires working together. The support that an advisory committee may offer to the institution guarantees the achievement of the goals proposed by the institution. However, despite its importance, three-quarters of the country's universities and university institutions have not implemented this kind of team work. Institutional internationalization policies and plans, if they exist at all, are determined by either the person in charge of international relations or by the rector when he or she leads the process.

The support that both public and private institutions give to international training of their teaching bodies to carry out master's degrees and doctorates abroad is significant. Eighty-four percent of the international relations offices support the mobility of professors traveling abroad. Attendance at international seminars and events is the activity that universities support most—giving Colombian universities a relatively high profile internationally—followed by support for studies abroad. However, there is no institutional policy to stimulate those who contribute and support the practice of internationalization itself.

Program Strategies

Those in charge of international relations in Colombia's higher education institutions develop various international academic activities. Despite their importance, however, many are not carried out and are not considered a priority.

ACADEMIC PROGRAMS
Fifty-eight percent of the institutions surveyed have developed international academic programs. Some have comparative studies programs and allow mobility and integration with universities abroad. However, many higher education institutions still operate very locally and give little support to academic programs abroad (Jaramillo 2002).

FOREIGN LANGUAGES
One of the greatest limitations for internationalization is the inadequate command of a second language by faculty and students. About three-quarters of the institutions confirm that the lack of a second language does not allow major mobility of faculty. As a consequence, important opportunities for professional training and participation in international projects are lost.

Aware of the role they must play in a global society without boundaries, 86 percent of the institutions have been creating centers to teach a second language and have made it an obligatory requirement for graduation. In a survey by the Association of Colombian Universities and the British Council, most of the 32 universities polled confirmed that they had established policies for strengthening mastery of English and other languages among students, faculty and researchers, and administrative staff. Almost 60 percent of students prepare a few subjects in English, while 91 percent develop modules supported by a bibliography in English (Jaramillo 2002).

INTERNATIONAL AGREEMENTS
Colombian institutions have signed almost 700 active international agreements (figure 6.2). Fifty-nine percent are with public universities, and all

Figure 6.2 Number of International Agreements Signed with Colombia

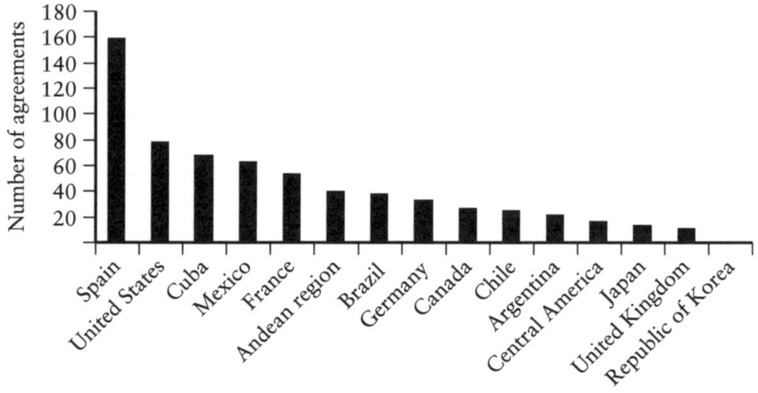

Source: I. Jaramillo (2003).

but 9 percent are bilateral, an indication of the lack of networking. Of the nearly 700 agreements, 287 agreements are with European countries and 273 are with other countries in Latin America. Most of the agreements are with Spain, followed by the United States, Cuba, Mexico, and France. Within Latin America Cuba is the country with the largest number of agreements (68), followed by Mexico (63) and Brazil (38). Despite these agreements, Latin American countries have not been considered the main destination for the academic community; cooperation relations have tended to be North-South, although the region has experienced an increment in alliances within the region (Jaramillo 2002).

Cooperation with Asian countries is scarce, despite its political and economic importance. Only one institution, in Bogota, has an agreement with a Korean university; 13 Colombian institutions have agreements with Japan. There is a growing demand for agreements with universities in Australia, a country that has recently shown interest in Latin America, particularly in Colombia. Little or no relations exist with institutions or organizations in Africa (I. Jaramillo 2003).

The areas of knowledge most represented in the agreements are social science and administration (22 percent), education and the humanities (19 percent), engineering and technology (18 percent), and the exact and natural sciences, health, and agriculture (41 percent) (figure 6.3). Private universities concentrate on social science and administration, engineering, and technological areas, while public universities concentrate on education

Figure 6.3 International Agreements, by Area of Knowledge 2002

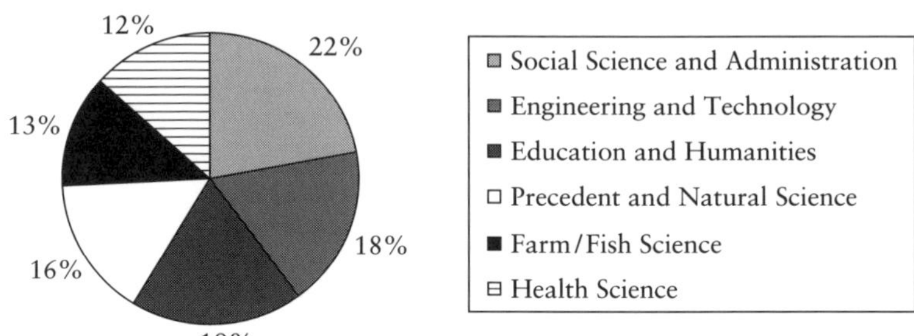

Source: I. Jaramillo (2003).

and the humanities, agriculture and the exact and natural sciences. These data are consistent with those provided by ICETEX, COLCIENCIAS, COLFUTURO, and the Fulbright Commission.

ACADEMIC MOBILITY

Academic mobility is based mainly on the movement of Colombian students and professors abroad rather than on reception of international students in Colombia. Only six of the institutions surveyed, five of them private, have foreign students. Current conditions in Colombia probably do not allow better performance in this area, but analysis is needed if institutions are to learn the real reasons for such low numbers. Despite the importance and significance that mobility has had for the internationalization process, there is no information system in Colombia that shows the number of students, professors, researchers, or even directors who have traveled to other countries to carry out academic activities.

EVALUATION AND INTERNATIONAL ACCREDITATION

Few of the mechanisms used in Colombia to guarantee the quality of programs and institutions are adequate for ensuring the quality of the process itself. In most institutions interviewed, there are no processes designed to review, evaluate, or follow up the internationalization process in order to improve it. Thirty-nine percent carry out some sort of evaluation and follow-up, but 61 percent are unaware or underestimate the value of a good internationalization process closely linked to the improvement of quality as an integral part of academic activity. Three-quarters have not subjected themselves to any kind of international accreditation.

Extracurricular Activities

Extracurricular activities allow students to interact with other students, enriching their academic development. Activities such as international weeks take place regularly, helping bring the world into the institution.

Alumni Programs

Sixty-eight percent of universities lack programs that include their alumni as agents of integration policy. Universities do recognize the capacity of alumni to strengthen relations with the productive sector and serve as a link between higher education institutions and international organizations and institutions.

Limiting Factors

Internationalization is being held back by a variety of factors (figure 6.4). Institutions cite such issues as inadequate command of a second language; the lack of adequate financing; inadequate planning; inflexible curricula; strict immigration policies; rigid or nonexistent legislation; inadequate information; and the unwillingness of Colombian institutions to recognize studies or degrees earned abroad.

Despite the lack of coherent government policy on internationalization, internationalization has advanced in Colombia in recent years. There is a greater commitment on the part of the authorities and the academic

Figure 6.4 Obstacles Holding Back Internationalization of Colombian Universities

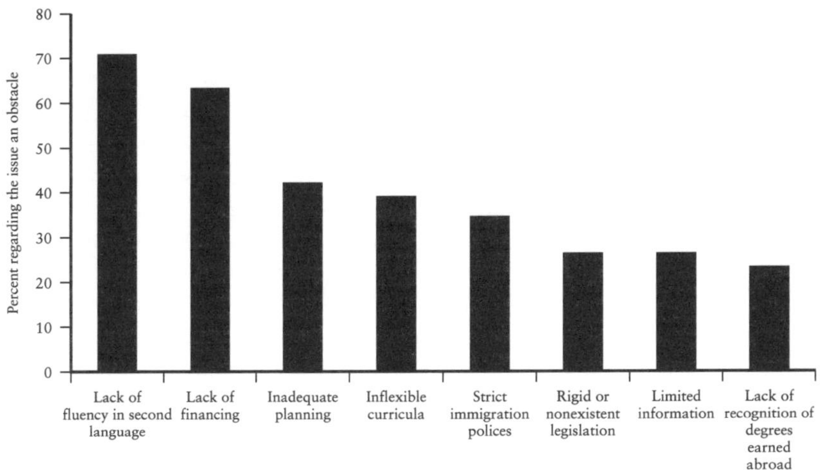

Source: I. Jaramillo (2003).

community in general, who have begun to see internationalization as an essential ingredient for improving the quality of higher education. The academic and organizational infrastructure has improved, and new technologies that support this task have been adopted.

Facing the Challenges

Higher education must integrate into global networks of knowledge and open its institutions and the higher education community to new trends. Institutions will have to be more creative in order to respond to these challenges. It is therefore necessary to consider certain proposals for strengthening and accelerating the internationalization process in a coordinated manner.

The Role of the Government

Internationalization of higher education cannot take place without the participation of the government. The government must ensure that its institutions enter the global world politically, economically, socially, and culturally, led by a clear national vision that recognizes education as a tool for achieving a place in the international arena. Government policies, mechanisms, and strategies that would strengthen the capacity of higher education in an international environment include the following:

- Coherent and structured policies are needed that do not disappear when the political leadership changes. The central government can integrate and promote internationalization, together with the various governmental organizations responsible for guaranteeing the process. These organizations include ICFES; ICETEX; COLCIENCIAS; the International Cooperation Office of the Ministry of Education; the Ministry of Foreign Affairs; the Administrative Security Department; the Ministry of Trade, Industry and Tourism; and the Colombian Agency for International Cooperation. It is the Ministry of Education's responsibility to develop overall coordination with the various administrative units responsible for proposing the criteria for strengthening the process and embarking on a new dynamic to interact with other central government organizations. With a shared objective in mind, these departments could act in a more coordinated way to encourage internationalization (Holm-Nielsen 2003).
- To orient policies and find mechanisms that facilitate the construction of an internationalization information system that leads not only to timely reception of information on international opportunities but also to learning about its quality and impact on Colombia's higher education institutions, it is necessary to collect and analyze information on

internationalization through the National Information System for Higher Education (SNIES). This data collection and analysis would enable all parties to monitor, evaluate, and provide information on the development of this process, with the support of various government organizations, in collaboration with other bodies, such as ASCUN/RCI. It is for this reason that the Network for the Internationalization of Higher Education will make available to offices responsible for internationalization an information system on internationalization that will allow them to obtain quantitative and qualitative information on advances achieved. If higher education institutions consider this information relevant, its inclusion in the SNIES will be proposed. The updating and follow-up of the SNIES will be the responsibility of the Ministry of Education.

- Academic mobility and exchange programs are not only costly, they have also contributed to brain drain. An appropriate financing program by the state, added to the support provided by higher education institutions and society in general, would facilitate the internationalization of higher education.

- International organizations have played an essential role in the conceptualization and rise of international cooperation (Sebastián 2001b). Support from multilateral organizations in strengthening international cooperation based on solidarity is particularly important at a time when Colombia is growing more isolated. The Ministry of Foreign Affairs needs to lobby these organizations and the diplomatic representations in Colombia in order to facilitate the provision of visas for Colombians interested in studying, teaching, or conducting research abroad. The difficulty of obtaining visas has become one of the main barriers to internationalization.

- The brain drain in recent years has increased the number of Colombian professionals living abroad. These expatriates can serve as links between the academic communities in Colombia and the countries in which they currently reside. Programs such as Colombia NosUne, recently established by the Ministry of Foreign Affairs, seek to strengthen links between Colombia and Colombian communities abroad (Ministry of Foreign Affairs 2004).

- The emigration process requires more attention from the government and the establishment of a policy that encourages the return of talented professionals, with the promise of better working conditions and research infrastructure support. Their return would contribute to Colombia's scientific and technological development (Ministry of Foreign Affairs 2004).

- With the gradual liberalization of teaching services and the arrival of new providers of higher education in Colombia, the central government will have to improve and strengthen its regulatory framework to ensure the quality and relevance of transnational academic programs. This new and challenging scenario demands the convergence of the national accreditation system and the evaluation of the internationalization process so that the internationalization process can be evaluated. What is needed is a system that will allow policymakers to assess the system in order to integrate it appropriately into the decisionmaking system. An incentive program is proposed that rewards institutions that develop their internationalization process, value and acknowledge internationalization, and encourage the continuous improvement of the process in teaching, research, and extension. Meanwhile, the Network for the Internationalization of Higher Education is preparing a model for evaluating the quality of the internationalization process in Colombia. In the medium term that model is expected to be integrated into institutional and program evaluation and the system of accreditation being developed.

- The forces of integration and globalization create a tension for higher education institutions in Colombia. The unilateral way of approaching other regions and international organizations has been characteristic of Latin America (González Arana, and Crisorio 2001). It is important for the central government to make progress in integrating educational systems, especially with regard to mutual recognition and certification. Unification of the Andean Community region, together with Mercosur, and extended to the Central American region, will allow a substantial advance in the formation of a common area for education. The proposal being developed within the Andean Community of Nations is expected to facilitate and regulate these new ways of delivering education.

- Interuniversity cooperation has grown considerably in recent years. Networks have become a strategic resource to conciliate the common interests of the institutions seeking to establish relations based on mutual trust and cooperation. Promoting the creation or strengthening of these networks would help institutions share knowledge and create integration processes regionally and internationally.

The Role of Institutions

The central government is responsible for fostering, regulating, and supervising higher education. Institutions of higher education are responsible for establishing policies and strategies aimed at guiding the development and the implementation of the international dimension, so that it will be integrated into university life in a central and systematic manner, generating true institutional international culture.

Systematic work by institutions will have to ensure that internationalization is reflected in the mission and the institutional vision, with clearly expressed mid-term and long-term strategies and actions. To do so, ASCUN/RCI have proposed a model for internationalizing Colombian universities (ASCUN 2003). The model, which seeks to make the sector aware of the value of internationalization in a setting adapted to Colombia's requirements, is expected to contribute to the development of a national agenda on internationalization. The granting of seed funds to support the launching of all cooperation projects would help make the process less sporadic.

The offices of international relations of Colombia's higher education institutions are mainly administrative units that carry out their functions in a scattered way. These offices lack autonomy and are not integrated into the core organic structure of the institution. If policies and structures to guide this process were available, these units could place themselves in the strategic positions they should have.

Mobility programs must be reviewed, bearing in mind that their objective is to develop human capacity among faculty and researchers. It is essential that these projects continue receiving support from the private and public sectors. However, because of the low number of students and faculty who benefit from these programs, higher education institutions must be innovative and design strategies to allow the integration and inclusion of an international dimension into their university communities. "Internationalization at home" is seen as a way of overcoming the exclusion of students who are not able to travel abroad but who nevertheless are expected to acquire certain abilities, including the capacity to become multilingual and multicultural. What should institutions do to strengthen command of a second language? The command of foreign languages not only allows a greater and better communication, it also permits a better understanding of other cultures and societies. It is essential for higher education institutions to strengthen programs for teaching foreign languages in order to guarantee greater competitiveness and better performance by their students and faculty.

Spanish has become an economic asset for countries that have discovered the important role it can play in the strengthening of their image, as a transmitter of culture, and as a source of economic development. Higher education institutions should take advantage of the high level of acceptance of the Spanish spoken in Colombia by promoting educational services for teaching Spanish as a second language to foreigners, who can play a fundamental role in the transmission of knowledge, whether face to face or virtually.

Higher education institutions should continuously evaluate the quality of internationalization in relation to their own purposes and objectives, based on institutional policy toward internationalization. The model for evaluating the quality of the internationalization process proposed by the Network for the Internationalization of Higher Education will be instrumental in reviewing, evaluating, and improving the quality of the internationalization process.

Coordination among the central government, higher education institutions, and other actors will determine the future of internationalization in Colombia. Many joint tasks will have to be developed in the near future to ensure continued internationalization of the higher education sector in Colombia.

An international presence can be achieved only through education, within a modernized regulatory framework, and, above all, with public investment to prepare the population as leaders of the new reality. Internationalization promises to develop the full potential of academic communities and improve Colombia's access to knowledge, the most valuable capital the world possesses today (I. Jaramillo 2003). It is essential that the central government and Colombian higher education institutions work closely together to build the framework and reinforce the process of internationalization in order to strengthen the quality, relevance, and effectiveness of higher education, for the benefit of students, faculty, and Colombia.

References

ASCUN (Association of Colombian Universities). 2002. "Agenda de políticas y estrategias para la educación superior Colombiana 2002–2006: De la exclusión a la equidad." Bogotá.

———. 2003. "Hacia una internacionalización de la universidad Colombiana con sentido propio." Bogotá.

Baeyens, Bernard, Mercedes Corpas, and Isabel Cristina Jaramillo. 1998. "Hacia una agenda sobre la cooperación internacional para fortalecer la educación superior." In *políticas y estrategias para la transformación de la educación superior en América Latina y el Caribe*. CRESALC/ASCUN, Bogotá.

British Council. 2004. *Programa Bogotá bilingüe*. www.britishcouncil.org/es/colombia/colombia-education.

CNA (National Council on Accreditation). 2001. "Lineamientos para la acreditación institucional." Bogotá.

COLCIENCIAS (Colombian Institute for the Development of Science and Technology). 2004. *Red caldas*. www.colciencias.gov.co

COLFUTURO (Foundation for the Future of Colombia). 2003. *COLFUTURO, 10 años*. Bogotá.

———. 1998. "Cambio para construir la paz." Plan Nacional de Desarrollo, Bogotá.

García Guadilla, Cármen. 2003. "Educación superior y AGCS: interrogantes para el caso de América Latina." In *El difícil equilibrio: la educación superior como bien público y comercio de servicios*, ed. García Guadilla, Cármen. Lima: Universidad de Lima–COLUMBUS.

García Guadilla, Cármen, Sylvie Didou-Aupetit, and Carlos Marquis. 2002. *New Providers, Transnational Education and Accreditation of Higher Education in Latin America*. Caracas, Venezuela: IESALC/UNESCO.

González Arana, Roberto, and Beatriz Carolina Crisorio. 2001. *Integración en América Latina y el Caribe. Análisis sobre procesos de regionalización*. Barranquilla, Colombia: Ediciones Uninorte.

Henao Willes, Myriam, and Myriam Velásquez Bustos. 2002. "La educación superior como objeto de reflexión e investigación." In *Educación superior, sociedad e investigación*. COLCIENCIAS/ASCUN, Bogotá.

Holm-Nielsen, Lauritz. 2003. "Higher Education." In *Colombia, the Economic Foundation for Peace*. Washington, DC: World Bank.

ICETEX (Colombian Institute for Educational Loans and Technical Studies Abroad). 2001. *Informe de labores 2000*. Bogotá.

ICFES (Colombian Institute for the Development of Higher Education). 2002 *Guía para la internacionalización de las instituciones de educación superior*. Bogotá.

Jaramillo, Felipe. 2003. "Los avances de las negociaciones del ALCA." Cámara de Comercio de Bogotá.

Jaramillo, Isabel Cristina. 2002. "Survey of Internationalization of Colombian Universities with Participation of 40 Private and Public Universities." Colombia.

———. 2003. "La internacionalización de la universidad Colombiana: un instrumento para el cambio." Association of Colombian Universities, Bogotá.

Jaramillo, Isabel Cristina, Patricia García, and Andreas Blom. 2003. *Colombian Higher Education in the Global Market*. Washington, DC: World Bank.

Ministerio de Comercio, Industria y Turismo. 2003. "Cátedra de negocios internacionales." www.mincomercio.gov.co.

Ministerio de Educación Nacional. 2002. "La revolución educativa: plan sectorial 2002–2006." Bogotá.

———. 2004. "Sistema nacional de información de la educación superior." http://www .mineducacion.gov.co.

Ministerio de Relaciones Exteriores. 2004. *Programa ColombiaNosUne*. www .minrelext.gov.co.

Ochoa Nuñez, Hernando. 1998. "La educación superior en Colombia y la cooperación internacional." In *Políticas y estrategias para la transformación de la educación superior en América Latina y el Caribe*. ASCUN-CRESALC/UNESCO, Bogotá.

Perilla Santamaría, Sonia. 2003. "Investigación avanza con las uñas." *El Tiempo*, November 16.

Presidencia de la República y Departamento de Planeación Nacional. 1994. "Las políticas del salto social." Plan Nacional de Desarrollo, Bogotá.

Revelo R., José. 1994. "Las relaciones internacionales de la universidad en el mundo actual." Colombian Institute for Educational Loans and Technical Studies Abroad, Bogotá.

Saavedra Guzmán, Ruth, Luis Eduardo Castro Zea, Olga Restrepo Quintero, and Alberto Rojas Rojas. 2001. *Planificación del desarrollo*. 2nd ed. Bogotá: Fundación Universidad Jorge Tadeo Lozano.

Sebastián, Jesús. 2001a. "La formación doctoral en América Latina y la colaboración de las universidades españolas." Universidad de Valladolid, Valladolid.

————. 2001b. "La internacionalización como instrumento para el desarrollo institucional de las universidades." In *Educación superior. Desafío Global y Respuesta Nacional*, Universidad de los Andes, Bogotá.

SNIES (National Information System for Higher Education). 2002. www.icfes.gov.co/snies/.

Tinjacá, C., ed. 2002. "Programa Latinoamericano de intercambio científico avanzado." COLCIENCIAS, MERCOCYT, Organization of American States, Bogotá.

World Bank. 2003. *La educación terciaria en Colombia: preparar el terreno para su reforma*. Washington, DC.

Yarce, Jorge, Carlos Mario Lopera, and Iván Pacheco. 2002. *La educación superior en Colombia*. Bogotá, IESALC/UNESCO.

7

Internationalization of Higher Education in Cuba

Raúl Hernández Pérez

This chapter traces the historical development of higher education in Cuba and examines the process of internationalization in Cuba. It provides an overview of the structure and functioning of Cuba's higher education system and examines the impact of internationalization on the activities of Cuban universities over the past four decades. It analyzes university activities related to internationalization processes, analyzes student mobility, and describes the academic service that Cuban institutions offer other countries.

The Higher Education System in Cuba

The first religious orders to settle in the New World were the Franciscans and the Dominicans. The Dominicans settled in Havana in the mid-sixteenth century. In the mid-seventeenth century, they began to offer convent-related studies at San Juan de Letrán Convent. The Dominicans needed royal approval to have the convent's curriculum raised to university level in order to issue university degrees. This led to the establishment of the Royal and Pontifical University of San Jerónimo in Havana in 1728.

In 1842 the University of Havana was secularized and became the Royal and Literary University of Havana. A teaching plan was designed for the islands of Cuba and Puerto Rico. In the early twentieth century, the University of Havana underwent major changes, including the introduction of programs in engineering, architecture, and agronomy.

By the early 1950s, three universities—the University of Havana (1728), the University of Oriente (1747), and the Central University of Villas (1952)—were offering higher education in Cuba. Nevertheless, the number of graduates and the composition of the degree courses failed to meet the country's needs for socioeconomic development. Another feature at the time was the almost total lack of scientific research by universities.

The author is grateful to Julio Achang Garcia, specialist in computer services, and to Dr. Ricardo Fundora, Head of the International Projects Group, at the Office of International Relations, Ministry of Higher Education, Cuba, for their collaboration.

The Cuban Revolution of 1959 found the universities in urgent need of profound changes to put them on a par with the transformations required to further the country's development. University reforms were adopted in 1962. The major objectives of these reforms were as follows (CEPES 2000):

- Establish universities in line with the needs of the country, with emphasis on scientific and technical programs.
- Transform the concept and practice of higher education.
- Guarantee faculty and student participation in university government.
- Train and upgrade faculty, and employ full-time faculty.
- Organize a broad system of university scholarships covering accommodation, meals, and other benefits.
- Increase enrollment.
- Create systematic linkages between higher and lower levels of education.
- Promote culture within society by means of university extension education.
- Promote scientific and cultural exchange with other countries.

At first this transformation of Cuban universities was associated with the wide-ranging development of international relations that would make it possible both to strengthen the academic and scientific foundation of the country's institutions and to gain insight into the advances taking place at universities in other countries around the world. This would serve as a point of reference for the proposed changes.

The 1960s witnessed substantial transformations in the socioeconomic and political spheres. These developments reinforced the need for highly skilled professionals and demanded that special attention be paid to higher education. Consequently, the Council for Higher Education and the Office of the Deputy Minister of Higher Education were created.

By 1975 the network of higher education centers had expanded to five institutions, and the universities soon started to form affiliates in the provinces, which formed the embryos of the country's current new universities. Enrollment rose sharply, as a result of the accumulated demand for education and the bold education development efforts undertaken during the revolutionary process, which granted the poor greater opportunities to study. Courses were designed for workers, and the teaching of medicine at the university level spread throughout the country.

Between 1976 and 1990, ties with Eastern Europe were strengthened. This development was beneficial to the country's economic development and helped reinforce the role of higher education as a factor for socioeconomic growth. It increased the public resources available to achieve these goals.

In 1976 the organizational restructuring process of the Cuban state was set in motion. A new system of economic management was implemented. Laws were passed to create the Ministry of Higher Education, the new structure of university programs, and a much broader network of higher education institutions.

Within a short period, these measures helped bolster higher education. They led to periodic and systematic enhancements of the teaching process; of curriculum development; of procedures governing admission to postsecondary studies; of the links between teaching, research, and production in the professional training process; and of the organization of faculty training and upgrading system.

From the mid-1970s to the 1980s, the higher education system underwent major expansion. The number of institutions, which rose to 28 during the 1976/77 academic year, increased to 42 during 1986/87.

During the second half of the 1980s, higher education continued to expand, albeit at a slower rate. This period was marked by the implementation of measures to ensure optimum performance of the subsystem. Major changes carried out during this decade included the following:

- broadening the profile of professional training, with an emphasis on basic training
- creating courses aimed at encouraging workers to pursue university studies
- strengthening the link between teaching, research, and production
- strengthening the role of higher education institutions in scientific research
- enhancing the external institutional evaluation system (also known as general inspection) and the way in which it is coordinated with other evaluation processes
- establishing a national computer development program.

Structure and Functioning of Higher Education

Higher education is one of the seven subsystems currently forming the national education system (the others are preschool education, general polytechnic and career education, special education, technical and professional education, faculty training and upgrading, and adult education). All educational institutions are public and offer their services to the Cuban people free of cost.

Law 15/76 dictates that the Ministry of Higher Education is responsible for implementing the government's policy on higher education. While the Ministry of Higher Education is the body responsible for higher education as a whole, higher education institutions are administratively subordinated to the ministries that employ most of their graduates. For example, the Ministry of Public Health is responsible for the Advanced Institutes of Medical Sciences; the Ministry of Education is responsible for the Advanced Institutes of Teaching; the Ministry of the Armed Forces is responsible for the Advanced Institute of Military; the National Institute of Sports, Physical Education and Recreation is responsible for the Advanced Institute of Physical Education; the Ministry of Foreign Affairs is responsible for the Advanced Institute of the Foreign Service; and the National Council of Culture is responsible for the Advanced Institute of Art.

The dynamic development continuously exhibited by higher education led to the creation of new institutions, which were assigned to existing or new agencies. Most of the new institutions were assigned to the Ministry of Higher Education, the Ministry of Education, the Ministry of Public Health, and the National Institute of Sports, Physical Education and Recreation.

The higher education subsystem is structured around a network of institutions. It is the responsibility of the Council of Ministers, at the proposal of the Ministry of Higher Education and through collective decisions, to approve the creation, merger, or elimination of a higher education institution.

The Ministry of Foreign Affairs and the Ministry of Foreign Investment and Cooperation are the main coordinating bodies for international cooperation with other countries and institutions. Higher education plays a vital role in more than 100 active governmental commissions with other countries.

Classification of Higher Education Institutions

Initially, universities, technical colleges, higher education institutes, and university centers were classified as higher education institutions. This classification subsequently underwent changes, as a result of the search for better solutions to socioeconomic demands (table 7.1). Institutions are currently classified as follows:

- *University:* Responsible for training professionals in various areas of knowledge, including the natural, exact, social, and agricultural sciences; the humanities; and accounting.
- *Advanced polytechnic institute:* Responsible for training professionals in the technical sciences and architecture.
- *Higher education institute:* Responsible for training professionals, with emphasis on certain areas of knowledge, such as medical sciences, teaching, physical education, and sports. In the case of military sciences, these institutions are sometimes called *schools* or *academies*.

Table 7.1 Number and Type of Institutions of Higher Education in Cuba, 2001/02

Type of institution	Number
University	11
Higher education institute	28
Technical college	1
School and academy	7
University center	2
University headquarters	1
University affiliate	2
Independent faculty of medical sciences	9
Latin American and international school	2
Total	63

Source: CEPES (2000).

- *University center:* Transitional institutions that meet the subjective and objective conditions necessary to develop into any of the types of institutions mentioned above.
- *University headquarters:* Geared toward the development of higher education–related activities in areas or territories. May be transformed into one of the institutions described above. Dependent on another educational institution.
- *University affiliate:* Dependent on another institution and may not necessarily develop into any other kind of institution.
- *Independent faculty of medical sciences:* Independent institutions that form a network in a medical specialty and possess responsibilities and functions similar to those of the higher education institutes, depending on the territory's needs for training and the needs of the public health services. Administratively, these institutions are independent. Academically, they are subordinated to a higher education institution specializing in the same area.
- *Latin American and international school:* There are two institutions of this kind, one in medicine and one in physical education and sports. Both train foreign students awarded scholarships. The expenses incurred for this training are defrayed by the Cuban government on the basis of joint cooperation with other developing countries. Cuban students also attend these institutions. Administratively, they are independent; academically, they are subordinated to a higher education institute specializing in the area.

During the 2000/01 academic year, 129,000 students, including 35,000 new students and 17,000 graduating students, were enrolled at Cuban institutions of higher learning.

Coordinating Bodies and their Characteristics

The Ministry of Higher Education is the governing body of higher education in Cuba. Ten other bodies (ministries and organizations) are responsible for various higher education institutions (see above).

The main NGOs are the Federation of University Students; the National Union for Education, Science and Sports Workers; the National Union for Science Workers; the National Union for Health Workers; other unions related to the area of specialization of the institution; and professional associations in teaching, psychology, law, economics and accounting, mathematics and computer science, veterinary medicine, architecture, engineering, medicine, and other fields. Membership in any of the NGOs is voluntary.

The Federation of University Students plays a vital role in representing students in university government and in major facets of national life. Faculty and researchers in the subsystem and in the unions associated with a particular higher education institution may also belong to the National Labor Union of Science. Professional associations bring graduates from various disciplines together and play a primary role in getting these graduates involved in Cuba's political and economic life, ensuring their professional upgrading, and granting support to scientific activity.[1]

Governing Bodies within Institutions

The university councils are the main advisory bodies of authority at the institutional and faculty levels. They are made up of representatives from the academy, the student body, and unions. Agreements reached by them are essential to institutional policy and possess considerable leverage in the decisionmaking process. The president of the university is the main authority of the institution; the deans are responsible for the faculty; and directors are responsible for science and technology units and study centers.

Make-up of Faculty

Teaching faculty hold the ranks of full professor, associate professor, assistant professor, or instructor. Researchers hold the ranks of full researcher, associate researcher, assistant researcher, or novice researcher. More than 90 percent of the teaching staff work full time. In 2002 there were about

---

[1] The most important of these organizations are the National Union of Construction Engineers and Architects, the National Union of Jurists of Cuba, the National Association of Economists and Accountants of Cuba, the Union of Journalists of Cuba, the Association of Sugar Specialists of Cuba, and the Cuban associations of mathematics, physics, chemistry, geology, and teaching.

22,000 faculty, with an average age of 45. Twenty-four percent of faculty work in teaching-related specialties, while 40 percent work in the medical sciences. More than half are women.

Access to Higher Education

The national system providing access to higher education is constantly being improved, in line with social and individual needs. It is part of a dynamic that combines stability and change in the quest to enhance the quality of incoming students, increase retention rates, increase efficiency, and achieve greater social equity. Greater access to higher education institutions is necessary to satisfy the need for a skilled workforce for the domestic economy and to better meet individual, cultural, and spiritual needs. The admission system for daily regular courses and for courses taken by workers is handled by the provinces, which deal with all matters relating to admission.

Distance learning has been used in Cuba for more than 20 years. It is available in law, history, economics, accounting, library science, and information sciences.

Scientific and Technical Information

In 1978 the Network of Scientific and Technical Information Centers of the Ministry of Higher Education was created. It started out as a simple organization but later became highly developed, thanks to the introduction of new information and communications technologies.

Two significant steps in the development of the network were the creation of the Scientific and Technological Information Program for Higher Education, in 1984, and the creation, in 1992, of the national university server through the University Network for Scientific and Technological Information of the Ministry of Education (REDUNIV), which coordinates the country's university library network. With regard to the virtual library, Cuba's most important experience is the telematic network for information access and management and access to information on the Cuban national health system, INFOMED.

Funding for Higher Education

As a percentage of GDP, the budget for operating expenses of higher education has been growing. In 2001 spending represented 2.25 percent of GDP.

Since 1990 Cuban universities have been suffering from a severe shortage of foreign exchange, which has adversely affected the ability to purchase laboratory equipment and materials, computers, books, and other materials that can be purchased only with foreign currency. The problem stems from the economic crisis that Cuba has been going through since the fall of socialism, in the wake of which the country lost 86 percent of the markets for its products and the opportunity to purchase goods and services for its universities on very favorable terms. Despite the change, the Cuban government has maintained an annual level of funding that enables it to cover minimum needs. It has prioritized the purchase of computers, facilitating the computerization of the country's universities. The harsh conditions caused by the economic blockade on Cuba have made the purchase of all these products costly and hampered economic progress.

Another measure taken in the wake of these difficulties was the development of a partial funding scheme in foreign currency earned from the sale of university goods and services. This measure, initiated in the 1990s, opened up a mutually beneficial sector for international cooperation with other foreign universities and institutions. Academic exchange and international projects, vital for universities under normal conditions, are essential to Cuban universities.

Graduate Studies and Research: The Link with the Outside World

International relations are vital for the continued development of higher education, particularly the development of graduate studies and research.

Graduate Studies

Cuba boasts a fully developed national graduate system supervised by national organizations, with the Ministry of Higher Education as the governing body. Graduate courses grew significantly during the 1990s. The increased volume, coupled with the country's weak economic conditions, has led to shortages of infrastructure and libraries. International cooperation is therefore of great importance.

One feature of graduate courses around the world is the interrelationship between institutions and the flow of information, faculty, and students. International access to knowledge and experience is vital, and graduate courses are a fundamental channel for gaining this access.

The growth of Cuba's graduate education and international ties has been marked by several important periods. In the late 1960s, several member states of UNESCO provided strong support to strengthen Cuban universities. They trained the first group of master's and doctoral students, who graduated from universities in former socialist countries, as students are trained in Canada, France, Great Britain, and other countries.

In the early 1970s, strong impetus was given to doctoral-level training in the Soviet Union, the German Democratic Republic, and elsewhere in

Eastern Europe. As of April 2003, 2,472 Cuban nationals had received PhDs abroad and 3,957 had received PhDs in Cuba. The year in which the highest number of PhDs were granted abroad was 1983, with 231 graduates (Ministry of Higher Education 2003).

Since the 1990s, this figure has fallen as a result of the break in academic relations with former socialist countries. Relations with countries such as Spain, Mexico, Canada, and Brazil were immediately strengthened and the number of research visits, joint events, and student exchanges increased. Nevertheless, the number of doctoral courses fell sharply. It has therefore been necessary to reinforce doctoral training in Cuba, which has led to an increase in the number of PhDs at universities and a return to training levels similar to those of the 1980s.

Since the mid-1990s, Belgium, Canada, and Germany have vigorously supported academic exchange, which has had an impact on doctorate-level training. In 1994 the master's program was approved as a graduate program in Cuba. As of the beginning of 2003, 12,000 students were enrolled in master's programs in Cuba. Several foreign master's degree programs have been offered in Cuba, with considerable impact on high-priority areas. International projects have also supported master's programs in Cuba.

Foreign doctoral degree programs in Cuba and joint doctoral degree programs were approved in the late 1990s. This has made it possible to cover areas with low rates of doctorates and to strengthen others. Twenty doctorates from Spanish universities have been approved in Cuba. Several joint doctorate programs with Spain are available, and this form of cooperation has been initiated in biology with the National Autonomous University of Mexico. One immediate objective is to increase cooperation with a greater number of Latin American countries, where the strengths of the participating universities may be fully tapped.

International networks have been beneficial to graduate work, particularly the Ibero-American Program of Science and Technology for Development program (CYTED), which fosters exchange between scientists, and the European Union's Latin America Academic Training (ALFA) program, which has strengthened the creation of graduate study networks, especially for multinational doctorates.[2] Since the establishment of the Ibero-American University Association of Graduate Education (AUIP), in 1989, both the Ministry of Higher Education, where the Association's Regional Office for Central America and the Caribbean is headquartered, and several Cuban universities have played important roles in the work of

---

[2] The ALFA Program fosters the establishment of networks between universities for the development of activities related to training, information exchange, and joint educational projects and, to a much lesser extent, research.

the association. This large network of universities has enabled the exchange of experiences and training in a broad range of subjects. Particularly since the early 1990s, the Self-Assessment Guide of the AUIP has been extensively applied to the evaluation of Cuban graduate programs and has served as a basis for accreditation processes.

Since 1998 graduate program accreditation has been developed within the framework of an ongoing quality improvement program. Relations have been established with accreditation agencies in different countries, including Brazil's Coordinating Agency for Graduate Education (CAPES), Colombia's National Accreditation Council, and the equivalent government agencies in the Dominican Republic, Ecuador, and other countries.

Since the early 1990s the demand for graduate courses has increased, especially within Latin America. A large number of master's and doctorate programs has been established, and Cuban scholars have helped strengthen national graduate programs. The number of foreign graduate students in Cuba has risen, with 800 foreigners pursuing master's and doctorate programs and more than 4,000 attending courses and training programs. Many students are from the United States, Canada, and Europe. Most come to Cuba because of their interest in Cuban culture and the Spanish language. More than 150 students from Argentina, Colombia, Mexico, Syria, and other countries in Latin America and Africa have also defended doctoral dissertations in Cuba.

Research in Higher Education

The development of science and technology as part of university activities in Cuba has been linked to international cooperation since the early 1960s. Important bilateral projects or projects undertaken by international organizations promoted the scientific development of such centers as the José Antonio Echeverría Advanced Polytechnic Institute (ISPJAE) (formerly the Faculty of Technology of the University of Havana), the National Center of Agricultural Health, the Faculty of Mathematics and Cybernetics (formerly the School of Mathematics of the University of Havana), the Institute of Animal Sciences, and the Faculty of Chemistry of the University of Oriente. Most of these projects were developed with Canada, Europe, and international organizations, such as UNESCO.

In the late 1960s, the increased exchange with former socialist countries enabled the large-scale opening of doctorate programs, especially in the basic sciences, in which Cuba had achieved limited development. The arrival in Cuba of faculty with doctorate degrees, coupled with the extended stay in Cuba of foreign consultants in various branches of science, produced, by the early 1970s, the beginning of vigorous scientific activity at universities, which from the start have been very closely related to the social, economic, and cultural development of the country.

The 1980s saw the consolidation of this development and ensured that more than 90 percent participated in scientific research. It also witnessed the strengthening of large national research centers engaged in higher education and smaller study centers at the universities. This trend enabled Cuban scholars to begin participating as equals in international scientific projects in association with scholars in Eastern Europe. In the mid-1980s, about half of the more than 300 Cuban doctoral students were studying in Cuba.

The break-up of the Soviet Union forced Cuban universities to establish closer scientific cooperation ties with Latin America, Canada, Spain, and other European countries. The mechanisms of bilateral and multilateral cooperation with these regions were vigorously activated. Cuba is active in multilateral programs such as the CYTED; it participates in the events and meetings of the Framework Program of the European Union; it conducts bilateral projects with universities in Mexico, Spain, Brazil, Argentina, Belgium, Germany, and other countries; and it engages in scientific exchanges, within the limits made possible by invitations extended by the Spanish Agency for International Cooperation, the German Academic Exchange Service, the ALFA Program networks, and other programs.

Within the context of international cooperation, the emphasis is on involvement in research and innovation projects that allow Cuban professors and researchers access to new technologies, up-to-date information, and modern laboratory equipment, while ensuring that Cuban science makes its own scientific contributions to the benefit of all parties involved. One of the main objectives is the participation of Cuban scientists in global networks that allow them to gain exposure through the most widely circulated publications in their own areas, to share patents, and to hold leadership positions in international events.

Stages of the Internationalization Process

The internationalization of Cuban universities is characterized by four distinct stages. In the early 1960s, Cuba had just 15,000 students and less than 1,000 faculty at three universities. It lacked research centers and had only limited graduate education. During this decade the literacy campaign was started, and young people from every level of society gradually began attending university, thanks to a university scholarship plan. International cooperation was undertaken to promote the training of faculty and students, and large-scale international projects geared toward strengthening institutions were carried out with support from Canada, UNESCO, and other sources.

In the 1970s large numbers of Cubans were sent abroad to enroll in master's and doctorate programs. University professors began to take summer courses given by scholars from Europe, mainly in France and Italy. During this stage, there was a strong presence of specialists from Eastern Europe at Cuban universities. The methodological and research structure was created through strong international cooperation, and there was a rise in the presence of foreign students at Cuban universities.

In the 1980s there was a sharp rise in the number of doctoral students trained abroad, and PhD programs were established in Cuba. The first scientific findings were made at universities and research centers. Cuban professors began providing technical assistance to other countries. University enrollment topped 300,000 students, and distance learning began.

The 1990s were marked by very harsh economic conditions in the wake of the fall of socialism in Eastern Europe. Bilateral agreements with these countries had ensured steady support for Cuba's higher education program; 70 percent of academic exchanges had been undertaken with universities in these countries. Cooperation and academic exchanges were quickly reinforced with Canada, Spain, Germany, Belgium, and other developed countries. Relations were fostered with Latin American universities, and bilateral exchanges were conducted with the leading universities in Argentina, Brazil, and Mexico. Cuba offered technical assistance to Latin American universities. Foreign students continued to be trained in Cuba, and training in medicine and sports was boosted.

Cuba entered the new millennium with more than 700,000 university graduates in a population of 11 million people, 73 universities, more than 5,000 PhDs in active service, and extensive international cooperation with more than 135 countries. More than 15,000 foreign students have graduated from Cuban institutions. Cuban professionals are participating in more than 500 international networks, and the country's international prestige has grown thanks to the quality of its education (Ministry of Higher Education 2002a).

In 1989 only 12 percent of cooperation-related activities were undertaken with Latin America and 9 percent with the European Union; 75 percent of cooperation-related activities were undertaken with the countries of Eastern Europe. In 2001, 72 percent were developed with the countries of Latin America and the Caribbean, and 14 percent were conducted with Spain. The rest of the European Union, Canada, and the United States accounted for 11 percent. Cooperation activities with Eastern Europe have almost disappeared completely (Ministry of Higher Education 2002b).

Impact of International Cooperation

The internationalization of higher education contributes to international support, to the promotion of an exchange of ideas at university and national levels, and to human development. Its most distinguishing features are faculty and student mobility and international cooperation.

Mobility is viewed as a way of preparing students and faculty to meet the demands of the twenty-first century. It involves providing students, scientists, and professors with the facilities needed to enable them to study, work, and learn outside Cuba. Mobility builds international confidence and boosts cultural levels and mutual trust. The downside to mobility is brain drain, as many students choose to work abroad after they complete their education.

International cooperation is manifested in the development of joint activities that ensure equal rights and shared technical and economic duties. The main indicators include the number and kinds of joint research projects, participation in networks, the number of framework agreements, and the number of joint graduate programs.

Faculty Mobility

In 2002, 77 percent of the participation of teaching staff, researchers, and academic officials in international cooperation–related activities were linked to international academic exchange, services, and events (figure 7.1). Most of the academic exchange of the higher education institutions and research centers attached to the Ministry of Higher Education was developed with Bolivia, Brazil, Colombia, Ecuador, and Mexico in the Americas and with France, Germany, and Spain in Europe. In 2002 the countries

Figure 7.1 Distribution of International Cooperation in Cuba, by Activity, 2001

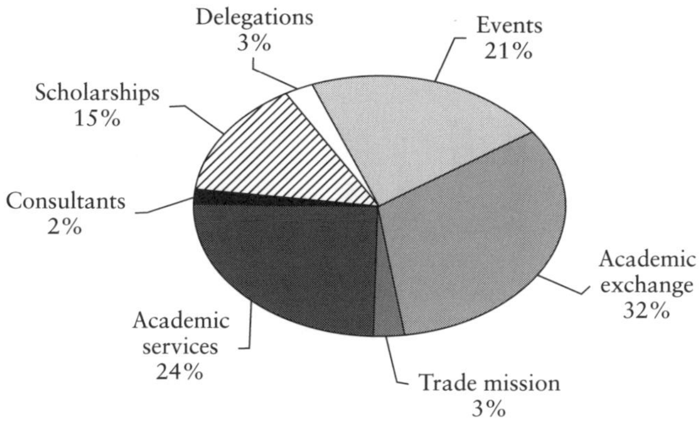

Source: Ministry of Higher Education (2002b).

Figure 7.2 Visits by Cuban Academics to Foreign Institutions of Higher Learning, by Country, 2001

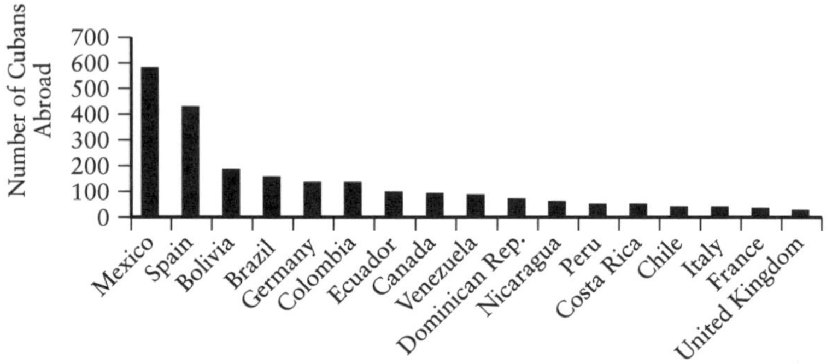

Source: Ministry of Higher Education (2002b).

with the highest levels of exchange were Canada, Ecuador, Mexico, and Spain (figures 7.2 and 7.3).

Involvement in scientific events is critical to the internationalization process. Participation in international events by professors, researchers, and specialists rose in 2002 (figure 7.4). The increase was due largely to the fact that greater advantage was taken of opportunities to participate in events organized through other cooperation-related activities, during

Figure 7.3 Visits by Foreign Academics to Cuban Institutions of Higher Learning, by Country, 2001

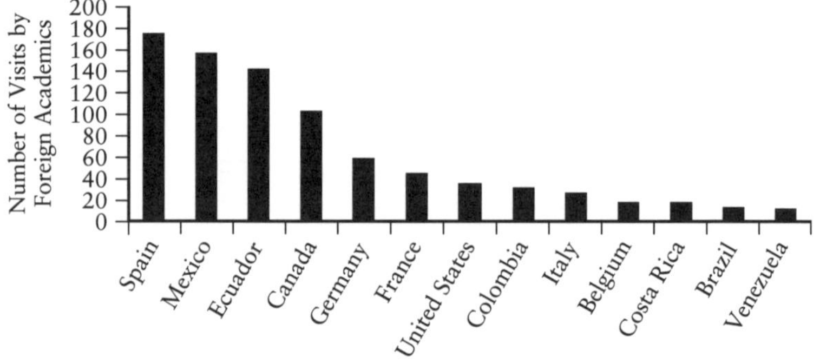

Source: Ministry of Higher Education (2002b).

Figure 7.4 Participation of Cuban Scholars in International Events, by Country, 2001

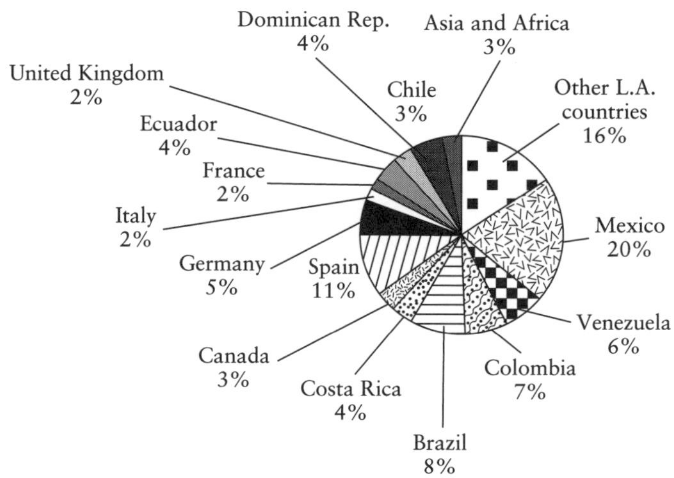

Source: Ministry of Higher Education (2002b).

visits abroad. The financial restrictions at universities and research centers prevent Cubans from taking part in most international events held abroad.

International scientific events are also developed by Cuban universities and research centers. In 2002 more than 100 such events were conducted, and efforts are being made to increase this activity. The biennial World Conference on Higher Education in Cuba enables the Ministry of Higher Education and its network of higher education and scientific centers to invite universities from all over the world. The 2002 event was attended by 960 scholars from outside Cuba.

Student Mobility

Student mobility in Cuba is encouraged through a national scholarship program.

FOREIGN SCHOLARSHIP HOLDERS IN CUBA

Evidence of the Cuban government's commitment to internationalism is its foreign scholarship program, established in 1961. The program targets developing countries and students from poor families who lack the opportunity

Figure 7.5 Number of Foreign Scholarship Holders Graduating from Cuban Institutions, 2003

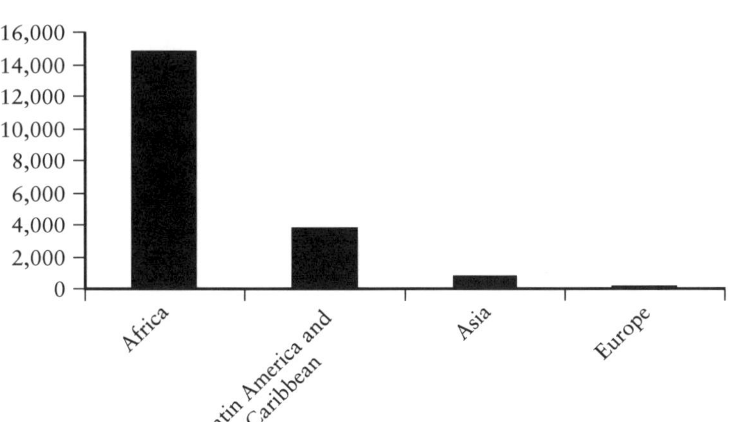

Source: ONABE (2003).

to study in their own countries or abroad. It has attracted students from more than 120 countries (figure 7.5). The program is aimed primarily at certain countries in Africa and at training secondary- and technical-level students in order to provide them with the foundation needed for entry into more advanced levels of training. Many of the students who have graduated from Cuba now hold major positions of responsibility in government, diplomacy, and business in their own countries.

In 1991, despite the difficult economic conditions faced at the time, government leaders decided to keep the 20,300 foreign scholarship holders in Cuba, more than 8,000 of whom were pursuing higher education programs, until they graduated. Since then, the program's figures have risen once again (figure 7.6).

In early 2002 the number of scholarship holders topped 11,000. These figures were achieved due to the establishment of the Latin American School of Medical Sciences and the International School of Sports and Physical Education.

Foreign students take part in cultural and sports-related events at Cuban universities. They also participate in national festivals and receive prizes and awards. The presence of students from many different countries enables foreign students to develop a more universal culture. It also allows Cuban students to draw on this culture and learn about other lifestyles and customs. Various activities are organized with foreign scholarship holders.

Figure 7.6 Enrollment by Foreign Scholarship Holders in Cuba, 1997–2002

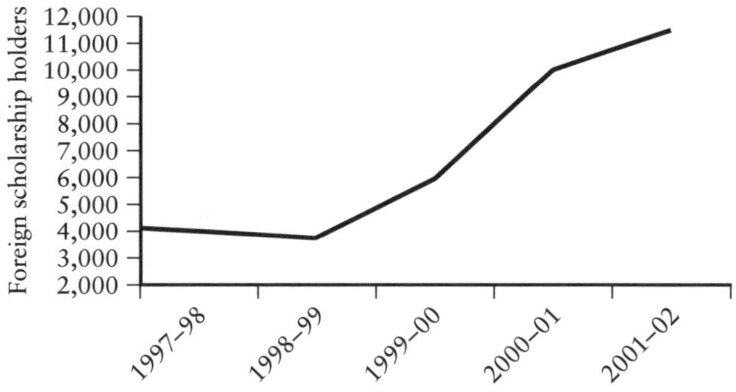

Source: ONABE (2003).

Foreign students studying in Cuba master Spanish as a second language. Several centers have facilities whose objectives include ensuring that, within a year, scholarship holders from non-Spanish-speaking countries are able to understand Spanish enough to pursue their studies.

At the end of each semester, each center selects the best foreign students in each field from each country and the most outstanding students overall. Several centers offer their best foreign students scholarship to continue their studies. These students receive various incentives and awards, and their selection is reported to the diplomatic representatives in their own country, some of whom provide their own incentives.

Every year more than 4,000 foreign university graduates enroll in graduate programs at Cuban universities. Cuban culture, history, music, and literature are topics of great interest in the United States, Canada, Europe, Japan, and other countries. Latin Americans are interested in education, health, and sports.

In 2001, 800 foreigners enrolled in master's and doctorate programs in Cuba. More than half of these students were in doctoral programs. The main countries of origin were Brazil, Colombia, and Mexico. More than 150 foreigners have defended their dissertations in Cuba.

CUBAN SCHOLARSHIP HOLDERS ABROAD
About 350 Cuban undergraduate and graduate students were granted scholarships to study abroad between 1996 and 2002 (figure 7.7). Cuban universities promote this kind of exchange, which is limited solely by the scant financial resources available. The vast majority of such scholarships have been financed by foreign counterparts.

Figure 7.7 Number of Cuban Scholarship Holders Studying Abroad, 1996–2002

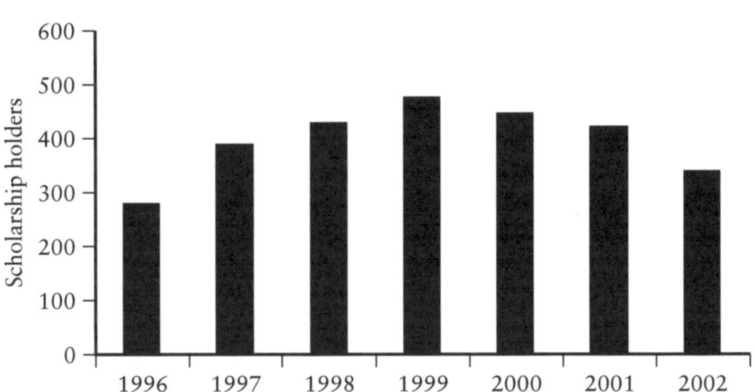

Source: Ministry of Higher Education (2002b).

Foreign Institutions of Higher Education in Cuba

Cuba seeks to attract foreign training programs that complement those offered by domestic institutions. Mechanisms have been designed for the approval of foreign or joint doctorate programs. Since this policy was implemented, in 1996, 20 foreign doctorate degree programs and 5 joint doctorate degree programs have been established. Dozens of doctorate students have graduated from these programs, in law, environment, education, international finance, and other fields. Almost all of these programs have been developed in conjunction with Spanish universities.

Cuban laws regulate such programs, in line with the needs of the country, the needs of the regions in which they operate, and the program's scientific contribution. Given the financial difficulties Cuba faces, with very few exceptions, the foreign party contributes most of the resources; only expenses associated with the visiting faculty members' stay in Cuba are covered by Cuba. Cuba is thus not a market for services of this kind unless they are provided within the framework of international academic cooperation.

The main difficulties arising from these activities are linked to inappropriate approaches to doctoral-level training. Too little emphasis has been given to the preparation of doctoral theses, leading to poor performance during doctoral defenses. Cuba's National Commission of Scientific Degrees is now enforcing stricter regulations on the preparation of theses. These regulations were applied to the last two doctorates approved, a PhD in biology conferred by the National Autonomous University of Mexico and a PhD in chemistry conferred by the University of Cadiz in Spain.

The concept of training networks has spread, both nationally and internationally, to the benefit of all parties involved. Examples of such networks are graduate courses taught by professors from Europe, North America, and several Latin American countries within the framework of cooperation networks; Cuba's active participation in more than 150 ALFA networks; and its participation in UNESCO's University Twinning and Networking Scheme (UNITWIN) professorships and networks, which encourage the study of development-related problems affecting education, innovation, tourism, and other sectors.

International Cooperation Agreements

Cuban institutions signed 1,165 international cooperation agreements in 2002, 62 percent of which are still in force (table 7.2). These agreements are periodically revised within the framework of bilateral exchanges or at meetings of university presidents.

The Ministry of Higher Education and its institutions have signed agreements with their main governmental counterparts and university president associations in almost all countries in Latin America, as well as in Belgium, Canada, China, Germany, Italy, Spain, and other countries with a high level of commitment and periodic supervision.

International Networks

A major indicator of the internationalization process is the participation of universities in academic and scientific networks that encourage faculty and student mobility, the development of academic activities, and scientific

Table 7.2 Number of Agreements between Cuban and Foreign Universities and Research Centers, by Country, 2002

Country	Number of agreements
Colombia	267
Spain	228
Mexico	218
Brazil	211
Ecuador	174
Bolivia	24
Germany	23
Canada	20
Total	1,165

Source: Ministry of Higher Education (2002b).

research. Networks also facilitate the recognition and accreditation of studies in different countries or groups of countries.

Cuban universities have joined many academic and scientific networks The main networks include those of the European Union's ALFA Program. Cuban universities participated in 121 of the 892 ALFA networks during the first phase of the program (1994–98).

CYTED is both an international and multilateral program. It was created in 1984, under a framework agreement signed by 21 Spanish- and Portuguese-speaking countries on both sides of the Atlantic. Research groups from Cuban universities and research centers have continued to participate actively in almost all the thematic networks and in the joint research projects in this program. The program has fostered cooperation in applied research and technological development, with the aim of facilitating the acquisition of scientific and technological findings that may be transferred to production systems and social policies in Latin America.

Cuba has engaged in a high level of academic and scientific exchange in the thematic teaching networks of the Spanish–Latin American Inter-University Cooperation Program. Cuban universities participate in 24 of the 60 networks approved at the 2002 meeting (Ministry of Higher Education 2000b).

The Scientific and Technological Cooperation with Developing Countries (INCO-DEV) subprogram is part of the European Union's R&D Framework Program. It fosters and finances joint research projects in selected areas, such as agriculture, health, and the environment. The projects are intended to integrate research groups from the European Union with those in Latin America, Africa, and Asia. The subprogram represents an important framework for scientific cooperation, since it finances both research and cooperation-related costs. It is not directed specifically at Latin America and is limited in terms of subjects and the number of projects approved. Three Cuban university institutions participate in six network projects forming part of the INCO-DEV Program of the Sixth Framework Program (2002–06).

Many Cuban professors and researchers are members of, or hold executive positions in, international organizations or institutions. These include the Latin American University Union, the Inter-American University Organization, the Ibero-American University Association of Postgraduate Education, the University Network of the Americas for Cooperative and Associative Studies, and the Latin American Faculty of Social Sciences.

In 2001 Cuban universities joined more than 150 international organizations, some deeply engaged in scientific or teaching exchange programs, others involved in global university policy publications or projects. Cuban professors and researchers participated in more than 100 international networks and in several projects conducted by international organizations (Ministry of Higher Education 2002b).

Presence of Cuban Institutions in Other Countries

Cuban higher education is present in more than 27 countries (figure 7.8). More than 800 professors a year work in these countries, the most important of which are Mexico, Bolivia, Colombia, Brazil, Ecuador, Peru, Nicaragua, Honduras, and Angola. They teach primarily graduate studies and provide consultancy services for institutions and governments. Since the Cuban Revolution, Cuban professors have also played an important role in developing countries.

The management of interuniversity, bilateral, and multilateral projects with international organizations began to develop intensely in 1996, when 213 projects were developed by Cuban universities with UN organizations and cooperation agencies in different countries. In 2002 this figure grew to 270 projects, more than 100 of which are with universities in Argentina, Brazil, Belgium, Canada, France, Germany, Italy, the Netherlands, and Spain.

Meetings of University Presidents

In the past two decades, binational meetings between Cuban and foreign university presidents have been vital to the development of academic

Figure 7.8 Cuban Professors Offering Services Abroad in 2002, by Country

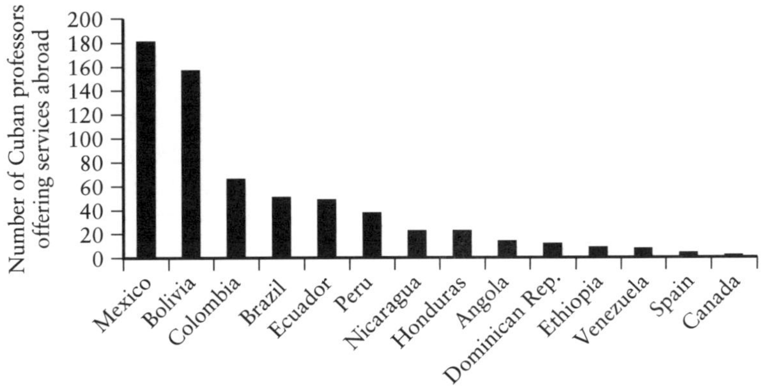

Source: Ministry of Higher Education (2002b).

exchange, scientific seminars, mobility, and the review and updating of agreements and letters of intent. Until a mechanism has been established, meetings are held annually, after which they are held biannually in alternating countries. Cuba currently holds meetings of university presidents with several countries, including Argentina, Bolivia, Brazil, Canada, China, Colombia, Ecuador, France, Germany, Italy, Mexico, Panama, Peru, Portugal, Spain, the United States, and Venezuela.

Accreditation and Recognition of Degrees, Diplomas, and Certificates of Studies

During the past 10 years, Cuban institutions have implemented regulations aimed at facilitating international exchanges. Formal processes exist for the accreditation of courses, modules, and programs taken abroad, and the foundations have been laid for the accreditation of graduate degrees, especially doctorates.

Cuba signed agreements governing accreditation and equivalency with UNESCO several years ago. It was an active member of the Institute for Higher Education in Latin America and the Caribbean (IESALC)–UNESCO Equivalencies Committee and continued relations and agreements entered into with the committee. Cuba has also been a part of the Andrés Bello Agreement since its implementation. That agreement aims to facilitate the establishment of equivalency of the undergraduate and graduate degrees granted in 10 Latin American countries. Bilateral agreements have been signed with several countries, and talks are underway with several others, primarily with regard to Cuba's willingness to sign all possible equivalency-related agreements.

Units and Structures that Promote and Facilitate International Cooperation

One of the main factors determining the achievement of tangible results in internationalization is the availability of international relations mechanisms with their own structure. These mechanisms needs to be managed by professionals who are conversant with international relations, who promote and maintain ongoing self-improvement, and who have the most advanced information media, such as the Internet, at their disposal.

Some universities possess a vice-president's department of international relations, others have an office or a department. Wherever the body is located, it is vital that it be closely linked to the university president and the primary mechanisms of the universities and that its main objective be strengthening the international scope of the institution's substantive activities.

International relations staff should strive for constant improvement. The fundamental areas of training are languages, information and communications technologies, project management, managerial skills in negotiation, marketing, strategic management, and, of course, extensive knowledge of the international relations of universities in the regions that concern them. It is valuable to have staffers from different specialties who are fluent in foreign languages.

The formation of a project management team with specialists in the area, a modern communications infrastructure, and immediate access to information sources are essential to strengthening international relations in each institution and in the ministry itself. This policy has been developed both at the ministerial level and at the level of the main Cuban universities.

Offices have been established at the ministerial level to provide aid for foreign students studying in Cuba. At the university level, dean's offices for foreign students or foreign student departments attached to international relations offices have been established.

Cuba provides free higher education to nationals of several countries, most of them in Africa. Since the early 1990s, it has also provided higher education on a mutually beneficial basis to nationals of dozens of countries in Latin America, Africa, and to a lesser extent Europe. This cooperation involves visits by Cuban professors, who help develop graduate programs, train local nationals, and provide consultancy services. A ministerial office has been created to deal with legal questions, financial issues, assistance to professors on sabbaticals in other countries, and related issues.

This office has ties with companies with which it shares developments and innovations stemming from scientific activities conducted by Cuban universities and research centers. Products offered include biotechnical products, complete production plants, machinery for the building industry, new materials, and medical equipment.

Cuba's Internationalization Policy

More than 65 percent of cooperation-related activities have been carried out with developed countries and top-level institutions. Foreign academics visiting Cuba work directly with the academic and scientific community, and the participation of Cuban faculty and researchers in international events continues to increase. While these indicators have been rising, they need to grow even more in the area of university exchange, which is vital to development.

Since 2003 the internationalization of higher education has been viewed as a key strategy in elevating the prestige of the Cuban higher education system. Within the framework of cooperation all Ministry of Higher

Education universities and research centers will create strategies that will help ensure that internationalization is reflected in their main substantive activities or key production areas. The Ministry of Higher Education's 2003 master strategy for internationalizing higher education includes the following specific strategies:

- Specify objectives for each country as the basis for the development of cooperation-related strategies.
- Develop academic networks, exchanges, and projects that will contribute to the training of professionals and to the development and optimal utilization of educational technologies, including distance learning, along international guidelines.
- Develop joint degree projects and scholarships for Cuban postdoctorate students, in line with the country's scientific policy.
- Participate in projects with top-level scientific institutions and in international networks and mega-projects.
- Develop the foreign scholarship program, ensuring proper training of scholarship holders.
- Take advantage of opportunities provided by the internationalization process to promote projects, academic services, and activities that improve infrastructure and strengthen economic and financial management in Cuba.

To ensure the implementation of specific strategies, Cuban universities and research centers will be developing independent analyses and devising medium- and long-term plans of actions. During the current stage, emphasis has been placed on strengthening network-related tasks for all substantive activities and, through the strengthening of national networks, exploiting the potential of international cooperation, which tend to give priority to the creation of regional and international cooperation networks.

The internationalization process of Cuban universities is fostered by strengths and opportunities. These include the good training of Cuban professionals, Cuba's good international contacts, its well-defined priorities, its rapid response to initiatives, its use of financing, and its capacity to cooperate with institutions throughout Latin American and the Caribbean.

As is normal in such a complex internationalization process, Cuban universities are also faced with challenges that must be addressed if they are to achieve the international and intercultural dimension they seek in their mission and substantive activities. Weaknesses include the lack of financing, inadequate infrastructure, the shortage of personnel with foreign language skills, scant familiarity with the area of networking and international projects, and the difficulty associated with transferring credits from one institution to another.

The Internationalization of the José Antonio Echeverría Advanced Polytechnic Institute

The Havana-based José Antonio Echeverría Advanced Polytechnic Institute (ISPJAE) is a technical university whose international relations policy may serve as an example. Like most Cuban universities, this university was created in the 1990s, in the midst of major changes. At the time of its creation, international cooperation was limited to the countries of Eastern Europe, with which Cuba had very stable agreements. Planning and annual budgets fostered and maintained bilateral technical and scientific exchanges and promoted the training of PhDs. Before the 1990s, a significant number of PhDs were trained at prestigious foreign universities, which helped strengthen Cuba's teaching and research faculty. At this time, there were no multilateral association networks and almost no undergraduate student mobility. Project execution levels were low outside of bilateral agreements. During the 1960s, projects were undertaken with Canada and UNESCO for faculty and university development. Universities were totally financed from the state budget, and there were no private contributions.

The experiences gained by universities worldwide in international cooperation have demonstrated that traditional models are being abandoned in favor of more modern cooperation-related models and policies. These new models have transformed cooperation from a recipient-oriented activity to an interactive activity. This new form of cooperation encourages bidirectional engagements and promotes mutual benefits. It facilitates joint programs, academic exchange, credit transfers, the recognition of degrees, and joint funding schemes based on the capabilities of the institutions themselves.

The ISPJAE possesses a clearly defined institutional international policy that is supported by its top authorities and that has been agreed upon by consensus within the university community and backed by an administrative and academic structure. It has developed activities in bilateral and multilateral cooperation, under different collaboration schemes. These include student and faculty exchange programs, technical assistance, joint research, joint programs, doctorate training programs in developed countries, training programs in Cuba for professionals from other countries, participation in networks, and the establishment of cooperation-related agreements.

None of the obstacles encountered over the years has impeded the development of this joint effort into an excellent example of South-South cooperation, with the training of professionals from developing countries representing an important activity. More than 1,700 engineers and architects from more than 40 countries, mainly in Africa, Asia, the

Middle East, and Latin America and the Caribbean have graduated from the ISPJAE. Many of these graduates occupy key positions in their own countries.

In 2002, 335 foreigners pursued undergraduate studies at ISPJAE and 314 students from 23 countries spent short periods there. In a program sponsored by the Project Trust Organization, students from Great Britain are helping the language department teach English while they take Spanish courses. Under the Academic Mobility and Exchange Program (PIMA) project of the Organization of Ibero-American States, students from the José Antonio Echeverría Advanced Polytechnic Institute, the University of Barcelona, the University of Chile, the University of Havana, and the University of San Juan (Argentina) are participating in exchange programs. Spanish students are received through programs sponsored by the Spanish Agency for International Cooperation. These exchanges have helped develop the skills of both students and faculty in international and intercultural affairs. Every year almost 200 scholars from prestigious universities carry out some kind of mainly graduate research or educational activity at the universities, while more than 100 of the university's own faculty teach in the master's programs of universities in 13 countries in Latin America and the Caribbean.

One example of international integration between enterprises and universities is the development of the diploma program in integral water management. The first phase of this project was successfully implemented, and the project is now in its second phase. Under the initiative, Aguas de Barcelona, in joint association with Aguas de la Habana and the Alicante and Castilla de la Mancha Universities in Spain, the chemical engineering faculty and ISPJAE's hydraulic research center train professionals in this important area. The Coahuila Autonomous University and the Aguas de Saltillo Company, both in Mexico, have now joined the effort.

The importance of training project agents for the university community and for other organizations has led to the center's developing of a diploma program in international cooperation management.

Professors at ISPJAE are involved in academic and scientific networks. In 2002 they participated in 12 of CYTED programs, in the telematic and educational network, in the Inter-American Organization of Higher Education's College of the Americas, and in 8 of the thematic teaching networks sponsored by Spain's Agency for International Cooperation. They also participate in 10 new networks in phase two of the European Union's ALFA program. Ten other Cuban universities and companies also participate in these networks or are linked to these projects.

Participation in international events is a priority for ISPJAE. Although resources are limited, some funds are still earmarked for this purpose. The presence of scholars in regional professional associations and international organizations is another priority. High levels of cooperation are maintained with several countries, the most important of which are Spain, Germany, Mexico, and Brazil.

Conclusions

The internationalization of higher education reflects the universal nature of learning and research. It has been reinforced by current political and economic integration processes, as well as by the growing need for inter-cultural understanding. The rising number of students, professors, and researchers working, living, and interacting within an international context attests to this trend. The expansion of different kinds of networks and of other forms of relationships between institutions, professors, and students has been facilitated by advances in information and communication technologies.

The development of higher education in Cuba has been closely linked to international relations and international cooperation. It has gone through different stages in which the global dimension has always been present in different ways. The level achieved by Cuban institutions in the internationalization process should be recognized.

In the special circumstances surrounding the current development of Cuba's universities, international relations and international cooperation are part of the strategy and policy of each institution. Internationalization is one of the master strategies to which Cuban education is committed in order to increase its strength and enhance its development. All the substantive activities of the system draw on, and contribute to, internationalization.

The development of international cooperation is viewed in Cuba as a fundamental strategy and as a process linking all universities and strengthening national and regional networks. The establishment of national networks is favored because it facilitates and helps ensure optimal use of foreign networks.

Despite the progress made, weaknesses are holding back the process. These include the lack of funding and infrastructure, inadequate command of foreign languages, and the lack of knowledge about international networks and projects.

International cooperation and collaboration are central to carrying out the mission of Cuba's institutions of higher education. Greater involvement is needed in international, regional, and subregional networks, and Cuba should continue to fulfill its commitments to the foreign scholarship program and to joint academic cooperation activities.

References

CEPES (Center for Studies on Higher Education Improvement). 2000. "Higher Education in Cuba in the 1990s." Advanced Learning Center of Higher Education, University of Havana.

Ministry of Higher Education. 2002a. "Status Report of the Cuban Ministry of Higher Education." Havana.

————. 2002b. "Status Report of the Office of International Relations." Havana.

————. 2003. "Master Strategy: Internationalization of Higher Education." Havana.

ONABE (Directora del Organismo Nacional de Administración de Bienes del Estado). 1961–2003. "Annual Reports of the National Foreign Scholarship Office." Havana.

8

Internationalization of Higher Education in Mexico

Jocelyne Gacel-Ávila

This chapter evaluates the current state of internationalization in Mexico. It describes the progress Mexico has made developing its higher education and the challenges it faces. To carry out this study, quantitative and qualitative methods were applied to answering the following questions: What is the international dimension in Mexico's national education policy? How advanced is the process of internationalization? What are the principal internationalization strategies adopted by Mexican institutions, particularly its public and private universities? What are the strengths, weaknesses, challenges, and perspectives of the internationalization process in Mexico?

The early years of the twenty-first century have witnessed an opening of international trade, an increase in information technology, and the creation of the knowledge society, all of which have increased demand for education. These changes have forced higher education institutions to restate their mission, agenda, and responsibilities and to seek innovative strategies for improving their quality and relevance.

This chapter examines whether the concept of comprehensive internationalization is genuinely understood by the main actors handling national and institutional educational policy or whether they continue to promote activities that are disconnected from and on the fringe of core institutional development. This is not a trivial distinction, because if internationalization strategies remain on the fringe, they have little chance of transforming higher education into the system the twenty-first century demands.

The Higher Education System in Mexico

Mexico's higher education system includes higher technical and associate professional degrees, *licenciatura* (bachelor's) degrees, and graduate degrees (master's and doctorates).

As of 1999, Mexico's higher education system comprised 1,250 institutions (counting only main institutions, not branches), 515 of which are state run and 735 are privately run (ANUIES 2000). The system comprises:

public universities, technological universities, private institutions, teacher training institutions, and other public institutions.

The subsystem of public universities is composed of 45 institutions. Most are autonomous public universities, which by law govern themselves. These institutions educate students, conduct research, and promote culture. This subsystem carries out more than half of all research in Mexico. Public universities educate 52 percent of all undergraduate students and 48 percent of graduate students.

The subsystem of technological education includes 147 institutions, which collectively serve the needs of 19 percent of all undergraduates and 6 percent of all graduates. This subsystem is coordinated for the most part by the federal government through the Sub-Department of Higher Education and Technological Research of the Department of Public Education, as well as by decentralized institutions of state governments.

The subsystem of technological universities is composed of decentralized public institutions that depend on state governments. All three levels of government—federal, state, and, in certain cases, municipal—have a say in their creation. Launched in 1991, the technological universities offer two-year programs. Mexico has 54 technological universities. The increase of educational opportunity in the public sector has occurred largely because of expansion of programs in this area, which has diversified higher education.

The subsystem of private education includes 598 institutions, not counting teacher training schools. Private institutions include universities (168), institutes (171), and centers, schools, and other institutions (259). The programs offered by these institutions must be recognized by the Department of Public Education or state governments or be incorporated into a public education institution. This subsystem accounts for 27.6 percent of undergraduate enrollment and 36.5 percent of graduate enrollment. Over the past few years, the importance of the private sector has been growing, particularly at the undergraduate level. Undergraduate enrollment at private institutions rose from 11.7 percent of total enrollment in 1975 to 27.6 percent in 1999, while graduate enrollment rose from 20.3 percent in 1985 to 36.5 percent in 1999. Growth has been disparate and fragmented. Some large elite institutions have developed, some with significant social prestige. But numerous small institutions, the quality of which is largely unknown, have emerged in response to specific local educational, economic, and political interests. Private institutions focus on the transmission of knowledge. Very few carry out research. For this reason most undergraduate programs and students are in the social and administrative sciences (68 percent in 1998); enrollment in health sciences is only 1 percent and that of natural and exact sciences is less than 1 percent.

The subsystem of teacher training schools prepares students to teach preschool, special education, and physical education. The group of institutions in this subsystem reached 357 schools in 1999, 220 of them state run and 137 privately run. They serve the needs of 11.5 percent of higher education students in Mexico.

According to Department of Public Education reports (http://sesic.sep.gob.mx/cgi-bin/index.pl), in the 2001/02 school year, 2,147,600 students were enrolled in higher education institutions in Mexico. This figure represents 22 percent of young adults 19–23. Sixty-eight percent of these students were studying at public institutions. In contrast with other Latin American countries, such as Brazil, Chile, and Colombia, the private sector in Mexico still educates a minority of students.

Public higher education in Mexico receives financing from both federal and state governments. The federal budget for higher education increased significantly in the past decade, rising from 0.42 percent of GDP in 1990 to 0.75 percent in 2002 (Secretaria de Educación Pública 2005).

The National Education Plan 2001–06

In the National Education Plan, the Department of Public Education sets the course for developing Mexico's national education system. The plan is based on three principles: the equitable expansion of access to education, the promotion of high-quality education for all, and the drive to federalize the educational system, transform management, and involve the community in education.

To widen access to higher education and extend its scope, the Department of Public Education sharply increased the number of scholarships and opened 45 new public institutions in 2001/02. The move added 90,000 places to the system.

Considerable resources have been allocated to scholarships for graduate study in order to raise the level of faculty at public institutions. Efforts include the Program to Improve Teaching Staff (PROMEP) and the Program to Raise the Level of Academic Staff (SUPERA). The purpose of these programs is to enhance the quality of full-time teachers in the public sector. The results are beginning to become apparent: 61.6 percent of full-time teachers now have graduate degrees (14.9 percent at the doctorate level and 46.7 percent at the master's level). By 2006, 100 percent of full-time faculty in higher education institutions will hold graduate degrees.

The Fund for the Modernization of Higher Education (FOMES) was created in 1989 to improve the infrastructure of higher education institutions in terms of modern technology, libraries, laboratories, language centers, computer centers, and buildings, as well as to develop programs to improve the operation of institutions, such as programs to conduct follow-up on graduates, systems of information to support educational decisionmaking, and evaluation of programs. Other programs support bi- and trilateral

Figure 8.1 Mexico's National Education Plan 2001–06

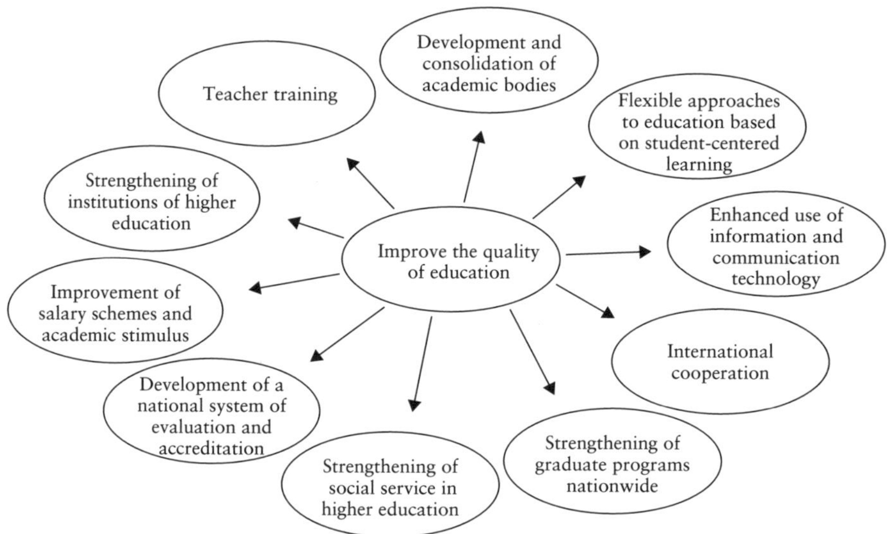

Source: Secretaria de Educación Pública (2002).

institutional collaboration, as well as a wide range of academic links. The National Education Plan 2001–06 includes international cooperation as a strategy for raising the quality of the higher education system (figure 8.1).

Quality Assessment

Quality assessment has been a priority for the Mexican higher education system in recent years. A number of bodies have been created to evaluate the quality of different products and programs. There is, for example, the Register of Graduate Programs of Excellence, supported by the Department of Public Education and the National Council for Science and Technology (CONACYT), the Interinstitutional Committees for the Evaluation of Higher Education, and the National Commission for Evaluation, an independent body that evaluates students at admission and on completion of studies as a means of diagnosing quality.

In 2000 the Council for the Accreditation of Higher Education was created. Its principal function is to establish a general framework for accreditation processes in higher education programs, as well as guidelines for the recognition of accreditation organizations for higher education programs. In tandem with these initiatives, the Federation of Private Mexican Institutions of Higher Education (FIMPES) established its program for the accreditation of institutions. At the same time, educational institutions were given incentives to submit to certification of their administrative and support processes by means of the International Organization for Standardization (ISO) 9000 standard. In another initiative, an agreement was signed between the Department of Public Education and FIMPES to simplify the administrative process for evaluating private institutions that wish to become incorporated into the subsystem of national higher education.

The International Dimension in National Policy for Higher Education

The international dimension has been incorporated in the National Education Plan, which recognizes international cooperation as vital for the continued development of higher education.

Rationale

The principal motivation for international cooperation is to improve the quality of education. According to the National Education Plan 2001–06, the quality of education will be improved by expanding international cooperation, forming strategic alliances in the areas of culture and education, strengthening exchange programs and student and faculty mobility, increasing joint international research and teaching programs at different academic levels, and establishing networks of collaboration in various academic fields. In a more recent document, importance is given to the need to develop competencies that will enable graduates to enhance the international status of Mexico and to be competitive with graduates from other countries in the face of the challenges created by NAFTA and Mexico's membership in the OECD.

The International Dimension of the National Education Plan

The National Education Plan seeks to improve the quality of education by means of "intensive interinstitutional collaboration through regional, national and international networks, and programs of student and staff mobility" (Secretaria de Educación Pública 2001, p. 198). The plan stresses the need to "make systematic schemes of international cooperation in order to increase the exploitation of such activities and take advantage of resources from abroad so as to strengthen the development of education in the country," citing "a lack of coordination between institutions and financial organisms" (Secretaria de Educación Pública 2001, pp. 215–16). It proposes the establishment of 20 international networks, without giving details of the types of networks envisaged or their objectives.

From this it follows that the Department of Public Education does not promote strategies of comprehensive internationalization as an integral part of its development policy.[1] The Department of Public Education guidelines promote a style of management of international cooperation that is designed to respond and give support to what international organizations offer. They emphasize the need to create schemes that make the accreditation and certification of studies easier and to establish equivalencies across international systems of education. No specific proposal to accommodate these needs has been put forward, however.

Programs of support and financing for higher education institutions proposed by the Department of Public Education do not include fundamental elements, such as internationalization of the curriculum and mobility of students and faculty, leaving initiatives to the institutions themselves. The only program of student mobility cofinanced by the Department of Public Education is the Program for the Mobility of Students in North America (PROMESAN). Its impact is limited, and the number of students supported is small. Moreover, the implementation of this program remains on the fringe of regular mechanisms and procedures for curricular innovation and institutional development.

National policy in Mexico is not innovative as far as internationalization is concerned. As a consequence, it does not support or reinforce this process at the institutional level.

Principal Actors in the Process

In addition to the Department of Public Education, a number of bodies promote international cooperation activities in Mexico. These include the National Science and Technology Council (CONACYT), the Foreign Relations Department, the National Association of Universities and Institutions of Higher Education (ANUIES), the Mexican Association for International Education (AMPEI), and the Mexican Federation of Private Institutions of Higher Education (FIMPES). All of these bodies promote or finance programs of international cooperation, the training and updating

---

[1] The concept of comprehensive internationalization developed by the Institute of Management for Higher Education of the OECD and the Center for Research and Innovation emphasizes that, in order to improve the quality of the higher education system and support reforms in response to its new globalized situation, internationalization strategies should be applied to three distinct levels: micro (the process of teaching and learning in the classroom), medium (the curriculum), and macro (decisive policies and institutional strategies) (Van der Wende 1994). This conceptualization goes beyond mere international cooperation and mobility of individuals: it recommends the development of policies and strategies of internationalization that are integrated into the mission and outlook of the institution and are a central part of its policies of institutional development.

of human resources, international collaborative research projects, and student and faculty mobility.

THE NATIONAL COUNCIL FOR SCIENCE AND TECHNOLOGY
Since its creation in 1971, CONACYT has provided Mexican universities with considerable financial resources for knowledge production, for scholarship programs for graduate studies in Mexican and foreign institutions abroad, for the promotion of international research projects, and for the national development of quality graduate programs. All of these programs have helped facilitate internationalization in Mexico.

Internationalization of Human Resources
The CONACYT awards 75 percent of all scholarships for graduate studies for Mexican students and faculty. The most popular place to study has traditionally been the United States, followed by the United Kingdom, Spain, and France (figure 8.2) (ANUIES 2000). In 2002, for the first time in the history of CONACYT a larger number of awards were given for graduate studies in the United Kingdom (740) than the United States (703). This was attributed to the successful promotion of studies by the British government through the Education UK project (http://www.embajadabritanica.com.mx/becas.htm). The knowledge areas most in demand are the exact and biological sciences, the social sciences, and engineering and technology (figure 8.3).

Figure 8.2 Geographical Distribution of CONACYT Graduate Scholarships

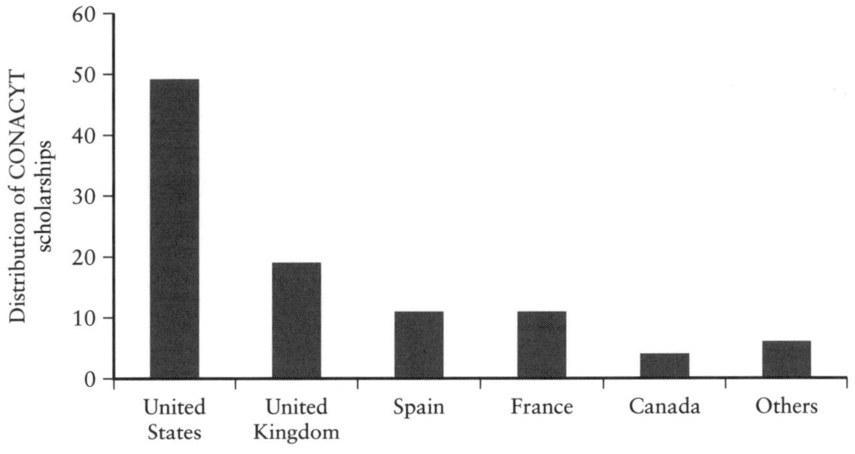

Source: ANUIES (2002).

Figure 8.3 Distribution of CONACYT Scholarship Holders by Knowledge Area

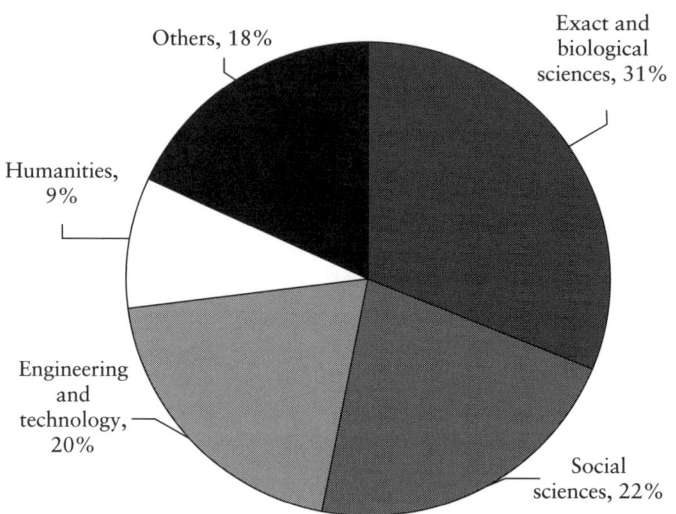

Source: ANUIES (2000).

Ninety-one percent of scholarship holders are at public institutions. Forty-one percent are between 25 and 29 years old. On their return home, 80 percent work in the public sector (68 percent in higher education), 14 percent in government, and 6 percent in industry and health. Of 26,000 scholarships awarded between 1971 and 2000, 10,900 (42 percent) were granted between 1990 and 2000.

Five percent of all scholarship holders failed to return to Mexico. To prevent this brain drain, Mexico has implemented a repatriation program to finance the return of students and give them support in the process of reincorporation into the national higher education system.

Mexicans who study abroad are a key element in the process of internationalization in higher education, particularly since 68 percent of them end up in higher education. On their return, these academics become ideal leaders of international initiatives and collaboration, thanks to their contacts and relations with the institution abroad where they studied. Unfortunately, there are no systematic national or institutional policies designed to take advantage of returning students in order to internationalize the curriculum.

Internationalization of Research

CONACYT finances joint international projects through bilateral agreements with countries in Europe, the Americas, and Asia. It has collaboration agreements for research with 21 scientific bodies in Europe (in Belgium, Bulgaria, the Czech Republic, France, Hungary, Italy, Germany, Poland, the Russian Federation, Spain, and the United Kingdom), giving Europe the leadership in matters of joint research projects with Mexican institutions. On the American continent, CONACYT maintains relations with 10 scientific bodies, in Argentina, Brazil, Chile, Cuba, Peru, the United States, and Venezuela. Moreover, it has collaborative relationships with six bodies in Asia (in China, Japan, the Republic of Korea, and Vietnam). CONACYT's support consists of providing public Mexican institutions with partial financing of research projects carried out jointly with foreign scientists (50 percent of transportation and travel costs). In 2001 CONACYT supported 462 joint research projects with foreign institutions, up from 300 in 1990 (table 8.1).

FOREIGN RELATIONS DEPARTMENT
The Foreign Relations Department receives and integrates proposed work agendas from Mexican higher education institutions, which it presents and negotiates with various intergovernmental commissions that represent the interests of the Mexican government and those of other countries in education, culture, science, and technology for the purposes of bilateral or multilateral collaboration. It also disseminates information to Mexican educational institutions regarding the availability of scholarships offered by foreign governments. In turn, it offers its own scholarships to foreigners who wish to study in Mexico. The Foreign Relations Department also has a program that enables Mexican students to intern at Mexico's consulates and embassies all over the world.

The Foreign Relations Department supports the internationalization of human resources in Mexico, the mobility of Mexican and foreign students, and faculty exchanges between Mexican and foreign institutions (tables 8.2 and 8.3). There is, however, a lack of coordination between these efforts and programs organized by the Department of Public Education and ANUIES.

Table 8.1 Number of Joint Research Projects Supported by CONACYT, 1990

Country	Number of projects
France	133
Germany	61
Spain	28
United States	28
Cuba	24
Argentina	15
Italy	12

Source: www.conacyt.mx

Table 8.2 Number of Foreign Students in Mexico and Mexican Students Abroad Supported by Government Grants, 2001 and 2002

Region	Foreign students in Mexico		Mexican students abroad	
	2001	2002	2001	2002
Africa	54	50	0	0
Asia	62	50	71	94
Caribbean	52	50	4	3
Central America	154	201	41	46
Europe	178	172	215	265
Middle East	6	10	17	3
North America	21	27	66	82
Pacific	4	3	11	11
South America	165	210	22	44

Source: Secretaria de Educación Pública (2005).

The patterns of geographical distribution are similar for students and academics. There is intense collaboration between Mexican universities and those in South America, Central America, and Europe. There has also been a significant increase in exchanges with Asian and Pacific countries. Mexico also supports development in Africa.

NATIONAL ASSOCIATION OF UNIVERSITIES AND INSTITUTIONS OF
HIGHER EDUCATION
The National Association of Universities and Institutions of Higher Education (ANUIES) is an NGO that represents the majority of public

Table 8.3 Number of Foreign Academics in Mexican Institutions and Mexican Academics Abroad, 2001 and 2002

Region	Foreign academics in Mexico		Mexican academics abroad	
	2001	2002	2001	2002
Africa	30	30	0	0
Asia	0	20	0	0
Caribbean	1	2	0	1
Central America	5	7	4	0
Europe	0	0	14	23
Middle East	0	7	0	0
North America	21	0	10	11
Pacific	0	6	0	0
South America	19	22	19	19

Source: Secretaria de Educación Pública (2005).

higher education institutions and many of the most prestigious private institutions in Mexico. It has 138 members. ANUIES is a highly representative body that has decisive impact on the design and implementation of national educational policy. Its ruling council, the Compatible Council of Public Universities and Institutions, which includes the heads of the principal institutions in Mexico, is instrumental in determining the orientation of educational programs. Its annual meeting, which brings together the most important actors in higher education, is the most important forum for debate of Mexico's major programs and policy.

According to ANUIES, the institutions with the greatest degree of international relations are those in the Federal District and in the states of Jalisco, Nuevo León, and Puebla (Pallán 1996). A 1997 study by ANUIES revealed that the United States was Mexico's most important partner: half of all academic exchanges were with the United States; one-third with European countries (the United Kingdom, France, and Spain); and 15 percent with Latin American countries. The majority of foreign students in Mexico were undergraduates from the United States taking short courses on Mexican history, culture, and literature or studying Spanish. The proximity of the United States, the strong social and economic ties between the two societies, knowledge of U.S. educational institutions, and the mutual recognition of academic degrees all contributed to the strength of this relationship (ANUIES).

Since 1997 the flow of Mexican and foreign students and academics to and from Europe, Canada, Asia, and Oceania has increased significantly; collectively these countries now outweigh the United States. The lack of nationwide reports after 1997 has made an accurate assessment of the situation difficult, however. Despite declarations about the importance of international cooperation, there appears to be very little interest in measuring the flow of Mexican and foreign students and academics.

The 1997 ANUIES report (ANUIES 2000, p. 101), notes that "from the 1990s onwards, the relevance and management of international activities has acquired strategic importance and is increasingly present in the framework of policies designed for the development of Mexican higher education, especially since the creation of regional economic communities, the opening of trade to the outside world and the internationalization of socioeconomic phenomena that influence the functioning of societies in a global manner." At the end of the 1990s, the importance of interinstitutional relations was reiterated in the official discourse of educational authorities as a strategic element to improve the quality of education. It is highly likely that the discourse reflects more official parroting than genuine conviction.

After polling major actors in higher education, in 2000 ANUIES presented a document titled "Higher Education in the Twenty-First Century: Paths for Strategic Development." The report proposes the implementation of four fundamental programs of educational policy at the national level: evaluation and accreditation, a national information network, academic networks and mobility, and the virtual university. The report is of particular importance given the fact that it was the basis on which the federal government defined its policy on higher education. The report sets the goal of establishing a National Network of Cooperation and Exchange with regional nodes that are the responsibility of the Regional Councils of ANUIES. These networks would design and implement strategies for internationalization and cooperation at the national and international level (ANUIES 2000). This plan proposed as a goal for 2001 that higher education institutions have an institutional strategic program for developing cooperation and exchange that emphasizes horizontal collaboration and exploitation of institutional areas of strength. Like the National Education Plan, the plan emphasized the need to create practical schemes for recognizing credits and academic equivalence in order to facilitate the mobility of students at the state, regional, and national level in all regions of ANUIES. It stressed the importance of establishing agreements for interinstitutional collaboration in order to strengthen research and doctoral programs. As a goal for 2002, it recommended that Mexican higher education institutions create programs for the mobility of faculty at the regional, national, and international level. It proposed that by 2003 all higher education institutions have innovative institutional models to increase the flexibility of their schemes of organization and administration for cooperation and exchange and that they create new curricula with flexible syllabuses in order to increase student mobility. For 2006 it proposed that these programs constitute the operational base of the higher education system (ANUIES 2000).

By 2004, three years after the plan was published, the objectives had not been reached. Regional mobility networks were created, but the number of students that had benefited from them was extremely small. In the Central Western Region, one of the most active in Mexico, for example, only 127 students participated in exchanges, of which 87 took place within the same region and 40 were with Spanish universities (ANUIES 2002). Attempts to establish a national system for accreditation and recognition of periods of study in other institutions failed completely, and it was not even possible to produce a proposal for discussion purposes. The program for mobility of academics at the regional, national, and international level was not implemented nor was the program for mobility of graduate students. ANUIES provides no financing for these programs: participation in these changes has been left to the initiative of the institutions themselves.

Despite the scant progress achieved, internationalization is repeatedly cited as a priority in visions and development plans. Some higher education institutions have actually incorporated strategic internationalization plans into their development plans.[2] Such schemes, however, reflect the initiative of the institutions themselves rather than any action by ANUIES.

ANUIES has given no consideration to improving the professionalism of the staff in charge of internationalization activities. There have been only sporadic workshops on managing international cooperation, which have not enabled administrators to develop the know-how to support the basic conception and adoption of internationalization strategies within their institutions. ANUIES has also failed to promote studies or publications on the theme of internationalization.

On the positive side, in research and human resource development, ANUIES has promoted horizontal cooperation projects with institutions in Central America through the ANUIES–Higher Council for Centro American Universities program. (A similar initiative launched by the American Council on Education failed.) ANUIES signed an agreement with the Council of Rectors of the Province of Quebec that allows Mexican students to study in Quebec without paying tuition. ANUIES was also a focal point for programs of collaboration with Europe, such as the Inter-University Cooperation Program (previously Intercampus), the Young Doctors of Spain Program, the German Academic Exchange Service, the Evaluation-Orientation of Scientific Cooperation Program of the French government, and the High Level Latin-American Scholarship Program (AlßAN), to cite just a few.

ANUIES is an important body for organizing international cooperation activities that encourage the internationalization of human resources and educational programs. It has focused mainly on disseminating information on opportunities for international cooperation offered by developed nations, however. It provides no financial resources for organizing or implementing programs for internationalization or for internationalizing the curriculum. ANUIES has not developed sufficient know-how to advise institutions on conceiving, designing, and adopting comprehensive internationalization strategies that are proactive and integrated into the academic development policies of Mexican educational institutions.

THE MEXICAN FEDERATION OF PRIVATE INSTITUTIONS OF HIGHER EDUCATION
The Mexican Federation of Private Institutions of Higher Education (FIMPES) includes the most prestigious private institutions in Mexico. It has less scope than the bodies mentioned above, since private institutions are in the minority in Mexico and only 10 percent of them belong to FIMPES.

---

[2] The Instituto Tecnológico de Estudios Superiores de Monterrey, the Universidad of the Americas at Puebla, the University of Guanajuato, the University of Guadalajara, and the University of Monterrey are examples.

FIMPES has developed procedures for evaluating and certifying the quality of private institutions in Mexico. It has formed commissions to develop agendas on research, academic links, information for promoting exchanges between researchers and national and international institutions, and networks of experts (http://www.fimpes.org.mx/investigacionVinc.htm).

The Mexican Association for International Education (AMPEI) was founded in 1992 at the initiative of a group of academics and professionals with interest in academic exchange and international cooperation. Its goal is to "improve the quality of higher education by integrating an international dimension into its substantive functions" (http://www.ampei.org.mx).

AMPEI has about 200 members, 51 percent from the private sector, 38 percent from the public sector, and 11 percent from foreign institutions. Nearly all of the higher education institutions in Mexico involved in international programs are members of AMPEI.

AMPEI has played a key role in promoting internationalization of higher education in Mexico. Among other activities, it organizes an annual meeting on education and international cooperation, with seminars and workshops to train and update members on internationalization, and publishes *Educación Global*. AMPEI has also conducted research, surveys, and questionnaires, including a census of foreign students in Mexico (1994–98); created profiles of departments responsible for academic exchange in Mexico; published a book, *Internationalization of Higher Education in Latin America and the Caribbean: Reflexions and Guidelines*, on cooperation with the Inter-American Organization for Higher Education; and published a directory, EduMexico, to promote Mexican higher education institutions abroad.

Thanks to AMPEI, Mexico is represented in a number of international forums on internationalization and international cooperation. It participates in the annual meetings of the National Association of International Educators (NAFSA) in the United States and the European Association for International Education (EAIE) in Europe. One feature that distinguishes it from the majority of organizations of this type in Latin America—such as the Forum for Consultation of Brazilian Universities on International Affairs, the Colombian Network for International Cooperation in Higher Education, and the Commission of International Relations of the Council of Rectors in Chile—is that it is an NGO that is independent of the national association of universities. Its organization is similar to that of international associations of international education, such as NAFSA and the Association of International Education Administrators in the United States or EAIE in Europe.

AMPEI does not receive financing from the Department of Public Education or ANUIES; it is financed by membership fees and support from international organizations, such as the Ford Foundation. This lack of support from the Department of Public Education and other government organizations makes AMPEI's financing insecure. It appears that there is no interest on the part of official Mexican bodies to support the development and maintenance of this type of organization, which has nevertheless succeeded in raising consciousness about internationalization of higher education in Mexico.

Strategies for Internationalization at the Institutional Level

Most Mexican institutions seek to internationalize in order to (in order of priority) improve the quality of education (as is the policy at national level); seek international accreditation; develop faculty, prepare graduates for a highly competitive, international labor market; increase revenues; and, at the bottom of the list, increase knowledge of other cultures.[3] The data presented below are based on quantitative and qualitative research on members of ANUIES and AMPEI (Gacel-Ávila 2002).

International Agreements

Public universities lead in the signing of international cooperation agreements (table 8.4), but 82 percent of these agreements are inactive. Among private institutions, 52 percent of agreements are inactive.

The public sector is also the leader in joint research agreements, faculty mobility, international research projects, and technical assistant projects.

Table 8.4 International Agreements Signed by Public and Private Universities in Mexico

Type of university	Public Sector	Private Sector
International agreements	1,294	907
Research agreements	533	60
International research projects	306	41
Faculty mobility	396	230
Student mobility	835	418
Development cooperation	81	5

Note: The number of agreements is an estimate, because not all institutions completed the questionnaire. The results are nevertheless sufficiently valid to draw general conclusions.
Source: Gacel-Ávila (2002).

---

[3] These results were obtained by polling individuals responsible for these areas in each institution.

Nationwide, public institutions carry out most of the research conducted in Mexico.

The fact that there are a greater number of agreements for faculty mobility in the public sector indicates recognition of the importance of retraining staff and bringing them up to date in order to raise the quality of education. Eighty-one percent of public universities provide their scholars with resources to attend conferences and various international academic events, compared with only 25 percent in the private sector. Two-thirds of public sector universities but just one-third of private institutions invest in scholarships to train their faculty. Ninety percent of the public universities and 35 percent of private universities provide sabbaticals.

Student Mobility

Private institutions are the leaders in student mobility, thanks to the greater economic means of students' parents. In order to offset this disadvantage, some public universities offer their students financial support to participate in student exchange programs.

The primary destination of Mexican students from public institutions is institutions in Latin America; students from private institutions overwhelmingly prefer the United States (table 8.5). These data differ markedly from those of the ANUIES 1997 survey, which shows the United States as the leading destination.

Private institutions have twice as many student mobility agreements as public institutions, seven times as many students on exchange visits abroad, and five times as many foreign students (table 8.6).

The only data on foreign students in Mexico (tables 8.7 and 8.8) come from the 1997/98 AMPEI survey (Gacel-Ávila and Rojas 1999a). According to these figures, 69 percent of foreign students are undergraduates who come to Mexico to study Spanish for a single semester. Only 10 percent come to Mexico for graduate studies.

Table 8.5 Preferred Destinations of Mexican Students Studying Abroad, 2002 (percent)

Region	Public institutions	Private institutions
Latin America	38	14
Europe	31	23
United States	22	46
Canada	7	12
Asia and Oceania	2	5

Source: Gacel-Ávila (2002).

Table 8.6 Measures of International Student Mobility at Public and Private Universities in Mexico

Type of institution	Public	Private	Total
Number of student mobility agreements	418	835	1,253
Number of Mexican students studying abroad	636	4,289	4,925
Number of foreign students	639	3,334	3,973

Note: Due to the small number of responses to this survey, the results should be used only as a measure of general trends.
Source: Gacel-Ávila (2002).

Table 8.7 Geographical Origin, Marital Status, and Age of Foreign Students in Mexico

Item	Percent of total
Geographical origin	
North America	61.7
South America	17.7
Europe	10.3
Asia	10.0
Oceania	0.3
Marital status	
Married	15
Single	85
Age	
16–21	35.8
22–27	49.5

Source: Gacel-Ávila (2002); Gacel-Ávila and Rojas (1999b).

Table 8.8 Number of Foreign Students in Mexico During 1998/99 Academic Year

Type of program	Public	Private	Total
Undergraduate programs (entire program)	193	2,983	3,176
Graduate programs (entire program)	126	295	421
Spanish and culture programs	3,714	955	4,669
Student exchange programs (one or two semesters)	672	3,397	4,069
Total	4,705	7,630	12,335

Note: Due to the small number of responses to this survey, the results should be used only as a measure of general trends.
Source: Gacel-Ávila (2002); Gacel-Ávila and Rojas (1999a).

The rest of the students, most of them Latin Americans, pursue undergraduate studies in health sciences (29 percent), exact sciences and engineering (28 percent), and administrative and economic science (24 percent). The majority of graduate students study engineering (50 percent) and administrative and economic science (39 percent).

The data indicate a greater number of foreign students in private institutions. There are a number of reasons for this. One is that private universities consider foreign students a valuable source of income. Another is that some private universities have promoted their programs and provided adequate institutional support. Finally, many private universities regard the presence of foreign students as a sign of prestige and a means of internationalizing their institutions.

The greater number of students in public sector institutions studying Spanish and Mexican culture can be explained by the fact that these universities have a stronger academic tradition in these areas.[4] The courses are organized as extension programs and are a source of income.

Internationalization of the Curriculum

The internationalization of higher education requires changes in the curriculum to ensure that the programs offered are in line with programs abroad.

LEARNING FOREIGN LANGUAGES

Learning foreign languages is obligatory in 77 percent of the universities surveyed (61 percent of public universities and 39 percent of private ones). Half of private institutions and just 13 percent of public ones expect students to have a command of English before commencing studies. Two-thirds of public institutions and 86 percent of private institutions require their students to acquire credits in a foreign language as a requirement for graduating. But only 9 percent of public and 28 percent of private universities demand a higher level of proficiency upon graduation than at matriculation, suggesting that the language requirement is probably more of an administrative requirement than a genuine policy to promote the learning of foreign languages.

CURRICULUM INNOVATION

None of the institutions surveyed reported curriculum modification or innovation designed to integrate an international, intercultural, and comparative dimension into its educational programs. As in national educational policy, institutions do not propose designing new programs to develop

---

[4] Universities with strong Spanish language programs include the National Autonomous University of Mexico, the University of Guadalajara, the University of Guanajuato, and the University of Veracruz.

global consciousness in order to prepare students to become citizens of the world (Gacel-Ávila 2003).[5]

Curricula in Mexico tend to be strongly focused on training professionals. Students lack flexibility and spend more hours in class than students in other OECD countries, a requirement that is particularly burdensome given the fact that most Mexican students are part-time students. All these factors make mobility and independent investigation by students difficult. Despite insistence that they adhere to UNESCO's guidelines, Mexican universities have failed to implement student-centered curricula or designed curricula according to the four pillars of the *Education of the Future*: learning to be, learning to do, learning to know, and learning to live together (Delors 1997).

Mexican universities usually consider as strategy of the internationalization of the curriculum student and faculty mobility programs, signing collaboration agreements, as well as joint study programs with foreign universities. The survey found no instances of the concept of "internationalization at home" (Nilson and Otten 2003), a concept with which Mexican universities are not familiar.

Programs of Study

Most foreign students in Spanish language programs spend one or two semesters in Mexico, for which they receive credit from their home institution. Virtual mobility is scarce.[6]

Double degrees, in which the degree is awarded by both institutions, seem to be more common than joint degrees, possibly because it is a means of overcoming the problems of certification requirements, graduation, and national accreditation.

Licenciatura *(Undergraduate) Level*
Eighty percent of the institutions surveyed report having no teaching program organized jointly with foreign institutions. Among the 20 percent with programs, private institutions dominate, offering courses in economics and administrative sciences; social sciences and the humanities; art, architecture, and design; and the exact sciences and engineering.

Graduate Level
Fifty percent of the institutions surveyed (57 percent of public institutions and 40 percent of private ones) report having at least one joint program.

---

[5] *Global consciousness* can be defined as comprehension and acceptance of foreign cultures, the availability of certain aspects of knowledge, or possession of information on certain aspects of socioeconomic and ecological world problems (Oxford Dictionary of New Words 1991).

[6] One example is the University of Guadalajara, in association with the Oberta University of Cataluña.

These statistics reflect the situation nationwide, where the public sector maintains leadership, since private universities make undergraduate studies their priority.

At public universities these programs are found in the social sciences and humanities (38 percent), economics and administrative science (31 percent), and biology and agricultural science (19 percent). At private universities economics and administrative science predominate (35 percent), followed by social sciences and the humanities (29 percent) and the exact sciences and engineering (18 percent).

The majority of double and joint award programs are at private universities[7] or at universities near the U.S. border.[8] These programs were spurred by NAFTA.

The North American Mobility Program (PROMESAN), which is financed by the governments of Mexico, the United States, and Canada, has led the way in organizing study programs with a North American dimension at Mexican, U.S., and Canadian universities. This program led to the creation of about 50 consortia of universities between 1995 and 2001 (CONAHEC 2002).

AREA STUDIES

A weakness in the curriculum of Mexican universities is the paucity of departments or centers of study specializing in foreign cultures or civilizations. Only 10 such centers exist, six focusing on North America, three on Asia, and one on Europe. Most of these centers are at public universities.

BRANCHES ABROAD

Only one university, the National Autonomous University of Mexico, has foreign campuses, two in the United States and one in Canada.[9] Mexican culture and Spanish are taught at these campuses.

The Instituto Tecnológico de Estudios Superiores de Monterrey has offices in a number of Latin American countries (Brazil, Colombia, Chile, Ecuador, Honduras, Panama, Peru, and Venezuela); in Europe (France); and in the United States (Miami). These offices represent the institute and sell on-line educational services. Other private universities, such as the Autonomous University of Guadalajara, have also set up recruitment offices abroad.

---

[7] Examples include the Centro de Enseñanza Técnica y Superior, the Instituto Tecnológico de Estudios Superiores de Monterrey, and the University of the Americas in Cholula.

[8] Examples include the Autonomous University of Chihuahua, the Autonomous University of Ciudad Juarez, the Autonomous University of Nuevo Leon, the Autonomous University of Tamaulipas, and the University of Sonora.

[9] The Permanent Extension School in San Antonio and the National Autonomous University of Mexico (UNAM) Extension School in Hull, Canada. Recently, the UNAM opened a small facility in Chicago.

THE TEACHING/LEARNING PROCESS
No university in either the public or private sector reports using innovative pedagogical methods using foreign students in the classroom. However, some universities organize extracurricular programs that facilitate interaction between local and foreign students.

Export of Educational Services

Only a few private universities have begun to export their services. The Instituto Tecnológico de Estudios Superiores de Monterrey, the leader in this area, offers degree programs and courses on line abroad, and it recently gave support to the creation of the University Tec Millennium and of Centers for Community Development, which will target alternative sectors of the educational market in Mexico as well as areas of the United States with large Mexican populations. In the case of public universities, which depend exclusively on federal and state funding, new information technology is used solely to increase their coverage locally and nationwide.

International Cooperation Networks and Membership in National and International Associations

About two-thirds of the institutions surveyed report participating in international cooperation networks. Fifty-two percent of the networking projects were in the public sector.

The universities surveyed belong to the following international associations (in order of importance): the Consortium for Collaboration in Higher Education in North America, the Inter-American Organization for Higher Education, the Inter-American Union of Universities of Latin America, the International Association of Universities, the International Association of University Presidents, the National Association of International Educators, and the Hispanic Association of Colleges and Universities.

Infrastructure for the Reception of Foreign Students and Academics

Only three universities report having residence facilities for foreign students (the University of Guadalajara, the University of the Americas, and the Monterrey Technological Institute). Among public universities, only the University of Guadalajara has an international house to receive foreign students and academics. Elsewhere, foreign students must choose between home-stay programs or renting accommodations. Lack of on-campus housing makes it difficult to attract foreign students and reflects the limited priority given to the reception of foreign students in Mexico.

Perceptions of Different University Actors

Surveys of and interviews with students, academics, and administrative staff reveal their perceptions of the process of national and institutional internationalization.

STUDENTS

Sixty-one percent of students at public institutions—and just 7 percent of students at private institutions—believe their university does not prepare them adequately for the challenges of globalization. Only 20 percent believe that coverage of internationalization in the syllabus is adequate (13 percent at public universities, 43 percent at private institutions).

During the course of their studies, only about half of all students had a visiting professor from abroad. The other half had a foreign professor only twice during their period of study. Sixty-eight percent of the visiting professors gave lectures, 27 percent gave full courses, and 3 percent gave tutorials.

Fifty-three percent of students report having had no contact with foreign students during their studies (67 percent at public universities, 5 percent at private ones). Ninety-eight percent of students consider international experience important but not very important (table 8.9).

FACULTY

Faculty members' main motivation for internationalization is to improve the quality of education (table 8.10). They also believe that internationalization helps prepare their students for the job market.

Half of all faculty at public institutions—but just 11 percent at private institutions—regard internationalization as not very important for the institution. As far as obstacles to the internationalization process are concerned, 100 percent of public institutions and 72 percent of private ones believe that the main obstacle is lack of a national policy to promote the process. Most attribute this failure to lack of vision by national authorities in the face of what are perceived as more pressing priorities. Faculty surveyed

Table 8.9 Student Motivations for Supporting Internationalization of Higher Education in Mexico

Motivation	Percent of all students
Improve quality of education	49
Prepare for the job market	33
Gain knowledge of other cultures	8
Gain personal experience	6
Learn a foreign language	3

Source: Gacel-Ávila (2002).

Table 8.10 Faculty Motivations for Internationalization of Higher Education in Mexico

Motivation	Percent of all faculty
Improve quality of education	48
Prepare for the job market	31
Gain knowledge of other cultures	12
Gain personal experience	6
Learn a foreign language	3

Source: Gacel-Ávila (2002).

consider the lack of financial resources the least important obstacle. In terms of geographical preferences, faculty in public institutions prefer cooperation projects with European universities, whereas the preference in private universities is with North America.

Some resistance to the idea of internationalization is evident in public universities, where 25 percent of academics regard it as a threat to national culture. At private institutions just 9 percent of faculty perceive internationalization as a threat.

In the opinion of academics, the number of student and staff mobility programs is insufficient. They cite among the greatest obstacles to student mobility the lack of family resources and scholarships and the rigidity of the curriculum, which makes recognition of studies carried out abroad difficult.

Seventy-four percent of professors regard their students' knowledge of foreign languages as insufficient; all professors at public institutions rate students' knowledge of languages as bad. They attribute this situation to the lack of motivation and the poor quality of teachers and language teaching programs. With certain exceptions, public institutions have not been able to develop policies to overcome this problem.[10] At private institutions, just 22 percent of faculty consider students' command of foreign languages poor.

Nearly all of the faculty surveyed (100 percent at public institutions, 85 percent at private ones) mention the lack of incentives for internationalization as a fundamental obstacle to progress. According to them, if this movement is to succeed, there must be more economic support, more recognition for international cooperation, and more emphasis on curriculum reform. Like students, 69 percent of faculty regard education inadequate to meet the needs of the twenty-first century. Forty percent consider

---

[10] In 2000 the Autonomous University of San Luis Potosi established an aggressive program to make the learning of a second language obligatory for all undergraduate students. These courses are integral to the curriculum and not merely an administrative requirement, as they are elsewhere.

Table 8.11 Administrative Staff's Motivation for Favoring Internationalization

Motivation	*Percent of all administrative staff*
Improve quality of education	71
Gain international accreditation	9
Foster individual development	9
Prepare students for the job market	6
Increase revenues	5

Source: Gacel-Ávila (2002).

that the organization of international activities is insufficient to provide students with competencies for the twenty-first century.

ADMINISTRATIVE STAFF

Administrative staff's main motivation for internationalizing is improving the quality of education (table 8.11). They highlight the lack of sufficient integration and coordination between international programs and the absence of a national policy to promote the process of internationalization. While administrative staff in the private sector recommend emphasizing student mobility, public sector administrators place greater priority on joint international research projects.

Seventy-five percent of the administrative staff believe that faculty demonstrate a low degree of participation, due to their individualistic attitudes. They believe that students attach some (not a great deal of) importance to student mobility programs, although some claim that many students have little interest in such programs. Administrators are unanimous in believing that the lack of scholarships is the chief factor holding back student mobility.

Organizational Structures of Internationalization at the Institutional Level

Universities and institutions have restructured their activities to include internationalization in their vision, education strategies, and management. Structural change and the introduction of new policies are difficult, however, and it will still take many years to fully integrate internationalization as a core dimension of higher education.

Internationalization Policies

In recent years internationalization strategies for improving the quality of education have achieved widespread support at all levels in Mexican universities. Most of the prestigious institutions have officially and explicitly incorporated internationalization into their vision and development plans. Some universities have developed internationalization plans that include specific definitions, programs, objectives, and goals, programmed step by step.

Careful examination of what is really happening, however, shows that none of these institutions has integrated the process of internationalization into their core development policies. Internationalization programs are still subject to institutional policies and administrators that respond to circumstances and lack continuity. While internationalization appears as a priority in university discourse and the institutional agenda, it has not been translated into concrete policies and organizational structures that are systematic and professional.

Rudzki (1998) proposes that internationalization be integrated into the following four aspects of the institution: organizational change, curriculum development, policies of human development, and student mobility. Few Mexican universities have done so. Structural change and the introduction of new policies are extremely difficult to achieve and very slow to emerge. As an example of this, despite the fact that some Mexican universities have submitted to examination of the quality of their international dimension through the Internationalization Process Quality Review, years later the recommendations made had not been implemented.[11] The incorporation of the international dimension into the design and content of the curriculum, which is one of the most important aspects of internationalization, is still missing.

Management of International Activities and Programs

In general, institutional mechanisms are lacking for initiating, adopting, and evaluating international activities. These activities are scattered throughout the institution without coordination or direction. International projects begin without planning or long-term vision. As a result, although many institutional agreements are signed, few are active or function properly. An institutional challenge for the future is to give coherence, sense, and direction to these initiatives, in order to transform them into an integral part of the agenda of the institution.

There is also a lack of clarity in identifying the institutional needs that could be addressed through internationalization strategies. As long as internationalization activities continue to be carried out on the periphery of institutional development policies, institutions will fail to allocate sufficient material, human, and financial resources.

---

[11] This was the case of the National Autonomous University of Mexico in 1997 and the University of Guadalajara in 1999.

The decision to declare internationalization as a priority has not been accompanied by debate on the subject by the community as a whole, which explains the lack of majority participation in the matter. Internationalization activities are the responsibility of a small group of academics and administrative staff committed to the idea, which makes this work look like an elitist activity. This situation is exacerbated by the fact that few staff members have university degrees, international experience, and adequate command of a foreign language.

Advances in the process of internationalization in Mexican universities in the past five years have focused on developing international activities and institutional cooperation. Despite the importance that authorities supposedly give to internationalization, however, institutions have not been able to develop sufficient know-how or knowledge to integrate their international activities into the mainstream of institutional development policies, their routine agendas, or their culture. The lack of a national policy in this area has slowed development.

Legal and Institutional Framework

One obstacle to the progress of internationalization is the rigidity of its legal and bureaucratic processes, especially in the public sector, which in some cases has made it impossible for institutions to adapt to new demands and new contexts. This lack of flexibility, which is typical of the Mexican higher education system, has made it difficult to attract foreign students, recognize studies pursued at foreign institutions, hire visiting professors from abroad, and obtain additional financial resources, to mention just a few problems. Together these factors limit the development of internationalization.

Planning and Quality Assessment of the Internationalization Process

Even when internationalization is part of the institutional development plan, it is not included in the regular processes of planning, programming, budgeting, and quality assessment. Educational institutions have not developed specific criteria or indicators to assess the quality of international programs. National policy, which in Mexico sets the guidelines for quality assessment, still does not include in its proceedings or criteria the evaluation of the international dimension. As a result, institutions pay no attention to establishing such criteria. The lack of adequate planning, evaluation, and follow-up suggest that international activities are still not incorporated into an internationalization policy that is central, widespread, integrated, and planned.

It is still difficult to determine the extent and nature of institutions' international activities. At both the national and institutional level, authorities are unaccustomed to creating and maintaining data banks on international activities, and concrete outcomes in university development. At best, offices of international affairs may have a list of cooperation agreements (both active and dormant), but this information cannot establish what actions have resulted from such agreements, much less assess their impact on the improvement of educational quality.

Sources of Financing

Few Mexican universities are able to state precisely how much money they allocate to internationalization strategies. In most cases, funds are scattered across the budgets of different university departments. Since there is no assessment of the impact of these activities on institutional quality, no one calculates the total amount spent. Some universities do not even provide a budget to support international activities, even when they state that internationalization is a priority. In such cases, universities rely on external resources provided by national and international bodies that fund international cooperation. As a consequence, international actions tend to be a response to whatever is offered by international organizations and institutions rather than a deliberate policy and strategy.

Human Resource Development

The survey examined evaluation criteria for professional development, official recognition, and incentives for participating in international activities. Only 37 percent of institutions surveyed recognized participation in international activities. Recognition tends to be in the form of points awarded for bonus schemes. Specific incentives for international activity, such as financial resources, reduced work hours, or points for developing new courses with an international dimension, were not found. This is related to the fact that no policies for curriculum development were found with an international or intercultural focus. For this reason, participation and involvement of university staff and faculty in the organization of international programs is limited. Despite the fact that many academics have studied abroad, no mechanisms have been put in place to take advantage of such international experience in order to internationalize teaching programs.

Administrative and Support Structures

Since they are peripheral to institutional development, departments in charge of international relations do not participate in decisionmaking over general institutional policies. In all of Mexico, there is only one Vice-Rectorship of International Relations (at the Instituto Tecnológico de Estudios Superiores de Monterrey). In the majority of institutions that have an international office, it tends to be at the fourth or fifth level in the hierarchy and generally has a limited number of staff assigned to it. If these offices are not given adequate representation, autonomy, or weight in the hierarchical structure, they are unlikely to be able to meet the strategic goals official discourse attributes to them.

At the same time, these offices lack professionalism. Staff lack specific training in this area, limiting their potential to promote international relations. Administrative leadership is inadequate to coordinate, design, and implement the policies and strategies needed.

A survey carried out on those in charge of academic exchange offices reveals that 70 percent of these staff have neither the experience nor the training necessary for this role, and they tend to stay in these positions for an average of only three years (Gacel-Ávila and Rojas 1999b), owing to the high turnover of directorial positions in university administrations. Their poor degree of attendance at international conventions and their almost nonexistent subscription to specialized journals in education indicates their lack of concern about keeping themselves professionally up to date. This situation results in a loss of experience at the institutional level that retards development and strengthening of international activities, which in turn limits the success of the internationalization process and its yield in academic terms.

Consensus Among University Members

Mexican universities are characterized by vertical decisionmaking from top to bottom. Faculty are seldom consulted over decisions about institutional policies or strategies, making it hard to reach genuine consensus. This is also the case with internationalization, where there is a lack of debate or search for consensus among the various actors involved. This can heighten resistance to actions and programs. In such cases, interinstitutional relations turn out to be simple declarations, with very little possibility of representing genuine interest or motivating the university community as a whole to participate actively. Perhaps this is why there is so little participation by academics.

Regional and Global Collaboration

Collaboration programs with countries in North America, Europe, and Latin American and other countries are critical to the internationalization process.

Collaboration in North America

It would be impossible to discuss internationalization in Mexico without mentioning collaboration with its northern neighbors, the United States and Canada. The signing of the NAFTA Treaty set off a series of actions designed to integrate the North American academic community. As part of this movement, three trilateral conferences were organized, in Wingspread (1992), Vancouver (1993), and Guadalajara (1996).

The 1993 Communiqué of Vancouver proposed the creation of a network for distance education and research, the North American Distance Education and Research Network (NADERN), trilateral mechanisms for recognizing degrees and professional accreditation, programs for collaboration between academic and administrative staff, an electronic network, the promotion of studies on North America, and a trilateral program for research and professional training of students. The six projects have developed unevenly during the 12 years since they were announced.

NADERN failed to do anything more than draft a proposal, due in part to technological differences. Particularly Mexico's lag behind its northern neighbors—but also because of lack of institutional interest. The initiative to develop trilateral mechanisms for recognizing degrees and professional certification has advanced very little, because of differences in professional certification structures in the three countries. Since 1994 the Mexican Committees for International Practice were developed to work with their counterparts in Canada and the United States toward the mutual recognition of degrees and certificates in actuarial science, agronomy, architecture, accounting, law, nursing, pharmacology, engineering, medicine, veterinary science, dentistry, and psychology. The results to date remain largely unknown.

The electronic information network has prospered, thanks to an electronic portal and information service operated by CONAHEC. It receives only marginal financial support from the three central governments, however.

The research projects and trilateral centers on North American studies were promoted initially by the William and Flora Hewlett Foundation. Parallel to this initiative, the Foreign Relations Department of the Mexican government, through the Inter-Institutional Program of Studies on the Region of North America, coordinated by the Colegio de Mexico, organized research and academic events on North American academic integration.

In the area of student mobility, the Regional Academic Mobility Program was set up, run by the Institute for International Education. This program organized mutual fee waivers between member institutions. This program enabled the mobility of 644 students between 1993 and 2003

(IIE 2003a). Despite lack of government support, the program still exists, and the number of students has increased in recent years, with a greater flow from Mexico toward its northern neighbors than vice versa.

PROMESAN, created in 1995, is the only program of this kind that receives financial support from the three national governments. An evaluation by CONAHEC (2002) reveals that this program has enabled the formation of 48 trilateral consortia, thanks to which 1,205 students were able to study in other countries. This represents an extremely small number of students for each project, particularly when compared with the matriculation of all students in the region. This small scale of the project is attributed to the fact that the three governments have not given the financial support originally hoped for (Mallea, Malo, and Pendergast 1998). PROMESAN has focused mainly on student mobility, paying scant attention to the longer term goal of integrating a North American dimension into the curriculum.

Few projects created by consortia have yielded innovative curriculum development, and only 25 percent of them have produced development or application of learning technologies to internationalize courses (León 2000). Only 47 percent of project directors consider the continuity of strategic alliances viable after government financing ends. Moreover, the complexity of managing trilateral projects among institutions is such that a large part of the resources are spent on administration and meetings of project directors. In the future it would make sense to establish a student mobility program whose financial resources are spent exclusively on student scholarships. Parallel to this, it might make sense to create a program for faculty mobility with the purpose of internationalizing their profile. Finally, the supposition that private firms in North America would become natural, active allies of universities and the governments has turned out to be false (Mallea, Malo, and Pendergast 1998).

Under NAFTA progress in cooperation in higher education has been modest, patchy, asymmetrical, and in most cases not institutionalized. Explicit clarification of the political will of the three governments is still lacking, as are the legal and financial mechanisms to promote mobility that depend on this will. This suggests that any effort in this direction is likely to be doomed to failure (Marmolejo 2000).

The signing of NAFTA increased mobility flows in North America, especially between Mexico and Canada. The number of students that studied in Canada between 1991 and 1996 increased by 134 percent, while Mexico's exchanges with the United States increased by only 30 percent and the number of U.S. students studying in Mexico increased 35 percent (León 2000). The 2002 *Open Doors* report (IIE 2003a) notes a 17 percent increase in Mexican students in the United States, especially in community colleges along the border, in Texas, New Mexico, Arizona, and California.

In 2002 the number of U.S. students in Mexico increased by 13.4 percent, ranking Mexico above Australia and Germany. Within Latin America, Mexico is the leading destination for U.S. students. As to the mobility of teaching and research staff between Mexico and the United States, Mexico ranks 17th out of 20, after Brazil and before Argentina (IIE 2003a).

Student and staff mobility initiatives have been affected by immigration policies and regulations, especially those affecting the issuance of, visas, after September 11, 2001.

Collaboration with the European Union

Collaborative activities between Mexico and the European Union have increased steadily since the 1990s. This has occurred mainly through the Latin American Academic Training (ALFA) Program. This program has facilitated the creation of collaborative networks between higher education institutions in the European Union and Latin American countries in various academic disciplines identified as priorities for the development of the region, such as institutional management, graduate programs, and the mobility of academics and graduate students. The program has promoted academic collaboration between Latin American institutions by means of these networks, combining both horizontal and vertical cooperation. Almost all major universities in Latin America have participated in ALFA projects.

The first phase of the program was launched in 1994, for a period of five years. The second phase began in 2000 and is envisaged to last until 2005, supported by a budget of €42 million.

The first phase of ALFA included 846 active projects. The leading coordinators of these projects were Spain (255 projects), France (86), Italy (81), the United Kingdom (70), and Germany (40). In Latin America, Argentina, Chile, and Mexico were in first place, with 28 projects each, followed by Brazil (19) and Costa Rica (13) (ALFA 2005).

Noteworthy also are programs that emerged from Ibero-American summits, such as the Ibero-American Program for Science and Technology for Development, in which 7,500 scientists participated in 46 different thematic networks; the Mutis Scholarship program for graduate study; Ibero-American Educational Television, with the participation of 250 educational institutions in the region; the Ibero-American Center for Strategic Urban Development, which promotes urban development in 56 cities in 18 Ibero-American countries; the Fund for Sustainable Development of the Indigenous Peoples of Latin America and the Caribbean, which channels financial resources through direct grants and NGOs; and adult literacy programs in Central America and the Caribbean.

In 2003 the European Union launched the new High-Level Latin American Scholarship (ALßAN) Program, which offers scholarships for graduate study at European universities to citizens of Latin American countries. By means of this program, the European Union plans to increase its presence in the region and challenge the leadership of the United States in incorporating students into graduate programs. During the program's first year, the countries most in demand were Spain (97 scholarships), the United Kingdom, (96), and France (20). Of the 251 scholarships granted, Mexico received 21 (8.4 percent), mainly in business, communications, and information sciences.

European countries have also developed cooperation programs through active bilateral collaboration organizations, such as the Spanish Agency for International Cooperation (AECI). Between 1994 and 2002 its Intercampus program mobilized 1,940 students, 879 professors, and 29 administrative staff. Other programs include those of the German Academic Exchange Service, the British Council, and the French Institut de Recherche pour le Développement, to mention only a few.

Mexico recently became an associate member of the European Union. This status offers great opportunities—yet to be explored—for establishing associations and strategic alliances between European and Mexican educational institutions.

All of these programs and initiatives demonstrate geopolitical and strategic interest in Latin America by the European Union. It is important that Latin American educational institutions and the European Union take advantage of these opportunities for academic cooperation and use them to strengthen their own capabilities, rather than simply responding to individual opportunities in order to secure financing.

Collaboration with Latin American and Caribbean Countries

Academic collaboration within Latin America and the Caribbean has increased in recent years, thanks largely to the establishment of academic networks but above all because of the influence of organizations outside the region (the European Union and EU member countries, such as Spain, France, and Germany). It is unfortunate that the governments of the region have not promoted interinstitutional collaboration. Some efforts have been made, such as the regional collaboration established between ANUIES and the Council for Central American Universities (CSUCA) and between ANUIES and the Association of Colombian Universities. Still, in general, despite a common language and culture, there have been no attempts to establish programs of student or faculty mobility in the region, to set up centers of excellence in key areas of development, or to create a regional system of recognition of studies, such as the European Community Transfer Scheme.

Collaboration with Countries in Asia and Oceania

CONACYT has signed collaborative agreements for science and technology with China, the Republic of Korea, Japan, and Vietnam, among other countries. Academic cooperation activities with Australia and New Zealand, especially student mobility, have increased significantly, as the popularity of these countries among Mexican students grows. Australian institutions have demonstrated great interest in opening up educational opportunities for Mexican students, both by recruiting students who wish to pursue graduate studies in Australia and by signing collaboration agreements for student and faculty exchange.

Mexico is receiving an increasing number of Asian students, chiefly from Japan and the Republic of Korea, who wish to learn Spanish. This is not the case with China, because Chinese students have great difficulty obtaining visas to enter Mexico. In recent years a number of Mexican public universities—including the National Autonomous University of Mexico, the University of Colima, and the University of Guadalajara—have created centers and programs for studies related to the Pacific Rim.

Mexico's location enables it to maintain privileged collaborative relations with the United States and Canada and with Pacific Rim countries. Its membership in the OECD and associate membership in the European Union create special ties with Europe. The political and economic stability of Mexico represents a powerful competitive advantage for mobility and academic integration schemes.

Transnationalization and the New Suppliers
of Higher Education

The introduction of foreign suppliers of education has been only a marginal topic of discussion among the various actors in the higher education system. The Department of Public Education has not publicly clarified its position on this matter, despite the fact that Mexico (through the federal Commerce Department) and Panama are the only two countries that proposed opening their educational market in 2004 in line with the General Agreement on Trade in Services (GATS). As part of chapter 12 of NAFTA, Mexico agreed to give suppliers of services (including education) from member countries the same treatment as nationals.

This might indicate that the Mexican government, far from opposing the introduction of foreign suppliers, might consider this to be an alternative means of increasing educational supply, which still remains insufficient. However, higher education, like public welfare, is an extremely sensitive subject for Mexicans, since Mexico continues to be one of the Latin American countries in which the majority of students (68 percent) study in public institutions. This is in contrast to Brazil, Chile, and Colombia, where private education predominates.

The Department of Public Education does not seem concerned about regulating, supervising, or controlling transnational educational services, as it does private education. Transnational education will probably become assimilated into private education and be considered a complement to what is offered in the public sector.

It is difficult to analyze the different modalities of transnational education in higher education in Mexico, because there is a lack of data and a system to classify various modalities, concepts, and categories. Mexico's need for imported education is greater than its capacity to export it. This is not surprising given that the export of educational services has traditionally been dominated by English-speaking countries (the United States, the United Kingdom, Australia, and Canada). Among Spanish-speaking countries, Spain is an important exporter, through the National Distance Education University and more recently through the Open University of Catalonia. These institutions tend to seek associative collaboration rather than simply sell services, however.[12]

The only Mexican institution to export educational services in a significant manner is the Instituto Technológico de Estudios Superiores de Monterrey (ITESM), through its virtual university. ITESM has also established a base of operations in the United States through its network of community centers.

The export of educational services is not a priority for the public sector agenda in Mexico, which has a tendency to be oriented toward internal needs. Its priorities are to increase access to education nationally and to improve the quality of education in general.

In recent years one strategy for improving the quality and widening the scope of education has been to form transnational alliances with foreign institutions for teaching courses and providing programs in association. These academic alliances are most common in economics and administration at the undergraduate level at private institutions and in the social sciences, exact sciences, and engineering at the graduate level at public universities. This tendency to form alliances has been enabled thanks principally to opportunities for international cooperation offered by international organizations of the European Union, Spain, Germany, and France; by PROMESAN; and by cooperation-facilitating bodies, such as CONAHEC and the Inter-American Organization for Higher Education (IAOHE).

Few foreign institutions have campuses in Mexico. Those that do—such as Endicott College, Westbridge University, and Alliant International

---

[12] For example, there are collaboration agreements between the Oberta University of Cataluña and the Universities of Guadalajara and Veracruz.

University, all of which are accredited by U.S. bodies—do not need official recognition by the Department of Public Education. Some foreign universities, mainly from the United States, have offices in Mexico to promote their programs and form alliances with Mexican institutions.

The purchase by Sylvan International of the Valley of Mexico University, one of the largest private universities in Mexico, represents penetration of the Mexican educational sector by a foreign commercial enterprise. The Valley of Mexico University now offers all of its students joint degrees with all universities in the Sylvan International network, suggesting that this type of association between Mexican and foreign institutions could produce greater internationalization of such institutions.[13]

Other enterprises, such as Apollo International, are also investigating purchasing Mexican universities.[14] The acquisition of well-established universities in Mexico that are well placed in the market and have official recognition could very well become an efficient means for foreign for-profit institutions to enter the Mexican educational market.

The phenomenon of transnationalization of higher education in Mexico is incipient but growing. Given the public sector's lack of capacity to absorb enough students, the lack of specific regulation in this area, and gaps, ambiguities, and contradictions in legislation, transnational institutions are likely to flourish. The government urgently needs to pay attention to this problem and find ways to regulate, supervise, and evaluate these institutions. Above all, it is necessary to subject the matter coolly to objective debate regarding its advantages and disadvantages, avoiding radical positions and conflict as far as possible.

Critical Aspects and Future Challenges

The challenges of internationalization in Mexico are closely linked to the challenges facing the system of higher education in general. Like other Latin American countries, Mexico needs to increase access to higher education, which, at 22 percent, is well below the average for other OECD countries (55 percent). One point in Mexico's favor is its significant advance in recent years, thanks mainly to the opening of 54 new technological universities and other types of institutions. In addition to increasing educational access, these institutions have helped diversify higher education. However, the financial cost of this expansion in the public sector has limited investment in new areas of development, such as internationalization

[13] The Sylvan International Universities network includes the European University in Spain, Les Roches University in Switzerland, the School of Higher Studies for Commerce in France, the University of the Americas in Chile, and Walden University in the United States.

[14] Apollo International is part of the same commercial group as the University of Phoenix, the largest for-profit university in the United States.

and international cooperation. This lack of finances is exacerbated by the fact that the public sector spends almost 90 percent of its budget on salaries, pensions, and administrative costs. Internationalization is thus competing for resources with increased access, research, development, curriculum improvement, equipment and infrastructure, development of human resources, cultural and extension programs, and other important programs.

At the same time, Mexico's higher education system suffers from low-quality programs, poorly qualified faculty, obsolete equipment, and lack of academic infrastructure, such as libraries and laboratories. These factors limit its ability to attract foreign students. As a consequence, Mexico sends more students abroad than it receives. At a time when 49 percent of Mexican students studying abroad chose to study in the United States (ANUIES 2002), only 5 percent of U.S. students studying abroad chose Mexico (IIE 2003a). In exchange programs such as PROMESAN, the flow of Mexican students toward the United States and Canada exceeds the number of American and Canadian students heading south. This deprives nonmobile students of the opportunity to have contact with students from other cultures, limiting their intercultural experience, which is so crucial in the twenty-first century.

Another aspect of the Mexican higher education system that has a negative impact on the process of internationalization is its lack of flexibility and innovative curricula. It is difficult to transfer credits even between programs and institutions in Mexico, much less internationally.

Curricula are poorly adapted to the job market and teacher centered. They emphasize the accumulation of knowledge, while failing to develop critical thinking and adaptability. The curriculum is highly specialized and goes against international tendencies to make undergraduate education more general and less specialized. Faculty need to modify the content of courses and their pedagogical approaches, as well as spend time coordinating international activities. It is recommended that the internationalized curriculum contain more general education (Gacel-Ávila 2003).

Almost half of all faculty are part time and hold a second job. This places severe limits on their ability to become truly professional teachers and reduces the time available to bring themselves up to date with new curricular approaches. Having full-time teaching staff is essential to the internationalization of curricula and student competence.

Technological higher education has not incorporated initiatives for internationalization. This implies that crucial sections of the Mexican economy remain unprepared for a global economy and job market.

Knowledge production in Mexico is still centered on specialized disciplines. It fails to follow modern international trends, such as the model for knowledge production recommended by Gibbons (1994), which focuses on problem solving.

The lack of professionalism in university management seriously weakens leadership and administration in the process of internationalization. In most Mexican institutions, particularly in the public sector, power and decisionmaking authority are in the hands of people who usually lack the experience and knowledge needed to promote the complex educational changes required by the twenty-first century (Altbach 2003). As a consequence, Mexican institutions are in a weak position to reap the benefits of the opportunities presented by the latest world trends. This is partly the cause of failure in the organizational and programming structures needed to sustain the strategies of internationalization.

Conclusions

Internationalization has grown in Mexico since the late 1990s, in an effort to improve the quality of education, at both the institutional and national level. Other reasons for internationalizing include, in order of importance, the need to build the nation's competitiveness in the face of challenges resulting from international trade agreements, to adapt to the new requirements of the global job market, to achieve international accreditation for Mexican educational programs, and, to a far lesser degree, to ensure that students master foreign languages, acquire knowledge of foreign cultures, and develop intercultural sensitivity.

Student and faculty mobility programs have increased, and international networks have been established. But efforts have generally been a response to external opportunities. Internationalization has developed on the fringe of institutional policies; it does not form a core part of universities' daily agenda. In general, the internationalization strategies adopted do not have an impact on and are not integrated into all levels of the educational process (teaching/learning approaches, curricular design, staff development policies, organizational and programming structures, or indeed decisionmaking on policies of institutional development), as recommended by the leading scholars in this area (Knight and de Wit 1995; Rudzki 1998; Van der Wende 1994). Very few Mexican universities have demonstrated organized and well-planned drives to recruit international students or promote and sell their educational services. The great majority of international activities are responses to offers made by international organizations or individual or independent initiatives. They lack a sense of direction or purpose and are disconnected from institutional policies and priorities. An international dimension is lacking in planning, budgeting, and quality assessment in national and institutional policy, and Mexican universities are still far from institutionalizing an international and intercultural dimension in their substantive functions and culture.

Obstacles to successful internationalization include the limited professionalism of the staff in charge of managing and administering the process, weak organizational and planning structures, curricula that fail to meet the needs of the twenty-first century, and poorly qualified, part-time faculty with little international experience. The rhetoric of institutional authorities notwithstanding, there are very few cases in which international strategies are a genuine priority in the agenda of the institution. Most of the main actors at Mexico's universities believe that the universities are not preparing students to meet the challenges of a changing world.

Despite official discourse about improving Mexico's higher education system, international programs are not organized around the concept of comprehensive internationalization, as prescribed by international organizations, such as the OECD's Institute for the Management of Higher Education. Internationalization must go beyond the traditional conception of international cooperation and mere mobility of people.[15]

The lack of leadership in national policy toward internationalization that is integrated into the core development of the institution is reducing the impact and potential of the process. Because public higher education institutions in Mexico depend on government subsidies, they have to follow the guidelines that national policy dictates. For this reason, national policy toward internationalization will determine its future. This policy has not supported the idea of innovative internationalization programs nor has it made sufficient resources and guidelines available to universities to internationalize their functions and the competencies of their graduates.

As Fullan (1991) notes, it is important to distinguish between strategies of change that have the capacity to affect the individual and those that affect the system. As long as both national and institutional policy choose strategies of international cooperation and mobility that affect individuals rather than the system, it will be impossible for these strategies to contribute to the improvement of the quality of education or affect the system's reform and innovation.

The Mexican educational system is not promoting a policy or making resources available to develop a global perspective among students regarding their professional and social roles. The failure is probably not deliberate but rather, as Van der Wende (1997) asserts, the result of the

---

[15] The National Education Plan 2000–06 does not use the term *internationalization* but *international cooperation* and *mobility*. This suggests that national policy continues to promote the organization of international programs based on the traditional concept of international cooperation rather than embracing the concept as part of institutions' priorities and development plans.

inability of decisionmakers to conceptualize the need for internationalization strategies that are comprehensive, wide-ranging, and integrated into all levels of the educational process. For this reason, it is vital that research be conducted on comprehensive internationalization, in order to gain a deeper understanding of its benefits for meeting the challenges of the twenty-first century. Research on this topic is relatively undeveloped in schools of education in Mexico. Publications such as this book therefore have an important function in increasing interest in the subject in Latin America.

Prospects for internationalization in Mexico are closely tied to progress in the higher education system itself, which appears to be improving. Access has increased, the qualifications of faculty are improving, the research budget has risen, evaluation is occurring at all levels, and infrastructure is being developed. Despite these encouraging results, however, the decline in education during the 1980s—the so-called lost decade—has not been reversed enough to close the gap with developed nations, and the gap could grow.

Decisionmakers should be aware of and follow the major trends of education in the world. OECD countries place internationalization at the center of their educational priorities, together with updated curricula and new approaches to teaching and learning. If Mexico fails to follow these trends, its system of education will not meet the requirements of the twenty-first century. For this reason, internationalization is not simply an option for Mexico but an obligation, in order to enable Mexican graduates to compete in a new, global context.

Internationalization strategies could enable Mexico to overcome its lag by means of strategic institutional alliances, which could provide students with the intercultural and global competences the twenty-first century demands. It is a matter of concern that Mexico is not educating its students to meet these new challenges, in contrast with developed countries.

Mexico needs innovative and creative approaches to upgrade its higher education system and to face the challenges of the future. Now is the time for decisionmakers to fully realize that internationalization could well be one of the roads to success.

References

ALFA (Latin America Academic Training). 2005. http://europa.eu.int/comm/europeaid/projects/alfa/index_en.htm

Altbach, Philip G. 2003. "The Decline of the Guru: The Academic Profession in Developing and Middle-Income Countries." 23–50. New York: Palgrave MacMillan.

ANUIES (National Association of Universities and Institutions of Higher Education). 2000. "La educación superior en el siglo xxi: líneas estratégicas de desarrollo." Mexico.

————. 2001. "Calidad e internacionalización de la educación superior." ANUIES and the National Autonomous University of Mexico, Mexico.

————. 2002. *Informe de la Red de Cooperación.* Mexico: University of Colima Press.

CONAHEC (Consortium for North American Higher Education Collaboration). 2002. "Neighboring in the 'Global Village': North American Cooperation and Collaboration in Higher Education. A Context for the Program for North American Mobility in Higher Education: Past, Present and Future." CONAHEC, Tucson, AZ.

Delors, J. 1997. "La educación encierra un tesoro." Paris: UNESCO.

De Wit, Hans. 1995. *Strategies for Internationalisation of Higher Education: A Comparative Study of Australia, Canada, Europe, and the United States of America.* Amsterdam: European Association for Internacional Education.

————. 1997. "Strategies for Internationalisation of Higher Education in Asia Pacific Countries: A Comparative Introduction." In *Internationalisation of Higher Education in Asia Pacific Countries,* ed. Jane Knight and Hans de Wit. Amsterdam: European Association for International Education.

————. 2002. *Internationalization of Higher Education in the United States of America and Europe: A Historical, Comparative, and Conceptual Analysis.* Westport, CT: Greenwood Publishing.

Didou, S. 2002. "Transnacionalización de la educación superior y aseguramiento de la calidad en México." *Revista de la Educación Superior* 31 (4): 11–23. ANUIES, Mexico.

Fullan, M. 1991. *The New Meaning of Educational Change.* New York: Teachers' College Press, Columbia University.

Gacel-Ávila, J. 1999. "Internacionalización de la educación superior en América Latina y el Caribe: reflexiones y lineamientos." Organization of Inter-American Universities, AMPEI, and the Ford Foundation, Guadalajara, Mexico.

————. 2000. "La internacionalización de las universidades Mexicanas: políticas y estrategias institucionales." ANUIES, Mexico.

————. 2002. "La dimensión internacional de las universidades mexicanas: un diagnóstico cuantitativo y cualitativo." *Educación Global* 6: 121–5. AMPEI, Mexico.

————. 2003. *La internacionalización de la educación superior: paradigma para la ciudadanía global.* Mexico: University of Guadalajara Press.

Gacel-Ávila, J., and R. Rojas. 1999a. "Características de los estudiantes extranjeros." *Educación Global* 3: 121–27. AMPEI, Mexico.

————. 1999b. "Las oficinas de intercambio académico en las instituciones de educación superior en México." *Educación Global* 3: 109–120. AMPEI, Mexico.

Gibbons, M. 1994. *The New Production of Knowledge: The Dynamics of Science and Research in Contemporary Societies.* London: SAGE.

IIE (Institute for International Education). 2003a. *Open Doors: Report on International Educational Exchange.* New York.

————. 2003b. "RAMP Impact Evaluation." May. New York.

Kälvermark, T., and M. Van der Wende. 1997. *National Policies for the Internationalisation of Higher Education in Europe.* Stockholm: Högskoleverket Studies, National Agency for Higher Education.

Knight, J., and H. de Wit. 1995. "Strategies for Internationalisation of Higher Education: Historical and Conceptual Perspectives." In *Strategies for Interna-*

tionalisation of Higher Education: A Comparative Study of Australia, Canada, Europe and the United States of America, ed. H. de Wit. Amsterdam: European Association for International Education.

León, F. 2000. "Movilidad académica en América del Norte: hacia nuevos modelos de integración y colaboración." *Educación Global* 4: 37–57. AMPEI, Mexico.

Mallea, J., Malo S. and Pendergast P. 1998. "The Vancouver Communiqué Revisited: An Assessment." Working Paper No. 8, Consortium for North American Higher Education Collaboration, Tucson, AZ.

Malo, S. 2000. "Reflexiones sobre el futuro para la educación superior en México." *Revista de la educación superior* 24 (1): 95–102, 113. ANUIES, México.

———. 2004. "La comercialización de la educación superior." In *El difícil equilibrio: la educación superior como bien público y comercio de servicios. Implicaciones del AGCS (GATS)*, Carmen García Guadilla, coordinator, pp. 101–08. Documentos Columbus. Universidad de Castilla-La Mancha, Cuenca.

Marmolejo, F. 2000. "Educación superior en América del Norte a seis años del TLCAN." *Educación Global* 4: 59–69. AMPEI, Mexico.

Nilson, B., and M. Otten. 2003. "Internationalisation at Home from a Swedish Perspective: Editorial." *Journal of Studies in International Education* 7 (1): 27–40.

Oxford Dictionary of New Words. 1991. Oxford: Oxford University Press.

Pallán, C. 1996. "Panorama y perspectivas del intercambio académico en las IES mexicanas." *Revista de la educación superior* 15: 31–41. ANUIES, Mexico.

Rudzki, R. 1998. "The Strategic Management of Internationalization: Towards a Model of Theory and Practice." PhD thesis, Newcastle School of Education, University of Newcastle-upon-Tyne, United Kingdom.

Secretaria de Educación Pública. 2001. "Programa nacional de educación 2001–2006." Department of Public Education, Mexico.

———. 2002. "Programa nacional de educación 2001–2006." Paper presented at the 33rd General Assembly of ANUIES, Autonomous University of Yucatan/ Technological Institute of Merida, October 17.

———. 2005. Educación superior. Institucional. *Estadisticas*. www.sep.gob.mx.

UNESCO (United Nations Educational, Scientific and Cultural Organization). 1998a. *Higher Education in the Twenty-First Century: Vision and Action*. World Conference on Higher Education, Paris, October 5–9.

———. 1998b. "Marco de acción prioritaria para el cambio y el desarrollo de la educación superior." Paris. www.unesco.org/education.

Van der Wende, M. 1994. "Internationalisation as a Process of Educational Change." In *Pilot Project on Regional Co-operation in Reforming Higher Education, Seminar II: Mobility in Higher Education*, pp. 37–49. Paris: European Commission/OECD.

———. 1997. "Missing Links: The Relationship between National Policies for Internationalisation and Those for Higher Education in General." In *National Policies for the Internationalisation of Higher Education in Europe*, ed. T. Kälvermark and M. Van der Wende. Stockholm: Högskoleverket Studies, National Agency for Higher Education.

9
Internationalization of Higher Education in Peru

Luis Jaime Castillo Butters, Leena Bernuy Quiroga, and Pamela Lastres Dammert

This chapter examines the way internationalization has been implemented at Peruvian universities. It describes the higher education sector, examines the key national level actors involved in or influencing the internationalization of higher education, looks at both organizational and program aspects of internationalization, summarizes key aspects of the international dimension of Peruvian universities, and concludes with a look at some of the positive trends and potential for the development of internationalization of Peruvian universities.

The term *international cooperation* is widely used in Peru. It usually refers to international development cooperation, which aptly describes the orientation and type of international work engaged in by Peru's higher education institutions. The international dimension of Peru's higher education system has been developed largely through international development cooperation involving bilateral and multilateral donor countries and agencies. Recently, this vertical type of international development cooperation has begun shifting toward horizontal cooperation. Horizontal cooperation may still involve technical assistance and it can be supported by external development or donor funds, but it is based more on a partnership and mutual benefit approach, and it often involves exchanges between developing countries.

At the same time that this shift is occurring, the importance of academic and research collaboration and mobility is growing. This type of collaboration is often based on institution-level relations and agreements for joint research and technological development. The internationalization process in Peru is thus characterized by both vertical and horizontal international development cooperation as well as growing collaboration and mutually beneficial partnerships for academic teaching and research purposes.

Internationalization in Peru is regarded as an end rather than a means. Peruvian universities seek to become internationalized, not international. This means that faculty and students have international exposure and experiences, institutions are recognized internationally as centers of excellence, faculty can be actors in a global environment, academic activities have an international component, and the international resources available are used effectively. In short, the international dimension needs to be incorporated into every aspect of higher education so that, through increased connectivity with Latin America and the rest of the world, new sources of innovative ideas and concepts, as well as new standards of quality and service, are taken advantage of.

Some risks are inherent in internationalization, particularly when it is implemented without regard to—or even in opposition to—national values and traditions. Internationalization in these circumstances can augment alienation. In developing countries, internationalization is sometimes regarded as a quest for foreign models to deal with national problems. Many universities in Latin America, particularly private and for-profit institutions, have been accused of being centers of alienation, breeding professionals who are divorced from reality and unable to contribute to their countries' development. A balance between these two extremes, national and international, is desirable but often difficult to achieve and sustain.

Methodology

Three methods of collecting information were used. A group of university officers was interviewed, some institutions completed a questionnaire, and site visits to different organizations and institutions were undertaken.

Interestingly, national organizations and agencies such as the Fulbright Commission have more complete and up to date information than Peruvian institutions themselves.[1] In many instances, institutions considered information about their international relations and internationalization efforts confidential and sensitive. Other institutions believed that releasing information could jeopardize their internationalization efforts. Most institutions simply did not keep records about their internationalization initiatives. This reflects the low importance attached to internationalization and the high turnover and modest qualifications of the people in charge.

Qualitative data come from meetings with international relations officers at universities and representatives from government departments, such as the Ministry of Foreign Affairs and the Peruvian Agency for International Cooperation. Special importance was given to interviews with the officers of the National Assembly of Rectors, as this institution has a major influence on the process of institutional development of the higher education system, including the international dimension.

---

[1] Because of the paucity of information on internationalization in Peru, this chapter is based partly on subjective generalization by the interviewees and the authors.

The Higher Education System in Peru

Higher education in Peru has experienced growth in both the public and private sectors.

Growth and Expansion of System

Peru's university system has expanded significantly since the 1940s. The quality of the system has lagged behind, however, and advances in education have been very uneven. Even with the explosive growth of enrollment, hundreds of thousands of people still lack even a minimal level of education.

Before 1960 Peru had 9 universities; 30 years later it had 46, and 5 more had been created but were not yet operational. By 2003 there were 78 universities, 25 of which had been created in the past decade (figure 9.1). Especially in the 1990s, the number of private universities grew rapidly. By 2003, 61 percent of all institutions of higher education in Peru were private, up from 45 percent in the 1980s. Between 1960 and 2003, the student population increased by a factor of 9.6.

Growth of Private Sector and Investment

The private sector plays a much more important role in higher education (both university and nonuniversity) than in more basic education,

Figure 9.1 Number of Universities in Peru, 1960–2003

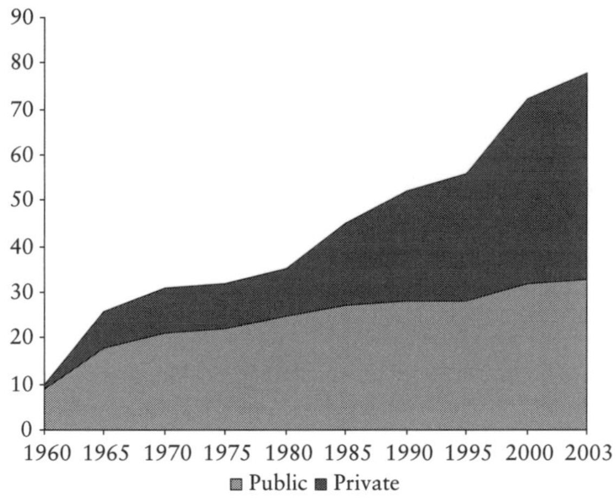

Source: Asamblea Nacional de Rectores (2005).

accounting for 43 percent of enrollment in higher education and just 12–15 percent of enrollment in primary and secondary schools. Agriculture, the exact and natural sciences, and engineering programs are offered mainly by public universities. Private universities concentrate on administration, law, and certain social science programs, which cost less to provide.

The main factor that paved the way for the private sector's entry into university education took place within the framework of the 1997 Act of Promotion of Investment in Education. This act amended the University Act of 1983. Under the amended law, individuals and corporations have the right to provide education, on a for-profit or not-for-profit basis. The amended act established that private universities were corporations with private rights and that it was no longer necessary to verify whether there was sufficient demand for yet another institution or whether qualified educational staff and the resources were available to ensure the quality of the services provided. Under the new legal framework, owners of private educational institutions need comply only with the "general specifications of the study plans, as well as with the minimum requirements of organization of educational institutions formulated by the State."

This new legal framework favored the creation of new university institutions, which saturated the higher education market. These new institutions generated intense competition in the education market. As a result, there was a diversification of programs and degrees, but this was not necessarily an indication of meeting new requirements for professional education or knowledge production. Diversification was more a result of marketing strategies to recruit students than consideration of the needs of society and the job market. In many cases the investment for developing new programs, including the acquisition of educational material and even the granting of scholarships, did not aim at improving educational quality but rather at justifying the tax benefits to investors stipulated in the new legislation.

Academic Quality of Peruvian Universities

The expansion of the university system, as well as the new legislation on investment in education, has a direct impact on the academic quality of universities, in several ways. One relates to the selection of applicants. The number of students reached its peak in 1985 and has stayed fairly stable, whereas the number of universities has nearly doubled since 1985. During the past decade, public universities accepted just 1 out of 100 applicants. The rate of acceptance at private universities rose from 46 percent in 1990 to 74 percent in 1997. In 2002, 229,107 students applied to public universities, and 62,149 applied to private universities. The preference for public universities may be explained by the low tuition costs and the high prestige attached to the oldest public universities. About 1 out of every 6 applicants enters a public university, while 1 out of every 1.4 applicants enters a private one (INEI and ANR 1997).

Another important indicator of the quality of the university system is the ratio between the number of students and the number of faculty. In the past 10 years, the student/faculty ratio at public universities in Peru was about 12–13 to 1. At private institutions the ratio rose from less than 10:1 in 1990 to 16:1 in 1991, remaining between 14:1 and 16:1 for the rest of the decade. As a result of the expansion of the private university system, the number of faculty at public universities remained virtually constant between 1991 and 2000, while the number of faculty at private institutions rose from 8,495 in 1991 to 14,335 in 2002. Many faculty are poorly qualified. Only 47 percent have graduate degrees. Among faculty with graduate degrees, just 17 percent have doctorates and 10 percent obtained their degrees abroad (Webb 2002).

Relatively little research is conducted at Peruvian universities. Only half of university professors are involved in research activities, with the average professor completing 2.4 research projects in a five-year period (Butters, Quiroga, and Dammert 2004).

Key National Actors in the Internationalization of Higher Education

Internationalization is not part of the planning process, at the governmental or institutional level. Rather, internationalization efforts have been a consequence of individual efforts and, for the most part, remain disorganized and disjointed.

In the 1960s and 1970s, higher education in Latin America, particularly in Peru, received technical assistance and resources from more developed countries. The focus of development was the modernization of higher education through the transfer of knowledge, institutional capacity building, and the education of human resources. Many universities created new programs and trained their professors with the support of development assistance. These efforts were not a result of medium- to long-term planning and policy development but rather reflected the desire to take advantage of available funds. This type of development assistance and international cooperation was based more on a reactive and ad hoc approach, which did not contribute to sustainable accomplishments or relationships. This scenario changed in the past two decades, as international development cooperation became more oriented to reducing poverty. The need to develop new partners and approaches to international cooperation began a gradual shift from vertical cooperation to horizontal cooperation.

To date the government has not developed a stable policy to carry out the process of internationalization in a consistent or sustainable manner. Since internationalization is not a national priority, there is not sufficient financing to promote it. According to the National Assembly of Rectors, during the past decade, higher education has not been perceived as fundamental to national development. The state has focused more attention on creating nonuniversity spaces for technological support, significantly weakening the capacity of most universities. This has negatively affected the ability of Peruvian scientists to establish ties with the international scientific community. According to the National Assembly of Rectors, there is, however, growing recognition of the need to reverse the situation, as evidenced by the liberalization of visa regulations for visiting scholars.

Governmental Level

At the governmental policy level, the actors participating in the process of internationalization are the Ministry of Foreign Affairs, the Peruvian Agency for International Cooperation, the National Council for Science and Technology (CONCYTEC), the National Institute for Scholarships and Education Credit (INABEC), and bilateral cooperation agencies.

MINISTRY OF FOREIGN AFFAIRS

The Ministry of Foreign Affairs is in charge of preserving and promoting national interests abroad, as well as developing foreign policies and coordinating their execution. It considers universities as key agents in foreign relations, especially those that handle scientific and cultural functions. One of the ministry's goals is to expand general agreements of cultural cooperation, a goal that has been transmitted to Peruvian embassies and consulates.

The Ministry of Foreign Affairs supports the development of cultural and educational affairs, as delineated in the Foreign Cultural Policy Plan. To make this plan successful, it has been decided to establish a working and coordination group with university representatives who meet at least twice a year to elaborate proposals and make appropriate evaluations. This working group is not yet fully functional. The Cultural Department of the Ministry of Foreign Affairs also supports the mobility of international experts by issuing visas to foreign students and professors from countries or institutions with which there are binational or interinstitutional agreements.

PERUVIAN AGENCY FOR INTERNATIONAL COOPERATION

The Peruvian International Cooperation Agency (APCI) was created in 2002, as a branch of the Ministry of Foreign Affairs. Its creation followed a period of turbulence and change in terms of the organizational structure and mandate for international cooperation. APCI recognized that universities and research centers have very limited participation in projects financed by bilateral and multilateral government agencies and NGOs. Several institutions have developed their own contacts and strategies for raising funds outside APCI channels. This funding has led to a series of small, isolated projects that are of little importance but that reflect the institutions' interest in working internationally. It is up to APCI to work with national institutions involved in higher education and science and technology to develop a plan to obtain and use support from international donors more efficiently. Doing so would recognize the important role universities must play in Peru's development.

NATIONAL AGENCIES

The National Council for Science and Technology (CONCYTEC) and the National Institute of Scholarships and Educational Credit (INABEC) are the key agencies responsible for internationalization. Both are dependent on the Ministry of Education for funding and policy direction. CONCYTEC is responsible for international scientific and technological developments and collaboration. INABEC is responsible for finding international training and mobility opportunities for scholars.

CONCYTEC promotes, coordinates, and executes policies on technological development. It receives funds from the national budget, loans, donations, the national fund for scientific and technological development, and international cooperation. Science and technology scholarships that are part of international cooperation projects must be requested through CONCYTEC, in coordination with the corresponding national bodies.

INABEC is an independent organization in charge of elaborating, proposing, and executing policies and programs related to the granting of academic scholarships from international technical cooperation sources. It has recently launched an important information awareness campaign and a decentralization process by developing agreements with the media, the regional Bureau of Education, and universities in different parts of the country. It has been proposed that in the future INABEC work more closely with APCI in processing scholarships and expanding its relations through interinstitutional agreements with foreign universities and foundations, embassies, and multilateral and bilateral agencies.

No single entity is in charge of receiving and distributing scholarships in Peru. As a result, there are no statistics on the number of Peruvians who have studied abroad. The extent of brain drain is not known, although the problem is believed to have grown in recent years.

National Assembly of Rectors

The National Assembly of Rectors is the coordinating entity of public and private universities in Peru. Its mission is to improve both academic quality and the management of Peruvian universities.

The National Assembly of Rectors has five regional councils, which represent all regions of Peru. These councils coordinate the creation of programs and professional degrees; appoint universities that can validate studies, degrees, and diplomas obtained abroad; evaluate new universities; resolve conflicts at Peruvian universities relating to the legitimacy of their governing authorities; and give opinions about legislative proposals related to higher education.

The National Assembly of Rectors considers internationalization of great importance for higher education and has had an International Technical Cooperation Office for several years. The association takes a comprehensive approach to internationalization and believes that international relations must not be limited to international mobility programs and agreements. It is essential for universities to relate to other realities and cultures, to get updated and enhance their programs, and to train professionals so that they can contribute to national development.

Some of the criteria used by the National Assembly of Rectors to evaluate the improvements in terms of internationalization of Peruvian universities include the following:

- Existence of a plan for internationalization covering the whole university.
- Evaluation of the management of the international relations offices.
- Updating of curricula, including foreign language instruction, study of other cultures, and world processes and their impact; deepening of specialized disciplines; use of new teaching technologies; and support for necessary administrative and organizational structures.
- Development of special programs to attract international students.
- Establishment of contacts and linkages with clear and effective guidelines and procedures, including professor and student mobility, joint research, and development of joint educational programs.
- Existence of clear mechanisms to evaluate the internationalization process.

The National Assembly of Rectors has developed a series of actions to promote internationalization of higher education in Peru. Among the most important are the following:

- Promote the integration of the international dimension in the overall university strategic plans in terms of their own priorities, vision, and expectations for the internationalization process.
- Promote greater stability in the offices and structures responsible for international affairs.
- Promote the teaching of languages in universities, especially in those outside the capital.

- Provide training at all levels on the management of internationalization and higher education in the global context.
- Promote greater links and cooperation within the Regional University Councils' administrative units that coordinate important regional issues for the universities that belong to the area.
- Strengthen the Interuniversity Regional Integration Network systematically.
- Promote debates on trade agreements such as the Free Trade Area of the Americas, Mercosur, GATS, Asia-Pacífico, and their implications and opportunities for higher education.

The National Assembly of Rectors makes an effort to encourage communication and integration between Peruvian universities. Its work is extremely important, since it is the only organization that brings Peruvian universities together and its policies have great influence on the system as a whole. Nevertheless, a lack of a clear policy on internationalization and limited resources and personnel dedicated to the international dimension of higher education constrain its effectiveness.

Consortia and Alliances

University consortia, alliances, and associations aim to bring together institutions of similar development, origin, or purpose. These associations address regional issues, such as academic quality, development of joint research projects, and exchange of students and professors, and undertake initiatives that build on the distinct aspects and strengths of each institution.

The first consortium in Peru was formed in 1996 by four private universities (Pontificia Universidad Católica del Perú, Universidad de Lima, Universidad del Pacífico, and Universidad Peruana Cayetano Heredia). Three public universities (Universidad Nacional Mayor de San Marcos, Universidad Nacional Agraria La Molina, and Universidad Nacional de Ingeniería) formed an alliance in 2002. Both of these groups bring together universities located in Lima. Regional consortia of universities are also active.

Bilateral Agencies

Bilateral aid organizations include the Japan International Cooperation Agency (JICA), the Korea International Cooperation Agency (KOICA), and Deutsche Gesellschaft für Technische Zusammenarbeit (GTZ), as well as horizontal cooperation from Argentina, Brazil, and Chile. These agencies work closely with the APCI.

In contrast, the European Union, which has offices in Lima, works directly with institutions of higher education. It offers extensive cooperation that include networks of research and teaching through the ALFA and ALßAN programs, in which Peruvian universities are actively involved. In terms of participation in the ALFA network, Peru ranks seventh in Latin America, behind Argentina, Brazil, Chile, Mexico, Cuba, and Colombia. Peru participated in 14 of 92 projects between 2000 and 2005. Ten of the higher education institutions participating are located in Lima and four are located in the provinces.[2]

Other agencies active in Peru are the British Council, the French Embassy, the Agency for International Cooperation (Spain), the Fulbright Commission (the United States), and Belgian Technical Cooperation.

The British Council has been very important in providing scholarships for study in Great Britain. Since it works independently of the government and has its own administrative structure, it obtains, receives, and approves resources according to its own priorities.

France, through its embassy and its scholarships for graduate students, has been a supporter of internationalization in Peru for many years. Aware of the importance of internationalization for universities in Peru, in 2001 the French Embassy created the University Cooperation Aggregate, which facilitates bilateral relations with Peru. Its goal is to promote scientific, academic, and institutional relations among Peruvian and French universities and research centers. In 2002 the French-Peruvian University Network was developed, with sponsorship by the French Ministry of Foreign Affairs, through the Embassy of France in Peru. This network, Network Raúl Porras Barrenechea, supports interuniversity projects related to the exchange of students and faculty, research projects, joint programs, and other activities. The French Embassy recently signed an agreement with the INABEC, which will manage some of its scholarships. Since 2002 the Embassy has organized a university fair through EduFrance, with the participation of prestigious French universities.

Spain, through its diverse mechanisms of support to Latin America, has been a valuable partner for internationalization. The Intercampus Program for students and professors was very successful in Peru and served as a first interinstitutional venture. It also allowed the strengthening of thematic networks, through projects with the Programa Iberoamericano de Ciencia y Tecnología para el Desarrollo (CYTED) and Programa Iberoamericano de Cooperación Universidad-Empresa (IBERCUE), among others. These programs, as well as the Mutis Scholarship Program and the programs of the Carolina Foundation, have been managed by the Spanish Agency for International Cooperation and the Spanish Embassy in Lima.

---

[2] http://europa.eu.int/comm/europeaid/projects/alfa/information/statistics/peru1_6 .pdf.

The Fulbright Commission for Educational Exchange between Peru and the United States is a binational nonprofit organization, established in 1956 through an agreement between the governments of Peru and the United States. Since its creation, it has granted more than 2,000 scholarships to Peruvian citizens and more than 1,000 scholarships to U.S. citizens to study, teach, and do research in Peru. Many of the best Peruvian students have been able to pursue graduate studies in the United States thanks to the support of the Commission. The Fulbright Commission also provides information about the American university system and offers Peruvian scholars the opportunity to visit American universities, an important step toward establishing contact among peers. The Fulbright Commission is planning to sign agreements with prestigious Peruvian universities in order to make more efficient and institutional use of its resources.

Belgium Technical Cooperation recently initiated a more coordinated approach to working with some Peruvian universities through its Centers of Excellence program. Belgium supports programs that have a strong impact on Peru's development, especially in the provinces. It provides technical advice, training, scholarships, and equipment.

Bilateral sources are of great importance for internationalizing higher education, but coordination at the national level is needed to make the most of these resources. The universities recognize the value of having an independent advocate and coordinator promoting cooperation between universities.

Internationalization at the Institutional Level

To become effective, the international dimension needs to be incorporated into every aspect of higher education. Most universities recognize this as a goal but find it difficult to implement in practice.

Goals and Rationales

Most Peruvian universities conceive internationalization as an integral process for institutional transformation in which the international and intercultural dimension becomes part of their mission and functions. They also see internationalization as a means of improving the quality of higher education in Peru. However, while these may be seen as the goals of internationalization, they do not reflect current priorities and practices. Universities look at internationalization in general and international cooperation in particular primarily as a means of establishing relationships that bring financial assistance to the higher education sector. The opportunity to establish collaborative research and academic initiatives is only a secondary motivation for internationalizing.

Approach to Internationalization

One of the challenges facing the Peruvian university system is the absence of mid- and long-term strategic planning in which the international dimension is included as core to the development of universities. This is a result of two main factors. The first is the lack of an entrepreneurial and dynamic approach to the management of both public and private universities. The second is the perception and understanding of international relations. In most cases international cooperation is seen only as a means of obtaining donor support. Therefore, more attention is paid to how and where to raise funds than to how to establish solid and sustainable relationships. The offices in charge of international relations at universities direct their efforts to fundraising, without exploring or developing opportunities for medium-term cooperation in terms of academic quality and research.

This type of ad hoc and short-term approach to internationalization is not only the result of a historical orientation to international development cooperation, it also reflects the subsistence conditions the universities currently face. This is true for both public universities, which are managed with very limited resources, and private universities, which have increased in such great numbers that they now face enormous competition for students and resources.

Planning and Policies

Most of the universities interviewed declared that they have an institutional strategic plan, and 75 percent reported that the internationalization is part of this plan. Despite awareness that internationalization is fundamental to improving the quality of education, however, many institutions are not clear on how to internationalize.

Mobility

Accurate figures are not available on the number of foreign students and faculty that come to Peru for academic or cultural purposes. A proxy for the figure is the number of applications for official visas. During 2002, 257 official visas were granted for academic or cultural purposes. About half of foreigners (both students and professors) come from Latin America or Spain.

INTERNATIONAL STUDENTS
Only 37 percent of the visas issued were for international students. All foreign students came to study at universities that perform research; no foreign students were enrolled at for-profit universities.

Figure 9.2 Number of U.S. Students Studying in South America, 1993–99

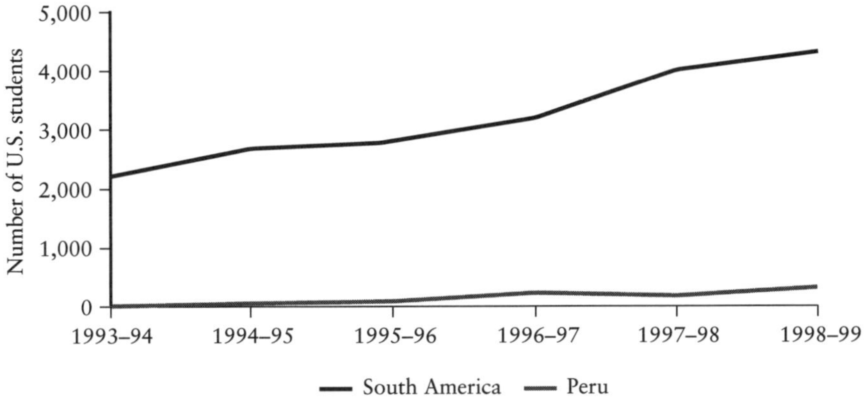

Source: http://opendoors.iienetwork.org.

The number of U.S. students studying at South American universities increased markedly in the past 10 years (figure 9.2). Numbers in Peru reflect the same rate of growth. Security issues are crucial push-pull factors in student mobility. The numbers of international students in Peru rose after September 1992, when Abimael Guzmán, the head of the Shining Path terrorist movement, was captured. These numbers declined in 1997, probably due to the hostage crisis at the Japanese Embassy in Lima (December 1996–April 1997).

VISITING FACULTY

About 60 percent of recipients of official visas to enter Peru in 2000 were professors, researchers, and lecturers. Within this group, about 80 percent were professors who were in Peru to develop academic activities at a Peruvian university. The remaining 20 percent worked with other public or private institutions. Sixty-nine percent of visiting scholars and scientists came to work in Lima (64 percent to private institutions, 36 percent to public institutions). Only 31 percent came to work in the provinces (26 percent to private universities, 74 percent to public universities) (Asamblea Nacional de Rectores 2005). These figures highlight two phenomena. First, foreign experts remain concentrated in the capital. Second, among universities in the provinces, public universities are the most active and the most interested in receiving foreign visitors. This may be explained by the fact that, despite their scarce resources, public universities in the provinces are interested in developing teaching and research, while most private provincial universities do not regard foreign visitors as important.

Peruvian professors do not receive financial support to attend conferences or to study abroad.

International Development Cooperation

A recent study of 14 universities in Peru (Lichowski and others 2004) shows that half had not received support from international cooperation organizations in the past few years. Among those that had received funding, 38 percent participated only in interuniversity cooperation projects related to mobility, training, or university networks; 62 percent were also involved with cultural, scientific, technological, and research cooperation.

All of the institutions surveyed consider international cooperation as very important. They believe that the most important factor limiting their participation has been lack of information. Universities do not know what rules to follow in order to obtain support or whom to speak to in order to get the necessary information about activities and mechanisms to fund their projects. Most of the universities report that although interuniversity cooperation is very important to them, their commitment to the development of their provinces is much more important.

Institutional Agreements

Peruvian universities believe that having agreements with universities abroad is one of the most immediate ways to internationalize. However, most institutions sign general agreements that represent the intention to cooperate but do not result in concrete activities (figure 9.3). They believe that simply signing these agreements increases the visibility of the

Figure 9.3 Number of Active Agreements Between Peruvian and Foreign Universities

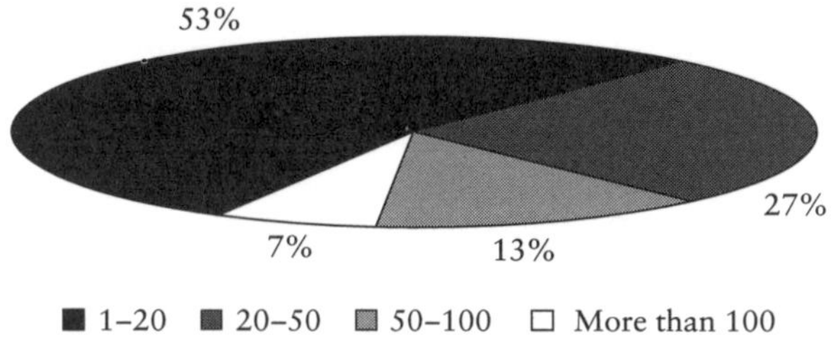

Source: Butters, Quiroga, and Dammert (2004).

institution. The competitiveness of the university marketplace in Peru has led to the perception that internationalization is a means to promote and improve the institutional image in order to better position the university among its competitors.

Research and Development

Research and development (R&D) includes the development of joint projects between local and foreign universities, as well as the establishment of strategic alliances with other institutions. Spending on R&D in Peru represented about 0.07 percent of GDP in 1997, about a tenth of the average for Latin America of 0.59 percent (Ismodes 2003). About 70 percent of spending went to government activities (research institutes); 30 percent went to universities.

Despite the low investment in R&D in Peru, Peruvian universities play a fundamental role in research. Unfortunately, no university has complete and centralized information on the research activities undertaken or the funding devoted to them. While all of the universities declare in their statutes that they consider academic education, research, and social service among their central activities, only 30 percent of universities engage in research.

Funds devoted to research at Peruvian universities are extremely limited. In most cases, resources are not allocated to support research projects that require investments in preparing bids or requests for proposals.

The results of the research projects performed at universities are limited, since researchers are not used to publishing, especially in the hard sciences and engineering. The publication of research is mainly in history, psychology, literature, and social science. Universities in Peru do not know how to take advantage of patents, since there is no culture of intellectual property in the country.

The policies for allocating state resources to public universities restrain initiatives and fail to support or promote research. In view of this situation, the most active public research universities, such as Universidad Nacional Mayor de San Marcos or Universidad Nacional Agraria La Molina, have decided to create foundations, which will allow them to compete for international funds, establish international networks, and appoint counterparts when necessary.

As for strategic alliances, the first systematic initiatives have been made at the national level. Joint research projects with foreign institutions have been undertaken by individual rather than institutional initiatives.

Distance Education

Universities regard distance education as a complement to face to face education. In 2003, about 10 percent of Peruvian universities offered some distance education programs (with or without e-learning platforms). These programs offer stand-alone classes, diploma programs, and specialization and graduate courses.

In a few programs, two or more education institutions participate. In most cases, the foreign university has been in charge of the design and content. Only one case is known in which the roles of the foreign and Peruvian university were equal.

Most distance education programs are given in Spanish. This explains why universities with distance education programs prefer making strategic alliances with Spanish or Latin American universities to develop joint programs. The Spanish Distance Education National University has entered into agreements with at least three Peruvian higher education institutions.

To what extent can distance education contribute to the internationalization of higher education? Fifteen professionals enrolled in distance programs as well as two authorities on the subject were consulted. They noted that the participation of international experts is what makes these programs attractive. They also value the fact that these programs bring together students from different cultural and social environments, which creates a very rich exchange of experiences and knowledge. Almost all of them highlight the importance of the certification obtained in these programs, since a diploma or degree obtained from a program that involves a foreign university is believed to have added value in Peru.

Accreditation

Globalization and technological development have made Peruvian university authorities more aware of the need to update education and ensure its quality. In 2002 the National Assembly of Rectors created the Rectors National Commission for Accreditation. The commission agreed to hire specialists in different professional areas, and it has held meetings to discuss the mechanisms used by Peruvian universities to improve the quality of higher education. The National Assembly of Rectors has asked each Peruvian university to create a new bureau or office for accreditation, focusing first on accreditation of master's degrees.

Accreditation is a very important issue. Most students regard higher education as a means of improving themselves personally and financially. Accreditation and evaluation of Peruvian universities would provide students and professors (both national and foreign) with information about higher education institutions. From the perspective of potential students, accreditation is necessary to determine whether a university meets the minimum conditions to provide a solid professional education. From the perspective of professors, accreditation is important to make them aware of the possibilities the university offers for support and development of teaching and research activities.

There is great interest in and discussion of the advantages of accreditation by a foreign body. The first reaction of university authorities has been rejection and fear of accreditation, probably because many are conscious of their limits.

Peru has no national accreditation agency, although a law has been proposed. Given the large number of new universities in Peru, in the near future accreditation will be an important tool, so that universities that provide high-quality programs can distinguish themselves from those that are mere educational businesses. Accreditation will enable universities that conduct research to make strategic alliances with foreign partners, carry out joint projects, and facilitate mobility of professors, researchers, and students.

Conclusions

Peru lags other countries in Latin America in terms of internationalization of its higher education institutions. The situation is characterized by an ad hoc and fragmented approach within and between institutions, the lack of concrete and realistic objectives, the limited institutional capacity to obtain and manage international cooperation or engage in international academic activities, and the lack of human and material resources. The problem starts at the highest level in the institutions, where there is a lack of understanding of, commitment to, and vision regarding why and how internationalization adds value to the teaching/learning, research, and service functions of the university and the wider higher education community. Few institutions are well positioned and competent to look at internationalization in a holistic way and to use it to contribute to the quality of their academic endeavors and their reputations, nationally, regionally, or internationally.

At the national level several institutions have expressed commitment to the internationalization of higher education. The Ministry of Foreign Affairs, the APCI, the INABEC, and the CONCYTEC have policy statements that commit them to the internationalization of higher education institutions. This formal commitment, however, has not been translated into activities and programs. Moreover, the lack of integration by these institutions makes even simple tasks difficult.

The National Assembly of Rectors understands the importance of internationalization, but it recognizes that there are many obstacles to making it a priority and turning verbal support into concrete action. Its interactions with other national agencies prevent it from becoming the lobbyist it should be on behalf of the interests of universities. However, it has been active in disseminating information from cooperation agencies.

At the level of the universities, some institutions explicitly declare their international focus and orientation and engage in international cooperation and international activities. But most have not gone beyond formal declarations.

The single greatest obstacle to internationalization is the lack of trained staff managing the process at universities. High turnover and a low level of professionalism limit the ability to manage internationalization effectively. Institutional memory is not preserved. In many instances, international officers are political appointees, and most of the activities remain in the hands of the rectors.

Universities are establishing new consortia and associations, and they are beginning to integrate into international associations, such as the Organization for Higher Education and the Latin American Universities Union. Some of these consortia, particularly those made up of regional universities in Peru, are aimed at reinforcing ties with institutions in neighboring countries. This kind of interaction forces them to engage in accreditation and to develop strategies to make their degrees compatible.

Universities, particularly those that regard research as one of their main activities, are finding it more important to train officers for positions in international relations. Cooperation agencies are providing opportunities for training aimed at making international institutional agreements and relationships more efficient and sustainable.

References

Agurto, Santiago. 1998. *La universidad en el Perú: conversatorio realizado en el congreso de la república de marzo a junio de 1998.* Lima: Editorial del Congreso de la República del Perú.

———. 1999. "Problemática universitaria: gobierno financiamiento y desarrollo universitario." Universidad Nacional Federico Villarreal, Lima.

Aljovín, Cristóbal, ed. 2002. "La universidad en el Perú." Universidad Nacional Mayor de San Marcos, Lima.

APCI (Peruvian International Cooperation Agency). 2002. "La Cooperación internacional orientada a universidades y centros científicos, una primera aproximación." Lima.

Asamblea Nacional de Rectores. 1988. "Perú: estadísticas universitarias 1960–86." Comisión de Coordinación Interuniversitaria. Secretaría Ejecutiva, Departamento de Informática y Documentación, Lima.

———. 1991. "Universidad peruana y desarrollo nacional." Lima.

———. 1997. "Legislación sobre la creación de universidades en el Perú." Lima.

———. 1999. "Hacia la modernización y acreditación integral de las universidades peruanas. Áreas o campos de acción." Lima.

———. 2000. "Datos estadísticos de las universidades del Perú." Lima.

———. 2005. "Estadisticas universitarias." Peru

Butters, Luis Jaime Castillo, Leena Bernuy Quiroga, and Pamela Lastres Dammert. 2004. "Survey of Peruvian Tertiary Institutions."

Consorcio de Universidades. 2001. "La universidad que el Perú necesita. Encuentros y seminarios 1999–2000." Foro Educativo, Consorcio de Universidades, Lima.

Cornejo, Raúl. 1994. "Las leyes universitarias en el Perú." Universidad Ricardo Palma, Lima.

INEI (Instituto Nacional de Estadística e Informática), and ANR (Asamblea Nacional de Rectores). 1997. "I censo nacional universitario 1996. Síntesis estadística." Lima.

———. 1999. *Perú: compendio de estadísticas sociodemográficas 1998–99*. Lima: Editorial Gráfica Monterrico.

Ismodes, Eduardo. 2003. "Redes de comunicación y desarrollo científico tecnológico en el Perú." MA thesis in communications, Pontificia Universidad Católica del Perú, Lima.

Lichowski, Luis, Leena Bernuy, Citlali Ayala, and Inmaculada Madera. 2004. "Las universidades Latinoamericanas y su papel en el ámbito de la cooperación internacional para el desarrollo." Paper presented on February 4, Cuba.

McLauchlan, Patricia. 1994. "La situación de las universidades peruanas." Group of Analysis for Development (GRADE), Lima.

Ortiz, René. 1998. *Universidad y modernización en el Perú del siglo XX*. Lima: Fondo Editorial de la Pontificia Universidad Católica del Perú, Lima.

Salgado, Cecilia. 1998. "Análisis de los problemas, retos y alternativas de la universidad peruana frente al siglo XXI." *Revista de psicología liberabit* 4 (4): 65–69.

Thorne, Cecilia. 2003. "Indicadores de calidad de la universidad a nivel internacional y el caso peruano." Pontificia Universidad Católica del Perú, Lima.

Webb, Richard, ed. 2002. *Perú en números 2002: anuario estadístico*. Lima: Cuanto.

10

Key Actors and Programs: Increasing Connectivity in the Region

Isabel Cristina Jaramillo and Jane Knight

The previous chapters focused on the role of national governmental and nongovernmental organizations and higher education institutions in the internationalization process. This chapter takes the region as the unit of analysis and examines the key actors and programs promoting and supporting the international dimension of higher education in Latin America.

It is important to examine the different levels and types of bodies involved for several reasons. First, the number and diversity of the actors in terms of purpose, function, and geographical scope has increased. Second, due to the nature of internationalization, issues have implications for international, regional, and domestic policies. Third, the boundaries separating these three levels are becoming blurred and porous. Thus any analysis of the international dimension of higher education must go beyond the national level and beyond the nation state as key actor.

This chapter identifies, describes, and analyzes the major international, interregional, regional, and subregional bodies and programs that reflect the international dimension and connectivity of Latin America. The framework for identifying and analyzing the key actors is based on the level of the actor or program and the type or status of the body (table 10.1).

While the analysis is meant to be inclusive, the group of actors reviewed is not exhaustive. The most active and best-known organizations, which are identified and discussed in the national reports, are included.

The terms *networks* and *networking* are frequently used in Latin America. They reflect and contribute to the increasing connectivity within the region and internationally. *Networks* are formal organizations, informal groups of institutions, and actors that come together around a specific task or issue. They are often used to achieve internationalization goals and are instruments for programs such as ALFA. Networks can therefore be used in the sense of an actor as well as a means or instrument of internationalization.

Table 10.1 Actors and Programs for Internationalization of Higher Education

Levels of actors and programs	*Type of actors and programs*
• International	• Intergovernmental bodies
• Bilateral	• Government departments and agencies
• Interregional	• Quasi-governmental bodies
• Regional	• NGOs
• Subregional	• Foundations
• National	• Treaties and conventions

A few words about how the different levels of actors are defined may be helpful. *International* is interpreted to mean actors with worldwide scope. This includes UN agencies, such as UNESCO and UNDP, as well as other bodies, such as the OECD and the World Bank.

Bilateral refers to foreign national government and nongovernment agencies that cooperate with individual countries in Latin America. Examples in this category include national government development agencies, such as the AECI or USAID, as well as other organizations, such as the British Council or the German Academic Exchange Service.

Interregional is used to denote cooperation between the Latin American region as a whole with other regional actors. This includes cooperation between Latin America and Europe, as illustrated by the AlßAN and ALFA programs, and Ibero-American cooperation, as illustrated by organizations such as the Ibero-American University Council (CUIB) and the Latin American Network for the Accreditation and Quality of Higher Education. Latin American and North American cooperation is often labeled inter-American and is exemplified by organizations such as the Inter-American Organization for Higher Education (IOHE) and the Organization of American States (OAS).

The Latin American region is defined in a cultural and geographical sense. It includes all the countries from Mexico to Argentina. Organizations such as the Latin American Universities Union and the Institute for Higher Education in Latin America and the Caribbean are good examples of regional organizations. Often regional cooperation is referred to as intraregional to distinguish it from interregional.

The last level is subregional. Organizations at this level include the Montevideo Group University Association (AUGM), the Association of Universities of the Amazon (UNAMAZ), and the Council of University Presidents for the Integration of the West-Central Sub-Region of South America (CRISCO). (The Caribbean is not a focus of this project, and actors specific to the Caribbean region are therefore not included.)

International Actors

International actors include intergovernmental organizations, NGOs, private foundations, and international programs.

Intergovernmental Organizations

Among the most important and active intergovernmental organizations are the International Organization for Migration; the Organisation for Economic Co-operation and Development; the United Nations Development Programme; the United Nations Education, Scientific and Cultural Organization; the World Bank; and the World Trade Organization.

INTERNATIONAL ORGANIZATION FOR MIGRATION

The International Organization for Migration (IOM) (www.iom.int) is not part of the UN system, but it maintains close working relations with UN bodies and operational agencies. It is the leading international organization working with migrants and governments to provide humane responses to migration challenges. The IOM supports academic mobility in the region through the movement of scholarship holders and the return of qualified nationals to their home countries. The goal of the IOM is to help Latin American countries better manage migration, with an emphasis on increased regional cooperation.

ORGANISATION FOR ECONOMIC CO-OPERATION AND DEVELOPMENT

The Organisation for Economic Co-operation and Development (OECD) (www.oecd.org) is an intergovernmental organization aimed at developing member countries' capacity and transforming it into economic growth and social development. Mexico, the ninth-largest economy in the world and the seventh largest in terms of its balance of trade, is the only country in Latin America that is a member of OECD.

Two organizations within the OECD have a special interest in internationalization. The first is the Program on Institutional Management in Higher Education (IMHE), which has institutional members in Brazil and Mexico. IMHE was involved in two regional studies on internationalization and continues its commitment to this topic by cosponsoring, with the World Bank, this publication.

The Center for Education Research and Innovation is the second unit in OECD that addresses the internationalization of the curriculum. It is currently undertaking regional studies on cross-border education and trade in education services.

UNITED NATIONS DEVELOPMENT PROGRAMME

The United Nations Development Programme (UNDP) (www.undp.org) is the United Nations' global development network. It connects countries to knowledge, experience, and resources so that people can build a better life. Its capacity-building strategy is applied in all of the 166 countries it works with.

UNDP maintains a very active presence in 24 countries in Latin America. Some of its 44 programs in operation in the region are being developed through academic centers in Latin America. Many government officials and academic leaders have benefited from UNDP fellowships to enhance their knowledge in science, technology, and development through studies abroad.

UNITED NATIONS EDUCATION, SCIENTIFIC AND CULTURAL ORGANIZATION

The United Nations Education, Scientific and Cultural Organization (UNESCO) (www.unesco.org/education) is the key UN body with the mandate for and competence in education. Made up of 190 member countries, it plays a significant role in addressing higher education policy issues, facilitating system reform, and building capacity in member states. A new section of the Education Division focuses on academic mobility, particularly studying abroad. In 2002 the section created the Global Forum on International Quality Assurance, Accreditation and Recognition of Qualifications in Higher Education. The forum is addressing the commercialization of and trade in education and the commodification of knowledge.

The regional office for higher education in Latin America is the Institute for Higher Education in Latin America and the Caribbean/UNESCO, in Venezuela. This office was responsible for important preparatory meetings and reports for the World Conferences of Higher Education held in Paris in 1998 and 2003. It promotes horizontal cooperation and mutual relations in order to help reduce asymmetric development among regions and educational systems worldwide.

WORLD BANK

The World Bank (www.worldbank.org) is an international financial organization that assists developing countries and transition economies improve their living standards through sustainable growth and investment in people. It is the largest international funder of education in the world. In Latin America the World Bank provides funding for projects at all levels of education. Among other things, it helps Latin American countries increase access to quality higher education in order to spur economic growth as a mechanism for sustainable poverty reduction. Higher education projects in the region make up 17 percent of the education portfolio in

Latin America and the Caribbean and are closely related to the Bank's support to science and technology.

The World Bank's priorities in higher education are building markets for higher education and improving the accountability and responsiveness of the public sector. Project components include institutional capacity building, competitive and performance-based funding, quality assurance mechanisms, information systems on labor market outcomes of graduates, and student loans.

The Bank is working or has recently worked with eight governments in the region (Argentina, Brazil, Bolivia, Chile, Colombia, Jamaica, Mexico, and Venezuela). It aims to enhance and strengthen their higher education systems as well as help them close the knowledge and income gaps with the leading economic regions of the world. During a recent assessment of the state of tertiary education in Colombia, internationalization was addressed and recognized as an important factor in the role of higher education in the knowledge society.

WORLD TRADE ORGANIZATION

The World Trade Organization (WTO) (www.wto.org) is the only international organization that deals with the trade of goods and services between nations. About two-thirds of its 146 members are developing countries. One of the WTO's principal objectives is to facilitate the removal of trade barriers in order to enhance the international flow of goods and services among countries.

The General Agreement on Trade and Services (GATS) includes education as one of the tradable service sectors. Several international studies have analyzed the potential risks and positive effects for higher education and the implications for the internationalization process. However, much more analysis needs to be done in the region on the consequences of trade, in terms of new opportunities and potential risks.

International Nongovernmental Organizations

Among the most important and active international NGOs are the International Association of Universities, the International Association of University Presidents, and the International Federation of Catholic Universities.

INTERNATIONAL ASSOCIATION OF UNIVERSITIES

Established in 1950, the International Association of Universities (IAU) (www.unesco.org/iau/internationalization) brings together universities from about 150 countries for the purpose of working together on common concerns related to higher education. It has official status as an NGO with

UNESCO and provides services to organizations, institutions, and higher education authorities, as well as individual policymakers and decision-makers, teachers, students, and researchers. It has an active membership in Latin America.

The IAU Statement on Internationalisation of Higher Education, adopted in 1998, supports the international dimension as a way to improve academic excellence and relevance. In 2003 the IAU conducted a survey of its institutional members on internationalization practices and priorities. The report provides a regional and comparative analysis of internationalization practices. The report and other useful documents and sources of information on internationalization are available on the IAU Web site.

INTERNATIONAL ASSOCIATION OF UNIVERSITY PRESIDENTS
Founded in 1964, the International Association of University Presidents (IAUP) (www.ia-up.org) seeks to strengthen the international mission of and quality of education provided by universities in an increasingly inter-dependent world. It also seeks to promote global awareness and compe-tence, peace, and international understanding through education. It has an active representation in Latin America, particularly in Argentina, Brazil, Chile, Colombia, and Mexico.

The University President's Exchange Program, launched in 2001, is an innovative initiative that facilitates international work-visits by university presidents. During the first two years of the program, more than half of IAUP members used this experience to share and learn from their col-leagues at universities around the world.

More recently, IAUP has focused international attention on the issue of international quality assurance and accreditation. Conference papers on internationalization are available on their Web site.

THE INTERNATIONAL FEDERATION OF CATHOLIC UNIVERSITIES
The International Federation of Catholic Universities (www.fiuc.org) is a worldwide organization with 200 members. It has six continental daugh-ter federations, as well as eight sector groups. It represents Catholic uni-versities in international associations and organizations and contributes to the development of Catholic higher studies, particularly the quality and scope of university work.

Private Foundations

The Ford Foundation (www.fordfound.org) is a worldwide philanthropic organization that has education as a focal point. Through its International Fellowship Program it provides opportunities for advanced and exceptional students from Asia, Africa, and Latin America to study abroad. The Ford Foundation is active in Latin America and has financed regional studies on the internationalization of higher education in Chile and Mexico.

Other private foundations have played important roles in establishing higher education and scientific institutions in Latin America. The Rockefeller Foundation helped establish university research and teaching units in Chile, Colombia, and Mexico during the 1960s. Since then it has supported other scientific developments. The Rockefeller Foundation and other private foreign foundations contribute to the internationalization of scientific research in Latin America.

International Programs

The International Association for the Exchange of Students for Technical Experience (IAESTE) (www.iaeste.org) was founded in 1948, at Imperial College in London. Since then it has grown to include more than 80 countries worldwide and has facilitated the exchange of more than 300,000 students.

Created in 1948, AIESEC (www.aiesec.org) is the world's largest student organization. This global network includes 50,000 members at more than 800 universities in more than 80 countries and territories. Every year AIESEC facilitates international exchange of thousands of students and recent graduates, who work in paid traineeships or as volunteers for nonprofit organizations. AIESEC contributes to development through its commitment to international understanding and cooperation.

Bilateral Actors

Bilateral actors include national development agencies, embassies, and international cooperation agencies.

National Development Agencies

The most important and active national development agencies in the region are the Agency for International Cooperation, the Canadian International Development Agency, the Japan International Cooperation Agency, the Korean International Cooperation Agency, the Swedish International Development Agency, other Nordic development agencies, and the U.S. Agency for International Development.

AGENCY FOR INTERNATIONAL COOPERATION
The Agency for International Cooperation (AECI) (www.aeci.es) was created in 1988 as the lead agency to execute Spain's policy for developmental cooperation. It is part of Spain's Ministry of Foreign Relations. AECI is

committed to fostering economic growth; contributing to the social, cultural, institutional, and political progress of developing countries, particularly to those with a Spanish background; and stimulating scientific and cultural cooperation and the harmonization of development policies. The agency supports scholarships and fellowships for Ibero-American professionals in Spain and Spanish professionals in Ibero-America.

AECI's efforts have had a significant influence on the internationalization process in most Latin American countries, not only because of the historical ties between Spain and Latin America but also because Spain serves as the link to future relations with the rest of Europe. This cooperation with Latin America and the Caribbean has boomed in the past several years and now absorbs about 60 percent of all funds allocated for international cooperation by the Spanish government. AECI's scholarship programs and its project on cooperation in education have strengthened solidarity among the countries in Ibero-America.

CANADIAN INTERNATIONAL DEVELOPMENT AGENCY

The Canadian International Development Agency (CIDA) (www.acdi-cida.gc.ca) is a governmental agency mandated to support sustainable development in developing countries in order to reduce poverty and contribute to a more secure, equitable, and prosperous world. The agency sponsors linkages and networks among Canadian and Latin American universities and related research centers through the University Program for Cooperation and Development.

The Americas branch, one of CIDA's four geographic branches, includes the Caribbean, including Haiti and Cuba; Central America; the Andean countries; the Southern Cone; Brazil; and Colombia. In Argentina CIDA is working to build a more skilled and educated workforce. In Brazil, Chile, Colombia, and Peru, it seeks to reduce poverty and inequities and encourage more sustainable and participatory environmental management.

JAPANESE INTERNATIONAL COOPERATION AGENCY

Japanese emigration to South America has a long history. Many people of Japanese descent, both permanent and temporary residents, live in Argentina, Bolivia, Brazil, Paraguay, and Peru.

The Japanese International Cooperation Agency (JICA) (www.jica.gov.jp) creates a bridge between Japan and the developing countries in Latin America to help build a more prosperous world. It has particularly strong ties to Brazil, Chile, Mexico, and Peru, which have important economic and commercial relations with Japan.

JICA provides international support to a large number of countries and higher education institutions in Latin America. Its provides infrastructure, mainly equipment, and scholarships for Latin American students interested in studying in Japan.

KOREAN INTERNATIONAL COOPERATION AGENCY

The Korean International Cooperation Agency (KOICA) (www.koica.or.kr), a government agency, was founded in 1991 to promote international cooperation with developing countries. It emphasizes human resource development as one of the most effective means of cooperation. It has supported projects in Mexico, Peru, and elsewhere in the region.

SWEDISH INTERNATIONAL DEVELOPMENT AGENCY

The Swedish International Development Agency (SIDA) (www.sida.org) is a government agency that reports to the Ministry of Foreign Affairs. It is responsible for most of Sweden's contributions to international development cooperation. SIDA has regional strategies for Central America, the Caribbean, and South America. It has financed research collaborations between Swedes and Latin Americans since the 1970s. The aim is to expand and reinforce skills at Latin American universities and research institutes. Sweden has helped train seismological researchers and social scientists, through the Latin American Council of Social Sciences, a network of social science research institutions in South America.

OTHER NORDIC DEVELOPMENT AGENCIES

Other Nordic development agencies, such as the Danish International Development Agency (DANIDA) (www.um.dk) and the Norwegian Agency for Development Cooperation (NORAD) (www.norad.no), are active in the region, particularly in Central America and some countries in South America. They develop higher education and research projects, provide scholarships, and develop joint projects through South-South cooperation programs.

U.S. AGENCY FOR INTERNATIONAL DEVELOPMENT

Since its inception in 1961, the U.S. Agency for International Development (USAID) (www.usaid.gov/our_work/education_and_universities/highered.htm) has been a key player in the development of higher education in aid-recipient countries. USAID has devoted substantial resources to creating university and college faculties and technical and vocational training institutions charged with developing host country capacity to support development objectives. USAID has 16 field missions in the Western Hemisphere, as well as operations in other countries, including Cuba.

The Association Liaison Office for University Cooperation in Development (ALO), established in 1992, assists the six major higher education associations in the United States build their partnership with USAID and help their member institutions foster cooperative development partnerships with colleges and universities abroad. In Latin America ALO works closely with Mexico and some countries in Central America.

Embassies

Embassies represent national interests and develop activities related to their countries' foreign policies. Many embassies in the region play an essential role in linking higher education institutions and facilitating the development of international agreements and networks. In North America, the U.S. and Canadian Embassies play key roles. In Europe, Spain, France, and the Ecos-Nord program promote cooperation on teaching and research projects. Germany, the Netherlands, and more recently Belgium and Italy have implemented initiatives to strengthen links between higher education institutions in their countries and Latin America. (An example is Fondo Mixto Italo-Argentino, established by the Italian Embassy in Argentina.) In Asia and Oceania, Japan, the Republic of Korea, and more recently Australia, China, and New Zealand are increasing their embassies' roles in Latin America. Several are promoting their higher education programs and services. Although all of these countries have different higher education systems and different interests in establishing international connections with Latin America, they work toward developing closer cooperation within higher education institutions in Latin America.

Bilateral International Cooperation Agencies

The most important bilateral international cooperation agencies are the British Council, the Canadian Education Centre, EduFrance, the German Academic Exchange Service, IDP Education Australia, L'Institut de Recherche pour le Développement, the Institute of International Education, the International Development Research Centre, the Netherlands Organizations for International Cooperation in Higher Education, and the Swedish Agency for Research Cooperation.

BRITISH COUNCIL
The British Council (www.britishcouncil.org), founded as a voluntary association in 1934, operates in 227 cities in 109 countries. It helps maintain the United Kingdom's international relations by supporting and complementing its diplomatic, commercial, and development efforts. The British Council's work focuses mainly on education and training, English language teaching, science, the arts, and governance. It creates linkages between British universities and higher education institutions around the world through a range of resources, including marketing and promotion, distance learning, support services, and scholarships for international students.

The British Council has worked in Latin America since 1935. It has offices in Brazil, Chile, Colombia, Mexico, and Venezuela. Since 1940 it has supported Anglophile societies and English schools in all of these countries.

CANADIAN EDUCATION CENTRE

The Canadian Education Centre (CEC) (www.studycanada.ca) promotes Canada as a destination for international students and as a source of contract training. The CEC Network operates with the support of Canadian education institutions and the government of Canada. More than 300 Canadian education institutions—public and private universities, university colleges, colleges, secondary schools, and language training providers—are members of the CEC Network. There are 17 Canadian Education Centres around the world, four of them located in Argentina, Brazil, Colombia, and Mexico.

EDUFRANCE

EduFrance (www.edufrance.fr) is a French agency created in 2000 that promotes the French higher education programs and services abroad. It welcomes international students, provides visas, secures work permits, helps find lodging for foreign students, and coordinates international cooperation with foreign countries. EduFrance has increased the number of international students studying in France. In Latin America, Brazil and Colombia send the highest number of students to France.

GERMAN ACADEMIC EXCHANGE SERVICE

The German Academic Exchange Service (DAAD) (www.daad.de) is a private, publicly funded, self-governing organization of higher education institutions in Germany. It was first founded in 1925 and reestablished in 1950. It promotes international academic relations and cooperation by offering mobility programs for students, faculty, administrators, and staff in higher education.

With more than 60,000 scholarships granted each year, the DAAD is one of the largest academic exchange organizations in the world. It provides scholarships for undergraduate and graduate students, PhD candidates, and faculty. It works in conjunction with partner organizations, such as the Alexander von Humboldt Foundation, which awards research fellowships to highly qualified scholars and scientists who hold PhDs.

The DAAD is becoming increasingly active in Latin America, particularly in Brazil and Mexico. Both the DAAD and the British Council have alumni networks, which support their programs and contribute to the development of more permanent ties that help develop long-standing relationships.

IDP EDUCATION AUSTRALIA

IDP Education Australia (www.idp.com/) is a world leader in international education, with a strong focus on recruiting students for Australian programs and institutions. IDP has more than 90 offices around the world and activities in some 50 countries. These offices provide international student services, development services, assessment and evaluation services, marketing, research, and consultancy services. In Latin America, IDP has offices in Brazil, Colombia, and Mexico.

INSTITUT DE RECHERCHE POUR LE DÉVELOPPEMENT

First established in 1943, l'Office de la Recherche Scientifique et Technologique d'Outre Mer later became L'Institut de Recherche pour le Développement (www.ird.fr). The institute has 34 offices around the world, six of them in Latin America (in Brazil, Bolivia, Chile, Ecuador, Mexico, and Peru); it has delegates in Colombia, Costa Rica, and Paraguay. It sponsors 1,106 researchers around the world, 140 of them based in Latin America. Their research focuses on water resources, climate change, biodiversity, ecology, development policies and globalization, and public health.

INSTITUTE OF INTERNATIONAL EDUCATION

The Institute of International Education (IIE) (www.iie.org), founded in 1919, is an independent, nonprofit organization that promotes education relations between the people of the United States and other countries. It established its Latin American office in 1974, in Mexico City.

IIE administers the Fulbright student scholarship program and the MacArthur scholarships. During the 1930s it established the first exchange program between the Soviet Union and Latin America, a program that has remained very active since then.

It works with a variety of institutions, foundations, organizations, and corporations in administering scholarship and student mobility programs in Argentina, Brazil, Chile, and Mexico.

INTERNATIONAL DEVELOPMENT RESEARCH CENTRE

The International Development Research Centre (IDRC) (www.idrc.ca) is a Canadian public corporation created in 1970 to help developing countries use science and technology to address social, economic, and environmental problems. IDRC has worked with 49 Latin America countries, especially in Mexico and the Southern Cone countries, since 1971. The Regional Office for Latin America and the Caribbean is located in Montevideo, Uruguay. In the past 30 years, IDRC has supported 1,957 research projects directed and managed by Latin American and Caribbean researchers and institutions.

Between 1993 and 2003 , IDRC also supported almost 200 scholars from the region, particularly in Chile, Colombia, and Peru.

NETHERLANDS ORGANIZATIONS FOR INTERNATIONAL COOPERATION IN HIGHER EDUCATION

The Netherlands Organizations for International Cooperation in Higher Education (NUFFIC) (www.nuffic.nl) was established in 1952 as a non-profit organization aimed at making education accessible around the world, particularly in countries where educational infrastructure is inade-quate. NUFFIC focuses on four areas: development cooperation, interna-tionalization of higher education, international recognition and certifica-tion, and marketing Dutch higher education. In the past, it has sponsored institution building projects in Latin America, particularly in Bolivia, Peru, and Central America. It is currently focusing mainly on Colombia and Guatemala. NUFFIC's scholarship programs have allowed students from Latin America to study in the Netherlands.

SWEDISH AGENCY FOR RESEARCH COOPERATION

The Swedish government has been supporting development research since 1975. This support is administered through the Department for Research Cooperation (SAREC), a department of SIDA (www.sida.se). SAREC supports research and acts as a resource in programs of develop-ment cooperation run by other departments of SIDA in which there is a focus on research.

SAREC allocates almost one-third of its appropriations for research cooperation to bilateral cooperation with developing countries, primarily to develop national research capacity. Another third is allocated to regional support and special programs. SAREC also supports special research programs and initiatives, international research programs, and development research in Sweden and the European Union. Assistance is targeted primarily at institutions and institution building, with the aim of increasing capacity in developing countries to run research programs of their own and to provide support to research that can help find solutions to important development problems. Support in Latin America is mainly in Bolivia and Nicaragua.

Bilateral Programs

Among the most important bilateral programs are the Academic and Pro-fessional Programs for the Americas, the Fulbright Academic Program, the Inter-University Cooperation Program, and the Undergraduate Stu-dent Agreement Program.

ACADEMIC AND PROFESSIONAL PROGRAMS FOR THE AMERICAS

Academic and Professional Programs for the Americas (LASPAU) (www.laspau.harvard.edu/sp-cont.htm) is a nonprofit organization affiliated with Harvard University. It designs, develops, and implements academic and professional exchange and scholarship programs on behalf of individuals and institutions in the United States, Canada, Latin America, and the Caribbean. LASPAU began in 1964 as a cooperative enterprise to enable talented Colombian high school students to obtain bachelor's degrees in the United States. Originally known as the Latin American Scholarship Program of American Universities, the organization changed its name in 1995 to reflect its wider scope of activities.

LASPAU's academic and professional programs serve more than 1,200 grantees annually. In addition, the organization consults on higher education issues in order to help strengthen institutions. These activities—sponsored by institutions such as the Fulbright Academic Exchange Program, the World Bank, the Inter-American Development Bank, Fundación Gran Mariscal de Ayacucho of Venezuela, Foundation for Science and Technology (FUNDACYT) of Ecuador, and the Colombian Institute for the Development of Science and Technology—involve hundreds of academic, research, and corporate institutions across the Americas.

FULBRIGHT ACADEMIC PROGRAM

The Fulbright Academic Exchange Program (www.fulbright.org) sponsors academic and cultural exchanges between students and academics from the United States and the rest of the world. It is the most widely known U.S. scholarship program. Since its inception in 1946, it has funded more than 255,000 participants from the United States and around the world. It has awarded grants to more than 13,000 Latin American and North American students and to experts from Argentina, Brazil, Chile, Colombia, and Peru, who have come from and gone to the United States to study, teach, and conduct research.

INTER-UNIVERSITY COOPERATION PROGRAM

The Inter-University Cooperation Program (PCI) (http://www.aeci.es) was created in 1994 as the Intercampus Program. It supports the creation of networks and the consolidation of joint activities among participating universities in Spain and Latin America. The Spanish Agency for International Cooperation (AECI) and the Ibero-American universities have contributed significant human and economic resources to the program. As of 2000 more than 80,000 applications had been received from Spanish students. Economy, law, and the social sciences are the most preferred disciplines. The majority of Spanish students and professors choose Argentina, followed by Mexico, Chile, Brazil, Peru, Colombia, and Cuba. Eighty percent of Latin American students and professors also come from these countries. Between 1994 and 2000, 223 Spanish administrators came to Latin America under PCI fellowships and 64 Latin Americans traveled to Spain. The experience gained through the implementation of the PCI stimulated the opening of international relations offices in some Latin American countries during the 1990s.

UNDERGRADUATE STUDENT AGREEMENT PROGRAM
The Undergraduate Student Agreement Program (PEC-G) (www.dce.mre.gov.br/PEC-G/PEC-G.htm), administered by the Brazilian Ministry of Foreign Affairs, was established in 1967 as a result of diplomatic resolutions directed to developing countries, particularly in the Caribbean, Africa, and Asia. As of 2000 the program had allowed more than 5,000 students, mainly from Latin America and Africa, to study at Brazilian universities. In 2002 an estimated 2,700 students were registered, 143 of them with scholarships from the Brazilian government. This program promotes exchanges and scientific cooperation. In 1981 a second program, the PEC-PG, was created in order to promote programs at the graduate level. More than 500 foreign students have enrolled in some 40 Brazilian universities.

Interregional Actors

Interregional actors include government agencies, NGOs and networks, trade agreements, and programs.

Government Agencies

Among the most important government agencies are the Andrés Bello Treaty, the European Commission, and the Ibero-American Organization for Education, Science and Culture.

ANDRÉS BELLO TREATY
The Andrés Bello Treaty (www.cab.int.co) was created in Bogota, Colombia, in 1970 as an international, intergovernmental entity with the purpose of integrating education, science, technology, and culture among its member countries. Bolivia, Chile, Colombia, Ecuador, Peru, Panama, Spain, and Venezuela are signatories to this treaty.

EUROPEAN COMMISSION
The European Commission (http://europa.eu.int) is the governing and administrative body of the European Union. It ensures that member countries maintain a close union and that the integration process is balanced between countries and regions, between business and consumers, and between different categories of citizens.

The external aid offered by the Commission is managed by the Europe Aid Co-operation Office. The Commission also negotiates international trade and cooperation agreements on behalf of member countries. Cooperation with Latin America is oriented toward social development and the strengthening of institutional capacities. Regional cooperation with Latin America is provided largely through the AlßAN program, which provides study awards, and the ALFA program, a cooperation program between universities on both continents.

IBERO-AMERICAN ORGANIZATION FOR EDUCATION, SCIENCE AND CULTURE
Founded in 1949, the Ibero-American Organization for Education, Science and Culture (OEI) (www.oei.es) is an international governmental organization that aims to strengthen knowledge, mutual understanding, integration, and solidarity among the Ibero-American people. Although it primarily serves the ministers of education throughout the region, it also works closely with universities, libraries, and research centers, helping them promote their own strategies on interinstitutional cooperation in order to harmonize the diverse higher education systems of the region.

Interregional Nongovernmental Organizations and Networks

The most important and active NGOs and networks in the region include Columbus, the Consortium for North American Higher Education Collaboration, the European University Association, the Ibero-American University Association of Graduate Education, the Ibero-American Network for the Evaluation and Accreditation of Higher Education, the Ibero-American University Council, the Inter-American Organization for Higher Education, the Interuniversity Center for Development, and Universia.net.

COLUMBUS
Created in 1987, Columbus (www.columbus-web.com) is a network of European and Latin American universities that aims to promote institutional development and multilateral cooperation. Its purpose is to help universities better respond to the challenges posed by scarce resources, demands for diversification, and internationalization. Universities in Argentina, Brazil, Chile, Colombia, Costa Rica, Mexico, Peru, Uruguay, and Venezuela participate in the program. More than 800 rectors and university managers have taken advantage of Columbus training opportunities in convergence of higher education systems, the application of information and communication technology to teaching and learning, continuing education, and internationalization, among other areas. UNESCO is one of the main supporters of Columbus.

CONSORTIUM FOR NORTH AMERICAN HIGHER EDUCATION COLLABORATION
The Consortium for North American Higher Education Collaboration (CONAHEC) (http://www.conahec.org) was established as a trilateral organization in 1997. It advises and connects institutions interested in establishing or strengthening academic collaborative programs among higher education institutions in Canada, the United States, and Mexico. It supports student exchange, program development, research projects, the ELNET network of universities, and international comparative research analysis. Its student exchange program promotes mobility for undergraduate and graduate students in all academic disciplines for one or two semesters, based on tuition reciprocity. CONAHEC also supports U.S.–Mexico borderlands grants for the development of binational projects on health, education, environment, economic development, and community issues.

EUROPEAN UNIVERSITY ASSOCIATION/IBERO-AMERICAN UNIVERSITY COUNCIL
The European University Association (www.eua.be/eua/en/about_eua.jsp), the representative organization of both the European universities and the national rectors' conferences, is the main voice of the higher education community in Europe. The organization has existed since 2001, when the Association of European Universities and the Confederation of European Union Rectors' Conferences merged. A main focus of the European University Association is to provide advocacy on behalf of its members, both at the European level to promote common policies and at the international level to promote increased cooperation and enhance the visibility of European higher education in a global context.

The European University Association and the Ibero-American University Council joined forces through a joint communiqué on partnership between the two regions. Since 2003 the partnership has aimed to create closer interuniversity cooperation in higher education and in scientific and technological research between the two regions by gradually improving education and training systems, promoting good-quality assessment, supporting mobility, strengthening basic and applied research, and promoting instruments of communication to foster the circulation of information and learning.

IBERO-AMERICAN ASSOCIATION OF POST-GRADUATE UNIVERSITIES
Founded in 1997, the Ibero-American University Association of Graduate Education (AUIP) (www.usal.es/auip) works out of regional offices in Brazil, Chile, Colombia, Cuba, Mexico, and Peru. Its members include 120 higher education member institutions from every country in Latin America and the Caribbean. This association is dedicated to the promotion, development, and evaluation of postgraduate programs in higher education

institutions in Latin America and the Caribbean, Portugal, and Spain. It facilitates mobility programs for students and university professors, particularly those involved in graduate and doctoral programs; provides technical assistance; and supports and organizes seminars and short courses. It also works on quality assurance, graduate distance programs, institutional management, and development and cooperative doctoral programs.

IBERO-AMERICAN NETWORK FOR THE EVALUATION AND ACCREDITATION OF HIGHER EDUCATION

The Ibero-American Network for the Evaluation and Accreditation of Higher Education (RIACES) (www.coneau.edu.ar/act_inter/riaces/riaces. html), established in 2003, brings together several Ibero-American evaluation and accreditation agencies from Argentina, Chile, Colombia, Cuba, Central America, Mexico, Spain, and other countries. The network aims to further the understanding of diverse higher education systems, address common issues related to evaluation and accreditation, improve the region's capacity for quality assessment, promote joint activities, and facilitate the development of processes for evaluating and accrediting programs and institutions. It also serves as a link with other agencies and networks around the world.

IBERO-AMERICAN UNIVERSITY COUNCIL

In 2002 the regional associations of universities and the rectors' councils created the Ibero-American University Council (www.crue.org/espacioib. htm) with the purpose of strengthening cooperation among member universities and other universities. The council promotes mobility for students, professors, researchers, and administrative staff and promotes initiatives that support regional integration. The Ibero-American University Council is undertaking an important new initiative, described below, to deepen cooperation with the European University Association.

INTER-AMERICAN ORGANIZATION FOR HIGHER EDUCATION

The Inter-American Organization for Higher Education (www.oui-iohe. qc.c) was created in 1979, in Quebec City, Canada. Its membership includes about 400 public and private universities, institutes of higher education, research centers, national and regional university associations, and rectors conferences from Canada to Argentina. It is present in 25 countries in the Americas.

Its principal objective is to promote cooperation between member institutions and to improve the quality of higher education in America. It offers professional development programs for university leaders, including international relations staff, and publishes resource materials on internationalization.

INTERUNIVERSITY CENTER FOR DEVELOPMENT

The Interuniversity Center for Development (www.cinda.cl) is an academic network of Latin American and European universities committed to economic and social development and the strengthening of links among members. Founded in 1975, it is one of the few organizations that has contributed to the understanding and implementation of international cooperation within the region. The center has three programs: the academic program, which analyzes the most important issues related to higher education; the mobility program, which supports the exchange of students, particularly within Latin America; and the service program, which facilitates knowledge exchange among members.

UNIVERSIA.NET

Universia.net (www.universia.net), established in Spain in 2000, is a private nonprofit company funded by Grupo Santander Central Hispano Bank. This new type of actor in the region is a portal that brings together 733 higher education institutions from several Ibero-American countries, including Argentina, Brazil, Chile, Colombia, Spain, Mexico, Peru, Portugal, Puerto Rico, and Venezuela, representing 8,040,000 students. Universia.net offers information on agencies, international programs and services, scholarships, and libraries. It has become a platform for interinstitutional communication, a source of innovation, and a channel through which to market the educational products and services offered by the universities.

Interregional Trade Agreements

Two interregional trade agreements—the Free Trade Area of the Americas and NAFTA—affect the region.

FREE TRADE AREA OF THE AMERICAS

The Free Trade Area of the Americas (FTAA) (www.ftaa-alca.org) is an effort to unite the economies of the Americas into a single free trade area. This unification process began in 1994, when the heads of state and government of the 34 democracies in the region agreed to construct the FTAA to progressively eliminate barriers to trade of goods and services. The agreement is currently being negotiated by the ministries of trade. If created, the FTAA would be the most far-reaching trade agreement in history. It would incorporate deregulation of services, including education.

NORTH AMERICAN FREE TRADE AGREEMENT

The North American Free Trade Agreement (NAFTA) (www.nafta-sec-alena. org) is an agreement between the governments of Canada, the United

States, and Mexico. First established in 1994 as a commercial treaty, NAFTA has influenced the way these three countries relate to one another in significant ways, but the original expectations regarding its impact on higher education have not yet been realized.

Interregional Programs

Among the most important and active interregional programs are the Academic Mobility and Exchange Program, the College of the Americas, the European Union Program of High-Level Scholarships for Latin America, the Ibero-American Science and Technology Program for Development, INCO-DEV, the Institute of University Management and Leadership, Latin America Academic Training, the North American Mobility Program, and the Student Mobility Program of the Interuniversity Centre for Development.

ACADEMIC MOBILITY AND EXCHANGE PROGRAM

The Academic Mobility and Exchange Program (PIMA) (www.campus-oei.org/pima), created in 2000 by the Organization of Ibero-American States for Education, Science and Culture, seeks to strengthen interinstitutional cooperation by fostering the multilateral exchange of graduate students in the region. Its mobility program includes 67 universities and moves more than 400 students a year, mainly from Argentina, Brazil, Chile, Colombia, Costa Rica, Ecuador, Guatemala, Mexico, Peru, and Uruguay to universities in Spain and Latin America. Equally important are the 24 networks in progress in Latin America.

COLLEGE OF THE AMERICAS

The College of the Americas (www.oui-iohe.qc.ca/Colam/en-index _apropos.htm) was created in 1997 by the Inter-American Organization for Higher Education (IGLU). Its objectives are to develop university cooperation through networks, research, and training; develop and improve university programs; encourage research on continental integration; and promote intercultural relations, the inter-American identity, cross-disciplinary approaches, and information and communication technologies applications.

As of 2003, 709 students had participated in 17 inter-American seminars, at which students from different countries and disciplines meet to discuss continental integration or problems specific to their region or sector of activity. Sixty-two IGLU member universities have been involved in the development of Inter-American Training Networks programs, with the participation of 1,247 students.

EUROPEAN UNION PROGRAM OF HIGH-LEVEL SCHOLARSHIPS FOR LATIN AMERICA

The European Union Program of High-Level Scholarships for Latin America (AlßAN) (www.programalban.org) was developed in 2002 as a joint scholarship program that enabled Latin American graduate students and professionals to improve their knowledge or skills at any European higher education institution or center of research. The European Union provides 75 percent of the scholarship funds, while the candidate has to come up with the remaining 25 percent. The program is expected to last until 2010 and is intended for Latin Americans who want to enroll in studies at the master's or doctorate level or pursue higher specialized training. Each of the 18 Latin American countries participating has a focal point office, which promotes the program. During 2003/04, 251 scholarships were awarded. Brazil obtained 63 (25 percent), Colombia 37 (15 percent), followed by Argentina, Chile, Mexico, and Venezuela. El Salvador, Guatemala, Honduras, and Panama obtained one scholarship each. Spain was the most popular destination (39 percent), followed by the United Kingdom (38 percent). Other countries selected were France, Germany, Italy, and the Netherlands.

IBERO-AMERICAN SCIENCE AND TECHNOLOGY PROGRAM FOR DEVELOPMENT

The Ibero-American Science and Technology Program for Development (CYTED) (www.cyted.org/) was created in 1984 by 21 Ibero-American countries. Its main objective is to foster cooperation among university research groups, research and development centers, and innovative firms in Ibero-American countries. It aims to achieve transferable science and technology results for productive systems and social policy and to serve as a bridge for cooperation between Latin America and the European Union through Spain and Portugal. It is made up of 16 thematic subprograms that range from aquaculture to science and technology management. To date, this program has created more than 76 networks and sponsored 95 research projects and 166 innovation projects, with the participation of more than 10,000 researchers from Ibero-America.

INCO-DEV

In November 1994 the European Council adopted the Specific Research and Technological Development Program in the Field of Cooperation with Third Countries and International Organizations (INCO) (www.europa. eu.int/comm/research/intco/achieve/edito_en.html). The objective of this initiative is to provide the Fourth Research and Technical Development Framework Program with a tool with which to respond to the growing globalization of science and the economy. INCO has been the interface of science and technology relations between the European Union and the rest of the world. It supports projects on health, the environment, and agriculture, in which Asian and Latin American countries work together with European countries.

INSTITUTE OF UNIVERSITY MANAGEMENT AND LEADERSHIP

The Institute of University Management and Leadership (www.oui-iohe. qc.ca/Iglu/en-index.htm), a program of the Inter-American Organization for Higher Education, is the only outreach program designed to improve the knowledge and skills of senior university administrators in Latin America. Since its creation, in 1983, the institute has trained about 1,300 university administrators in strategic university management, accreditation and quality assessment, the relationship between the university and the community, internationalization of higher education and reengineering of the university, and other issues.

LATIN AMERICA ACADEMIC TRAINING

International cooperation with the European Union increased significantly during the past several years. Several European Commission programs have provided funds to strengthen relations between European and Latin American academics through scholarships and the creation of networks that improve cooperation between higher education institutions. One of the most important of these programs is Latin America Academic Training (ALFA) (http://europa.eu.int/comm/europeaid/projects/alfa/index_en.htm). Created in 1994, ALFA involves 15 European and 18 Latin American countries.

ALFA is implemented through networks of higher education institutions in the region. The networks must fulfill certain requirements, particularly the participation of at least three higher education institutions from Latin America and three from the European Union. Each network is coordinated by a participating institution.

ALFA has helped increase participation by Latin American universities in international networks and helped the institutions learn to work in coordination and collaboration with peer institutions. The cost of the first phase of ALFA was about €60 million. Between 1994 and 1999, 1,434 networks were created and 2,918 projects submitted. Thirty percent were coordinated by Spain and 10 percent by French and Italian institutions. Together with Portugal, these countries form the "Latin bloc," which together coordinated 471 projects (55 percent of the total). The countries in Latin America with the highest number of coordinators are Argentina, Chile, and Mexico, with 28 projects each. The European Union contributed about 84 percent of the funds, with Latin American institutions providing the rest.

During the second phase of ALFA (2000–05), 279 proposals were submitted for evaluation, 92 of which were accepted. Almost 400 higher education institutions were involved. In Europe, Spain remains the country with the highest number of projects (82), followed by Portugal (46). In Latin America, Argentina and Brazil continue to be the countries with the highest participation rate, with 62 projects between them. Fifteen percent of these projects deal with academic evaluation, 29 percent with the relationship between the university and the private sector, and 51 percent with development of course plans and academic management.

ALFA supports networks that are coordinated by one or in some cases two higher education institutions. Spain coordinates 28 projects, Italy manages 12, and Austria, Belgium, and Germany each manage 5. In Latin America, Chile coordinates seven projects, followed by Argentina and Brazil with five each. Cuba is involved with one-third of all projects. Twenty-five projects are coordinated by Latin American higher education institutions, and 73 are coordinated by higher educations institutions in 13 European countries.

NORTH AMERICAN MOBILITY PROGRAM
The North American Mobility Program (PROMESAN) (http://sesic.sep. gob.mx/dges/ddu/movilidad2003/index2.htm) is supported by Human Resources Development Canada, the Fund for the Improvement of Post-Secondary Education (FIPSE) in the United States, and the Secretary of Public Education in Mexico. It was created in 1995 to improve opportunities for study abroad by students in Mexico, Canada, and the United States. The program stimulated the creation of more than 50 consortia between 1995 and 2001.

STUDENT MOBILITY PROGRAM OF THE INTERUNIVERSITY CENTER FOR DEVELOPMENT
In 2003 the Interuniversity Center for Development (CINDA) set up a mobility program (www.pucp.edu.pe/estudiantes/cinda/) among its 29 university members. The program, which provides 10 scholarships a year, seeks to stimulate the exchange of undergraduate and graduate students by promoting mobility within Latin America and by supporting not only studies but also research by students. In 2003, 25 universities participated in the program, offering 184 very diverse options.

Regional Actors

Regional actors include intergovernmental bodies, NGOs, and networks and programs.

Regional Intergovernmental Bodies

Among the most important intergovernmental bodies are the Inter-American Development Bank, the International Institute for Higher Education in Latin America and the Caribbean, and the Organization of American States.

INTER-AMERICAN DEVELOPMENT BANK

Established in 1959, the Inter-American Development Bank (www.iadb. org) is the oldest and largest regional development bank and the principal source of multilateral financing for economic, social, and cultural development in Latin America and the Caribbean. It has played a leading role in strengthening regional integration. It administers two scholarship programs: the Japan Scholarship Program for graduate students in development-related fields and scholarships to attend social development courses offered by the Inter-American Social Development Institute.

INTERNATIONAL INSTITUTE FOR HIGHER EDUCATION IN LATIN AMERICA AND THE CARIBBEAN

The mission of the International Institute for Higher Education in Latin America and the Caribbean (IESALC/UNESCO) (www.iesalc.unesco. org.ve) is to achieve important, permanent reforms in higher education in the region and to strengthen the relationships among higher education institutions and the academic community of the region. Like UNESCO, IESALC works toward regional integration by encouraging the mobility of academics, mainly from the least developed countries in the region, and facilitating the recognition of studies, degree equivalencies, and credit transfer. IESALC's work focuses on research and policy reform rather than the direct implementation of programs. Resource materials on the international dimension of higher education are available on the institute's Web site.

ORGANIZATION OF AMERICAN STATES

At the regional level, the only supranational organization is the Organization of American States (OAS) (www.oas.org), which is made up of 35 independent countries, including Cuba.[1] Created in 1948, the OAS works closely with national governmental bodies in administering multinational fellowships and training programs. These programs support graduate

---

[1] Both the Organization of American States and the Inter-American Development Bank could be classified as interregional organizations, as North America is involved. They have been listed as regional intergovernmental actors, because their services and programs target countries in Latin America.

studies and research, undergraduate studies, and short-term training at various centers. The OAS played an important role in establishing national science councils in Latin American countries. It has not been a major funder of activities that could promote regional academic integration. In recent years it has been involved mainly in macro political issues.

Regional Nongovernmental Organizations and Networks

Among the most active NGOs and networks in the region are the Latin America and Caribbean Association of Universities for Integration, the Latin American Council of Social Sciences, the Latin American Faculty of Social Sciences, the Latin American Macro Universities Network, the Latin American Macro Universities Network, the Latin American Network of University Cooperation, and the Union of Latin American Universities.

LATIN AMERICA AND THE CARIBBEAN ASSOCIATION OF UNIVERSITIES FOR INTEGRATION

The Latin America and Caribbean Association of Universities for Integration (AUALCPI) (www.aualcpi.org) was created in 1993 to improve regional integration. More than 100 institutions in 20 Latin American and Caribbean countries participate in common actions aimed at strengthening regional integration. The AUALCPI has supported research, agreements, exchange programs, and seminars.

LATIN AMERICAN COUNCIL OF SOCIAL SCIENCES

The Latin American Council of Social Sciences (CLACSO) (http://www.clacso.org/wwwclacso/espanol/html/grupos/fgrupos.html), is a nongovernmental network dedicated to promoting research, discussion, and academic diffusion in several areas of social sciences. Founded in 1967 by 35 Latin American institutions, CLACSO now includes more than 130 research institutes and graduate programs in social sciences in 19 countries in Latin America and the Caribbean.

LATIN AMERICAN FACULTY OF SOCIAL SCIENCES

The Latin American Faculty of Social Sciences (FLACSO) (www.flacso.org), established in 1957, is an autonomous cooperative initiative of UNESCO and 14 countries in Latin America and the Caribbean. Its basic functions are to provide training in the social sciences through graduate and specialization courses, conduct research on Latin American problems, disseminate advances in the social sciences, promote the interchange of social science teaching material in and for Latin America, and collaborate with universities and other regional and national bodies, both governmental and private, to encourage development in the social sciences.

LATIN AMERICAN MACRO UNIVERSITIES NETWORK
In 2002, on the initiative of the National Autonomous University of Mexico
and with the support of IESALC/UNESCO, several important regional
universities created the Latin American Macro Universities Network
(LAMUN). This network brings together the largest universities in the
region (institutions with at least 40,000 students), collectively representing
institutions with more than 9 million students. Member institutions cover
all areas of knowledge, do most of the research in the region, receive their
funding from the state, and share similar cultural and historical patri-
monies. The 23 universities in the network—located in Argentina, Brazil,
Colombia, Costa Rica, Cuba, the Dominican Republic, Ecuador, El Salvador, Guatemala, Mexico, Nicaragua, Panama, Paraguay, Peru, Uruguay,
and Venezuela—seek to strengthen academic cooperation through mobility and research, mainly on the internationalization and commercialization of higher education.

LATIN AMERICAN NETWORK OF UNIVERSITY COOPERATION
The Latin American Network of University Cooperation (RLCU)
(www.rlcu.org.ar), created in 1997, is a regional association of 26 private
universities from 14 countries (Argentina, Bolivia, Brazil, Chile, Colombia,
Costa Rica, Ecuador, El Salvador, Honduras, Mexico, Nicaragua, Panama,
Paraguay, and Puerto Rico). Its purpose is to provide mutual support for
achieving academic excellence and regional integration. Its main activities
deal with accreditation, advance studies, the virtual university, management, mobility, and recognition of studies and degrees.

UNION OF LATIN AMERICAN UNIVERSITIES
The Union of Latin American Universities (UDUAL) (www.unam.mx/
udual) was established in 1949, with the recognition of UNESCO. With
more than 160 universities from 19 countries in Latin America, UDUAL
represents 2 million students, 200,000 professors, and about 5,000 undergraduate and 3,800 graduate programs. It promotes Latin American integration by providing scientific and academic awards to strengthen
regional research and the higher education sector, publishing reports, and
sponsoring a mobility program for students, known as PAME–UDUAL.

Regional Conventions

In 1974 the Latin American and Caribbean states signed a Regional Convention on the Recognition of Studies, Diplomas and Degrees in Higher
Education with the purpose of strengthening and increasing cooperation in
education, recognizing academic qualifications between countries, enhancing mobility, and increasing integration within the region. The convention

requires updating and revising, as it does not address changes in cross-border education, mobility, qualification recognition, or quality assurance.

Regional Programs

Among the most important regional programs are the Academic Program for Student Mobility and the Common Market of Scientific and Technological Knowledge Program.

ACADEMIC PROGRAM FOR STUDENT MOBILITY
The Academic Program for Student Mobility (PAME) (www.unam.mx/udual/PAME/Pame.htm), established in 2002, supports student exchange based on the recognition of experiences and credits. In 2003, 24 of the 150 Latin American institutions that belong to the Latin American Universities Union participated in the program. The Latin American Universities Union has also established support programs, including programs for distance education and for the evaluation and accreditation in higher education institutions in Latin America.

COMMON MARKET OF SCIENTIFIC AND TECHNOLOGICAL KNOWLEDGE PROGRAM
Created in 1994 by OAS states, members of the Common Market of Scientific and Technological Knowledge Program (Mercocyt) promote contact among universities and research centers in the Western Hemisphere. Mercocyt promotes cooperation, provides training, shares information, and promotes scientific and technological development and innovation.

The Mercocyt program supports two major projects. The first, on scientific and technological integration, supports research, graduate-level training, networks of centers of excellence, and contacts and exchanges between highly qualified professionals, as well as information, intercommunication, and dissemination. The second, on innovation, is intended to create a systematic innovation-oriented collaborative effort involving academic and technical institutions and businesses and public agencies. The project includes support for technological initiative, innovation in small- and medium-size businesses, and modernization of government agencies.

Subregional Actors

Subregional actors include NGOs, agreements, and programs.

Subregional Nongovernmental Organizations

Among the most active NGOs in the region are the Association of Universities of the Amazon, the Council of Central American Universities, the

Council of University Presidents for the Integration of the West-Central
Sub-Region of South America, and the Montevideo Group of Universities.

ASSOCIATION OF UNIVERSITIES OF THE AMAZON
Since 1987 the Association of Universities of the Amazon (UNAMAZ)
(www.campus-oei.org/guiauniv/red011.htm) has developed scientific,
technological, and cultural cooperation among 72 universities and
research centers in Bolivia, Brazil, Colombia, Ecuador, Guyana, Peru,
Suriname, and Venezuela. UNAMAZ receives support from the German
Academic Exchange Service for a scholarship program; develops environmental projects jointly with universities in Brazil, Canada, and Colombia;
and participates actively in an ALFA network made up of four UNAMAZ
and six European universities.

COUNCIL OF CENTRAL AMERICAN UNIVERSITIES
The Council of Central American Universities (CSUCA) (www.csuca.edu
.gt), created in 1948, is a regional NGO that includes all public universities
in Belize, Costa Rica, El Salvador, Guatemala, Honduras, Nicaragua, and
Panama. Its main objective is to promote the integration and modernization
of higher education in Central America. It seeks to strengthen the quality of
higher education and facilitate relations with universities and national and
international organizations around the world. The Meso-American Program
of Academic Exchange with the Association of Universities and Higher
Education Institutions in Mexico (ANUIES) was established to increase
cooperation between the two subregions on research and training.

COUNCIL OF UNIVERSITY PRESIDENTS FOR THE INTEGRATION OF THE
WEST-CENTRAL SUB-REGION OF SOUTH AMERICA
Established in 1997, the Council University Presidents for the Integration
of the West-Central Sub-Region of South America (CRISCO) (www.
campus-oei.org/guiauniv/red005.htm) is a network whose main purpose
is to integrate universities in the subregion in order to promote policies,
programs, and projects among its members. Twenty-four public and private universities in Argentina, Bolivia, Chile, and Peru belong to the council. Almost 400 students have taken part in its student mobility program.

MONTEVIDEO GROUP OF UNIVERSITIES
Established in 1991, the Montevideo Group of Universities (AUGM)
(www.grupomontevideo.edu.uy) is a network of 17 public universities in
Argentina, Brazil, Chile, Paraguay, and Uruguay. More than 500 professors have participated in the group's mobility program. Since 2000 more
than 200 students have participated in its ESCALA exchange program,
described below.

Subregional Agreements

Among the most important subregional agreements are the Andean Community and the Common Market of the South.

ANDEAN COMMUNITY

The Andean Community (www.comunidadandina.org) was created in Cartagena, Colombia, in 1959. This subregional treaty includes Bolivia, Colombia, Ecuador, Peru, and Venezuela. Its main objectives are to promote more balanced and harmonious development among member countries under equitable conditions, to enhance participation in the regional integration process with a view to the progressive formation of a Latin American common market, and to strive for a steady improvement in the standard of living of their inhabitants.

The Andean Community is in the process of setting up a mutual agreement for regional accreditation, a move that would facilitate the movement of students, academics, providers, and professionals. The liberalization of trade in services is a basic element for consolidation of this subregional integration, as it fosters participation in the international trade in service and promotes effective positioning in the global market.

COMMON MARKET OF THE SOUTH

Created in 1991 as an economic and political project, the Common Market of the South (Mercosur) (www.mercosur.org.uy) is the most important international educational project for its member countries. The Educational Sector of Mercosur, which includes Argentina, Brazil, Paraguay, and Uruguay, as well as Bolivia and Chile as associate members, is a good example of subregional cooperation and integration. The results of the programs for education and science and technology are still nascent, and the scope of the mobility program for students and professors, accreditation of programs, and collaboration for the creation of joint graduate programs is being developed. The ministries of education focus on four areas of interest: internships and mobility for students and professors; accreditation of programs, mainly in agronomy, engineering, and medicine; creation of the European–Latin America Common Space; and support for interinstitutional cooperation for graduate programs, scientific research, and human resources.

Subregional Programs

Among the most important subregional programs are the Common Academic Space Program and the Student Mobility Program.

COMMON ACADEMIC SPACE PROGRAM

Founded in 2000, the Common Academic Space Program (ESCALA) (www.grupomontevideo.edu.uy) is a student exchange program founded by the universities that are part of the Association of Universities of the Montevideo Group. This program facilitates the exchange of 100–150 students per semester. The broadening of the program to cover student mobility within the southern subregion is playing a crucial role in the development of a subregional integrating dimension of higher education, supported and stimulated by Mercosur. Higher education institutions linked to the program have begun to take this mobility into account in establishing their structures and aims. The mobility of professors and researchers is in an early phase.

STUDENT MOBILITY PROGRAM

In 1997 the Council of University Presidents for the Integration of the West-Central Sub-Region of South America created the Student Mobility Program (www. ucsm.edu.pe/criscos), which facilitates study abroad by undergraduate students. Between 1998 and 2003 more than 400 students have taken part in this program, which has fostered regional integration around social, cultural, scientific, and educational issues.

National Actors in Latin America

The key actors at the national level are described here in general terms. Country-specific descriptions are included in the country studies (chapters 3–9).

Government Departments

The key government departments are ministries of education and related ministries, agencies of international cooperation, science foundations and councils, national export agencies, scholarship agencies, and quality assurance and accreditation agencies.

MINISTRIES

The national ministries or secretaries of education in the region are the highest education authority at the national level. They implement education policies, regulations, and programs. Ministries of education are increasingly challenged by the changing conditions of the global world, as are other ministries that have a growing interest in the higher education sector (foreign relations, trade, science and technology, heritage and culture, commerce, immigration, and employment). Other equally important organizations are the state agencies for the promotion of higher education.

Few national policies explicitly address the internationalization of higher education. The ministries of education are more concerned with domestic issues, such as access, quality, funding, cross-border education, and equity. Even these aspects are affected by the international arena, however, especially cross-border education. There is evidence that more attention is being given to the international dimension of higher education in the region.

AGENCIES OF INTERNATIONAL COOPERATION

International cooperation is usually channeled through an agency or government department with a mandate for such cooperation. As a rule, these agencies are closely linked to the Ministry of Foreign Relations. These agencies include the General Directorate of Cooperation in Argentina (www.me.gov.ar/), the Brazilian Cooperation Agency (www.abc.mre.gov.br), the Chilean Agency for International Cooperation (www.agci.cl), the Colombian Agency for International Cooperation (www.acci.gov.co), and the Peruvian Agency for International Cooperation (www.apci.gob.pe). Their role is to facilitate links between local agencies, including higher education institutions, and international donors and contributors.

SCIENCE FOUNDATIONS AND COUNCILS

National councils or foundations for the development of science and technology are responsible for the internationalization of research activities and researchers. The primary function of these councils is to fund research. Because of the international nature of most state of the art research, these councils have a tradition of being involved in international cooperation. Examples of these bodies include the Scientific and Technical Research Council (www.conicet.gov.ar) in Argentina, the National Council for Scientific Development (www.cnpq.br) in Brazil, the National Commission of Science and Technology (www.conicyt.cl) in Chile, the Colombian Institute for the Development of Science and Technology (www.colciencias.gov.co), the National Council for Science and Technology (www.conacyt.mx) in Mexico, and the National Council for Science and Technology (www.concytec.gob.pe) in Peru.

These bodies maintain and stimulate collaborative alliances with peer organizations within and outside the region. Efforts have been made to create and sponsor Latin American networks in several major fields. UNESCO and the International Council of Scientific Unions (through the Committee on Science and Technology in Developing Countries) have supported these networks. Members discuss policies and problems affecting the scientific community in Latin America, foster interregional exchanges by young scientists, administer government support, and generate mechanisms for the integration and financing of joint efforts in science and technology.

NATIONAL EXPORT AGENCIES

National agencies for the promotion of nontraditional exports of services promote higher education services and programs abroad. The Chilean Trade Commission (ProChile) (www.prochile.cl) and PROEXPORT (www.proexport.com.co) in Colombia actively sponsor the presence of higher education institutions internationally, particularly in Central America, the Caribbean, and other countries in the region.

SCHOLARSHIP AGENCIES

In some Latin American countries, the government has set up decentralized units that administer scholarships offered by international organizations and countries. Examples of this type of agency include the Colombian Institute for Educational Loan and Technical Studies Abroad (www.icetex. gov.co), the National Institute of Scholarships and Educational Credit (www.inabec. gob.pe) in Peru, and the Fundación Gran Mariscal de Ayacucho (www.fgma. gov.ve) in Venezuela. In other countries, such as Cuba and Mexico, these activities are under the responsibility of the central government.

New organizations have arisen as a result of the limited funds available for study abroad. The Foundation for the Future of Colombia (COLFUTURO) www.colfuturo.org) was created in 1991, as a nonprofit organization offering financial aid for students who want to pursue a graduate degree abroad or improve their English. It is a joint effort by private and public firms and some higher education institutions. Since its creation, it has helped 1,182 Colombians upgrade their skills.

QUALITY ASSURANCE AND ACCREDITATION AGENCIES

Quality assurance and accreditation agencies help develop theory and practice in the assessment, improvement, and maintenance of quality in higher education. They provide information on the standards set by higher education institutions and their capacity to fulfill and sustain them. They provide evidence of the quality of programs and institutions.

Several quality assurance and accreditation agencies have been established since the mid-1990s. They include the National Commission for Evaluation and University Accreditation in Argentina (www.coneau .edu.ar), the National Undergraduate Accreditation Commission in Chile (www.cnap.cl), the National Council of Accreditation in Colombia (www.cna.gov.co), the National Accreditation Body of the Republic of Cuba, the Central American Higher University Council (www.csuca.edu.gt) in Guatemala, and the National Higher Education Accreditation Council in Mexico (www.copaes.org.mx).

Nongovernmental Organizations

NGOs include university associations and international relations networks.

UNIVERSITY ASSOCIATIONS

In all countries except Cuba, universities belong to national associations of universities or councils of rectors. The primary tasks of these organizations is to strengthen cultural, academic, and scientific cooperation among members; to contribute to the establishment of national and international cooperation with governmental and nongovernmental organizations and higher education institutions locally, regionally, and internationally; and to serve as centers of thought and analysis of higher education issues and trends. The nature and activities of these associations differ from country to country. In some countries, they are private NGOs; elsewhere they are public organizations with the capacity to influence national policies.

Most of these associations have become leading national driving forces for the establishment and promotion of the international dimension of their higher education systems. Examples include the Inter-University Argentinian National Council (www.cin.edu.ar) and the Council of Rectors of Argentinian Private Universities (www.crup.org.ar); the Association of Private Universities (www.anup.com.br), the Brazilian Association of Community Universities (www.abruc.org.br), the Council of Rectors of Brazilian Universities (www.crub.org.br), the National Association of Federal Universities of Higher Education (www.andifes.org.br), and the Rectors Association of State Universities in Brazil; the Rectors Council of Chilean Universities (www.cruch.cl); the Association of Colombian Universities (www.ascun.org.co); the Mexican Federation of Private Higher Education Institutions (www.fimpes.ur.mx) and the National Association of Universities and Higher Education Institutions (www.anuies.mx) in Mexico; and the National Assembly of Rectors in Peru (www.anr.edu.pe).

INTERNATIONAL RELATIONS NETWORKS

As the associations of universities and the councils of rectors find internationalization strategic for developing and improving institutions, most of them have helped establish networks of international relations offices. Examples of these networks include the Network of Heads of International Cooperation of National Universities (www.redciun.edu.ar) in Argentina; the Brazilian Universities Consulting Forum on International Affairs (www.ci. com.br/faubai); the Commission for International Cooperation (www.cruch.cl/) in Chile, which operates under the umbrella of the Council of Rectors; and the association of Colombian Universities (www.ascun. org.co/rci). Mexico created the Mexican Association for International Education (AMPEI) (www.ampei.org.mx), composed of academics and professionals interested in promoting international cooperation and exchange programs. It includes both individuals and institutions.

Analysis of Key Actors and Programs

A key theme of this analysis is the diversity in the level and types of actors and programs. Table 10.2 shows the most relevant actors in the international dimension of higher education in Latin America.

Table 10.2 Key Actors in the Internationalization of Higher Education in Latin America

Level	International	Bilateral	Interregional	Regional	Subregional
Intergovern-mental	• UNESCO • World Bank • UNDP • WTO • OECD • IOM		• European Commission	• OAS • IESALC • IDB	
Government department or agency		• AECI • USAID • CIDA • SIDA • JICA • KOICA • Embassies	• OEI • Andrés Bello Treaty		
Nongovermental or quasi-government organization	• IAU • IAUP • IFCU	• British Council • DAAD • NUFFIC • EduFrance • IDP • CEC • IIE • IDRC • SAREC • IRD	• COLUMBUS • CUIB • EAU/CUIB • AUIP • CINDA • CONAHEC • RIACES • IOHE	• UDUAL • CLACSO • FLACSO • RLCU • LAMUN • AUALCPI	• CSUCA • UNAMAZ • AUGM • CRISCO
Treaty or convention	• GATS		• FTAA • NAFTA	• UNESCO Convention	• Mercosur • CAN
Program	• IAESTE • AIESEC	• Fulbright • LASPAU • PCI • PEC	• ALFA • AlßAN • CINDA • PIMA • CYTED • INCO-DEV • IGLU • COLAM • PROMESAN	• PAME • Mercocyt	• ESCALA • PME

The presence and importance of the international dimension in the teaching/learning process, the curriculum, research, scholarship, and service to society are key elements in the model of internationalization used in this book. These elements include campus-based activities as well as the mobility of students, faculty, and programs across national borders. Development assistance projects (vertical cooperation), exchanges and partnerships (horizontal cooperation), and commercial ventures are all modes of internationalization. Given this scope, it is understandable that a wide variety of actors is involved in a broad spectrum of activities and related issues. Actors include science and technology organizations, university associations and rectors conferences, student mobility and exchange groups, development assistance agencies, student recruitment bodies, quality assurance agencies, graduate organizations, international relations networks, research and development entities, export agencies, and cultural cooperation bodies.

An important trend is the attention being given to student mobility, at both the undergraduate and graduate level. New mobility programs, such as PIMA, ESCALA, PROMESAN, and the interregional program of CINDA, are good examples. The emphasis on providing scholarships for graduate students and junior faculty members is still strong (good examples are the programs provided by Mercocyt). However, national-level agencies may be stronger in this area than regional actors. The Inter-American Organization for Higher Education and other regional university associations remain active in management training, but this does not appear to be a key area of growth.

Many of the regional university and rectors' organizations were established more than five decades ago (table 10.3). In 2003 UDUAL created a new program, which supports the mobility of students through exchange and linkage programs. This is an example of a long-established organization attempting to address a new internationalization priority.

The first few years of the twenty-first century mark a new phase in the development and evolution of actors. New organizations with a specialized theme have been established. Examples include a focus on quality assurance by the Latin American Network for the Accreditation and Quality of Higher Education and on graduate education by the Ibero-American University Association of Graduate Education, two new Ibero-American organizations. The presence of three new bilateral agencies in the region dedicated to student recruitment efforts (IDP, EduFrance, and the Canadian Education Centre) illustrates another rather new area of focus. It is important to add that long standing bilateral organizations such as the British Council, the German Academic Exchange Service, and the Netherlands Organizations for International Cooperation in Higher Education are also emphasizing student recruitment as a more important activity.

In recent years two new interregional programs with Europe were established—ALFA, established in 1994, and AlßAN, established in 2002.

Table 10.3 Date of Establishment of Organizations and Programs

1940 and 1950s	*1960 and 1970s*	*1980–94*	*1995–2004*
Actors			
• UDUAL			
• OEI	• IOHE	• COLUMBUS	• CUIB
• CSUCA	• CLACSO	• UNAMAZ	• EUA/CUIB
• FLACSO	• CINDA	• AUALCPI	• AUIP
• IAU	• IDRC	• INCO-DEV	• CONAHEC
• British Council	• IAUP		• RIACES
• NUFFIC	• Andrés Bello Treaty		• Universia.net
• DAAD	• SIDA/SAREC		• AUGM
• IRD			• CRISCO
• IIE			• LAMUN
			• EduFrance
			• IDP
			• CEC
Programs			
• Fulbright Program	• LASPAU	• CYTED	• PIMA
• IAESTE	• PEC-G	• IGLU	• PROMESAN
• AIESEC		• ALFA	• ESCALA
		• PCI	• PAME
		• Mercocyt	• AlßAN
		• INCO-DEV	• CINDA
			• COLAM
			• PME

Note: Does not include intergovernmental bilateral governmental agencies, foundations, or agreements.

A new interregional partnership that brings together the Ibero-American Council of Universities and the European University Association was also created in 2003.

Increased activity is also occurring at the subregional level. The development of AUGM and CRISCO and the new PME and ESCALA programs are examples of new subregional initiatives. Given the absence of any regional organization or network dedicated to international education (such as the European Association for International Education), one wonders whether the catalyst for such a network will come from the subregional level and then grow to the regional level. Alternatively, an Ibero-American association of international education could be an option, given that RIACES and CUIB were created at the interregional, not the regional, level. This is an important issue to reflect on, as it reveals that rather than taking the initiative to create regional organizations and networks, Latin America looks to Spain to create and support Ibero-American initiatives.

The number of programs and actors that are international has increased since 1994. Some are providing or promoting international education activities, others are addressing issues directly related to internationalization or have international membership, which is resulting in more international connectivity.

The large number of organizations and networks in the region creates the potential for duplication or overlap. In fact, however, different bodies handle different functions (scholarships, research and development, management training, mobility, graduate program development); they cover a large geographical area; and they establish different cultural, political, and economic ties. Thus the overall picture is one of complexity rather than duplication.

Are these organizations and programs actively fulfilling their missions, or are they little more than paper-based entities? The answer is hard to determine, as many of the organizations were created only in the past decade and need time to gain a solid footing in order to mature into active and sustainable bodies.

Interregional Actors

The large number of actors from Ibero-American, Latin American, North American, Hispanic, and European countries reflects the long history of cultural, political, and linguistic ties between higher education institutions and bodies in Latin America and other regions. This is a feature that illustrates the cultural richness and political heritage of the region and in some respects distinguishes it from other regions of the world.

The longstanding relationship between Spanish and Latin American universities is evident in the number of Ibero-American organizations, networks, and programs. At the interregional level, Ibero-American organizations are the most numerous (table 10.2). These relationships continue to be strong, as evidenced by the creation of four Ibero-American organizations since 1994 (table 10.3). As many of the country studies note, Spain is the leader in these relationships, with Portugal playing at best a minor role. The historical importance of the Spanish universities is fundamental to the Latin American higher education system, and this influence continues today, especially with the role of Spain as a gateway to Europe. To the traditional cultural, linguistic, and historical ties with Spain have been added new political and economic drivers. It is not clear to what extent Spain acts as a bridge to other European countries, as the European Commission has itself made new efforts to develop closer cooperation with the Latin American higher education system. The ALFA and AlßAN programs show the growing importance of interregional cooperation between Europe and Latin America.

The recent growth and importance of interregional cooperation with Europe has not been duplicated with other regions, such as North America. In many ways, it is surprising that more Inter-American organizations and programs are not being developed. There seems to be significant movement in terms of economic relationships between the regions, as evidenced by new bilateral and multilateral trade agreements. But the number of higher education regional actors is not growing and remains limited to the longstanding relationships developed through Inter-American Organization for Higher Education and the Organization of Ibero-American States for Education, Science and Culture.

The lack of growth in inter-American actors during the past decade does not mean that there are not important bilateral connections at the institutional level between Latin America and North America, especially the United States. This does not mean that they do not exist but rather that they have not increased at the same rate as the connections with European institutions and organizations. In the mid-1990s it was expected that NAFTA would generate increased trilateral cooperation over higher education by Mexico, the United States, and Canada. This has not been the case. CONAHEC and PROMESAN program have been the principal regional actors during this period, but the level of activity has been lower than expected. Mexico does not seem to be acting as a bridge to the rest of North America in the way that Spain is trying to serve as a link to Europe.

Regional and Subregional Actors

The growth in interregional actors in the internationalization of higher education has not been mirrored by growth in regional actors. IESALC, UDUAL, CLACSO, and AUALCPI are regional actors, but they do not address the international dimension of higher education in a formal or direct way. It is by virtue of their international membership that they are increasing the international connectivity of their members, not necessarily by concrete activities. The exceptions to this lack of attention to international initiatives are UDUAL's new but very small mobility program, the research that IESALC is conducting on new providers and cross-border mobility of programs and providers in the region, and the creation by the RLCU of a regional network of private universities.

More is happening at the subregional level. AUGM and CRISCO are promoting and supporting internationalization activities in a small way. ESCALA, a new student exchange program of AUGM, is a good example. Other important subregional actors include CSUCA and UNAMAZ, which are addressing important issues and implications of internationalization, such as the need for stronger quality assurance and accreditation frameworks.

Bilateral Agencies

There has always been a strong emphasis on development cooperation by bilateral government and nongovernment agencies. These technical assistance–type initiatives continue, but there has been a shift from vertical cooperation to horizontal cooperation, through support for exchanges, linkages, and mutually beneficial partnerships. Horizontal support includes an increasing emphasis on South-South cooperation, such as Brazil's development cooperation initiatives.

An important new trend is the emergence of bilateral student recruitment agencies in the region. These agencies were created in response to a new focus on generating revenues from international students. In addition to the international agencies, such as EduFrance, IDP, and the British Council, governmental export agencies in Chile and Colombia are focusing on promoting programs and facilitating mobility in the region.

Conclusions

Growing numbers of players are increasing connectivity in the region. These actors are promoting and examining policy issues of the international dimension of higher education. These new players are active at different levels—national, regional, interregional, and international—and have a broad scope of interests, missions, and functions.

There is evidence that issues such as quality assurance, accreditation, qualification recognition, student exchange, new international providers, brain drain, commercialization and trade of education, to name but a few, are no longer the sole purview of national-level actors in terms of monitoring and policy. There is clearly a need to look at how national-level frameworks can be strengthened and perhaps augmented by regional-level actors and policies.

The increased international connectivity of the region with other countries and regions of the world is reflected in the new actors and programs operating on a bilateral and interregional level. While there are new developments at the subregional level, there is less activity in terms of internationalization at the regional level. Most striking is the absence of any organization or network that brings together the national-level networks dedicated to promoting and supporting international education. The development of such a body may be a logical next step in the internationalization of higher education in Latin America, but it is unclear whether the impetus for such an organization will come from a subregional grouping, by an Ibero-American body, or by national-level networks coalescing to form a regional network. This will be an important issue to monitor, as the development of such a network could play a significant role in supporting the international dimension of higher education, through financing, training, information exchange, advocacy, and policy analysis.

11

The Latin American Way: Trends, Issues, and Directions

Jocelyne Gacel-Ávila, Isabel Cristina Jaramillo, Jane Knight, and Hans de Wit

Since the 1980s, and particularly in the 1990s, there have been several attempts to reform higher education in Latin America in response to the challenges posed by globalization. However, as Altbach (2002) observes, although globalization is having an increasingly significant impact in the region, Latin America remains peripheral to the international centers of research and knowledge dissemination. Latin American higher education faces the challenge of positioning itself within these developments and making use of its own strengths and opportunities—doing things the Latin American way.

In several comparative studies, the future of higher education in Latin America is identified as a central priority on the agendas of different national systems (see, for example, Brunner 2001 and López Segrera 2002). Despite the advancement and the results proclaimed by these studies, however, none of them deals with the development and characteristics of the internationalization of higher education in the region.

Little is known about how diverse or similar, how heterogeneous or uniform, how complex or simple higher education and its international dimension have become in Latin America. This volume examines higher education at both the national and institutional level. The countries analyzed (Argentina, Brazil, Chile, Colombia, Cuba, Mexico, and Peru) represent about 90 percent of the region's population, suggesting that this analysis is representative of the region as a whole. (Specific circumstances affect the internationalization process and migratory patterns of the smaller Caribbean and Spanish-speaking Central American countries, and the study does not cover the particularities of the French- and English-speaking Caribbean countries.)

This chapter highlights the most important characteristics found in the country studies and those that illustrate aspects that are specific to the region. It overviews key issues in the international dimension of higher education institutions in the region.

International Influences on Latin American Higher Education in the Past

Latin American universities inherited several common characteristics that distinguish them from universities elsewhere. The first institutions of higher education in Latin America were established in Santo Domingo in 1538 and in Mexico and Peru in 1551. At the time, the Old World had only 16 such institutions, and there were none in what is now the United States. The establishment of these institutions responded to the need to evangelize and to offer educational opportunities that were more or less equivalent to those in Spain. The goal was to link the colonies culturally to the empire and to provide adequate professional training to the civil servants needed by the colonial, civil, and ecclesiastical bureaucracy.

Salamanca and Alcalá de Henares, the two most famous Spanish universities of the colonial era, served as models for the universities founded in the New World. Their influence is reflected in some ways in the current division into state and private (fundamentally Catholic) universities (Tünnermann 1995). The organization of national universities in Latin America was inspired by the Salamanca tradition, while Alcalá de Henares is considered the model of the Catholic university. The co-existence of national universities and private universities of a primarily Catholic character dominated the higher education landscape in the region for a long time. Only in the twentieth century did other private universities enter the sector, in response to the increased demand for higher education.

A liberal movement in Argentina in the early twentieth century (1918), the so-called Cordoba Reform, gave Latin American higher education one of its main distinctive characteristics: university autonomy. It also introduced student participation in decisionmaking about university administration and increased the role of the university in social development.

Most experts agree that there is no such thing as a typical Latin American university, as the universities reflect the enormous differences across countries in the region. Nevertheless, they share characteristics that result from being located on a dependent, underdeveloped continent that has not yet reached a sufficient level of scientific and technological development for its universities to be independent centers of thought.

The current organization of Latin American higher education was influenced by European models (mainly Spanish and French). The basic model adopted was the Napoleonic one, which can be described as vocationally oriented and national and nationalistic in nature. As Schwartzman (1999) notes, the public universities trained students for the professions (law, engineering, medicine), while the Catholic universities provided general education to a small elite. Together they trained the new intelligentsia of Latin America and strongly influenced a national, as opposed to regional or international, approach to higher education until the end of the twentieth century.

Beginning at the end of the nineteenth century, some members of the economic and social elite did travel and study abroad, mainly at European universities. In the twentieth century this elite was still going to Europe, but it began to opt increasingly for universities in the United States. Students who studied abroad were meant to become leaders and key actors in the intellectual life of the region. They helped spread foreign schools of thought, new knowledge from European and North American scholars, and new sources of information. However, because only a small social elite studied abroad, they had only a marginal effect.

The post–World War II period saw the expansion of international cooperation activities, organized mainly around the concept of development cooperation. These activities were intended to help Latin American countries improve their social and economic development. The programs offered scholarships for graduate studies, granted technical assistance, and supported development research.

An analysis of the international dimension of Latin American higher education has to take into account these historical influences: the colonial past (the common language and culture, the adoption of European academic paradigms, the coexistence of national and private universities); the impact of the Cordoba movement on university autonomy; the limited international orientation of universities in the nineteenth century; and the influence of development cooperation and technical assistance on higher education.

Program Strategies

Program strategies refer to academic programs that enable the internationalization of the curriculum, study plans, student mobility, staff development, community services, and extracurricular activities. Program strategies are an indication of the level of involvement of the institution in the realization of its internationalization policies. While organizational strategies reflect *how* internationalization is done by the institution, program strategies provide insight into *what* is done.

Institutional Agreements

The country reports indicate a high number of interinstitutional and international agreements, although a significant proportion are reported to be inactive. In many cases, the signing of an agreement is seen as more protocol than a real commitment to collaboration.

For public institutions, most agreements are in the area of research. Institutions in the private sector focus on student mobility. Traditional Catholic private universities focus on both research and mobility.

As the country studies demonstrate, the geographical regions of preference vary across countries in Latin America. The United States is the most favored partner for Mexico, although cooperation with European countries has become increasingly important in recent years, as has cooperation with other Latin American countries. In Argentina, Brazil, Chile, Colombia, and Peru, the most frequent academic partners are European countries. Chile has 715 agreements with institutions in the European Union, 472 with institutions in South America, and 260 with institutions in North America. Colombia has a large number of agreements with Spain, the United States, Cuba, Mexico, and France. Socialist countries were involved in 75 percent of Cuba's international activities during the 1970s, but today 72 percent are developed with Latin American and Caribbean countries (Colombia and Mexico being the principal partners) and Spain.

Collaboration and exchange programs with countries in Asia and Oceania are still in their infancy, but they are increasing in number. This can be observed in relations with Australia and New Zealand (which have cooperated with Chile and Mexico), as well as with Japan, China, and the Republic of Korea, on a smaller scale.

Student Mobility

Latin American students tend to choose European countries, except students from Mexico, for whom the United States is the favorite destination (understandably, given the proximity of the two countries). Latin American students prefer to go to Europe or North America rather than to neighboring countries. A few programs are dedicated to promoting student mobility within the region and in subregions, but they reach only a very small number of students. Worth mentioning is the North American mobility program PROMESAN, financed by Canada, the United States, and Mexico. This scheme is aimed at financing student mobility and initiatives to build a North American dimension in the curriculum. There is also a mobility program for students and faculty among the southern Latin American members of Mercosur, implemented through the Association of Universities of the Montevideo Group (AUGM). There is no intraregional scheme for the recognition of studies and credits, although Mercosur is working on creating one.

In addition to sending students abroad, countries in Latin America host students from outside the region. The numbers are small, however. The majority of international students come from the United States, Germany, France, Spain, and Scandinavia. Latin America is becoming an increasingly attractive place for foreign students who wish to take Spanish-language or regular credit courses, however. Political and economic instability has been a major obstacle to attracting foreign students, however.

Despite the gradual progress made in recent years, student mobility remains a marginal activity. It is seen as an area of great potential, however, as there is a growing demand from students.

Faculty Mobility and Human Resource Development

Most of the country studies note that opportunities for faculty mobility exist. For public universities, it is a higher priority than student mobility, but it is aimed mainly at the elite of the university, primarily researchers at the international level or faculty educated abroad. Unfortunately, most academics never benefit from an opportunity for an international experience. Some public and traditional private universities report that resources are available to encourage the participation of tenured academics in international symposia and conferences, as well as in exchange programs with foreign institutions. Fewer opportunities appear to be available at the new private universities, where most of the teaching staff are part time and do not conduct research. Mobility opportunities for scholars have increased in recent years, mainly as a result of international cooperation funds provided by Spain, Germany, France, the European Union, the United States, Canada, and other countries.

Although most of these opportunities are promoted at the national level, some of the larger universities, particularly in the public sector, have their own scholarship programs for sending faculty and researchers abroad. Despite the common language and cultural background, other Latin American universities are not favored destinations.

By sending junior faculty abroad for master's and doctoral studies, institutions create the critical mass required to develop their own programs. Ensuring that students or faculty who study abroad return to their home institutions and remain there requires effective national and institutional policies, however, lest internationalization contribute to brain drain. Such policies are in place in Brazil and Mexico, but they are not common elsewhere in the region.

International Networks for Research and Teaching

Networking has become an important program strategy for Latin American universities, as all of the country studies indicate. There appears to be a lack of clear focus with respect to the meaning and content of networks. When institutions refer to their participation in networks, they mention both their membership in international and regional institutional associations, such as Columbus and the Latin American Universities Union (UDUAL) and their participation in multilateral agreements, programs and projects, such as the Latin America Academic Training (ALFA) program and the Inter-University Cooperation Program (PCI). Participation of Latin American institutions in international networks has increased in recent years, and all the country studies mention various international networks.

Through these networks, Latin American institutions are stimulated to work together in research programs on regionally relevant topics and on the consolidation of quality academic programs. They can serve as a model for expanding internationalization. The most active countries are Argentina, Brazil, and Mexico, probably because they represent the largest higher education systems and the greatest capacity for research in the region. The intense activity of Cuban institutions in this field should also be noted: in 2002 Cuban universities participated in 24 of the 60 academic networks approved by the Spain–Latin America Interuniversity Cooperation Program. Cuba is also an active participant in the ALFA program of the European Union.

Networks are viewed as important instruments for international contacts, cooperation, and exchange. The emphasis is still on contacts rather than activities. Where programmatic cooperation is taking place, there is criticism of the bureaucracy and inefficiency of both national and regional programs for international cooperation—for example, the EU programs— under which these networks have been set up. There is also concern about the sustainability of such networks, given limited institutional and national capacities.

These networks are, however, of great benefit to the institutions of the region. They are a mixture of horizontal and vertical international cooperation, but most are still based on reactive responses to the programs of international donors and national governments rather than on proactive institutional initiatives. As far as participation in regional associations is concerned, there is a great diversity of regional higher education networks but also a lack of coherence and an emphasis on political statements rather than concrete action (see chapter 10).

Internationalization of the Curriculum

In Europe and the United States, institutions have internationalized their curricula. In contrast, very little curricular change has occurred in Latin America.

INTEGRATION OF AN INTERNATIONAL DIMENSION IN CURRICULUM DESIGN
Few institutions include international topics or international, global, intercultural, or comparative subjects in their curricula. The internationalization

of the curriculum is taking place mostly through the limited instruments of student and faculty mobility. Given the extremely limited numbers of mobile faculty and students in the region, as well as the low probability that these numbers will increase substantially in the near future, internationalization of the curriculum and the teaching and learning process could be an opportunity to create an international dimension for the vast majority of the students (see chapter 1).

JOINT ACADEMIC PROGRAMS

In recent years there has been increasing interest in Latin American and foreign institutions establishing joint undergraduate and graduate programs. This is a very positive development, as it internationalizes the program content and the faculty and gives students opportunities for study abroad.

Private institutions have created joint programs in administrative science and economics for undergraduates. Public universities are developing joint graduate programs in all fields of study. The most common option is the double degree, which grants the student a degree from both institutions. This option ensures that the diploma is recognized domestically; in some countries laws require that the diploma be issued by the domestic institution in cooperation with the partner institution.

Because many students and professors are insufficiently proficient in English, most of these programs are organized with Spanish-speaking institutions, with Spain the favorite partner. Cuba has been seeking more intense international cooperation in order to strengthen its graduate programs following the loss of assistance from socialist countries. The development of graduate studies and the organization of joint doctorates with institutions from Spain, Mexico, Canada, France, Brazil, and other countries has become a priority for Cuba.

The use of new information and communication technologies is still in its infancy in the region, but it holds great promise for the future. In some countries, institutions are developing graduate programs based on new modalities, such as on-line course delivery, but these courses are mainly for the national market, based on joint programs primarily with North American and European universities. In continuing education, however, some universities are starting to develop programs for neighboring countries using distance delivery.

Offering courses in English as an internationalization option for local students and to attract foreign students is common in Europe and Asia. It is an option that has not taken root in Latin American institutions. This should not be seen as an obstacle, given that Spanish and to a lesser extent Portuguese are widely used languages, both as the first language in the region and as a second language in other parts of the world (the

United States, Europe, and in the case of Portuguese Africa). Spanish and Portuguese therefore represent more of an opportunity than a risk in the internationalization process.

TEACHING OF FOREIGN LANGUAGES
Most of the country studies identify the lack of proficiency in foreign languages among students, faculty, and staff. This has a negative impact on the international competencies of Latin American students and scholars and on their ability to take advantage of opportunities for international cooperation. For this reason, the teaching of English as a second language is key. Many programs have been launched in recent years to improve the level of English.

TEACHING AND LEARNING PROCESS
Generally speaking, teaching and learning are still very traditional in Latin American institutions, usually centered on the transmission of knowledge through an expert-novice relationship. The move toward teaching that is focused on the learning process, as recommended by most international educational guidelines, has not yet taken place, but efforts are being made in this direction. This will be a requirement for, and should go hand in hand with, the implementation of new forms of delivery and recognition of the international and multicultural dimensions of teaching and learning.

Given the relatively small numbers of foreign students in the region, faculty cannot use them as a means of internationalizing the classroom. Extracurricular activities that facilitate interaction by local and foreign students would be beneficial, but very few institutions offer them. A more interactive and critical pedagogy, as well as extracurricular activities with foreign students, is therefore highly recommended for the benefit of local students and as a way of achieving internationalization at home.

DISTANCE EDUCATION AND VIRTUAL MOBILITY
Although more and more universities have incorporated new technologies for information and communication into their teaching in order to extend access to greater numbers of students, they are used mostly for national purposes. The internationalization of such academic programs is still at an early stage. In only a few countries (such as Chile and Mexico, which are working with Spanish and North American counterparts) are institutions beginning to implement joint academic programs using the Internet.

COLLABORATIVE AND DEVELOPMENT RESEARCH COOPERATION
Research collaboration in the region reveals a high level of international cooperation. International cooperation in this area is far more developed

in public sector institutions and in a small number of traditional private universities (such as the Catholic universities in Brazil and Peru), since research is done primarily by these institutions.

Since the 1980s there has been a move away from development cooperation toward collaborative research cooperation. Having developed their research capacity to a higher level of competence, institutions in the region are now increasingly considered by their counterparts in developed countries to be equal partners rather than recipients of technical or development cooperation. In terms of the number of joint research agreements and projects being undertaken and the level of participation in international networks for research, the leading countries are Argentina, Brazil, Chile, Cuba, and Mexico. These are the countries with the largest populations or the most developed higher education systems. Other countries, such as Peru, continue to be primarily recipients of development cooperation in research.

The institutions make use of national organizations dedicated to the advancement of science and technology. Some of these organizations actively support collaborative and development cooperation projects and make funds available for individual researchers to carry out international projects.

The major foreign partners are principally European countries (Spain, France, Germany, Italy, and the United Kingdom) and, to a smaller extent, the United States, Canada, and Japan. There are very few intraregional collaborative research programs and projects, except for some institutions in Argentina, Brazil, Chile, Paraguay, and Uruguay.

Some countries in the region are also cooperation donors. Mexico provides assistance to the Central American countries, and Cuba provides support to Bolivia, Colombia, Ecuador, and some Caribbean countries, including Haiti and Santo Domingo. Argentina and Chile are donors of cooperation to Bolivia, Ecuador, and Peru, providing both research and staff development programs.

Organizational Strategies

Organizational strategies refer to the administrative systems, institutional policies, and systems that make the integration of an international, intercultural, and global dimension in the primary functions of the university (teaching, research, and community services) possible.

Institutional Policies

By institutional policy, Knight (chapter 1) refers to all statements, directives, or planning documents that address the implications for, or of, internationalization. Internationalization of higher education is frequently mentioned in speeches and official declarations by educational authorities. It is seen as a key strategy for enhancing the quality of teaching, learning, and research in order to meet the demands and challenges of the twenty-first century. Despite this recognition, there is an absence of explicit policies for internationalization. Very few institutions have formulated comprehensive plans and policy statements on the internationalization process; at most, the internationalization strategy is expressed in the institutional development plan. Few institutional documents fully describe the internationalization process, its rationales, priorities, objectives, programs, regulations, and planning and quality assessment procedures.

International activities seem to be managed and organized in a marginal way. They are not integrated into the core of institutional development policies or in the mainstream of primary functions. In most cases international activities seem to respond to proposals from outside, mainly from international organizations or institutions in developed countries, such as the EU countries, the United States, and Canada. Horizontal cooperation and intraregional projects are limited in number. Some horizontal cooperation projects that were set up on the initiative of third countries (the ALFA program, promoted by the European Union, for instance) have given Latin American universities the opportunity to work together and start up regional networks for teaching, research, and human resources development. The sustainability of these networks once donor funding ceases is questionable, however.

INSTITUTIONAL PLANNING

The country studies suggest that international activities and programs are not yet integrated into regular planning procedures.[1] International activities do not address the specific priorities of the institutional agenda, and they are organized in an ad hoc manner, left mainly to the initiatives of individual faculty members. Many programs are simply responses to opportunities offered by international institutions or organizations. Higher education institutions are not yet used to planning their own international activities in a systematic way and setting objectives based on their needs, requirements, and financial resources in the short, medium, or long term. As a whole, the international dimension is not seen as a transversal

---

[1] In the discussion of the remaining organizational strategies, the internationalization process of higher education institutions is analyzed based on a broader definition of institutional policy. This definition refers to an institutional integrative and sustainable approach to internationalization that includes the implementation of a broad range of policy and procedure statements covering quality assurance, planning, resourcing, staffing, faculty development, admission, research, curriculum, student support, and contract and project work (see chapter 1).

strategy in academic development policy, and so it is not systematically integrated into institutional development policies. These elements can be classified as reactive, as ad hoc, or as an activity approach.

QUALITY ASSURANCE AND ACCREDITATION

All the country studies report efforts toward establishing and implementing quality assurance systems aimed at evaluating the quality of academic programs, graduates, and institutions. Quality assurance of the internationalization process or of internationalization activities is not specifically mentioned. There appears to be a mismatch between the declarations made about internationalization as a key strategy for improving the quality of teaching and research and the fact that national quality assurance policies for institutional development and academic programs do not yet consider the international dimension as a relevant indicator of improvement. There is still a lack of strategic development of internationalization, and quality review of existing strategies is lacking, although some institutions are starting to conduct such reviews. Worth mentioning are two Mexican universities, the National Autonomous University of Mexico and the University of Guanajuato, which have undergone the Internationalization Quality Review Process established by the International Management of Higher Education program of the OECD. (For more information on the Internationalization Quality Review Process, see OECD 1999 or the Spanish translation published by ANUIES 2001).

In national guidelines for institutional and program accreditation, the international dimension is generally neglected or featured only as fragmented elements. This has a negative impact on institutional plans and quality assurance systems. At the same time, more and more institutions are looking for international accreditation of their programs by international bodies and agencies, particularly in professional fields (business administration, medicine, engineering). These international accreditations provide status and recognition, both at the national level and in the international market. More awareness of the international reputation of international bodies and agencies is needed, however, to avoid linking up with the accreditation mills that have emerged in response to the growing demand for international status and recognition.

FINANCING

There appears to be an inherent contradiction between official discourse, which declares internationalization to be a priority, and funding, which is inadequate to implement internationalization activities. When a priority is high on the institutional agenda, educational authorities usually make the necessary financial resources available; such is the case, for instance, for new information and communication technologies. When internationalization is seen primarily as an externally funded activity or as an income source, there is less inclination or awareness of the need to invest in it.

The country studies point out that very few international offices have the financial resources or seed money needed to support internationalization activities. In Argentina funds for internationalization activities do not exceed 0.3 percent of the institutional budget. In Mexico most large public universities are increasing budgets for internationalization, but this is not the case for the majority of private sector universities. Only 20 percent of the international offices in Colombia are reported to have even a limited budget. More than 80 percent of international relations offices in Chile received larger budgets in recent years, as internationalization activities have become more relevant on the institutional agenda, but much of this funding is used to support collaborative research activities and human resource development; only a small proportion of these resources is invested in the internationalization of the curriculum or in student mobility. Most of the country studies note the lack of national programs aimed at student mobility, which relies largely on the availability of international cooperation funds or students' own economic resources.

Administrative Offices for the Management of Internationalization Activities

Almost all of the country studies note the low level of professionalization of the staff managing international activities and programs. The situation is reported to be due mainly to a high turnover in senior staff positions in the region. Institutions are therefore unable to develop the know-how needed to conceive, design, and implement the internationalization process.

International offices occupy a low position in institutional flowcharts, found on the fourth or fifth tier of the hierarchy. This position does not give these offices the autonomy and authority required to implement strategies.

These offices tend to be dependent on academic or planning provosts, who generally do not have the training, knowledge, and practice that internationalization requires. As a consequence, the international dimension is not taken into consideration at the time of decisionmaking on orientation and development policies. The position of Vice-Chancellor or Vice-Provost for International Relations, for example, which some European and American universities have created, is rare in Latin America.

Policies on Human Resource Development

As Knight points out in chapter 1, policies on the internationalization of human resource development should cover recruitment and selection procedures that recognize international expertise, reward and promotion policies that recognize faculty and staff contributions, faculty and staff professional development activities, and support for international assignments and sabbaticals. The country studies indicate that recruitment and selection procedures do not emphasize a preference for international expertise above and beyond the general perception that it is an asset for any academic and will therefore be taken into consideration by any institution.

Higher education institutions in the region have been sending faculty and scholars abroad for graduate studies for many years, and there are therefore academics with international expertise and experience. Academics who have pursued graduate studies abroad are an elite, but they do exist. Universities could develop and implement institutional policies designed to use this elite in the internationalization process. Academics who had studied abroad could be ideal change agents in the internationalization process. Unfortunately, once home, the great majority of these scholars work at research centers. Since research tends to be disconnected from teaching in Latin America (although there is a clear trend toward change in this area), they are not used sufficiently in the internationalization of the teaching process or curriculum design.

In most of the countries studied, the procedures for evaluating academic productivity focus on individual achievements and do not reward involvement in international cooperation projects, student counseling, or the organization of student mobility programs. These activities are time consuming and need to be rewarded if the institution wants them to develop. Faculty involvement is key to the future of a deeper and wider internationalization process.

Opportunities for faculty and staff professional development activities, such as participation in international conferences and opportunities to spend an exchange period or a sabbatical abroad, are another key element in the internationalization process. This is a crucial aspect for institutions and needs to be properly addressed. Most of the country studies report the existence of budget lines to support this kind of activity. However, the provision is generally inadequate, even though participation in international conferences, as well as publishing and being cited in international journals and books, have become key indicators within the planning and quality review processes of institutions. Unfortunately, access to these opportunities is limited to full-time faculty, who usually represent only about half of all instructors at Latin American universities.

Key Rationales, Approaches, Issues, and Opportunities for Institutions

Several key rationales, approaches, issues, and opportunities can be identified that are relevant to the future development of internationalization.

There appears to be consistency between the driving rationales at the national level and institutional levels, particularly for public universities. The main rationales at the national level are nation-building and positioning of the country in the global knowledge economy. At the institutional level they are institution-building, moving up to international standards, and quality enhancement. At both levels, human resource development and strategic alliances appear to be a means and an end in connection to these rationales. In general, trade and income generation—other than by way of technical assistance and grants—are not yet important driving forces for internationalization at the institutional level.

Institutional Approaches

Latin American institutions still appear to be reacting to initiatives coming from national and, in particular, international organizations. There is a need for a gradual shift from this approach to a more proactive approach to internationalization.

The approach to activities tends to be fragmented, with little connection between participation in different programs, projects, and strategies. Strategies are not part of the central plan and are marginal. Only recently have some institutions started moving toward a more coherent process approach and bringing internationalization into the center of institutional policy and planning.

There is a gradual shift from considering international activities and projects primarily as a source of income (development cooperation, sponsored cooperation projects, trade) toward looking at internationalization as an integrated and coherent process. Related to that, awareness is emerging that institutional investment is required for internationalization strategies.

Issues and Opportunities

The large numbers of activities, projects, and programs indicate that the international dimension is very much alive in Latin American higher education. However, the emphasis is still largely on mobility, there is a lack of coherence across program strategies, and the programs are still peripheral to the overall plans of the institutions.

Some of the key issues that require attention at the institutional level are presented here.

QUALITY ASSURANCE AND ACCREDITATION
Quality enhancement is a key driver of internationalization in the region. However, assurance of the quality of the international dimension of higher

education and inclusion of the international dimension in the various quality review systems of the universities are still not widely recognized as important. In general, accreditation appears to be more of a driving force than quality improvement.

Linkages and Alliances

Institutions need to re-examine their approach to bilateral linkages and multilateral alliances. Linkages and networks are still seen more as instruments for profile heightening and information gathering than as foundations for concrete programs, projects, and activities. Many linkages and networks exist only on paper or follow bureaucratic agendas. Others have been created in response to external funding sources and lack sustainability after funding stops. A more strategic approach is needed, and a clearer distinction between different types of networks and programs should be developed.

An "at home" approach to internationalization—one that includes changes in the curriculum, the teaching and learning process, and extracurricular activities—is lacking. The current focus is on an "abroad" approach, primarily oriented to outward mobility of faculty and students. In the International Association of Universities survey (IAU 2004), Latin American respondents mentioned mobility and research as the two priority growth areas for internationalization, confirming the abroad focus in the region.

The movement for internationalization at home started in Europe, in response to the emphasis on mobility and the lack of attention given to the 95 percent of students and faculty who do not take part in mobility. In Latin American universities awareness has recently started to emerge that more than 95 percent of faculty and students will not have an opportunity to go abroad and that more attention should therefore be paid to the internationalization of the curriculum and the teaching and learning process.

Intraregional Cooperation

A disproportionate amount of cooperation effort and activity is directed toward North America and Europe. There is a growing awareness of the importance of and the opportunities for intraregional activities. Opportunities for the intraregional delivery of both traditional and continuing education courses and joint programs are not being seized.

Cultural and Linguistic Identity

Institutions are increasingly identifying the opportunities that the region's cultural and linguistic identity provides for setting up language and culture programs for international students.

Internationalization from a National Perspective

There appears to be open-mindedness toward internationalization in Latin America. Solidarity is a traditional and still important driving force for internationalization, as expressed, for instance, in the support from Latin American higher education and government representatives for the 1998 World Conference of Higher Education of UNESCO.

By contrast, globalization is still viewed negatively, especially in Brazil and Cuba, where it is often perceived as equivalent to imperialism or dependency and therefore viewed as a threat rather than an opportunity. Related is the concern about trade in education and the appearance of new foreign providers, which have an impact on the international dimension of higher education in the region not only at the institutional but also at the national level. Combined with the strong notion of autonomy by Latin American universities, these new developments can result in sometimes highly polemic debates about the impact of globalization on higher education, particularly at public universities. At the same time, a more pragmatic approach can be observed (in Colombia and Mexico, for instance) that tries to incorporate the benefits of a more global knowledge society into the traditional, more national, and autonomous culture of higher education.

National Rationales

At the national level, the main rationales for the internationalization of higher education are nation-building and positioning the country in the global knowledge economy. However, different stages in development can be observed and, related to these, various ways of approaching their realization. In Peru development cooperation is still the most important driving force, while Cuban national policies are driven by an ideology of solidarity and cooperation. In Chile, Colombia, and Mexico, the emphasis is on international cooperation and, more recently, on trade. In most countries there is a strong human resource development and connectivity drive for internationalization.

Development cooperation/technical assistance was an important rationale in most countries until the 1980s, and it is still important in Bolivia, Ecuador, Peru, and Central America. Until recently, academic cooperation was based primarily on the agenda of, and funding from, the North. Only in recent years has there been a gradual move toward South–South cooperation and to setting an agenda together with the South (López Segrera 2002).

The Inter-American Development Bank was the most important investor in the 1960s–1980s. Between 1962 and 1984 it invested $541 million in higher education in the region, not including science and technology and research. It continues to be one of the region's main investors. Until the early 1970s, it funded primarily national universities; since then it has funded private institutions as well (López Segrera 2002).

During the 1990s the Inter-American Development Bank shifted its attention toward the introduction of community colleges and other short-cycle colleges in the region, and its lending program for higher education declined. During this period, the World Bank became a major player, making large investments in higher education in Argentina, Chile, Colombia, Mexico, and Venezuela (World Bank 2003). The World Bank has increased its lending to research and to science and technology in Brazil, Chile, Mexico, and Venezuela. These investments support the modernization of higher education in major countries of the region and include student aid, university grants, and research grants. The World Bank's investments have amounted to more than $1.5 billion over the past decade, and its portfolio is growing.

The shift from recipient to contributor can be observed in Argentina, Brazil, Chile, and Mexico, although the amounts are rather limited and these countries also continue to be recipients. Cuba is a special case. In the past, Cuba received technical assistance from the former Soviet Union and other communist states in Central and Eastern Europe—and also from Western Europe and Canada. It also provided support to students and universities in Latin America and Africa. Since the collapse of the Soviet Union, support has dried up completely. The change has made it difficult for Cuba to provide aid, although it still is making an effort to do so.

Another rationale is that internationalization is a means of improving national standards. Quality, standards, and profile and status are all mentioned as important rationales at both the national and institutional levels. Being connected to the leading higher education systems and institutions in the region and the world is a driving rationale. A danger of this approach is the tendency to look for comparison and linkages with the most prestigious universities in the United States and Europe instead of looking for institutions of similar quality, culture, scope, and size. Shooting too high may create false expectations and limit the scope for cooperation.

Connectivity (strategic alliances) is another rationale in most countries. This issue is addressed below, as it is considered one of the key factors in the development of internationalization in the region.

In most of the country studies there is only implicit reference to the issue of national and regional cultural identity. In the IAU study (2004), Latin American respondents ranked cultural aspects as the number one benefit (increasing cultural awareness) and the number one risk (losing cultural identity) of internationalization. At the national policy level, one would therefore expect greater attention to the cultural dimension of internationalization, but not many expressions of this can be noted.

Key Issues and Opportunities

Several key issues and opportunities emerge from the country reports.

NATIONAL AND REGIONAL UNIVERSITY ASSOCIATIONS

In the past, national and regional university associations in Latin America were perceived as too political, fragmented, and inefficient to stimulate internationalization. As a result, they did not play an active role in influencing the creation of national and regional internationalization policies, particularly at the regional level. At the same time, they were seen as important networks for bringing universities together at the national level and across the region and linking universities with the rest of the world. Recently, national and regional associations have started to develop and set up cooperation and mobility programs, an indication that they are attaching increasing importance to internationalization. Most national associations have also supported the establishment of national networks of international relations officers.

NETWORKS OF INTERNATIONAL RELATIONS OFFICERS

Most countries in the region, especially the larger ones, have national networks of international relations officers. Except in Mexico, they are linked to and dependent on rector or university associations.

There are informal contacts between the different national networks of the region, and their representatives meet one another at events such as those sponsored by ALFA and ALßAN. These contacts remain rather ad hoc, however. The influence of these networks on national and regional policies is mainly indirect, through the institutional associations to which they are linked. The creation of a Latin American association, a network of international relations officers, or a network of their national bodies might have a stimulating impact on the emergence of intraregional policies and programs and encourage the regional university associations to take a more active position with respect to internationalization. Such a regional network could help overcome the lack of experience, professional development opportunities, continuity, and qualified academics in international education by developing training programs and facilitating the exchange of information and experiences.

QUALITY ASSURANCE, ACCREDITATION, AND CREDIT TRANSFER

Mechanisms for quality assurance (recognition of degrees, establishment of standards, development of systems for accreditation) need to be established for both traditional institutions and new providers and forms of delivery.

Until the early 1990s, quality was not an issue in Latin American higher education. Planning and development were based mainly on quantitative indicators and related to the economic and social developments in the different countries. The call for a more qualitative approach to quality assurance came in the 1990s, influenced by and modeled after instruments developed in North America and, in particular, Europe. For instance, the Brazilian model of quality review is inspired by the Dutch system (see chapter 4).

During the 1990s most Latin American countries established bodies and mechanisms for quality assurance and accreditation. In the past 10 years Argentina, Brazil, Colombia, Chile, Costa Rica, and Mexico have developed accreditation mechanisms. Other countries are in the process of doing so.

The creation of Mercosur, which includes higher education among its fields of cooperation, was an important regional development. In 1992 a three-year plan for the education sector was approved, intended to address the compatibility of education systems, the recognition of studies, and the official approval of degrees. The plan aimed at facilitating the free movement of students and professionals in the region. Accreditation was mentioned as one of the instruments to reach these goals, and in 1998 a memorandum was signed for the realization of an experimental mechanism for accreditation for the countries in Mercosur.

These efforts notwithstanding, the quality of internationalization strategies and policies at the national and institutional levels and the contribution that internationalization can make to the overall quality of higher education continue to receive little attention. Credit transfer between Latin American countries remains a problem. The development of a Latin American version of the European Credit Transfer System would stimulate cooperation and exchange in the region and beyond.

COMMON LANGUAGE AND CULTURE

Higher education in Latin America could make more effective use of its common culture and a common language to stimulate the internationalization of its education. There appears to be much heterogeneity in higher education and little evidence of regional harmonization and regulation. Little emphasis is given to intraregional cooperation and exchange. Countries and institutions tend to look outside the region, mainly to the United States and Europe, although some forge ties with institutions in Argentina, Brazil, and Cuba.

STUDENT MOBILITY

Outward student mobility remains limited in Latin America (table 11.1). Latin Americans represent less than 4 percent of the total number of foreign

Table 11.1 Outward Student Mobility in Latin America, 2000

Country	Number of students abroad	Percentage of all students	Percentage of all students studying abroad studying in English-speaking countries
Argentina	6,676	0.6	56.0
Brazil	16,756	1.0	62.3
Chile	4,115	1.4	48.0
Colombia	10,735	1.9	70.6
Mexico	15,264	1.0	84.4
Peru	5,748	0.8	50.1

Source: Davis (2003).

students enrolled in reporting OECD and partner countries, a much lower percentage than the 45 percent for Asian students, 30 percent for European students, 11 percent for African students, and 6 percent for North American students (OECD 2004). Increased demand for higher education in Latin America and the Caribbean seems to be absorbed more by the growing numbers of local private universities than by foreign providers or study abroad.

There are indications, however, of an increase in demand for study abroad, particularly at the graduate level. In Brazil the number of students studying abroad rose from 0.7 percent in 1995 to 1.0 percent in 2000; in Mexico the figure rose from 0.8 percent in 1995 to 1.0 percent in 2000. The figure fell only in Peru (from 1.1 percent to 0.8 percent), which might be due to the political instability in the country up to 1995, which increased outward mobility (1995 data from Task Force on Higher Education and Society 2000; Davis 2003)

In all countries except Chile, the majority of students studying abroad are in English-speaking countries. The United States is by far the most popular destination for Latin American students, followed by Spain for all countries except Brazil, where there is a greater diversity of destinations, including France, Germany, the United Kingdom, Portugal, and Spain. Intraregional destinations are not high in the listings.

Inbound student mobility is marginal. The number of U.S. students studying in Latin America increased 11 percent in 2002, to 22,387. Mexico is the only country in the region that received more than 8,000 students (up 13 percent). Costa Rica received 3,641, up 6 percent (IIE 2002). Students from outside Latin America studying in the region are primarily exchange students and students in American junior year abroad programs. The political and economic instability in the region is an obstacle to attracting foreign students.

Governments and institutions could do more to explore opportunities for intraregional mobility as an alternative to the traditional cooperation and exchange with North America and Europe.

INCOME GENERATION, TRADE, AND THE PRESENCE OF INTERNATIONAL PROVIDERS

Policies with respect to income generation, trade in higher education, and the presence of international providers require special attention. These new developments are recent phenomena, and the landscape is rapidly changing. UNESCO/IESALC (http://www.iesalc.unesco.org.ve) has contributed to this area by publishing several reports on this issue.

Latin America is a region of contrasts. There are excellent public universities as well as weak ones. There is a growing private sector that includes both prestigious Catholic universities and substandard institutions that simply absorb demand. Alongside these institutions, new local and international providers have appeared. Together they form an interesting mix of public and private, national and international institutions of higher education.

Traditionally, public universities were funded exclusively by the government. In some countries, including Argentina, Brazil, Cuba, and Mexico, this is still the case. Elsewhere some public institutions have been forced to supplement their income by charging tuition.

The decline in governmental financial support for the sector is stimulating the expansion of private higher education institutions and attracting international private providers.

Many new types of providers are operating in Argentina and Mexico. Argentina has formed alliances with universities in Europe (predominantly Spain) and the United States. In Mexico alliances have been initiated by the Open University of the United Kingdom, the Universidad Nacional a Distancia of Spain, and Phoenix, Atlantic International, and Newport University of the United States. In Mexico commercial international providers, including Endicott College, Westbridge University, and Westhill University, have established branches. One of the most visible providers is the Apollo International Group, primarily through its subsidiary the University of Phoenix in Arizona, which offers undergraduate programs that prepare students for the labor market, particularly in business administration and engineering. Sylvan International Universities, a U.S. provider, is active in Chile, Costa Rica, Mexico, and Panama. Oracle University is active in Argentina, Brazil, Chile, Colombia, Costa Rica, Ecuador, Mexico, Paraguay, Uruguay, and Venezuela. International entrepreneurs have initiated contacts with local institutions in order to buy and resell their shares once the institutions have achieved a certain level of recognition in the country. In Brazil, for instance, Advent International and

J.P. Morgan Partners have increased their holdings in the ownership of higher education institutions.

Although higher education across borders is not common in Latin America, some countries, including Chile, Colombia, Cuba, and Mexico, have begun to expand their presence in neighboring nations through franchises, distance education, and online programs. The Instituto Tecnológico de Monterrey in Mexico has stimulated the participation of other recognized institutions in this new trend. It offers at least 15 master's programs over the Internet, reaching 50,000 students all over Latin America (World Bank 2002).

For the region as a whole, the role of international providers is still quite small. The impact of this presence has yet to be studied and analyzed. Despite the rigidity and complexity of the legal systems, these new providers have managed to overcome some of the bottlenecks and have forced local institutions to undertake drastic transformations in governance, organizational structure, and modes of operation (Salmi 2001; World Bank 2002).

Trade in higher education and the presence of new foreign suppliers in the region is growing, but it remains marginal. The national higher education systems in the region have not yet developed quality assessment procedures to regulate the establishment of these types of educational service providers, leaving citizens unprotected as potential buyers of these services.

Several European universities, particularly those in Spain, as well as some American universities are working closely with universities in the region (in Argentina, Brazil and Chile, for instance) on joint and double degree programs.

Some Latin American universities have established offices abroad with the idea of strengthening interinstitutional relations. The National Autonomous University of Mexico has two campuses in the United States, and some Chilean universities have opened offices in Spain, Argentina, and the United States.

Latin American Higher Education and Its Links to the Rest of the World

Higher education in Latin America is linked with the rest of the world through ties with a variety of countries.

Spain

Despite its colonial past and its cultural influence on Latin America, for many years Spain played only a minor role in the higher education of the region. Strong contacts with Spain developed only after the end of the Franco dictatorship, in 1975, in particular since Spain's admission to the European Union, in 1990.

Expansion of ties between Spain and the Spanish-speaking countries of Latin America has had many positive effects. The downside of this close connection with Spain for cooperation and exchange is that it might stimulate parochialism.

France and Other European Countries

Linguistic and historical cultural links between Latin America and France make France the second most important country after Spain in terms of internationalization of higher education. Over the years, France's role has diminished, but there appears to be a revival taking place as a result of initiatives by Alliance Française, French embassies, and EduFrance, the agency promoting French higher education abroad.

Germany provides Latin American students with scholarships for study, faculty exchange, joint research and staff development in Germany. The Netherlands and Sweden provide technical assistance and scholarships. Cooperation in these programs tends to be bilateral and lacks networking within the region.

The European Union

The European Union creates programs and tenders to stimulate international cooperation in higher education between the European Union and Latin America, particularly through the ALFA and ALßAN programs. These efforts have been instrumental in redirecting attention in the region toward a broader Europe and away from the focus on cooperation with the United States, Spain, and to a lesser extent Portugal. Contacts with Central and Eastern Europe are still marginal, but it is expected that this will gradually change as these countries are integrated into the European Union.

The creation of a European, Latin American and Caribbean Common Space for Higher Education in 2002 by the Madrid Summit and its reconfirmation in 2004 in Guadalajara, Mexico, in connection with the meeting of heads of states of the three regions is intended to strengthen the cooperation in higher education between these regions. Among the objectives of the Common Space are the encouragement of intra- and interregional mobility of students, professors, researchers, and administrative staff. Several initiatives are underway to promote the realization of the Common Space. These include the 6 × 4 project initiated by the National Center for the Evaluation of Higher Education (CENEVAL) in Mexico and Columbus in Europe.[2]

The project intends to establish operational conditions that foster the compatibility and convergence of Latin American and Caribbean higher education systems and a comparison and closer connection between them and those of the European Union, through dialogue and collaborative work between institutions and associations from both regions.

North America

Cooperation between Latin America and Canada and the United States has fluctuated over the past 50 years. In Canada the provision of technical assistance dominated its role in the post–World War II period. Canada's relations with Mexican universities have increased since NAFTA. The new emphasis over the past decade on recruiting international students has led to new interest in the region, which may lead to a major change in Canada's linkages with Latin America.

Several programs support scholarships and internships in the United States. The best known, especially in Latin America, is the Fulbright program, which has reached more than 200,000 grantees since its creation in 1946. Other U.S. programs and organizations active in the region are the Institute of International Education and Academic and Professional Programs for the Americas (LASPAU).

Asia

There is little cooperation between Latin America and Asia, although there is increasing demand from China for educational opportunities in Latin America. Recently, Australia and, to a lesser extent, New Zealand have come into the picture as partners, largely as providers of training opportunities for Latin American students.

Africa

Few academic alliances have been established between Latin American and African higher education institutions. Traditionally, Brazil and Cuba were active in this area, mainly for political, economic, and cultural reasons. Since the 1990s Cuba has developed graduate programs in which many African students have participated. Its doctoral programs are its most popular programs.

---

[2] The project is called 6 × 4 because it analyzes six fields of study (public and business administration, electronic engineering or similar professions, medicine, chemistry, history, and mathematics) from four axes (professional competencies, academic credits, evaluation and accreditation, and training in innovation and research) (CENEVAL-Columbus 2004).

Internationalization of Higher Education in Latin America from a Global Perspective

Is there a distinctive Latin American way of approaching the internationalization of higher education? Or are developments in the region similar to those elsewhere in the world?

Findings from a survey of internationalization among IAU member institutions (Knight 2004) reveal the following:

1. Mobility of students and teachers is the most important reason for making internationalization a priority and the fastest growing aspect of internationalization.
2. Brain drain and the loss of cultural identity are seen as the greatest risks of internationalization.
3. Student, faculty, and staff development; academic standards and quality assurance; and international research collaboration are the three most important benefits of internationalization.
4. Lack of financial support at the institutional level is the greatest obstacle for internationalization.
5. Distance education and the use of information and communication technologies are key areas for new developments.
6. Faculty are the driving force behind internationalization, more active than administrators and students.
7. Two-thirds of member institutions appear to have an internationalization policy and strategy in place, but only about half of these institutions have budgets and a monitoring framework to support implementation.
8. Rationales based on academic considerations for internationalization are more common than rationales based on political or economic considerations.
9. Intraregional cooperation is the first priority for Africa, Asia, and Europe. Europe is the primary partner for interregional collaboration.
10. Issues requiring attention include development cooperation, quality assurance and accreditation, funding, and research cooperation.

These findings provide an institutional perspective to internationalization from members of the IAU. Are the findings presented in this volume consistent with these results? With the exception of the emphasis on intraregional cooperation, the IAU findings largely reflect the institutional perspective on the internationalization of higher education in Latin America. The top 12 reasons for internationalization cited in the IAU survey are also important in Latin America:

1. mobility and exchange by students and teachers
2. teaching and research collaboration
3. academic standards and quality
4. research projects
5. cooperation and development assistance
6. curriculum development
7. international and intercultural understanding
8. promotion and profile of institutions
9. source of faculty and students
10. regional issues and integration
11. international student recruitment
12. diversification of income.

So can we speak of a distinctive Latin American way of approaching internationalization when its priorities appear to match those elsewhere and the only difference appears to be that the region is not (yet) giving priority to intraregional cooperation? At first glance the answer to this question would appear to be no. However, as the country studies make clear, certain issues appear to be of greater importance in Latin America than elsewhere, although they are not unique to the region:

- Connectivity (belonging to networks, associations, and programs) is a key expression of international involvement of higher education in Latin America. The primary focus appears to be on networking and information gathering, however, rather than on strategic choices and alliances.
- National policies are still more relevant in defining and implementing international cooperation than institutional policies, especially in the public sector.
- There appears to be a discrepancy between pragmatism and reality on the one hand and a debate over competitiveness and trade in higher education on the other.
- There is a strong feeling of cultural awareness and fear of loss of cultural identity, as the IAU study found.

In Latin America there is a sharp distinction between public universities and the small number of traditional private universities with a strong research orientation on the one hand and the rapidly growing number of new, primarily local, private providers, which are mainly teaching institutions, on the other. This distinction is expressed in different internationalization strategies, with the first group focusing primarily on faculty and research collaboration and the second on student mobility and curriculum development.

Another distinction is between the poorer developing countries and the more developed ones, which is reflected in national and institutional policies. For the poorer countries, including most of Central America, Bolivia, Ecuador, and Peru, international cooperation is still primarily vertical, based on international development cooperation. For the more developed countries, including Argentina, Brazil, Chile, and Mexico, horizontal international cooperation is more common, although this cooperation is more reactive to initiatives from outside the region than based on active regional or national policies.

The continuing political and economic instability in many countries of the region is affecting the internationalization process. Recently, Argentina, Colombia, Cuba, and Peru have been affected by this factor.

Regional integration, cooperation, and transparency are still at an early stage of development. Latin America looks to the European Union and the Bologna process for the reform of higher education in Europe, as an example of regional integration and cooperation in higher education. So far intraregional cooperation in Latin America remains limited, but Mercosur may be an example for future broader integration, cooperation, and transparency in higher education. The agreement on the Common Space of Higher Education of the European Union, Latin America and the Caribbean, signed by 48 ministers of education, is gaining momentum in Latin America as a way to stimulate both interregional and intraregional cooperation in higher education.

Internationalization of higher education in the region is still very much focused on internationalization abroad, and the region is primarily an importer of higher education. Internationalization of the curriculum and of the teaching and learning process is still low on the agenda of the higher education sector.

The training and upgrading of faculty and research development are considered more important than internationalizing the student body. Given limited resources, nation- and institution-building can best be accomplished by focusing on human resource development and research.

In designing regional, national, and institutional strategies for internationalizing higher education, clear weaknesses and risks need to be taken into account. These include political and economic instability, the fear of innovation and change, and the lack of regional integration. But higher education in the region also provides opportunities that are not being fully exploited, such as a well-established public sector of research universities combined with a growing private sector of teaching institutions; a strong presence in regional and international networks; a common history, culture, and language of interest to the rest of the world; and good prospects for regional integration, cooperation, and transparency.

There may not be *a* Latin American way to internationalize higher education. The country studies and the overview of actors and programs reveal that there are several ways to do so.

References

Altbach, Philip. 2002. "La educación superior Latinoamericana desde una perspective internacional." In *Educación superior latinoamericana y organismos internacionales: un análisis crítico*, ed. Francisco López Segrera and Alma Maldonado Maldonado, pp. 3–5. UNESCO, Universidad de San Buenaventura Cali, and Boston College, Cali.

ANUIES (National Association of Universities and Institutions of Higher Education), Jane Knight, and Hans de Wit, eds. 2001. *Calidad y internacionalización de la educación superior*. ANUIES, Mexico.

Brunner, J.J. 2001. "Globalización y el futuro de la educación." In *Análisis de prospectivas de educación en América Latina y el Caribe*. UNESCO, Santiago.

CENEVAL-Columbus. 2004. "6 × 4 UEALC Six Professions in Four Axes: A Dialogue of Universities Project." National Center for the Evaluation of Higher Education, Mexico.

Davis, Todd M. 2003. *Atlas of Student Mobility*. New York: Institute of International Education.

IIE (Institute of International Education). 2002. *Open Doors*. New York: Institute of International Education.

Knight, Jane. 2004. "Internationalization Practices and Priorities: 2003 IAU Survey Report." International Association of Universities, Paris.

López Segrera, F. 2002. "El impacto de la globalización y de las políticas educativas en los sistemas de Educación Superior en América Latina y el Caribe." In *Educación superior Latinoamericana y organismos internacionales: un análisis crítico*, ed. Francisco López Segrera and Alma Maldonado Maldonado. UNESCO, Universidad de San Buenaventura Cali, and Boston College, Cali.

OECD (Organisation for Economic Co-operation and Development). 2004. *Education at a Glance. OECD Indicators 2004*. Paris: OECD.

OECD, Jane Knight, and Hans de Wit, eds. 1999. *Quality and Internationalisation of Higher Education*. Paris: OECD.

Salmi, J. 2001. "Tertiary Education in the Twenty-First Century: Challenges and Opportunities." *Higher Education Management* 13 (2): 105–30.

Schwartzman, Simon. 1999. "Latin America: National Responses to World Challenges in Higher Education." In *Higher Education in the Twenty-First Century: Global Challenges and National Responses*, ed. Philip Altbach and Patti McGill Peterson, 47–58. IIE Research Report No. 29, Institute of International Education, New York.

Task Force on Higher Education and Society. 2000. *Higher Education in Developing Countries, Peril and Promise*. Washington, DC: World Bank.

Tünnermann, C. 1995. *Universidad y sociedad: balance historico y perspectivas desde Latinoamerica*. Universidad Central de Venezuela, Caracas.

World Bank. 2002. *Constructing Knowledge Societies: New Challenges for Tertiary Education*. Washington, DC: World Bank.

———. 2003. *Tertiary Education in Colombia: Paving the Way for Reform*. Washington, DC: World Bank.

Index

Note: *t* indicates tables, *f* indicates figures.